EVIDENCE AND CASEWORK SKILLS

Inns of Court School of Law

BLACKSTONE
PRESS LIMITED

First published in Great Britain 1989 by Blackstone Press Limited,
9–15 Aldine Street, London W12 8AW. Telephone 081-740 1173

© The Council of Legal Education, 1989

ISBN: 1 85431 272 3

First edition 1989
Second edition 1990
Third edition 1991
Fourth edition 1992
Fifth edition 1993

British Library Cataloguing in Publication Data
A CIP catalogue record for this book is available from the British Library.

Typeset by Style Photosetting Ltd, Mayfield, East Sussex
Printed by Loader Jackson Printers, Arlesey, Beds.

Foreword

These Manuals are published in conjunction with the Vocational Course for the Bar which is run at the Inns of Court School of Law. The course, which was introduced in 1989, was specifically designed to equip students with the procedural and evidential knowledge and the practical skills they will need to start their professional careers. It is gratifying to find that this course has been greeted as a major step forward in legal vocational training, and that it has attracted substantial interest.

These Manuals have been produced specifically to support this course, and they have been written both by teaching staff at the Inns of Court School of Law and by a range of members of the Bar. The Manuals are designed to cover all the areas of skill and knowledge which research showed were important for the new practitioner, and the emphasis throughout is on the practical, professional approach. Although the Manuals are produced for a specific course, their range is such that they should be of interest to all those concerned with legal training.

The Manuals are revised annually, to keep them up-to-date, and to improve content with the benefit of experience and of the many useful comments made by practitioners and by students. The development of legal vocational training can only be an ongoing process for all those concerned in achieving and maintaining high standards, and further comments are always welcome. Such comments may be addressed either to the Dean or the Course Director at the Inns of Court School of Law.

The enthusiasm of the staff of Blackstone Press Ltd and their efficiency in arranging the production and publication of these Manuals is much appreciated.

The Hon. Mr Justice Phillips
Chairman of The Council of Legal Education
September 1993

Introduction

This Manual contains materials both on a 'knowledge' area, evidence, and on two 'skills' areas, legal research and fact management, with the joint title of 'casework skills'. The link between these three areas may not be immediately obvious, but they are not put together at random. In fact, these areas are very closely inter-related in a way that is absolutely fundamental to practice as a barrister, and coming to appreciate this inter-relationship is fundamental in moving from an academic to a practical study of law.

Initially, you will study these three areas separately, and they will seem very different, as evidence inevitably involves the study of technical rules, whereas fact management and legal research involve practical analytical skills. However, by the end of the course you should be using all three areas together at the same time in dealing with cases, as you will go on to do in practice.

Evidence is a knowledge area in that you will have to learn detailed rules as to what is and what is not admissible to prove a case in court. This inevitably involves consideration of both statute law and case law. Rather than approaching the subject in a very academic way, this course seeks to be practical, concentrating on those rules the lawyer must carry in his or her head as they may need to be applied on the spur of the moment in court, although the course also sets out to make you aware of all the evidential principles that as practitioners you might need to look up if necessary for a particular case.

Legal research is a skill that a lawyer will obviously need. This Manual seeks to show how skills acquired as a student will need to be developed to a professional level, dealing with a range of practitioner books, and also learning more complex research techniques that practitioners may require to check the details of law in force. The course looks at how to set about a research task properly, even if there is no obvious starting point. At the academic stage of training, one will normally know that the answer to a particular problem might be found in a tort or a contract textbook, but the practitioner may have no substantial clue where to start researching the law relevant to a particular brief.

Fact management deals with an element that is as important as the law in any real case, but which tends to play a lesser role in academic legal study, and that is the facts of the case. In a real case, facts cannot be dealt with quickly and superficially, with any gaps filled by assumptions, so that one can move on to look at legal principles as quickly as possible, but they must be fully investigated and analysed to identify precisely what the case is about.

The basic link between these three areas is that they are all involved in the preparation of a case. All three must be covered before the practitioner can write an opinion, draft, negotiate or advocate a case in court. However, this link is not a simple one, but a very complex and fundamental one, where all three eventually weave together almost inseparably.

Facts and law jointly rather than separately form the foundation of a case. In dealing with facts, you must have legal objectives in view, or you are doing no more than any layman could do. Facts must be organised in terms of what is of most legal use to the client, for example in terms of potential causes of action or potential defences.

Equally, there is no point in carrying out legal research without a careful consideration of the facts of the case. You will waste a lot of time if you simply set out to research a general area, such as the enforceability of an exclusion clause, unless you have started by considering carefully the acts relating to the clause and the circumstances in which it is sought to be enforced. A fact management exercise is required to identify precisely what legal points need to be researched.

The inter-relation of facts and evidence is equally close. The principles of evidence as such may seem somewhat esoteric, but they should spring into sharp focus when related to the facts of a particular case. There is no point in building a legal argument on alleged facts if you cannot prove those facts in court. The principles of evidence guide you on to what you can and cannot prove. A fact management exercise needs to take the principles of evidence into account, to decide what facts alleged by your client may be relied on in court and what may not. In this way evidence is relevant to both fact management and legal research — you can only use facts that you can prove to justify a legal argument. When related to these skills, the principles of evidence become very practical tools.

As the Course progresses, you should begin to develop the ability to deal with all three areas at the same time in your mind, as any barrister does in practice. This does not mean confusing the three or blurring the distinctions between them, but developing sufficiently advanced abilities in all to be able to deal precisely and efficiently with all three without needing to look at each entirely separately.

With this close inter-relation of knowledge and skills areas, this Manual clearly illustrates something which is central to a Vocational Course — that one uses blocks of knowledge and blocks of skill to build an overall professional approach that will be of most use to a real client.

Contents

CONTENTS

CONTENTS

CONTENTS

CONTENTS

CONTENTS

CONTENTS

Table of Cases

EVIDENCE

1   Introduction

1.1   General

I know a parrot who can learn the rules of Evidence in half an hour and repeat them in five minutes.

That was the view of Edmund Burke at the trial of Warren Hastings. But that was in 1794. Today, nearly two centuries later, evidence is anything but a straightforward subject to learn. Part of the difficulty stems from the fact that it is highly integrated: individual topics are often incomprehensible without reference to some other topics which are, in turn, incomprehensible when viewed in isolation. Another difficulty is the absence of a code: evidence is a set of common law principles interlaced with a variety of statutory provisions, a combination which often does little to promote either coherence or clarity. A third problem is that evidence has more than its fair share of seemingly irreconcilable authorities.

Evidence cuts across the whole field of substantive law, regulating the means by which facts may be proved in courts of law and tribunals.

A thorough mastery of all the basic principles of evidence is essential to the practitioner because there is rarely time to consult a book and look up rules, statutes or cases. Evidential problems can arise in court without warning and, when they do, must be resolved instantly. For example, questions put to a witness which seek to elicit inadmissible evidence require a speedy objection to prevent the witness answering before the issue of admissibility has been considered by the court. Similarly, objections made to questions which have been put to a witness require the speedy formulation of an answer to the objection.

Evidential problems also arise in the preparation of cases and must be considered before the trial even begins. Knowing that your client has a valid claim or defence is not enough: counsel must also know how, or how best, to prove it. Police statements in a criminal trial must be scrutinised to identify any material which is considered to be inadmissible. If that material is crucial to the prosecution case, admissibility will have to be determined as a preliminary issue immediately after the jury has been empanelled and, if the material is excluded, the prosecution may be forced to offer no evidence. In many cases, advance notice must be given to an opponent before evidence can be adduced.

The materials on evidence in this Manual are designed to help students of the subject to do two things: first, to acquire a thorough knowledge of all the principles of evidence (to the level that would be expected of a barrister in the early years of practice); and secondly, to be able to apply that knowledge practically. All major areas of the subject are covered. Broadly speaking, the material is of three kinds:

(a)   Text accompanied by authorities, including statutory materials and extracts from leading judgments, Rules of the Supreme Court, County Court Rules and the Codes of Practice. This material, originally designed for the benefit of students attending the evidence lectures at the Inns of Court School of Law, is also free-standing: in addition to summarising all the leading principles, it provides a framework for private research into a variety of subsidiary case-law and other material. In appropriate circumstances, diagrams and charts (including flow-charts) are employed; and 'transcript' is provided to show how the rules are actually used in court. One of the best ways of approaching the subject is to consider first the sorts of questions which it seeks to answer. For this reason, at the start of each chapter a series of questions is posed to alert you to the critical relevance which the law of evidence has to practice.

(b)   An outline of the objectives of the problems and questions (to be found at the end of each chapter) together with suggested further research to be undertaken prior to attempting to answer those problems and questions.

(c)   A variety of problems and questions (including multiple-choice questions of the type used on the Bar vocational course) specifically designed to ensure that you have not only acquired the relevant knowledge, but are also in a position to apply it realistically. Suggested answers to some of the questions are contained in **Appendix 1**.

2   Preliminary Matters

What facts, if any, have to be proved by a party to litigation?

May the other party admit such facts and, if so, how?

May a party adduce evidence of other facts from which it is possible to infer the facts which that party seeks to prove?

May you adduce evidence of facts affecting the credibility of your opponent's witnesses, that is, to show that such witnesses are not worthy of belief?

Does the judge have any *discretion* to admit or exclude evidence or is the judge entirely bound by rules of *law?*

Which questions, relating to the evidence, are for the judge and which for the jury?

2.1   What is Evidence?

Evidence is information which may be presented to a court or tribunal in order that it may decide on the probability of some fact asserted before it, i.e. information by which facts tend to be proved or disproved.

2.2   The Fact-Finding Process

Approaching this subject for the first time, you would be forgiven for thinking that it is relatively straightforward: the two parties come before the court with their versions of the facts in dispute, whereupon the court embarks upon a discovery of the truth by taking into account all available evidence which is relevant. This, however, would be to make two enormous errors. First, it assumes, wrongly, that there is a scientific investigation for the discovery of the truth. Secondly, it is to ignore the fact that most of the English law of evidence comprises rules which exclude relevant, even highly relevant evidence.

2.2.1   FACT-FINDING AND THE DISCOVERY OF THE TRUTH

A number of factors intrinsic to any fact-finding process and common to all legal systems militate against a scientific investigation of the truth. For example:

(a)   The facts in question may be witnessed by no-one.
(b)   The facts in question may be witnessed, but the capacity of the witnesses for accurately observing and remembering them may be weak.

5

(c)   The witnesses' capacity for accurate observation and recall may be strong but they may have no desire to tell the truth.

(d)   The tribunal of fact is limited to the evidence adduced by the parties to the litigation — it cannot inform itself by adducing its own evidence.

(e)   The tribunal of fact has no training in the investigation of facts.

(f)   The tribunal of fact may prefer to be at work or at home (watching the Wimbledon semi-finals).

(g)   The parties, who are hardly impartial, decide what evidence to adduce and what evidence to withhold.

(h)   The evidence may be inadequate or inconclusive but the court must nonetheless come to a decision.

(i)   Time.

(j)   Cost.

(k)   Emotions — fact-finding is a human, and not purely intellectual exercise.

2.2.2   EXCLUSIONARY RULES

The reasons for the mainly exclusionary nature of the English rules of evidence are partly historical and partly based on policy considerations extrinsic to the efficiency of the fact-finding process.

2.2.2.1   History

The scales used to be loaded against the defence; and the judicial desire to protect the accused resulted in the adoption, by the judiciary, of a paternalistic attitude towards the jury. At common law therefore, much evidence, the significance of which the jury may overrate, such as evidence of out-of-court statements, evidence of the accused's bad character and evidence, by non-experts, of opinion (as opposed to fact), is inadmissible. The exclusionary mentality has been further nurtured by a near-obsessional fear, on the part of the English judiciary, of the deliberate manufacture of evidence by parties and their witnesses.

2.2.2.2   Policy

Policies extrinsic to the efficiency of the fact-finding process, when accommodated by the law, result in the exclusion of relevant evidence. For example:

(a)   Relevant evidence is excluded because its disclosure would be injurious or prejudicial to the public interest (national defence, good diplomatic relations etc.).

(b)   The client of a lawyer has a privilege not to reveal communications between himself and his lawyer, the policy being to encourage full and frank communication in the obtaining and giving of legal advice.

In order to understand the law of evidence, it is necessary to begin with a number of preliminary matters of general importance. First, what are the facts which may be proved or disproved in an English court?

2.3   Facts Open to Proof or Disproof

Under English law the facts open to proof (or disproof) are facts in issue, relevant facts and collateral facts.

2.3.1   FACTS IN ISSUE IN CRIMINAL CASES

Facts in issue in criminal cases are those which it is necessary for the prosecution to prove if it is to succeed in the prosecution together with those which it is necessary for the defence to prove if it is to succeed in the defence.

R v *Sims* [1946] KB 531, CCA per Lord Goddard CJ at p. 539:

> Whenever there is a plea of not guilty, everything is in issue and the prosecution has to prove the whole of their case including the identity of the accused, the nature of the act and the existence of any necessary knowledge or intent.

(Evidence which can directly establish a fact in issue is often referred to as direct evidence (as opposed to circumstantial evidence see **2.3.4**).)

2.3.2 FACTS IN ISSUE IN CIVIL CASES

Facts in issue in civil proceedings should be identifiable from the pleadings, the whole point of which is to set out the parties' allegations, admission and denials so that before the trial everyone knows exactly what essential matters are left in dispute and therefore open to proof or disproof.

(Evidence which can directly establish a fact in issue is often referred to as direct evidence (as opposed to circumstantial evidence, see **2.3.4**).)

2.3.3 FORMAL ADMISSIONS

A fact which is formally admitted ceases to be in issue. Evidence to prove such a fact is neither required nor allowed.

2.3.3.1 Civil cases
In civil cases, formal admissions can be made in a number of ways, for example, by the pleadings, or default thereof; in answer to an interrogatory or a notice to admit facts; or by agreement before or at the trial by the parties or their representatives. Concerning the last, see:

Ellis v *Allen* [1914] 1 Ch 904.

Swinfen v *Chelmsford (Lord)* (1860) 29 LJ Elx 383.

Urquhart v *Butterfield* (1887) 37 ChD 357, CA.

H. Clark (Doncaster) Ltd v *Wilkinson* [1965] Ch 694, CA.

2.3.3.2 Criminal cases
A plea of guilty obviously amounts to an admission of the offence charged, but it is *not* an admission of the facts stated in the depositions (*R* v *Riley* (1896) 18 Cox CC 285).

Criminal Justice Act 1967, s. 10:

> *(1)   Subject to the provisions of this section, any fact of which oral evidence may be given in any criminal proceedings may be admitted for the purpose of those proceedings by or on behalf of the prosecutor or defendant, and the admission by any party of any such fact under this section shall as against that party be conclusive evidence in those proceedings of the fact admitted.*
>
> *(2)   An admission under this section—*
>
> > *(a)   may be made before or at the proceedings;*
> > *(b)   if made otherwise than in court, shall be in writing;*
> > *(c)   if made in writing by an individual, shall purport to be signed by the person making it and, if so made by a body corporate, shall purport to be signed by a director or manager, or the secretary or clerk, or some other similar officer of the body corporate;*
> > *(d)   if made on behalf of a defendant who is an individual, shall be made by his counsel or solicitor;*
> > *(e)   if made at any stage before the trial by a defendant who is an individual, must be approved by his counsel or solicitor (whether at the time it was made, or subsequently before or at the proceedings in question).*

7

(3)   An admission under this section for the purpose of proceedings relating to any matter shall be treated as an admission for the purpose of any subsequent criminal proceedings relating to that matter (including any appeal or retrial).

(4)   An admission under this section may with the leave of the court be withdrawn in the proceedings for the purpose of which it is made or any subsequent criminal proceedings relating to the same matter.

2.3.4   RELEVANT FACTS

Relevant facts are those from which it is possible to infer the existence or non-existence of a fact in issue, i.e. they *tend* to prove or disprove facts in issue. Evidence of such facts is often referred to as 'circumstantial' evidence.

Teper v *R* [1952] AC 480, PC per Lord Normand:

Circumstantial evidence must always be narrowly examined.

R v *Exall* (1866) 4 F & F 922 per Pollock CB at p. 929:

It has been said that circumstantial evidence is to be considered as a chain, and each piece of evidence as a link in the chain, but that is not so, for then, if any one link broke, the chain would fall. It is more like the case of a rope composed of several cords. One strand of the cord might be insufficient to sustain the weight, but three stranded together may be of quite sufficient strength.

Thus it may be in circumstantial evidence — there may be a combination of circumstances, no one of which would raise a reasonable conviction, or more than a mere suspicion; but the three, taken together, may create a conclusion of guilt with as much certainty as human affairs can require or admit of.

2.3.5   COLLATERAL FACTS

Collateral or 'subordinate facts' are:

(a)   Facts affecting the credibility of a witness or the weight of evidence. See *Thomas* v *David* (1836) 7 C & P 350.
(b)   Facts affecting the competence of a witness. See *R* v *Yacoob* (1981) 72 Cr App R 313, CA.
(c)   Preliminary facts (to be proved as a condition precedent to the admissibility of certain kinds of evidence). See *Brewster* v *Sewell* (1820) 3 B & Ald 296; and *Bartlett* v *Smith* (1842) R LJ Ex 287.

2.4   Types of Judicial Evidence

The types of evidence by which facts are open to proof or disproof are known collectively as judicial evidence. The principal labels given to the varieties of judicial evidence are as follows.

2.4.1   TESTIMONY

Statements of a witness made orally in court and presented as evidence of the truth of what he or she states.

2.4.2   DIRECT TESTIMONY

Statements of a witness about a fact of which he or she has or claims to have direct, personal or first-hand knowledge.

2.4.3   HEARSAY

Any out-of-court statement offered as evidence of the truth of its contents.

2.4.4   ORIGINAL EVIDENCE

Evidence of an out-of-court statement tendered for any relevant purpose other than that of proving the truth of the facts contained in it.

2.4.5   REAL EVIDENCE

Real evidence usually takes the form of a material object produced for inspection by the court.

2.4.6   DOCUMENTARY EVIDENCE

Documents produced for inspection by the court, either as items of real evidence or as hearsay or original evidence.

2.4.7   PRIMARY EVIDENCE

Evidence of the best or highest kind, applied, for example, to the original of a document.

2.4.8   SECONDARY EVIDENCE

Evidence of an inferior kind, applied, for example, to a copy of a document or a copy of such a copy.

2.5   Relevance

The most fundamental and important rule of the English law of evidence is that all evidence of facts in issue and all evidence which is sufficiently relevant to prove or disprove facts in issue is admissible *unless* one or more of the exclusionary rules applies or the evidence in question is excluded as a matter of discretion.

According to art. 1 of Stephen's *Digest of the Law of Evidence*, 'relevance' means that:

> Any two facts to which it is applied are so related to each other that according to the common course of events one either taken by itself or in connection with other facts proves or renders probable the past, present or future existence or non-existence of the other.

DPP v *Kilbourne* [1973] AC 729, per Lord Simon at p. 756:

> Evidence is relevant if it is logically probative or disprobative of some matter which requires proof. It is sufficient to say, even at the risk of etymological tautology, that relevant (i.e. logically probative or disprobative) evidence is evidence which makes the matter which requires proof more or less probable.

Consider the following examples of relevance and irrelevance:

Beresford v *St Albans Justices* (1905) 22 TLR 1.

Noble v *Kennoway* (1780) 2 Doug KB 510.

Hart v *Lancashire & Yorkshire Railway Co.* (1869) 21 LT 261.

Hollingham v *Head* (1858) 27 LJ CP 241.

R v *Blastland* [1986] AC 41, HL.

R v *Kearley* [1992] 2 All ER 345, HL.

Agassiz v *London Tramway Co.* (1873) 21 WR 199.

Hui Chi-ming v *R* [1991] 3 All ER 897, PC.

2.5.1 MULTIPLE ADMISSIBILITY

If an item of evidence is, under the rules of evidence, admissible for one purpose but inadmissible for another, it remains admissible for the former purpose. The principle is referred to, somewhat inappropriately, as 'multiple admissibility'. For example, a confession which implicates both its maker and a co-accused is admissible for the truth of its contents as against its maker (by way of exception to the hearsay rule), but is no evidence against the co-accused.

2.5.2 CONDITIONAL ADMISSIBILITY

Sometimes an item of evidence, by itself, appears to be irrelevant but in conjunction with another item of evidence can be shown to be relevant. If the other item has yet to be admitted, the judge will admit the first item on the undertaking of counsel to show its relevance at a later stage, failing which the tribunal of fact will be directed to ignore it. The evidence is said to be admitted conditionally or *de bene esse*.

2.6 The Best Evidence Rule

This exclusionary rule, which operates to prevent the admissibility of evidence where better evidence is to hand, is now virtually defunct. See *Omychund* v *Barker* (1745) 1 Atk 21.

The only remaining instance of the rule is that a party seeking to rely on the contents of a document must rely on primary evidence, secondary evidence only exceptionally being admissible (*Kajala* v *Noble* (1982) 75 Cr App R 149, DC). See also *R* v *Governor of Pentonville Prison, ex parte Osman* [1989] 3 All ER 701, QBD at p. 728.

But, for a rare example of the application of the best evidence rule in modern times, see *Greenaway* v *Homelea Fittings (London) Ltd* [1985] 1 WLR 234.

2.7 Discretion

2.7.1 INCLUSIONARY DISCRETION

An inclusionary discretion is a power to admit as a matter of discretion, evidence which is inadmissible as a matter of law. Under English law, statute occasionally confers such a power. There is no such power at common law. See:

Sparks v *R* [1964] AC 964, PC.

Myers v *DPP* [1965] AC 1001, HL.

2.7.2 EXCLUSIONARY DISCRETION

An exclusionary discretion is a power to exclude as a matter of discretion evidence which is admissible as a matter of law.

2.7.2.1 Civil cases

An exclusionary discretion in civil cases is virtually non-existent. See:

Helliwell v *Piggot-Sims* [1980] FSR 356.

Attorney-General v *Mulholland* [1963] 2 QB 477, CA.

D v *National Society for the Prevention of Cruelty to Children* [1978] AC 171, HL.

British Steel Corporation v *Granada Television Ltd* [1981] AC 1096, HL.

2.7.2.2 Criminal cases

In criminal cases, by contrast, there is no doubt that at common law the trial judge has a general discretion to exclude legally admissible evidence tendered by the prosecution. In *R* v *Sang* [1980] AC 402 it was held that:

(a) A trial judge, as part of his duty to ensure that an accused receives a fair trial, always has a discretion to exclude evidence tendered by the prosecution if, in his opinion, its prejudicial effect outweighs its probative value. See, e.g. *R* v *List* [1966] 1 WLR 9.

(b) Save with regard to admissions and confessions and generally with regard to evidence obtained from the accused after the commission of the offence, the judge has no discretion to exclude relevant admissible evidence on the ground that it was obtained by improper or unfair means.

In committal proceedings, however, examining magistrates had no power at common law to exclude as a matter of discretion any admissible evidence. See *R* v *Horsham Justices, ex parte Bukhari* (1981) 74 Cr App R 291, DC (see now for the position under s. 78, Police and Criminal Evidence Act 1984, *R* v *Kings Lynn Justices, ex parte Holland* (1993) 96 Cr App R 74 infra).

The discretion may be invoked by a *trial judge* to exclude statements tendered in committal proceedings: *R* v *Blithing* (1983) 77 Cr App R 86. However, the judge's power to exclude the sworn deposition of a deceased witness should be exercised with great restraint. Neither the inability to cross-examine, nor the fact that the deposition contains the only evidence against the accused, nor the fact that it is identification evidence will of itself be sufficient to justify exercise of the discretion. The crucial factor is the quality of the evidence in the deposition: *per* Lord Griffiths in *Scott* v *R* [1989] AC 1242 at pp. 312–3, applied in *R* v *Neshet* [1990] Crim LR 578, CA (see **9.2, - Hearsay Exceptions in Criminal Cases, 9.2.2 - Statutory Exceptions**, and **9.2.2.4 - Criminal Justice Act 1925, s. 13(3))**.

The discretion has been exercised by judges in relation to evidence otherwise admissible under Theft Act 1968, s. 27(3) (**6.1.4, Similar Fact Evidence, 6.1.5, Statutory Provisions**). See *R* v *Perry* [1984] Crim LR 680, CA.

Exercise of the discretion is particularly important in relation to cross-examination of the accused on his bad character under Criminal Evidence Act 1898, s. 1(f)(ii) (see **Chapter 7, Character Evidence**). For guidance on the exercise of the discretion in this context, see *Selvey* v *DPP* [1970] AC 304, HL.

Note that the discretion can only be used to exclude evidence tendered by the prosecution. There is no discretion to exclude at the request of one co-accused evidence sought to be tendered by the other: the defendant, in seeking to defend himself, should not be fettered in any way. See *Murdoch* v *Taylor* [1965] AC 574, HL; *R* v *Miller* [1952] 2 All ER 667 and *R* v *Neale* (1977) 65 Cr App R 304, CA.

In addition to the common law discretion now under discussion, the Police and Criminal Evidence Act 1984, s. 78, provides that:

(1) In any proceedings the court may refuse to allow evidence on which the prosecution proposes to rely to be given if it appears to the court that, having regard to all the circumstances, including the circumstances in which the evidence was obtained, the admission of the evidence would have such an adverse effect on the fairness of the proceedings that the court ought not to admit it.

(2)   Nothing in this section shall prejudice any rules of law requiring a court to exclude evidence.

Note that this section applies to evidence on which the prosecution *proposes* to rely. In *R* v *Harwood* [1989] Crim LR 285, the Court of Appeal doubted whether s. 78 could in any circumstances entitle a judge to withdraw evidence already adduced when the judge had *not* been invited to refuse to allow that evidence to be given. Although s. 78 applies to committal proceedings, examining magistrates should only exclude evidence under s. 78 in exceptional circumstances i.e., where they are satisfied that the admission of the evidence at trial would be so obviously unfair that no judge properly directing himself could admit it'. See *R* v *Kings Lynn Justices, ex parte Holland* (1993) 96 Cr App R 74.

From its wording, it is clear that this section overlaps with the common law discretion. One example of evidence which would have 'an adverse effect on the fairness of the proceedings' would be evidence the prejudicial effect of which outweighs its probative value.

Thus s. 78 is not concerned exclusively with police misconduct, but embraces circumstances which need not involve any improper conduct (whether on the part of the police or anyone else): see *R* v *Brine* [1992] Crim LR 122, CA.

However, s. 78 clearly goes beyond such cases; and *may* be relied upon when it is sought to exclude prosecution evidence obtained by illegal or improper means (see **Chapter 10, Confessions and Illegally or Improperly Obtained Evidence**). In *R* v *Quinn* [1990] Crim LR 581 Lord Lane CJ said:

The function of the judge is . . . *to protect the fairness of the proceedings*, and normally proceedings are fair if a jury hears *all* relevant evidence which either side wishes to place before it, but proceedings may become unfair if, for example, one side is allowed to adduce relevant evidence which, for one reason or another, the other side cannot properly challenge or meet, or where there has been an abuse of process, e.g. because evidence has been obtained in deliberate breach of procedures laid down in an official code of practice.

2.8   Functions of Judge and Jury

The general rule is that legal questions are for the judge, factual questions for the jury.

2.8.1   QUESTIONS OF LAW

Apart from resolving questions of substantive law and directing the jury on this in the summing up, issues of law for the judge include:

(a)   whether a witness is competent to give evidence:

(b)   whether evidence is admissible:

(c)   the sufficiency of evidence (see below);

(d)   in the summing-up, directing the jury on a variety of evidential points including, e.g. that law is for him and facts for them and that the burden of proof is on this or that party and must be satisfied to this or that standard of proof.

In *R* v *Jackson* [1992] Crim LR 214, the Court of Appeal commended the following specimen direction of the Judicial Studies Board on the respective functions of judge and jury.

It is my job to tell you what the law is and how to apply it to the issues of fact that you have to decide and to remind you of the important evidence on these issues. As to the law, you must accept what I tell you. As to the facts, you alone are the judges. It is for you to decide what evidence you accept and what evidence you reject or of which you are unsure. If I appear to have a view of the evidence or of the facts with which you do not agree, reject my view. If I mention or emphasise evidence that you regard as unimportant disregard that evidence. If I do not mention what you regard as important, follow your own view and take that evidence into account.

Note that as in the case of other specimen directions, this one may require adaptation to meet the precise circumstances of the particular case.

Consider also the following cases:

R v *Donoghue* (1987) 86 Cr App R 267, CA.

R v *Turnbull* [1977] QB 224, CA.

R v *Harris* [1986] Crim LR 123, CA.

R v *O'Donnell* (1917) 12 Cr App R 219.

R v *Canny* (1945) 30 Cr App R 143.

DPP v *Stonehouse* [1978] AC 55.

R v *Gent* [1990] 1 All ER 364, CA.

2.8.2 PRELIMINARY FACTS AND THE *VOIR DIRE*

Preliminary facts (facts to be proved as a condition precedent to the admissibility of certain kinds of evidence) are decided by the judge in a hearing on the *voir dire* (or 'trial within a trial'). A trial within a trial is called a hearing on the *voir dire* because the witnesses give their evidence on a special form of oath known as the *voir dire*. (See further **Advocacy, Negotiation and Conference Skills Manual, Chapter 53**.)

The jury will be asked to retire because it is almost impossible to discuss the admissibility of evidence in their presence without revealing to them the very nature of the evidence to which objection is made. Such evidence may be prejudicial to the accused, or indeed prosecution, but, in the event, ruled inadmissible. One exceptional case in which the jury should be present is when evidence is given on whether a child is competent to give evidence (*R* v *Reynolds* [1950] 1 KB 606, CCA).

Concerning the appropriateness of a *voir dire* in a magistrates' court, see the following cases:

F v *Chief Constable of Kent* [1982] Crim LR 682, DC.

R v *Epping & Ongar Justices, ex parte Manby* [1986] Crim LR 555, DC.

Vel v *Chief Constable of North Wales* [1987] Crim LR 496, DC.

R v *Liverpool Juvenile Court, ex parte R* [1988] QB 1, DC.

R v *Oxford City Justices, ex parte Berry* [1988] QB 507, DC.

2.8.3 THE SUFFICIENCY OF EVIDENCE

Questions of sufficiency of evidence (i.e. whether a party has adduced sufficient evidence to justify a finding on a particular fact in his favour) are for the judge.

If the evidence is such that the jury *could* find in favour of the party on that fact, the judge leaves it to the jury to decide if the fact has been proved. If the evidence is insufficient, the matter cannot even be submitted to the jury but is withdrawn from them and they are told to return a finding on the fact in favour of the other party. See *Metropolitan Railway* v *Jackson* (1877) 3 App Cas 193.

In a Crown Court trial, the question of sufficiency of evidence may be raised by the defence, after the prosecution has adduced its evidence, in what is known as a submission of no case to answer. The submission should be made in the absence of the jury and, if the trial proceeds, should not be referred to by the judge in his summing up (*R* v *Smith & Doe* (1987) 85 Cr App R 197, CA).

R v *Galbraith* [1981] 1 WLR 1039, CA:

(1)   If there is no evidence that the crime alleged has been committed by the defendant there is no difficulty — the judge will stop the case. (2) The difficulty arises where there is some evidence but it is of a tenuous character, for example, because of inherent weakness or vagueness or because it is inconsistent with other evidence: (a) where the judge concludes that the prosecution evidence, taken at its highest is such that a jury properly directed could not properly convict on it, it is his duty on a submission being made to stop the case; (b) where, however, the prosecution evidence is such that its strength or weakness depends on the view to be taken of a witness's reliability or other matters which are generally speaking within the jury's province and where on one possible view of the facts there is evidence on which the jury could properly conclude that the defendant is guilty, then the judge should allow the matter to be tried by the jury.

See also *R* v *Cockley* (1984) 79 Cr App R 181, CA.

Practice Direction [1962] 1 WLR 227, DC: as a matter of practice justices should be guided by the following considerations:

A submission that there is no case to answer may properly be made and upheld: (a) when there has been no evidence to prove an essential element in the alleged offence: (b) when the evidence adduced by the prosecution has been so discredited as a result of cross-examination or is so manifestly unreliable that no reasonable tribunal could safely convict on it.

For a useful case on the sufficiency of evidence see *Chief Constable of Avon & Somerset* v *Jest* [1986] RTR 372, DC.

Special rules apply to civil cases. See *Alexander* v *Rayson* [1936] 1 KB 169 and *Young* v *Rank* [1950] 2 KB 510. See also *Payne* v *Harrison* [1961] 2 QB 403, CA.

2.8.4   SPECIAL CASES

In a number of special cases, questions of fact are decided, either wholly or in part, by the judge.

2.8.4.1   The meaning of words
In *Brutus* v *Cozens* [1973] AC 854, HL, the appellant, during the annual tennis tournament at Wimbledon, went on to court number two while a match was in progress, blew a whistle and threw leaflets around. When he blew the whistle, nine or ten others invaded the court with banners and placards. The appellant then sat down and had to be forcibly removed. Charged with using insulting behaviour whereby a breach of the peace was likely to be occasioned under the Public Order Act, 1936, but the magistrates dismissed the information on the grounds that the behaviour was not insulting. On appeal by case stated, the question was whether the decision was *legally* correct. The Divisional Court ruled against the appellant but the House of Lords allowed his appeal. Lord Reid held that although the proper construction of a statute was a question of law, the meaning of an ordinary word of the English language like 'insulting' was a question of fact. His Lordship envisaged two exceptional cases where the meaning of a word would be a question of law:

(a)   where the context shows that the word is used in an unusual sense, in which case the judge must decide what that unusual sense is; and

(b)   where, the tribunal of fact having decided that the words in question do apply to the facts proved, it is argued on appeal that their decision was perverse in the sense that no tribunal acquainted with the ordinary use of language could possibly have reached that decision.

See *R* v *Feely* [1973] QB 530, CA.

Subsequently, however, both the Court of Appeal and the House of Lords have reached decisions involving elaborate legal definition of ordinary words without reference to *Brutus* v *Cozens*. This has prompted one commentator to observe that *Brutus* v *Cozens*, after a mute inglorious career of 15 years or so, seems to have come to an ignominious end (see Professor D. W. Elliott [1989] Crim LR 323).

See: *R* v *Callaghan* [1988] 1 WLR 1, CA.

2.8.4.2   Defamation

In criminal proceedings for libel and also, as a result of the House of Lords decision in *Nevill* v *Fine Arts & General Insurance Co. Ltd* [1897] AC 68, in civil libel proceedings, it is for the judge to decide whether the document in question is capable of bearing the defamatory meaning alleged and for the jury to decide whether it does in fact bear that meaning and is, therefore, a libel.

2.8.4.3   Perjury

See Perjury Act 1911, s. 11(6): 'The question whether a statement on which perjury is assigned was material is a question of law to be determined by the court of trial'.

2.8.4.4   Foreign law

Administration of Justice Act 1920, s. 15:

> *Where, for the purpose of disposing of any action or other matter which is being tried by a judge with a jury in any court in England or Wales, it is necessary to ascertain the law of any other country which is applicable to the facts of the case, any question as to the effect of the evidence given with respect to that law shall, instead of being submitted to the jury, be decided by the judge alone.*

2.8.4.5   Reasonableness

Subject to minor exceptions, questions of reasonableness are questions of fact for the jury. For one such exception, see *Herniman* v *Smith* [1938] AC 305, HL.

2.8.4.6   Corroboration

See **Corroboration, Chapter 12**.

Questions

OBJECTIVES

This chapter is designed to ensure that you have a sound understanding of:

(a)   the basic terminology of the law of evidence;
(b)   the facts that are open to proof or disproof under English law;
(c)   the distinction between the concepts of relevance, admissibility and weight;
(d)   the division of functions between the judge and jury; and
(e)   the discretion to exclude evidence (apart from evidence obtained by illegal or unfair means).

RESEARCH

(a)   Read the materials contained in **Chapter 2** of this Manual.

(b)   Read:

Keane, *The Modern Law of Evidence* (2nd ed., 1989), ch. 1 and 2, OR

Murphy, *A Practical Approach to Evidence* (4th ed., 1992), ch. 1; AND

Carter, *Cases and Statutes on Evidence* (2nd ed., 1990), ch. 1 and 5 and the Supplement (1992), OR

Heydon, *Evidence Cases & Materials* (3rd ed., 1991).

(c)   On the basis of this research, answer the following questions.

Question 1
Which of the following propositions, all of which relate to formal admissions in civil proceedings, is *not* true?

[A]   They can be made by either party in their pleadings.
[B]   They can be made by agreement before or at the trial.
[C]   They can be made in answer to an interrogatory.
[D]   They require proof, at the trial, of the facts stated therein.

Question 2
John is charged with indecently assaulting Kate, who is four years old, in a playground near her home. He has two previous convictions for indecent assaults on young girls and, when questioned by the police about the assault on Kate, and on being told that he had been identified leaving the playground shortly after the assault, admitted that he had been in the locality. Some time after the alleged offence, Kate told her mother that the person who had attacked her had red hair and a curly ginger beard. John is clean-shaven and has black hair. The trial judge rules that Kate is too young to be called as a witness in the proceedings against John. He also rules that evidence of Kate's conversation with her mother is inadmissible hearsay. Is John entitled to rely on the statement made by Kate to her mother (in which she described her assailant)?

[A]   Yes, because it is relevant.
[B]   Yes, because the judge has a discretion to include such evidence.
[C]   No, because it is not sufficiently relevant.
[D]   No, because the judge has no inclusionary discretion.

Question 3, Part 1
Alan Smith has been charged with the theft of a bottle of claret from Walter's Wine Warehouse, Hackney. He intends to plead not guilty. The prosecution proposes to call, among others, Mrs Edwina Walter, the owner of the Warehouse, WPC Duncan, Mr Hughes and Inspector Jenkins.

The following are extracts from the witness statement made by Mrs Walter:

> In late April 1992, I had an argument with a customer, Alan Smith, who claimed that I had short-changed him. I denied this. He became very angry and started swearing. He insisted that I was mistaken and said that I would live to regret it . . . Mr Smith has been back in the Warehouse many times since then and I suspect that he has been up to no good . . . My takings have been considerably lower than normal in the three months of May, June and July 1992. At about 1.20 p.m. on 7 August 1992, I saw Mr Smith enter the Warehouse. He was wearing a baggy brown coat. He went to the far end of the shop where we keep our best claret. He bent down behind some wine crates, out of my line of vision, then got up and hurriedly left the shop. Later that day, WPC Duncan showed me a bottle of claret priced £17.50 which I identified as having come from the Warehouse. She also asked me for a till roll to see if it showed the sale of any item priced £17.50. It did not.

WPC Duncan, in her witness statement, says:

I was passing the Warehouse at about 1.25 p.m. on 7 August when a man wearing a large brown trenchcoat emerged. He looked startled to see me and rushed off. I followed him. He kept looking over his shoulder and then ran off. I ran after him. He turned into Cambridge Passage but by the time I got to the Passage, he had disappeared. I inspected some dustbins there and inside one of them I found a bottle of claret bearing a small price sticker bearing the words 'Walter's Wine Warehouse', and a price, £17.50 '... At 4.15 p.m. I arrested and cautioned Alan Smith. He was still wearing the trenchcoat. I subsequently discovered inside the coat there was a false pocket, inexpertly stitched by hand, and measuring some 12 inches by 8 inches.

The statement of Mr Hughes, a higher scientific officer from the Police Forensic Science Laboratory, is to the effect that the bottle found by WPC Duncan bears fingerprints matching those taken from Alan Smith.

The statement of Inspector Jenkins relates to three interviews with Alan Smith at the police station. The written record of the third interview, which Alan Smith read over and signed as correct, concludes as follows:

Q. Come on Al, don't waste any more of our time.

A. OK. OK. My hands are up. It was me. I took the bloody wine. That's what you thugs want to hear isn't it. Now lay off.

Alan Smith proposes to testify that he was, at the time of the alleged offence, with Mr Evans, whom he intends to call, at the Slug and Lettuce public house, Islington. He will say that Mrs Walter is lying because he once caught her out short-changing him, and proposes to cross-examine her about that and about the fact that she is blind in one eye and short-sighted in the other. He will also say that he confessed to the crime because Inspector Jenkins, exasperated by his constant denials in all three interviews, had threatened to punch him where it would hurt: a confession seemed the only way to prevent this from happening.

    (a)   What are the facts in issue in this case?
    (b)   Of the facts which the parties are proposing to prove, which, if any, may be referred to as being:

        (i)   collateral;
       (ii)   preliminary?

    (c)   What direct (as opposed to circumstantial) evidence is there of the offence charged?
    (d)   Of the evidence which the parties propose to adduce, which items, if any:

        (i)   are properly classified as:
          (1)   hearsay (whether or not admissible hearsay);
          (2)   original evidence;
          (3)   circumstantial evidence;
       (ii)   will be ruled inadmissible because irrelevant?

    (e)   What real evidence, if any, would you advise the parties to adduce?
    (f)   Which items of evidence, if any, require a *voir dire* to determine their admissibility?

Question 3, Part 2
Alan Smith was convicted of theft. The following are extracts from the summing-up of the trial judge:

At the end of the prosecution case, I rejected the defence submission that there was no case to answer as being entirely without foundation. So now it falls to you, members of the jury, to decide whether the accused is guilty or not ... Another vital element that the prosecution must prove is dishonesty and we all know what that is, it's knavery, deceitfulness or fraud ... And so we come to the testimony of Inspector Jenkins. Do you really think that he would jeopardise his long and distinguished career by threatening to beat up a suspect? Bear in mind, if you will, that that is the likely result if you decide to reject his account of how the confession came to be made . . . And what did you make of the evidence of Mr Evans? He contradicted himself more than once about the precise times at which the accused arrived at and left the public house. Did he not strike you as somewhat hesitant and unconvincing? I would not believe him but that is not to the point because this is not a matter for me but a question of fact entirely for you.

Draw up a list of the grounds on which Mr Smith may appeal.

Question 4

(a)   Ian is charged with indecently assaulting John, a boy of 13. His defence is mistaken identity. The prosecution is able to prove that Ian is a homosexual.

To what extent, if at all, is this evidence relevant?

Give a reason for your answer.

(b)   Kevin is charged with the rape of Linda. His defence is mistaken identity. The prosecution is able to prove that Kevin is a heterosexual.

To what extent, if at all, is this evidence relevant?

Give a reason for your answer.

Question 5

In what circumstances, if any, is a *voir dire* appropriate in

(a)   a summary trial;
(b)   committal proceedings?

[Suggested outline answers to these questions can be found in **Appendix 1** to this Manual.]

3 The Burden and Standard of Proof

Which party has the obligation to prove which facts (the burden of proof)?

If a party bears such a burden, what degree of cogency or persuasiveness is required of the evidence adduced by that party before the burden is discharged (the standard of proof)?

Are the answers to the above two questions the same in civil and criminal cases?

What is the position at a trial within a trial?

3.1 The Burden of Proof

The question for consideration here is simply this: which party has the obligation to prove which facts in issue? The answer is not quite so simple and calls for a distinction to be drawn between two different burdens, the legal and evidential.

3.1.1 THE LEGAL BURDEN

The legal burden is the obligation on a party to prove a fact in issue. Whether the burden has been discharged is decided at the end of the trial by the tribunal of fact.

The legal burden is also known as the burden of proof, the persuasive burden, the probative burden, the ultimate burden, the burden of proof on the pleadings, or the risk of non-persuasion!

3.1.2 THE EVIDENTIAL BURDEN

The evidential burden is the obligation to adduce sufficient evidence on a fact in issue to justify, as a possibility, a favourable finding on that issue by the tribunal of fact. Whether the burden has been discharged is decided, during the course of the trial, by the judge.

The evidential burden is also known as the burden of adducing evidence, or the duty of passing the judge.

3.2 The Incidence of the Legal Burden

Which party bears the legal burden on which facts in issue?

3.2.1 CIVIL CASES

The general rule is that the legal burden on any fact in issue is borne by the party asserting and not denying: he who asserts must prove, not he who denies. The incidence of the legal burden is usually clear from the pleadings. See *Wilsher* v *Essex Area Health Authority* [1988] AC 1074, HL.

3.2.1.1 Statute

The incidence of the legal burden may be fixed by statute. For example, if, in proceedings referred to in s. 139(1) of the Consumer Credit Act 1974, the debtor or any surety alleges that the credit bargain is extortionate, it is for the creditor to prove the contrary: s. 171(7), *ibid*. See *Coldunell Ltd* v *Gallon* [1986] 1 All ER 429, CA; 1 WLR 994, HL.

3.2.1.2 Contract and insurance policy cases

In contract cases, which party bears the legal burden on a certain issue may be fixed by the express terms of the contract. Questions of construction have arisen in contracts of insurance and contracts for the carriage of goods but cases here are not entirely clear. For example, if the defendant relies on an exemption clause in a contract, does he have to show that the facts come within it or does the plaintiff have to show that they don't? See *Hurst* v *Evans* [1917] 1 KB 352, *Munro Brice Co.* v *War Risks Association* [1918] 2 KB 78 and *The Glendarroch* [1894] P 226, CA.

3.2.1.3 Negative assertions

He who asserts must prove: this remains the case even if the assertion is negative. See: *Abrath* v *North Eastern Railways Co.* (1883) 11 QBD 440, CA; affirmed (1886) 11 App Cas 247, HL.

Sometimes a party may try to avoid a legal burden by so drafting his pleadings as to make assertions of his own look like assertions of his opponent. Consider *Soward* v *Leggatt* (1856) 7 C & P 613:

  (a) Plaintiff (landlord): the defendant (tenant) 'did not repair' the premises.
  (b) Defendant (tenant): the defendant 'did well and sufficiently repair'.
  (c) Abinger CB: the plaintiff could as easily have pleaded the defendant 'allowed the house to become dilapidated' i.e. P was alleging D had broken the covenant and P had to prove it.

3.2.1.4 Policy

In many cases it is difficult to know whether facts in issue are essential to the case of one party or to that of his opponent. In these cases, the courts have tended to put the legal burden on the party who would be expected to find its discharge least difficult. See:

Amos v *Hughes* (1835) 1 Mood & R 464.

Joseph Constantine Steamship Line Ltd v *Imperial Smelting Corpn Ltd* [1942] AC 154, HL.

Coldman v *Hill* [1919] 1 KB 443, CA.

Brook's Wharf & Bull Wharf Ltd v *Goodman Brothers* [1937] 1 KB 534, CA.

Levison v *Patent Carpet Cleaning Co. Ltd* [1977] 3 WLR 90, CA.

3.2.2 CRIMINAL CASES

3.2.2.1 The general rule

The general rule is that the prosecution has the burden of proving the guilt of the accused. The rule applies to both negative and positive assertions. See *R* v *Horn* (1912) 7 Cr App R 200 and *R* v *Donovan* [1934] 2 KB 498.

Woolmington v *DPP* [1935] AC 462, HL, *per* Lord Sankey LC at p. 481:

> Throughout the web of the English criminal law one golden thread is always to be seen, that it is the duty of the prosecution to prove the prisoner's guilt subject to what I have already said as to the defence of insanity and subject also to any statutory exception . . . No matter what the charge or where the trial, the principle that the prosecution must prove the guilt of the prisoner is part of the common law of England and no attempt to whittle it down can be entertained.

3.2.2.2   Exceptions

(a)   Insanity: *M'Naghten's Case* [1843] 10 Cl & F 200, HL. See also *R* v *Burns* (1973) 58 Cr App R 364, CA

(b)   Express statutory exceptions, for example:

'unless the contrary is proved',
'unless the accused proves',
'the proof whereof shall lie on the accused'.

The Misuse of Drugs Act 1971, s. 6, provides that it is an offence to cultivate any plant of the genus *cannabis*. Section 28(2) of the Act provides that it is a defence for the accused to prove that he neither knew of nor suspected nor had reason to suspect the existence of some fact alleged by the prosecution and which it is necessary for the prosecution to prove to secure a conviction. Must the prosecution prove that the accused knew that the plant was of the genus *cannabis* or must the accused prove that he or she did not know that the plant was of the genus *cannabis*? See *R* v *Champ* (1981) 73 Cr App R 367, CA: the accused must prove that he/she did not know that the plant was of the genus *cannabis*.

Another example is provided by the Prevention of Terrorism (Temporary Provisions) Act 1989, s. 10(1):

A person is guilty of an offence if he—

(c)   enters into or is otherwise concerned in an arrangement whereby money or other property is or is to be made available for the benefit of . . . [a proscribed] organisation.

Section 10(2) provides that:

. . . in proceedings against a person for an offence under subsection 1(c) above it is a defence to prove that he did not know and had no reasonable cause to suspect that the arrangement related to a proscribed organisation.

(c)   Statutes creating offences subject to exceptions, provisos etc., for example:

'. . . without lawful authority or excuse'.
'. . . provided that'.
'. . . other than'.

Magistrates' Courts Act 1980, s. 101 (formerly Magistrates' Courts Act 1952, s. 81):

Where the defendant to an information or complaint relies for his defence on any exception, exemption, proviso, excuse or qualification, whether or not it accompanies the description of the offence or matter of complaint in the enactment creating the offence or on which the complaint is founded, the burden of proving the exception, exemption, proviso, excuse or qualification shall be on him: and this notwithstanding that the information or complaint contains an allegation negativing the exception, exemption, proviso, excuse or qualification.

Sometimes this statutory provision occasions difficulty. Consider, for example, the following sections of the Factories Act 1961:

(i)   section 155(1): it is an offence not to comply with s. 29(1);
(ii)   section 29(1): any workplace 'shall, so far as is reasonably practicable be made and kept safe for any person working therein'.

Is the phrase 'so far as is reasonably practicable' an excuse or qualification? If so, the accused employer has to prove it was not reasonably practicable to keep the premises safe. If not, the prosecution has to prove it was reasonably practicable to keep the premises safe. See *Nimmo* v *Alexander Cowan & Sons Ltd* [1968] AC 107, a Scottish case, in which the House of Lords, by a majority, took the former view.

On its wording, s. 101 is confined to summary trials. For the position at trials on indictment, see *R* v *Edwards* [1975] QB 27 *per* Lawton LJ at pp. 39–40:

> . . . this line of authority establishes that . . . the common law . . . has evolved an exception to the fundamental rule of our criminal law that the prosecution must prove every element of the offence charged. This exception . . . is limited to offences arising under enactments which prohibit the doing of an act save in specified circumstances or by persons of specified classes or with specified qualifications or with the licence or permission of specified authorities. Whenever the prosecution seeks to rely on this exception, the court must construe the enactment under which the charge is laid. If the true construction is that the enactment prohibits the doing of acts, subject to provisos, exemptions and the like, then the prosecution can rely upon the exception.

> In our judgment its application does not depend upon either the fact, or the presumption, that the defendant has peculiar knowledge enabling him to prove the positive of any negative averment . . .

> Two consequences follow . . . First, as it comes into operation upon an enactment being construed in a particular way, there is no need for the prosecution to prove a prima facie case of lack of excuse, qualification or the like: and secondly, what shifts is the onus: it is for the defendant to prove that he was entitled to do the prohibited act. What rests on him is the legal or, as it is sometimes called, the persuasive burden of proof. It is not the evidential burden.

See also the following examples pre-dating *R* v *Edwards:*

R v *Scott* (1921) 86 JP 69: selling cocaine without a licence.

R v *Oliver* [1944] KB 68: dealing in sugar without a licence.

R v *Ewens* [1967] 1 QB 322: possessing drugs without a prescription.

The merits of the decision in *Edwards* are debatable. One good consequence of the decision is that the test is now the same in summary trials and trials on indictment — there is, after all, no good reason why there should be a difference. On the other hand, it is the view of some that the accused should never bear more than an evidential burden. If the accused merely bears the evidential burden, and discharges it, the judge will direct the jury that the prosecution bears the legal burden of disproving the particular defence in question and must satisfy the jury in that respect beyond resonable doubt. If the accused bears the legal burden, the judge directs the jury that it is for the accused to prove the defence on a balance of probabilities. Thus in a case like *Champ* (1981) 73 Cr App R 367, CA, where the only issue was guilty knowledge, the judge would be entitled to say to the jury: 'If you are unable to conclude that the defence case is more probable than not, you must convict.'

Since *R* v *Edwards* there has been a further and important development, the decision of the House of Lords in *R* v *Hunt* [1987] AC 352 concerning the following statutory provisions:

    (i)   Misuse of Drugs Act 1971, s. 5: subject to any regulations under s. 7, it is an offence for a person to have a controlled drug in his possession.
    (ii)   A controlled drug is defined by the Act to include a preparation or other product containing morphine.
    (iii)   Misuse of Drug Regulations 1973: s. 5 shall have no effect in relation to, *inter alia*, any preparation of morphine containing not more than 0.2% of morphine.

The burden is on the prosecution to prove that the facts do not come within the above exception.

Lord Griffiths, at p. 374:

> I would summarise the position thus far by saying that *Woolmington* did not lay down a rule that the burden of proving a statutory defence only lay on the defendant if the statute specifically so provided: that a statute can, on its true construction, place a burden of proof on the defendant although it does not do so expressly and that if a burden of proof is placed on the defendant it is the same burden whether the case be tried summarily or on indictment, namely a burden that has to be discharged on the balance of probabilities.
>
> The real difficulty in these cases lies in determining on whom Parliament intended to place the burden of proof when the statute has not expressly so provided. It presents particularly difficult problems of construction when what might be regarded as a matter of defence appears in a clause creating the offence rather than in some subsequent proviso from which it may more readily be inferred that it was intended to provide for a separate defence which a defendant must set up and prove if he wishes to avail himself of it. This difficulty was acutely demonstrated in *Nimmo* v *Alexander Cowan* . . . their Lordships were in agreement that if the linguistic construction of the statute did not clearly indicate on whom the burden should lie the court should look to other considerations to determine the intention of Parliament, such as the mischief at which the Act was aimed and practical considerations affecting the burden of proof and, in particular, the ease or difficulty that the respective parties would encounter in discharging the burden. I regard this last consideration as one of great importance, for surely Parliament can never lightly be taken to have intended to impose an onerous duty on a defendant to prove his innocence in a criminal case, and a court should be very slow to draw any such inference from the language of a statute.

See also *R* v *Cross* (1990) 91 Cr App R 115, CA.

3.3 The Incidence of the Evidential Burden

A party bearing the legal burden on a particular issue usually bears the evidential burden on that issue as well. Two important categories of exception are (a) presumptions and (b) (in criminal cases) certain defences. Presumptions are considered below. Concerning many criminal defences, the evidential burden of adducing sufficient evidence to leave the defence before the jury is on the accused and, if that burden is discharged, the legal burden of disproving the defence is on the prosecution. See:

Bratty v *Attorney-General for Northern Ireland* [1963] AC 386, HL (non-insane automatism).

Mancini v *DPP* [1942] AC 1, HL (provocation).

R v *Lobell* [1957] 1 QB 547, CCA (self-defence).

Kennedy v *HM Advocate* (1944) JC 171 (drunkeness).

R v *Gill* (1963) 47 Cr App R 166, CCA (duress).

R v *Bennett* (1978) 68 Cr App R 168, CA (impossibility in cases of common law conspiracy).

There are dicta in *R* v *Johnson* [1961] 1 WLR 1478, CCA that the accused bears an evidential burden in relation to a defence of alibi; but see *R* v *Price* (1993) 96 Cr App R 264.

See also:

DPP v *Morgan* [1976] AC 182, HL.

Bullard v *R* [1957] AC 635, PC.

3.4 The Burden of Proof in a Trial within a Trial

The burden of proving preliminary facts is borne by the party alleging their existence and seeking to admit the evidence in question. See *R* v *Yacoob* (1981) 72 Cr App R 313, CA (the competence of a prosecution witness).

See also *R* v *Shephard* (1993) 96 Cr App R 345: a party seeking to adduce a statement in a document produced by a computer under Police and Criminal Evidence Act 1984, s. 69, has the burden of proving that the computer was operating properly. Section 69 provides that such a statement shall not be admissible as evidence of any fact stated therein 'unless it is shown', *inter alia*, that the computer was operating properly at all material times.

However, where a witness claims to have a privilege it seems that it is for the party disputing the privilege to show that the claim cannot be sustained. See *R* v *Ataou* [1988] 2 WLR 1147, CA.

3.5 The Right to Begin

The incidence of the burden of proof affects the question of which party has the right to begin adducing evidence in court. See RSC Ord. 35, r. 7(6):

> *Where the burden of proof of all the issues in the action lies on the defendant or, where there are two or more defendants and they appear separately or are separately represented, on one of the defendants, the defendants or that defendant, as the case may be, shall be entitled to begin.*

3.6 The Standard of Proof

The standard or proof is the degree of cogency or persuasiveness required of the evidence adduced by a party in order to discharge a burden of proof borne by him.

3.6.1 CRIMINAL CASES

3.6.1.1 The legal burden

(a) Borne by the prosecution:

Woolmington v *DPP* [1935] AC 462, HL: 'the prosecution must prove the case beyond reasonable doubt'.

Miller v *Minister of Pensions* [1947] 2 All ER 372 *per* Denning J at pp. 373–4:

> It need not reach certainty, but it must carry a high degree of probability. Proof beyond reasonable doubt does not mean proof beyond the shadow of doubt. The law would fail to protect the community if it admitted fanciful possibilities to deflect the course of justice. If the evidence is so strong against a man as to leave only a remote possibility in his favour which can be dismissed with the sentence 'of course it is possible, but not in the least probable', the case is proved beyond reasonable doubt, but nothing short of that will suffice.

R v *Kritz* [1950] 1 KB 82, CCA; *R* v *Summers* [1952] 1 All ER 1059, CCA: the jury 'must be sure' or 'should be satisfied so that they feel sure'.

See also:

R v *Hepworth and Fearnley* [1955] 2 QB 600, CCA.

R v *Gray* (1973) 58 Cr App R 177.

R v *Stafford* (1968) 53 Cr App R 1, CA.

R v *Ching* (1976) 63 Cr App R 7, CA:

> A reasonable doubt, it has been said, is a doubt to which you can give a reason as opposed to a mere fanciful sort of speculation such as 'Well, nothing in this world is certain, nothing in this world can be proved' . . . It is sometimes said the sort of matter which might influence you if you were to consider some business matter. A matter, for example, of a mortgage concerning your house, or something of that nature.

Walters v *R* [1969] 2 AC 26, PC:

> a reasonable doubt is that quality and kind of doubt which, when you are dealing with matters of importance in your own affairs, you allow to influence you one way or the other.

(b)   Borne by the accused:

R v *Carr-Briant* [1943] KB 607, CA, *per* Humphreys J at p. 612:

> . . . in any case where, either by statute or at common law, some matter is presumed against an accused person 'unless the contrary is proved', the jury should be directed that it is for them to decide whether the contrary is proved, that the burden of proof required is less than that required at the hands of the prosecution in proving the case beyond a reasonable doubt, and that the burden may be discharged by evidence satisfying the jury of the probability of that which the accused is called upon to establish.

3.6.1.2   The evidential burden
Jayasena v *R* [1970] AC 618 *per* Lord Devlin:

> the prosecution in order to stop an issue from being withdrawn from the jury must adduce such evidence as would be sufficient, if believed and left uncontradicted, to justify as a possibility a finding by the jury in their favour.

Bratty v *Attorney-General for Northern Ireland* [1963] AC 386, HL, *per* Lord Morris of Borth-y-Gest:

> where the accused bears the evidential burden alone, he must adduce such evidence as would, if believed and left uncontradicted, induce a reasonable doubt in the mind of the jury as to whether his version might not be true.

3.6.2   CIVIL CASES

3.6.2.1   The legal burden
Denning J in *Miller* v *Minister of Pensions* [1947] 2 All ER 372 at p. 374:

> It must carry a reasonable degree of probability, but not so high as is required in a criminal case. If the evidence is such that the tribunal can say: 'We think it more probable than not', the burden is discharged, but, if the probabilities are equal, it is not.

The degree of probability required, however, can vary from case to case. See *Bater* v *Bater* [1951] P 35.

In some exceptional cases, the criminal standard is used. See *Re Bramblevale Ltd* [1970] Ch 128, CA, and *Dean* v *Dean* [1987] 1 FLR 517, CA (where an order is sought to commit a person to prison for a civil contempt): and *Mahadervan* v *Mahadervan* [1964] P 233 (where it is sought to rebut the presumption as to the formal validity of a marriage).

The variable nature of the degree of probability required is exemplified by civil cases in which an allegation of crime is made. See *Hornal* v *Neuberger Products Ltd* [1957] 1 QB 247, CA:

> The more serious the allegation the higher the degree of probability that is required (*per* Denning LJ at p. 258).

> ... the very elements of gravity become a part of the whole range of circumstances which have to be weighed in the scale when deciding as to the balance of probabilities (*per* Morris LJ at p. 266).

See also *The Michael* [1978] 1 WLR 411, and *Re Dellow's Will Trusts* [1964] 1 WLR 451:

> The more serious the allegation the more cogent is the evidence required to overcome the unlikelihood of what is alleged and thus to prove it.

Matrimonial proceedings are another category of case which has caused difficulty and here the authorities remain in conflict. See:

Ginesi v *Ginesi* [1948] P 179, CA.

Preston-Jones v *Preston-Jones* [1951] AC 291, HL.

Blyth v *Blyth* [1966] 1 All ER 524, HL.

F v *F* [1968] P 506.

Bastable v *Bastable* [1968] 1 WLR, CA (a case concerning adultery). Although the ordinary civil standard applies, the court should require a degree of probability proportionate to the subject matter; and since adultery is a serious matrimonial offence, it calls for a high standard of proof.

See also: *Re G* [1987] 1 WLR 1461 (an allegation that a child has been sexually abused by a father with legal custody): *W* v *K* (1987) 151 JP 589 (rebuttal of the presumption of legitimacy): *Serio* v *Serio* (1983) 13 Fam Law 255, CA (an issue of paternity); and *Lawrence* v *Chester Chronicle* (1986) *The Times*, 8 February 1986, CA (defamation actions).

In *H* v *H and C; K* v *K* [1989] 3 All ER 740, the Court of Appeal held that in custody and access applications in the matrimonial jurisdiction, the appropriate standard of proof for determining whether sexual abuse of children by a father has taken place is the ordinary civil standard and not a lesser standard of a real possibility of abuse or a real risk that the allegations might be true. However, when exercising his discretion in deciding whether future access by a father should be permitted the judge, applying the principle that the welfare of the child was paramount, could take into account evidence which, while insufficient to show abuse on a balance of probabilities, pointed to a real possibility or risk of abuse in the future.

For the problems that can arise on interlocutory applications, see *Attock Cement Co. Ltd* v *Romanian Bank for Foreign Trade* [1989] 1 All ER 1189, CA: concerning the standard of proof that applies when an action falls within RSC Ord. 11 r. 1. At the *ex parte* stage the Master sees whether the facts in the plaintiff's (P's) affidavit bring the case within the rule and if so grants leave (unless P's evidence is incredible). If the defendant applies to set aside leave to serve the writ out of the jurisdiction and there is a disputed question of fact essential to determining whether the action falls within Ord. 11 r. 1, P must establish 'a good arguable case', i.e. the court, before allowing service to stand, must reach a provisional or tentative conclusion on all the admissible material before it that P was probably right.

3.6.2.2   The evidential burden

3.6.3   THE STANDARD OF PROOF IN A TRIAL WITHIN A TRIAL

In civil cases the standard is on a balance of probabilities; in criminal cases where the prosecution bears the burden the standard is proof beyond reasonable doubt and where the accused bears the burden the standard is proof on a balance of probabilities. See *R* v *Ewing* [1983] QB 1039, CA. (Contrast *R* v *Angeli* [1979] 1 WLR 26, CA; and *R* v *Yacoob* (1981) 72 Cr App R 313, CA).

These cases must be distinguished from cases in which the judge, before allowing certain items of evidence to be admitted, must be satisfied by *prima facie* evidence. See *R* v *Robson* [1972] 1 WLR 651, CA: in order to admit tape recordings the judge must 'satisfy himself that a *prima facie* case of originality has been made out by evidence which defines and describes the provenance and history of the recordings up to the moment of production in court.

As to the use in criminal trials of tape recordings and transcripts of police interviews, see also *R* v *Rampling* [1987] Crim LR 823, CA; the *Code of Practice for Tape Recording of Police Interviews*, SI 88/1200; *Practice Note* [1989] 2 All ER 415, QBD; and *R* v *Emmerson* (1991) 92 Cr App R 284, CA.

The requirement in *Robson* appears not to apply in the case of photographs and video tapes, where all that is required is proof that such material relates to the events in question. See generally *New Law Journal* (1989), Vol. 139, pp. 1079–82.

Questions

OBJECTIVES

By the conclusion of this chapter, you should be able:

   (a)   to analyse the facts in issue in both civil and criminal cases and indicate who bears the legal burden of proof and who bears the evidential burden on each fact in issue;
   (b)   to decide who has the right to begin adducing evidence in a trial;
   (c)   to identify the standard of proof appropriate to a burden;
   (d)   to understand and to use properly the terminology applicable to both burdens and standards of proof.

RESEARCH

   (a)   Read the materials contained in **Chapter 3** of this Manual.
   (b)   Read:

Keane, *The Modern Law of Evidence* (2nd ed., 1989), ch. 3, OR

Murphy, *A Practical Approach to Evidence* (4th ed., 1992), ch. 3; AND

Carter, *Cases and Statutes on Evidence* (2nd ed., 1990), ch. 2 and 3 and the Supplement (1992), OR

Heydon, *Evidence Cases & Materials* (3rd ed., 1991).

   (c)   On the basis of this research, answer the following questions.

Question 1
Noah and Max were en route to a party in a well-known gay bar. As they were walking to the entrance, a group of skin-heads shouted abusive taunts at them and called them 'a pair of pansies'. The gang approached them in a menacing manner and Noah punched out at one of the skin-heads, breaking his nose and cutting his face. Later Noah was charged with inflicting grievous bodily harm contrary to Offences Against the Person Act 1861, s. 20. At his trial, Noah intends to raise the defence of self-defence. Who will bear the burden of proof on this particular issue?

[A]   Noah bears both the legal and evidential burden.
[B]   Noah bears the evidential burden only.
[C]   Noah bears the tactical burden only.
[D]   Noah bears the legal burden only.

Question 2
Which of the following propositions is *not* true?

[A] Where an accused raises the defence of duress an evidential burden only lies on the accused.
[B] Where the legal burden on a particular issue is borne by the accused it is discharged by the defence satisfying the jury on a balance of probabilities.
[C] Where the defence bears the legal burden of proving insanity, it is only discharged by proof beyond all reasonable doubt.
[D] A statutory provision may expressly place the legal burden on the defendant.

Question 3
Table 3.1 has been used to separate a number of facts in issue and assign legal and evidential burdens and standard of proof in respect of the example given.

For example, Alan is charged with possessing an offensive weapon, contrary to the Prevention of Crime Act 1953, s. 1. He is alleged to have had a chisel with him in a public street. He was found with the chisel at 2 a.m. He does not deny this but says he is a sculptor and while he was at a party, inspiration had struck him for a sculpture and he was on his way to his studio. He adds that he always carries a chisel in case he is attacked.

The Prevention of Crime Act 1953, s. 1(1), provides:

> *Any person who without lawful authority or reasonable excuse, the proof whereof shall lie on him, has with him in any public place any offensive weapon shall be guilty of an offence.*

Section 1(4) of the Act defines an offensive weapon as:

> *any article made or adapted for use for causing injury to the person, or intended by the person having it with him for such use by him.*

Table 3.1

For each fact in issue, indicate:

Fact in issue	Who must discharge the evidential burden	Who must discharge the legal burden of proof	The standard of proof on the legal burden
Possession of chisel	Prosecution	Prosecution	Beyond reasonable doubt
Public place	Prosecution	Prosecution	Beyond reasonable doubt
Offensive nature	Prosecution	Prosecution	Beyond reasonable doubt
Reasonable excuse	Defence	Defence	Balance of probabilities

Fill in a table for each of the following problems

(a)   Arabian Ltd, the charterers of a ship, is suing Bulk Traffic Co., the owners of the ship, for breach of contract: the ship blew up and sank during its voyage. No one is able to determine the cause of the explosion.

Bulk Traffic alleges that the contract is frustrated by the explosion. Arabian Ltd says that any frustration was self-induced and does not afford a defence to its action.

Table 3.2

Fact in issue	Evidential burden	Legal burden	Standard of proof on legal burden
1.			
2.			
3.			
4.			
5.			

(b)   Following a collision between his car and a lamp-post, Charles is accused of driving without due care and attention. He told the police officer who interviewed him at the hospital that he remembered nothing of the incident. Later, he told the police that his doctor told him that in all likelihood he simply blacked out (non-insane automatism).

Table 3.3

Fact in issue	Evidential burden	Legal burden	Standard of proof on legal burden
1.			
2.			
3.			

(c)   Daphne is the sole beneficiary of a trust, established by her late uncle, Edward. Frank is the trustee and Daphne wishes to sue him for misuse of the trust fund. She alleges that he has deliberately mixed money from the fund with his own in his bank account and has spent it. Frank denies these allegations.

Table 3.4

Fact in issue	Evidential burden	Legal burden	Standard of proof on legal burden
1.			
2.			
3.			
4.			

Question 4

Using the same type of table as in question 3, explain the burdens and standard of proof in the following case.

In an action by A for breach of contract for the carriage of a consignment of television sets by lorry from London to Manchester, the contract provided that B, a lorry owner, was not liable for loss caused by fire provided that the lorry owner's servants were not negligent. The lorry and its load were destroyed by fire in a service area on the motorway. B claims that he is not liable for the loss. A asserts that B was facing bankruptcy and that the lorry was deliberately set on fire so that B could claim on his insurance from the insurers of the lorry. Alternatively A asserts that the fire was caused by the carelessness of the lorry driver.

Question 5

Michael is charged with an offence which reads:

A person who promotes or takes part in a competition or trial (other than a race or trial of speed) involving the use of motor vehicles on a public highway shall be guilty of an offence unless the competition or trial is authorised, and is conducted in accordance with conditions imposed, by or under regulations under this section.

Michael admits that he took part in a trial involving the use of a vehicle on a public highway but says that:

(a)   it was a race or trial of speed; and
(b)   the vehicle was not a *motor* vehicle.

Who will bear the burden of proof on each of these issues?

What standard of proof will be required to discharge them?

[Compare your answer to Question 3 with that contained in **Appendix 1** to this Manual.]

4   Presumptions, Competence and Compellability

When, if at all, can the court treat a fact as having been proved not withstanding that no evidence or insufficient evidence has been adduced to establish it (presumptions)?

Which persons can be called to give evidence and which can be forced to do so (competence and compellability)?

When can witnesses give their evidence unsworn (that is, without having taken the oath or made an affirmation)?

4.1   Presumptions

On the operation of a presumption, a fact may or must be taken to have been proved notwithstanding that no evidence or insufficient evidence has been adduced to establish that fact. Put simply, the presumption can assist a party who might be expected to bear the burden of proving a particular fact by imposing a requirement of disproof on the other party. Three types of presumption need to be distinguished.

(a)   Presumptions of fact.
(b)   Irrebuttable presumptions of law.
(c)   Rebuttable presumptions of law.

4.1.1   PRESUMPTIONS OF FACT (OR PROVISIONAL PRESUMPTIONS)

Presumptions of fact are nothing more than frequently recurring examples of circumstantial evidence: see **Chapter 2**.

*Proof or admission of primary (basic) fact = another fact *may* be presumed in the absence of sufficient evidence to the contrary.

4.1.1.1   Presumption of intention
DPP v *Smith* [1961] AC 290.

R v *Steane* [1947] KB 997, CCA.

Criminal Justice Act 1967, s. 8:

> *A court or jury, in determining whether a person has committed an offence—*
>
> *(a)   shall not be bound in law to infer that he intended or foresaw a result of his actions by reason only of its being a natural and probable consequence of those actions; but*

(b)   shall decide whether he did intend or foresee that result by reference to all the evidence, drawing such inferences from the evidence as appear proper in the circumstances.

4.1.1.2   Presumption of guilty knowledge

On a charge of theft or handling, if it is proved that the accused was found in possession of goods which were recently stolen and the accused offers no explanation or the jury is satisfied that the explanation he gives is false, the jury *may* infer guilty knowledge. See *R* v *Aves* (1950) 34 Cr App R 159; and *R* v *Cash* [1985] QB 801, CA.

4.1.1.3   Presumption of continuance of life

If a person is proved to be alive on a certain date, it may be inferred, in the absence of contrary evidence, that he or she was alive on a subsequent date. See:

R v *Lumley* (1869) LR 1 CCR 196.

4.1.2   IRREBUTTABLE PRESUMPTIONS OF LAW (OR CONCLUSIVE PRESUMPTIONS)

Irrebuttable presumptions of law are simply rules of substantive law.

*Proof or admission of primary (basic) facts = another fact *must* be presumed as a matter of law.

R v *Waite* [1892] 2 QB 600: in criminal proceedings boys under 14 years of age are conclusively presumed to be incapable of sexual intercourse or buggery.

4.1.3   REBUTTABLE PRESUMPTIONS OF LAW

*Proof or admission of primary (basic) fact = another fact *must* be presumed in the absence of sufficient evidence to the contrary.

Concerning disproof of the presumed fact, the party against whom the presumption operates bears *either* a legal burden (a 'persuasive' or 'compelling' presumption) *or* an evidential burden (an 'evidential' presumption).

An example of a rebuttable presumption of law is that of *doli incapax*. See:

J.M. v *Runeckles* (1984) 79 Cr App R 255, DC.

H v *Chief Constable of South Wales* (1986) *The Times*, 5 July 1986, DC.

A v *DPP* [1992] Crim LR 34, DC.

4.1.3.1   Presumption of marriage

(a)   Formal validity

Formal validity of a marriage means compliance with the formal requirements of the *lex loci celebrationis*, e.g. in a Church of England marriage in England, banns must be published and a common licence obtained. If not, the marriage may be made void.

*This presumption arises on proof or admission of the primary facts that a marriage ceremony, whether English or foreign, was celebrated between persons who intended to marry. See *Piers* v *Piers* (1849) 2 HL Cas 331; and *Mahadervan* v *Mahadervan* [1964] P 233.

(b)   Essential validity

Essential validity of a marriage means compliance with requirements such as the parties' capacity to marry and the reality of their consent, e.g. under English law the parties should not be related within the prohibited degrees and neither should be a party to another marriage. If they are, the marriage is void.

*This presumption arises on proof or admission of the primary fact that a formally valid marriage ceremony was celebrated. See *Re Peete* [1952] 2 'All ER 599; and *Taylor* v *Taylor* [1967] P 25.

   (c) Cohabitation
*There is also a presumption of marriage arising from a man and woman cohabiting with the repute of man and wife. See *Re Taylor* [1961] 1 WLR 9, CA.

4.1.3.2 Presumption of legitimacy
*The presumption arises on proof or admission of the basic fact that the child in question was born or conceived during lawful wedlock.

The Poulett Peerage Case [1903] AC 395.

Maturin v *Attorney-General* [1938] 2 All ER 214.

Hetherington v *Hetherington* [1887] 12 PD 112.

Family Law Reform Act 1969, s. 26:

> *Any presumption of law as to the legitimacy or illegitimacy of any person may in any civil proceedings be rebutted by evidence which shows that it is more probable than not that the person is illegitimate or legitimate as the case may be and it shall not be necessary to prove that fact beyond reasonable doubt in order to rebut the presumption.*

T. (H.H.) v *T. (E.)* [1971] 1 WLR 429.

R v *Inhabitants of Mansfield* (1841) 1 QB 444.

4.1.3.3 Presumption of death
Sachs J in *Chard* v *Chard* [1956] P 259 at p. 272:

> That presumption in its modern shape takes effect (without examining its terms too exactly) substantially as follows. Where as regards 'A.B.' there is no acceptable affirmative evidence that he was alive at some time during a continuous period of seven years or more, then if it can be proved first, that there are persons who would be likely to have heard of him over that period, secondly that those persons have not heard of him, and thirdly that all due inquiries have been made appropriate to the circumstances, 'A.B.' will be presumed to have died at some time within that period.

This is *probably* an evidential presumption. See *Prudential Assurance Co.* v *Edmonds* (1877) 2 App Cas 487, HL.

This presumption establishes death but not, in the absence of additional evidence, that the deceased died on any particular date during the seven-year-period: see *Re Phené's Trusts* [1870] 5 Ch App 139 at p. 144. Is the date of presumed death the date of the legal proceedings in which the presumption arises (view 1) or the date at the end of the seven-year period (view 2)? The authorities conflict. See *Lal Chand Marwari* v *Mahant Ramrup Gir* (1925) 42 TLR 159, PC; *Re Westbrook's Trusts* [1873] WN 167; and *Chipchase* v *Chipchase* [1939] P 391, DC.

Additional to the common law presumption of death, there exist analogous and related statutory provisions:

   (a) The proviso to Offences Against the Person Act 1861, s. 57:

Provided that nothing in this section shall extend . . . to any person marrying a second time whose husband or wife shall have been continually absent from such person for the space of seven years then last past, and shall not have been known by such person to be living within that time.

R v *Curgerwen* (1865) LR 1 CCR 1.

(b)   Matrimonial Causes Act 1973, s. 19(3):

. . . the fact that for a period of seven years or more the other party to the marriage has been continually absent from the petitioner and the petitioner has no reason to believe that the other party has been living within that time shall be evidence that the other party is dead until the contrary is proved.

(c)   Law of Property Act 1925, s. 184:

In all cases where, after the commencement of this Act, two or more persons have died in circumstances rendering it uncertain which of them survived the other or others, such deaths shall (subject to any order of the court), for all purposes affecting the title to property, be presumed to have occurred in order of seniority, and accordingly the younger shall be deemed to have survived the elder.

Hickman v *Peacey* [1945] AC 304.

4.1.3.4   Presumption of regularity (*omnia praesumuntur rite esse acta*)

*On proof or admission that a person acted in a judicial, official or public capacity, it is presumed, in the absence of contrary evidence, that the act complied with any necessary formalities and that the person in question was properly appointed. See, for example:

Johnson v *Barnes* (1873) LR 8 CP 527.

R v *Cresswell* (1873) 1 QBD 446, CCR.

R v *Roberts* (1874) 14 Cox CC 101, CCR.

R v *Gordon* (1789) Leach 515.

There is also a presumption that mechanical and other instruments were in working order at the time of their use. See *Tingle Jacobs & Co.* v *Kennedy* [1964] 1 WLR 638 n (traffic lights) and *Nicholas* v *Penny* [1950] 2 KB 466 (speedometers).

The authorities are in conflict as to whether this presumption can be used by the prosecution to prove the existence of facts central to the offence charged. See *Gibbins* v *Skinner* [1951] 2 KB 279, DC; and *Scott* v *Baker* [1961] 1 QB 659, DC. The Privy Council, in *Dillon* v *R* [1982] AC 484 has answered this question in the negative.

4.1.3.5   *Res ipsa loquitur*

Erle CJ in *Scott* v *London & St Katherine Docks Co.* (1865) 3 H & C 596 at p. 601:

There must be reasonable evidence of negligence.

But where the thing is shown to be under the management of the defendant or his servants, and the accident is such as in the ordinary course of things does not happen if those who have the management use proper care, it affords reasonable evidence, in the absence of explanation by the defendants, that the accident arose from want of care.

What sort of presumption is this, a presumption of fact, an evidential presumption or a persuasive presumption? The authorities are in conflict. See:

Langham v *The Governors of Wellingborough School* (1932) 101 LJ KB 513.

The Kite [1933] P 154.

Barkway v *South Wales Transport Co. Ltd* [1948] 2 All ER 460.

Ng Chun Pui v *Lee Chuen Tat* [1988] RTR 298, PC.

Wilsher v *Essex Area Health Authority* [1988] AC 1074, HL.

4.1.4   CONFLICTING PRESUMPTIONS

Where two presumptions apply to the facts of a case, the one leading to a conclusion which conflicts with that of the other, do they neutralise each other so that the court should then proceed on the basis that no presumption at all is involved? Again, the authorities are not entirely clear. See:

R v *Willshire* (1881) 6 QBD 366, CCR.

Monckton v *Tarr* (1930) 23 BWCC 504, CA.

Taylor v *Taylor* [1967] P 25.

4.2   Competence and Compellability

A witness is competent if he or she can as a matter of law be called by a party to give evidence. A witness is compellable if, being competent, he or she can as a matter of law be compelled by the court to give evidence.

4.2.1   THE GENERAL RULE

The general rule has two limbs:

(a)   all persons are competent; and
(b)   all competent witnesses are compellable.

4.2.2   THE EXCEPTIONS

4.2.2.1   The accused

(a)   For the prosecution.

An accused or co-accused is incompetent to give evidence for the prosecution. The only way in which a co-accused can become competent for the Crown is if he or she ceases to be a co-accused. See:

R v *Rhodes* [1899] 1 QB 77, CCR.

R v *Payne* (1872) LR 1 CCR 349.

In *R* v *Pipe* (1966) 51 Cr App R 17, CA it was held that an accomplice against whom proceedings are pending but who is not being tried in the proceedings in question, should not be called by the prosecution unless they have given an undertaking that proceedings will be discontinued against that accomplice. It was held to be wholly irregular, therefore, in a prosecution for theft, to call for the prosecution the alleged receiver of the stolen goods, who had been charged and would face separate trial on some later date, to give evidence for the prosecution against the alleged thief of the goods. However, the Court of Appeal in *Pipe* and in *R* v *Turner* (1975) 61 Cr App R 67, CA, were of opinion that the rule was one of practice and not law, i.e. a matter of discretion for the judge.

(b)   For the defence.

An accused is competent but not compellable to give evidence in his or her own defence.

Criminal Evidence Act 1898, s. 1.

Every person charged with an offence shall be a competent witness for the defence at every stage of the proceedings, whether the person so charged is charged solely or jointly with any other person. Provided as follows:-

(a)   A person so charged shall not be called as a witness in pursuance of this Act except upon his own application:
(b)   The failure of any person charged with an offence to give evidence shall not be made the subject of any comment by the prosecution.

An accused may give evidence-in-chief against a co-accused and such evidence may also be elicited from him or her by the prosecution in cross-examination. See *R* v *Paul* [1920] 2 KB 83.

An accused is competent to give evidence for a co-accused but not compellable (unless he or she ceases to be an accused person). See: *R* v *Richardson* (1967) 51 Cr App R 381.

(c)   Comments on failure to testify.

The words 'any comment' in proviso (b) to the Criminal Evidence Act 1898, s. 1, mean what they say. Thus there should be no comment whatsoever by the prosecution, whether favourable or unfavourable; but if the prosecution does make a comment, then in so far as any harm has been done, the judge may make good the damage done in his summing-up: see *R* v *Riley* (1990) 91 Cr App R 208, CA, where the prosecution made a comment which was *not* unfavourable.

Proviso (b) to the Criminal Evidence Act 1898, s. 1 does not prevent comment by a co-accused. See *R* v *Wickham* (1971) 55 Cr App R 199, CA.

The judge also may comment on the accused's failure to give evidence. The nature and degree of the comment, if any, is a matter of discretion for the judge: *R* v *Rhodes* [1899] 1 QB 77, CCR. The discretion, however, is not totally unfettered. In *Waugh* v *R* [1950] AC 203, PC it was held that where a judge does comment, it should be pointed out to the jury that the accused is not bound to give evidence and that it is for the prosecution to make out their case. In *R* v *Bathurst* (1968) 52 Cr App R 251 Lord Parker CJ, in an *obiter dictum*, said that the approved form of comment is to tell the jury that the accused is not bound to give evidence, that he can sit back and see if the prosecution have proved their case and that while they, the jury, have been deprived of the opportunity of hearing his story tested in cross-examination, they must not assume that he is guilty because he has not gone into the witness box. These words, however, were not intended to be a judicial directive; depending upon the facts, in some cases the interests of justice may call for a stronger comment: *per* Lawton LJ in *R* v *Sparrow* [1973] 1 WLR 488. See also *R* v *Mutch* [1973] 1 All ER 178, CA.

Although in most cases it is advisable for the judge to make some comment, comment is *not* obligatory: *R* v *Harris* (1986) 84 Cr App R 75, CA: and *R* v *Squire* [1990] Crim LR 341, CA. It is a matter of discretion whether the judge directs the jury at all about the effect of a defendant not giving evidence.

An accused who declines to answer police questions or to give evidence does not thereby add credibility or weight to the evidence of an accomplice giving evidence for the prosecution or any other prosecution witness. It is improper, therefore, to suggest that the jury might find the silence of the accused a relevant factor in deciding whether the accomplice is telling the truth: *R* v *Hubbard* [1991] Crim LR 449, CA.

4.2.2.2   The spouse of the accused
Police and Criminal Evidence Act 1984, s. 80:

(1)   In any proceedings the wife or husband of the accused shall be competent to give evidence—

(a)   subject to subsection (4) below, for the prosecution; and
(b)   on behalf of the accused or any person jointly charged with the accused.

(2)   In any proceedings the wife or husband of the accused shall, subject to subsection (4) below: be compellable to give evidence on behalf of the accused.

(3)   In any proceedings the wife or husband of the accused shall, subject to subsection (4) below: be compellable to give evidence for the prosecution or on behalf of any person jointly charged with the accused if and only if—

(a)   the offence charged involves an assault on, or injury or a threat of injury to, the wife or husband of the accused or a person who was at the material time under the age of 16; or
(b)   the offence charged is a sexual offence alleged to have been committed in respect of a person who was at the material time under that age; or
(c)   the offence charged consists of attempting or conspiring to commit, or of aiding, abetting, counselling, procuring or inciting the commission of, an offence falling within paragraph (a) or (b) above.

(4)   Where a husband and wife are jointly charged with an offence neither spouse shall at the trial be competent or compellable by virtue of subsection (1)(a), (2) or (3) above to give evidence in respect of that offence unless that spouse is not, or is no longer liable to be convicted of that offence at the trial as a result of pleading guilty or for any other reason.

(5)   In any proceedings a person who has been but is no longer married to the accused shall be competent and compellable to give evidence as if that person and the accused had never been married.

(6)   Where in any proceedings the age of any person at any time is material for the purposes of subsection (3) above, his age at the material time shall for the purposes of that provision be deemed to be or to have been that which appears to the court to be or to have been his age at that time.

(7)   In subsection (3)(b) above 'sexual offence' means an offence under the Sexual Offences Act 1956, the Indecency with Children Act 1960, the Sexual Offences Act 1967, section 54 of the Criminal Law Act 1977 or the Protection of Children Act 1978.

(8)   The failure of the wife or husband of the accused to give evidence shall not be made the subject of any comment by the prosecution.

(a)   For the prosecution.

A spouse is competent to give evidence against the accused or any co-accused (Police and Criminal Evidence Act 1984, s. 80(1)(a)). The only exception is where the husband and wife are jointly charged (s. 80(4)).

A spouse is compellable to give evidence against the accused or any co-accused only in the circumstances specified in s. 80(3)(a) to (c). The only exception is where the husband and wife are jointly charged (s. 80(4)).

(b)   For the accused.

A spouse is competent for the accused (s. 80(1)(b)).

A spouse is compellable for the accused. The only exception is s. 80(4).

(c)   For a co-accused.

A spouse is competent for any co-accused (s. 80(1)(b)).

A spouse is compellable for any co-accused only in the circumstances specified in s. 80(3)(a) to (c). The only exception is s. 80(4).

On the meaning of 'jointly charged' in s. 80(3) (and also s. 80(1)), see *R* v *Woolgar* [1991] Crim LR 545. W and M were jointly indicted. W was charged with criminal damage. M was charged with assault. The judge ruled that M's wife was not compellable to give evidence for W. W was convicted. The appeal against conviction was allowed. The Court of Appeal held that M's wife was a compellable witness because the words 'jointly charged' in s. 80(3) mean 'jointly charged with an offence' and W and M were not jointly charged with anything. Whatever the merits of this construction, the difficulty with this case is that even if the construction is accepted, *it does not follow that M's wife was competent and compellable*. This is because on the construction adopted, the case is simply not covered by the statute — it falls outside both s. 80(1)(b) (on the question of competence) and s. 80(3) (on the question of compellability). That being so, one must turn to the authorities at common law. In particular, see *R* v *Thompson* (1872) LR 1 CCR 377: A & B charged with theft, C with receiving. Held: C's wife *not competent* to give evidence for A and B.

(d)   Failure to testify.

See s. 80(8), re-enacting parts of proviso (b) to s. 1, of the Criminal Evidence Act 1898. Under the earlier provision, it was held by the Court of Appeal in *R* v *Naudeer* [1984] 3 All ER 1036 that where prosecution counsel in his/her final speech does comment on the failure of the accused to call the spouse as a witness, the trial judge must correct that breach in the summing-up and make the true position plain. Note, however, that s. 80(8) applies only as against the prosecution. The judge may make such comment as he thinks fit in all the circumstances.

(e)   Former spouses.

See s. 80(5). See *R* v *Khan (Junaid)* (1987) 84 Cr App R 44, CA and *R* v *Cruttenden* [1991] 3 All ER 242.

4.2.2.3   The former spouse of a party to civil proceedings
Although nowadays it seems absurd, the common law authority is that in civil proceedings a former spouse is incompetent if the evidence in question concerns events which occurred during the subsistence of the marriage. See *Monroe* v *Twistleton* [1802] Peeke Add Cas 219. See also *R* v *Ash* (1985) 81 Cr App R 294, CA.

4.2.2.4   Children

(In this paragraph it is necessary to distinguish between competency to give sworn evidence and competency to give unsworn evidence. Almost invariably adult witnesses must give sworn evidence; whereas, subject to the rules to be considered in this paragraph, a child will often give unsworn evidence. For the meaning of sworn evidence see **4.2.3.1**.)

(a)   Civil cases.

Children Act 1989, s. 96:

(1)   Subsection (2) applies where a child who is called as a witness in any civil proceedings does not, in the opinion of the court, understand the nature of an oath.
(2)   The child's evidence may be heard by the court if, in its opinion —
  (a)   he understands that it is his duty to speak the truth and;
  (b)   he has sufficient understanding to justify his evidence being heard.

A 'child' is a person under the age of 18: s. 105.

On matters of procedure and on the question whether a child does not understand the nature of an oath, for the purposes of s. 96(1), the courts are likely to be guided by authorities drawn from criminal cases at a time when the position was similar to that laid down in s. 96 (for the current situation in criminal cases see below at (b)). Thus the question being for the judge, he or she should put to the child preliminary questions so as to be able to form an opinion: *R v Surgenor* (1940) 27 Cr App R 175. Whether a child is sufficiently young to warrant examination to see whether he or she can give sworn evidence is a matter for the judge to decide on the particular facts of the case. However, in *R v Khan* (1981) 73 Cr App R 190, CA it was held that although much depends on the type of child before the court, as a general working rule inquiry is necessary in the case of a child under the age of 14.

The test to determine whether the child understands the nature and consequences of an oath was reviewed by the Court of Appeal in *R v Hayes* [1977] 1 WLR 238. The test laid down in *Hayes* is 'whether the child has a sufficient appreciation of the solemnity of the occasion and the added responsibility to tell the truth, which is involved in taking an oath over and above the duty to tell the truth which is an ordinary duty of normal social conduct'. If, in civil proceedings, a child fails this test, his or her evidence may be given unsworn if the conditions in s. 96(2) are satisfied. It seems likely that the 'duty to speak the truth' in s. 96(2)(a) will be interpreted to mean the duty to tell the truth which is an ordinary duty of normal social conduct.

(b)   Criminal cases.

The position now in criminal cases is governed largely by s. 33A of the Criminal Justice Act 1988 (which was inserted by s. 52(1), Criminal Justice Act 1991)

> *33A. – (1) A child's evidence in criminal proceedings shall be given unsworn.*
> *(2)   A deposition of a child's unsworn evidence may be taken for the purposes of criminal proceedings as if that evidence had been given on oath.*
> *(3)   In this section "child" means a person under fourteen years of age.'*

Section 33A(1) is mandatory: in criminal proceedings, the evidence of any child under 14 years of age *shall* be given unsworn. There is no question of the child giving sworn evidence, even if the child might satisfy the test in *Hayes*. For children aged 14–17 inclusive, the *Hayes* test will be applied but there will be no question of giving unsworn evidence if that test is failed.

Section 33A provides no test for deciding whether a child under 14 years is capable of giving unsworn evidence (unlike s. 33A's predecessor (s. 38, Children and Young Persons Act 1933), which was repealed by s. 52(2), Criminal Justice Act 1991). By reason of s. 52(2), whereby s. 38(1) of the 1933 Act shall cease to have effect, the court is no longer *required* to consider whether the child is possessed of sufficient intelligence to justify the reception of his or her evidence or whether he or she understands the duty of speaking the truth. Section 52(2), however, goes on to provide that the power of the court to determine that a particular person is not competent shall apply to children of tender years as it applies to other persons, i.e. adults. Presumably this refers to the power of the court to determine that a particular person is incompetent to testify by reason of unsound mind or the inability to communicate in an intelligible and coherent manner.

The question of intelligibility and coherence is of particular relevance in the case of very young children. In deciding whether a child is too young to give evidence at all, the courts are likely to be guided by the case law prior to the 1991 Act.

In *R v Wallwork* (1958) 42 Cr App R 153, it was held most undesirable to call a child as young as five years old. See also *per* Ognall J, *obiter*, in *R v Wright and Ormerod* (1990) 90 Cr App R 91. However, in *R v Z* [1990] 2 All ER 971, Lord Lane CJ held that the decision in *Wallwork* had been overtaken by events, in particular by the system of video links (see Chapter 5 at 5.1(g)) and by the repeal to the proviso to Children and Young Persons Act 1933, s. 38(1) (which required corroboration where the unsworn evidence of a child was given on behalf of the prosecution). These developments reflected a change of attitude by the public in general to the acceptability of the evidence of young children and an increasing belief that their testimony, when all precautions have been taken, may be just as reliable as that of their elders. Lord Lane CJ said:

> ... the younger the child the more care the judge must take before he allows the evidence to be received. But the statute lays down no minimum age, and the matter accordingly remains in the discretion of the judge in each case.

The judge, in deciding under s. 52(2) whether a child is competent to give evidence at all, should examine the child in open court so that the jury can make up their minds on what weight to give to the evidence of the child, if subsequently allowed to be given: see *R* v *Reynolds* [1950] 1 KB 606, CCA, which may be taken to have survived the 1991 Act.

4.2.2.5 Persons of defective intellect
The test, here, is whether such a person understands the nature and sanction of the oath. See *R* v *Hayes* (supra).

See *R* v *Bellamy* (1986) 82 Cr App R 222, CA.

4.2.2.6 The sovereign, heads of sovereign states and diplomats

4.2.2.7 Bankers
Bankers' Books Evidence Act 1879, s. 6: bankers shall not, in legal proceedings to which the bank is not a party, be compellable to produce any bankers' book the contents of which can be proved under the Act, or to appear as witnesses to prove the matters etc. therein recorded, unless by order of a judge made for special cause.

4.2.3 OATHS AND AFFIRMATIONS

4.2.3.1 Sworn evidence
Evidence given by a witness who has taken an oath or has made an affirmation is known as sworn evidence. The present law is governed by the Oaths Act 1978.

Section 1(1) provides for oaths in the case of Christians and Jews. Such an oath will be administered, without enquiry on the part of the judge, unless the witness objects or is physically incapable of taking the oath: s. 1(2). For those of other religious beliefs, the oath shall be administered 'in any lawful manner': s. 1(3). Whether the oath is administered in a lawful manner does not depend on the intricacies of the particular religion in question (e.g. for Muslims, strictly an oath should be taken on a copy of the Koran *in Arabic*) but on:

(a) whether the oath appears to the court to be binding on the conscience of the witness, and
(b) whether it is an oath which the witness himself considers to be binding on his conscience: *R* v *Kemble* [1990] 3 All ER 116, CA.

4.2.3.2 Unsworn evidence
The general rule is that evidence must be sworn: a conviction or judgment founded on unsworn evidence, therefore, will be set aside as a nullity. To the general rule, however, there are exceptions, notably the exceptions applying to children: see the Criminal Justice Act 1988, s. 33A and the Children Act 1989, s. 96 (see **4.2.2.4**).

Questions on Presumptions

OBJECTIVES

By the conclusion of this section, you should be able:

(a)   to classify presumptions;
(b)   to know when to apply a presumption to a given set of facts;
(c)   to indicate correctly the effect which a presumption has on the incidence of the legal and evidential burdens.

RESEARCH

(a)   Read the materials contained in **4.1** of this Manual.
(b)   Read:

Keane, *The Modern Law of Evidence* (2nd ed., 1989) ch. 20, OR

Murphy, *A Practical Approach to Evidence* (4th ed., 1992), ch. 17; AND

Carter, *Cases and Statutes on Evidence* (2nd ed., 1990), ch. 4 and the Supplement (1992); OR

Heydon, *Evidence Cases and Materials* (3rd ed., 1991).

(c)   On the basis of this research, answer the following questions.

Question 1

In a civil suit, the plaintiff, Paula, is seeking to establish her legitimacy. She alleges that she was born at a time when her mother, Enid, was married to a man called Fred. David, the defendant, formally admits these allegations but adduces evidence that at the time at which Paula was conceived, Fred was impotent. At the end of the trial, the judge concludes that on all the evidence before him the probability that Fred was impotent at the time of Paula's conception is equal to the probability that he was not. Should the judge rule that Paula is legitimate?

[A]   Yes, because the legal burden is on David and he has failed to discharge it.
[B]   Yes, because the legal burden is on Paula and she has discharged it.
[C]   No, because the legal burden is on Paula and she has failed to discharge it.
[D]   No, because the legal burden is on David and he has discharged it.

Question 2

On 1 January 1986 Mr and Mrs Bush (aged 22 and 24 respectively) set off from Folkestone, England in their yacht, *Mermaid*, to cruise to Australia. On 16 August 1988 the *Mermaid* was discovered adrift in open seas off the island of Bali in the Indian Ocean. Mr and Mrs Bush were not aboard.

Neither set of parents has heard from the couple since they left Folkestone, although Mrs Bush sent her parents a picture postcard of Cape Town which was postmarked '1 April 1987'. Title to Mr and Mrs Bush's house is registered at the Land Registry in Mrs Bush's name alone. Mr Bush's parents now claim:

(a)   their son and daughter-in-law owned the house jointly and that the title deeds are incorrect;
(b)   as neither Mr Bush junior nor his wife have been heard from, save for the postcard, since they left Folkestone, they should be given up as dead;
(c)   that their son and daughter-in-law made mutual wills in which all property went to whichever outlived the other; that their son's will bequeathed the house to his parents should he survive his wife; and that since their son probably outlived his wife, they should inherit the house.

Advise Mr and Mrs Bush senior as to any presumptions of fact or law which may assist or hamper them in establishing their claims.

Question 3

Create a rebuttable presumption which assists the prosecution in a statute which makes it an offence to sell solvents to people under 18 years old knowingly for abuse.

Questions on Competence and Compellability

OBJECTIVES

By the conclusion of this section, you should be able:

(a)   to identify when, during the course of a trial, the issue of competence is likely to arise;
(b)   to know the procedure for determining the competence of a witness;
(c)   to know whether a given witness in given circumstances will be competent; and
(d)   to know whether a given witness in given circumstances will be compellable.

RESEARCH

(a)   Read the materials contained in **4.2** of this Manual.
(b)   Read:

Keane, *The Modern Law of Evidence* (2nd ed., 1989) ch. 4, OR

Murphy, *A Practical Approach to Evidence* (4th ed., 1992), ch. 3; AND

Carter, *Cases and Statutes on Evidence* (2nd ed., 1990), ch. 8 and the Supplement (1992), OR

Heydon, *Evidence Cases & Materials* (3rd ed., 1991).

Consider also the following Table (**Table 4.1**). It shows how the Police and Criminal Evidence Act 1984, s. 80, operates in relation to the compellability of the spouse of an accused and the spouse of a co-accused who is called for the prosecution (column 1), the accused (column 2) and the co-accused (column 3). The table assumes that A & B are jointly charged with the same offence.

Table 4.1

General case	For prosecution	For defence For A	For B
Mrs A	No 80(3)	Yes 80(2)	No 80(3)
Mrs B	No 80(3)	No 80(3)	Yes 80(2)
Assault on Mrs A			
Mrs A	Yes 80(3)(a)	Yes 80(2)	Yes 80(3)(a)
Mrs B	No 80(3)	No 80(3)	Yes 80(2)

(c)   On the basis of this research, answer the following questions.

Question 1
Brian is charged with indecently assaulting his neighbour's 15-year-old son, Charles. The prosecution wishes to call as a witness, Daphne, Brian's wife; and Brian wishes to call as a witness, Edwina, Charles' mother. Both of these potential witnesses would prefer not to give evidence. Can they be compelled to do so?

[A]   Daphne can be compelled to testify, but not Edwina.

[B]   Edwina can be compelled to testify, but not Daphne.
[C]   Both Daphne and Edwina can be compelled to testify.
[D]   Neither Daphne nor Edwina can be compelled to testify.

Question 2

Richard and Timothy are jointly charged with inflicting grievous bodily harm on Richard's wife, Sue. Richard pleads not guilty; Timothy pleads guilty. The prosecution wishes to call as witnesses, Sue and Timothy's wife, Ursula. Are Sue and Ursula competent and compellable for the prosecution?

[A]   Both Sue and Ursula are competent and compellable.
[B]   Both Sue and Ursula are competent but not compellable.
[C]   Sue is competent and compellable; Ursula is competent but not compellable.
[D]   Sue is competent but not compellable; Ursula is competent and compellable.

Question 3

(a)   Can a spouse be compelled to give evidence for the prosecution against her defendant husband when:

(i)   He is charged with assaulting her.
(ii)   He is charged with handling stolen goods.
(iii)   He is charged with sexually assaulting their neighbour's 14-year-old daughter.
(iv)   He is jointly charged with his wife of assaulting their 14-year-old son.
(v)   He is charged with attempting unlawful sexual intercourse with a girl under 16, and he is living apart but not yet divorced.

(b)   In what circumstances may a person who is alleged to have jointly committed the offence with the accused be competent and compellable to give evidence for the prosecution against the accused?
(c)   What is the test for determining whether a child is capable of giving sworn evidence?
(d)   John is 11 and is about to be called for the prosecution. Describe the procedure to be adopted before he will be allowed to give evidence.

Question 4

Ellen leaves her husband, Edgar, and goes to live with George and his 12-year-old son, Gary. Edgar and his brother, Harry, are jointly charged with assaulting Gary, seriously wounding George, and attempting to kidnap Ellen.

(a)   Advise the prosecution whether Ellen and Gary may be called to give eye-witness evidence of these three offences.
(b)   Edgar and Harry both wish to call Harry's wife, Hilda, to give evidence in their favour. Hilda is now estranged from Harry and is reluctant to testify for the defence. Can she be compelled to do so?
(c)   In what circumstances can Harry be called as a prosecution witness?
(d)   Advise whether Harry can be called as a defence witness either on his own behalf or for Edgar.

43

5   Examination, Cross-Examination and Re-Examination

May you call your witnesses in any order you choose?

Must your witnesses be called before the close of your case?

May the judge call witnesses?

What are the rules governing the questions that you ask of your witnesses (examination-in-chief)?

May a witness refresh his or her memory by reference to notes made before the case came to court?

What can you do if a witness you call fails to prove a certain matter or proves the opposite (unfavourable and hostile witnesses)?

What are the rules governing the questions that you can ask of your opponent's witnesses (cross-examination)?

5.1   Procedural Issues

(a)   Does a party to litigation have any property in the evidence of a witness?

The short answer is no. See *Harmony Shipping Co. SA* v *Saudi Europe Line Ltd* [1979] 1 WLR 1380, CA. However, once a witness in criminal proceedings has given evidence for the prosecution, he or she cannot be called to give evidence for the defence: *R* v *Kelly* (1985) *The Times*, 27 July 1985, CA.

(b)   Are the parties under any obligation to call competent witnesses or do they have an unfettered choice?

In civil proceedings they have an unfettered choice.

In criminal proceedings the accused may call such witnesses to support his case as he thinks fit.

In criminal proceedings, the prosecution is obliged to ensure that 'witnesses whose names appear on the back of the indictment' (i.e. witnesses who gave evidence for the prosecution in committal proceedings or who made statements served on an accused who was committed without consideration of the evidence) are brought to court (unless they are prevented from doing so by circumstances outside the prosecution's control). The prosecution must call these witnesses if their testimony is essential to the narrative of its case. If not essential, the prosecution has a discretion whether or not to call them and, if called, whether to examine them in chief or simply to tender them for cross-examination by the defence: see *R* v *Oliva* [1965] 1 WLR 1028, CCA. The prosecution has no obligation to call witnesses whose witness statements had never formed part of the prosecution case but had been served on the defence as unused material. See *R* v *Richardson* (1993) *The Times*, 9 June 1993.

(c)   Are there any rules as to the order in which competent witnesses should be called?

Parties are generally free to call the witnesses in the order of their choice. The only major restriction relates to the order of defence witnesses in criminal trials. Police and Criminal Evidence Act 1984, s. 79, provides that:

If at the trial of any person for an offence—

  (a)   the defence intends to call two or more witnesses to the facts of the case; and
  (b)   those witnesses include the accused.

the accused shall be called before the other witness or witnesses unless the court in its discretion otherwise directs.

See also *Bayer* v *Clarkson Puckle Overseas Ltd* (1989) NLJ Feb 24, 256 QBD: if the issues in a commercial action are such that professional experts will be asked to express an opinion on the professional competence of someone else in the same profession, the High Court has power to order that all the oral evidence as to the facts be given by both sides before the expert evidence of either side is given.

(d)   Must all of a party's witnesses be called before the close of the party's case?

The general rule is that all of a party's evidence should be adduced before the close of the party's case. A party will not be allowed at some later stage to remedy defects in his case, or contradict the evidence of his opponent, by adducing evidence available to him from the start and foreseeably relevant to his case. See: *R* v *Day* [1940] 1 All ER 402, CCA.

However, the court will normally allow evidence in rebuttal to be called in order to make good a purely formal omission: see *Price* v *Humphries* [1958] 2 QB 353, DC.

Also, the judge has a discretion to allow a party to call evidence in rebuttal of a matter which has arisen *ex improviso*, i.e. which could not reasonably have been anticipated or foreseen. See: *R* v *Scott* (1984) 79 Cr App R 49, CA; and *R* v *Hutchinson* (1986) 82 Cr App R 51, CA.

The discretion of a trial judge to allow the prosecution to call further evidence after the close of its case is not confined to the above two exceptions. The judge has a wider discretion, the limits of which should not be precisely defined, but which should be exercised only rarely outside the two established exceptions (*R* v *Francis* [1991] 1 All ER 225, CA), especially when the evidence is tendered after the case for the accused has begun (*R* v *Munnery* [1992] Crim LR 215, CA). In *R* v *Francis*, evidence having been given that at a group identification the man standing at position number 20 was identified, the prosecution was allowed to recall the inspector in charge of the identification to say that it was the appellant who was standing at position number 20. Counsel for the prosecution was under the impression that the name of the person standing at that position was not in issue.

Note also that it is the practice, in the case of evidence which did not form part of the evidence upon which an accused was committed for trial, but which is capable of forming part of the affirmative case for the prosecution, to give notice of that additional evidence to the defence *before* it is tendered: *R* v *Kane* (1977) 65 Cr App R 270, CA. The fact that the accused might then trim his/her evidence is not a reason for witholding the material until he/she testifies. The rationale for the principle is that an accused needs to know in advance the case against him/her if he/she is to have a proper opportunity of answering that case to the best of his/her ability. The accused is also entitled to such knowledge when deciding whether to testify. It is better in the interests of justice that an accused is not induced, by thinking he/she is safe to do so, to exaggerate, or to embroider, or to lie. To do so might be to ambush the accused: *R* v *Phillipson* (1990) 91 Cr App R 226. See also *R* v *Sansom* (1991) 92 Cr App R 115, CA.

As to the prosecution's duty to disclose *unused* material see *R* v *Ward* [1993] 2 All ER 577 and **11.1.3.7**.

(e)   Is the judge entitled to call witnesses?

In civil proceedings, the general rule is that the judge can call witnesses if he has the consent of all parties. See *Re Enoch & Zaretsky, Bock & Co.'s Arbitration* [1910] 1 KB 327, CA.

In criminal proceedings the judge, without the consent of either party, may call and examine any witness not called by the parties. See *R v Chapman* (1838) 8 C & P 558; and *R v Harris* [1927] 2 KB 587.

Note there is a sacrosanct rule that when the jury or justices have retired to consider their verdict, no witness may be called or re-called, even if the jury has requested it and the defence consents. This rule extends to material, other than evidence, designed to assist them, as when the jury ask for scales to conduct weighing experiments with exhibits: see *R v Stewart* (1989) 89 Cr App R 273, CA. However, a magnifying glass, a ruler or a tape-measure does not normally raise the possibility of experiments with exhibits and there can be no objection to their use in the jury room: *R v Maggs* (1990) 91 Cr App R 243, CA.

(f)   Exchange of witness statements.

In criminal cases the prosecution must always furnish the defence with a witness statement of any witness they propose to call at trial (see generally the **Criminal Litigation Manual**). In general there is no duty of disclosure on the defence (although there are special rules regarding expert witnesses: see **chapter 11** at **11.1.3.7**).

In civil cases in the High Court the position is governed by RSC Ord. 38, r. 2A as amended by RSC (Amendment No. 2) 1992 (there are equivalent rules for the County Court in CCR Ord. 20, r. 12A). RSC Order 38, r. 2A provides:

2A   Exchange of witness statements
(1)   The powers of the Court under this rule shall be exercised for the purpose of disposing fairly and expeditiously of the cause or matter before it, and saving costs, having regard to all the circumstances of the case, including (but not limited to)—
   (a)   the extent to which the facts are in dispute or have been admitted;
   (b)   the extent to which the issues of fact are defined by the pleadings;
   (c)   the extent to which information has been or is likely to be provided by further and better particulars, answers to interrogatories or otherwise.
(2)   At the summons for directions in an action commenced by writ the Court shall direct every party to serve on the other parties, within 14 weeks (or such other period as the Court may specify) of the hearing of the summons and on such terms as the Court may specify, written statements of the oral evidence which the party intends to adduce on any issues of fact to be decided at the trial.
The Court may give a direction to any party under this paragraph at any other stage of such an action and at any stage of any other cause or matter.
Order 3, rule 5(3) shall not apply to any period specified by the Court under this paragraph.
(3)   Discretions under paragraph (2) or (17) may make different provision with regard to different issues of fact or different witnesses.
(4)   Statements served under this rule shall—
   (a)   be dated and, except for good reason (which should be specified by letter accompanying the statement), be signed by the intended witness and shall include a statement by him that the contents are true to the best of his knowlddge and belief;
   (b)   sufficiently identify any documents referred to therein; and
   (c)   where they are to be served by more than one party, be exchanged simultaneously.
(5)   Where a party is unable to obtain a written statement from an intended witness in accordance with paragraph (4)(a), the Court may direct the party wishing to adduce that witness's evidence to provide the other party with the name of the witness and (unless the Court otherwise orders) a statement of the nature of the evidence intended to be adduced.
(6)   Subject to paragraph (9), where the party serving a statement under this rule does not call the witness to whose evidence it relates, no other party may put the statement in evidence at the trial.
(7)   Subject to paragraph (9), where the party serving the statement does call such a witness at the trial—

(a)   except where the trial is with a jury, the Court may, on such terms as it thinks fit, direct that the statement served, or part of it, shall stand as the evidence in chief of the witness or part of such evidence;

(b)   the party may not without the consent of the other parties or the leave of the Court adduce evidence from that witness the substance of which is not included in the statement served, except—

(i)   where the Court's directions under paragraph (2) or (17) specify that statements should be exchanged in relation to only some issues of fact, in relation to any other issues;

(ii)   in relation to new matters which have arisen since the statement was served on the other party;

(c)   whether or not the statement or any part of it is referred to during the evidence in chief of the witness, any party may put the statement or any part of it in cross-examination of that witness.

(8)   Nothing in this rule shall make admissible evidence which is otherwise inadmissible.

(9)   Where any statement served is one to which the Civil Evidence Acts 1968 and 1972 apply, paragraphs (6) and (7) shall take effect subject to the provisions of those Acts and Parts III and IV of this Order.

The service of a witness statement under this rule shall not, unless expressly so stated by the party serving the same, be treated as a notice under the said Acts of 1968 and 1972; and where a statement or any part thereof would be admissible in evidence by virtue only of the said Act of 1968 or 1972 the appropriate notice under Part III or Part IV of this Order shall be served with the statement notwithstanding any provision of those Parts as to the time for serving such a notice. Where such a notice is served a counter-notice shall be deemed to have been served under Order 38, rule 26(1).

(10)   Where a party fails to comply with a direction for the exchange of witness statements he shall not be entitled to adduce evidence to which the direction related without the leave of the Court.

(11)   Where a party serves a witness statement under this rule, no other person may make use of that statement for any purpose other than the purpose of the proceedings in which it was served—

(a)   unless and to the extent that the party serving it gives his consent in writing or the Court gives leave; or

(b)   unless and to the extent that it has been put in evidence (whether pursuant to a direction under paragraph (7)(a) or otherwise).

(12)   Subject to paragraph (13), the judge shall, if any person so requests during the course of the trial, direct the associate to certify as open to inspection any witness statement which was ordered to stand as evidence in chief under paragraph (7)(a).

A request under this paragraph may be made orally or in writing.

(13)   The judge may refuse to give a direction under paragraph (12) in relation to a witness statement, or may exclude from such a direction any words or passages in a statement, if he considers that inspection should not be available—

(a)   in the interests of justice or national security,

(b)   because of the nature of any expert medical evidence in the statement, or

(c)   for any other sufficient reason.

(14)   Where the associate is directed under paragraph (12) to certify a witness statement as open to inspection he shall—

(a)   prepare a certificate which shall be attached to a copy ('the certified copy') of that witness statement; and

(b)   make the certified copy available for inspection.

(15)   Subject to any conditions which the Court may by special or general direction impose, any person may inspect and (subject to payment of the prescribed fee) take a copy of the certified copy of a witness statement from the time when the certificate is given until the end of 7 days after the conclusion of the trial.

(16)   In this rule—

(a)   any reference in paragraphs (12) to (15) to a witness statement shall, in relation to a witness statement of which only part has been ordered to stand as evidence in chief under paragraph (7)(a), be construed as a reference to that part;

(b)   any reference to inspecting or copying the certified copy of a witness statement shall be construed as including a reference to inspecting or copying a copy of that certified copy.

(17)   The Court shall have power to vary or override any of the provisions of this rule (except paragraphs (1), (8) and (12) to (16)) and to give such alternative directions as it thinks fit.'.

See also the *Practice Direction* [1992] 4 All ER 679.

See generally the **Civil Litigation Manual**.

(g)   Live television links.

Normally a witness must give evidence from the witness box but, exceptionally, a live television link is permissible. The Criminal Justice Act 1988, s. 32(1) and (2) provides:

(1)   A person other than the accused may give evidence through a live television link on a trial on indictment or an appeal to the criminal division of the Court of Appeal or the hearing of a reference under section 17 of the Criminal Appeal Act 1968 if—

(a)   the witness is outside the United Kingdom; or

(b)   the witness is under the age of 14 and the offence charged is one to which subsection (2) below applies,

but evidence may not be so given without the leave of the court.

(2)   This subsection applies—

(a)   to an offence which involves an assault on, or injury or a threat of injury to, a person;

(b)   to an offence under section 1 of the Children and Young Persons Act 1933 (cruelty to persons under 16);

(c)   to an offence under the Sexual Offences Act 1956, the Indecency with Children Act 1960, the Sexual Offences Act 1967, section 54 of the Criminal Law Act 1977 or the Protection of Children Act 1978; and

(d)   to an offence which consists of attempting or conspiring to commit, or of aiding, abetting, counselling, procuring or inciting the commission of, an offence falling within paragraph (a), (b) or (c) above.

An alternative to a live television link is to erect a screen which is positioned so as to ensure that the witness cannot see the accused: see *R* v *XYZ* (1989) 91 Cr App R 36 and H. O. Circular 61/1990.

For other circumstances in which such a screen might properly be erected see *R* v *Watford Magistrates' Court, ex parte Lenman* [1993] Crim LR 388.

Regarding the position on television links in civil cases in the High Court see *Garcin* v *Amerindo Investment Advisors Ltd* [1991] 4 All ER 655.

5.2   Examination-in-Chief

5.2.1   LEADING QUESTIONS

Leading questions are those which suggest the answer sought, which put to the witness some matter in dispute in such a way as only to permit the reply of 'yes' or 'no', or which are framed in such a way that they assume certain facts not yet established. (See **Advocacy, Negotiation and Conference Skills Manual, 33.4.1**). Such questions are not generally permitted in examination-in-chief.

5.2.2   REFRESHING MEMORY

5.2.2.1   In court
A witness may refresh his or her memory in the witness box by reference to a document that the witness made or verified provided that:

(a)   the document was made or verified at the time of the events in question or so shortly thereafter that the facts were fresh in the witness's memory;

(b)   the document is produced in court for inspection; and

(c)   if the original is available, the document is, in cases where the witness has no recollection of the events in question, but simply gives evidence as to the accuracy of the contents of the document, that original.

The rule applies not only where 'present recollection is revived' (i.e. on sight of the document the witness's train of memory is triggered), but also in the case of 'past recollection recorded' (i.e. the witness, his memory being a perfect blank, swears to the accuracy of the statement made in the document). See: *Maugham* v *Hubbard* (1828) 8 B & C 14.

Topham v *McGregor* (1844) 1 Car & Kir 320.

A witness may even be allowed to refresh his or her memory in re-examination – see *R* v *Sutton* [1991] Crim LR 836, CA.

As to 'making' or 'verification' (which can be visual or aural), see:

R v *Whalley* (1852) 3 Car & Kir 54.

R v *Kelsey* (1982) 74 Cr App R 213, CA.

R v *Eleftheriou* (1993) *The Times*, 2 March 1993.

'Contemporaneity', in the literal sense, is not a necessary requirement. See:

R v *Richardson* [1971] 2 QB 484, CA.

The jury may see the document if this would assist them in estimating the witness's credibility. See: *R* v *Bass* [1953] 1 QB 680, CA. It may also be used by them as an *aide memoire* in cases where the witness's evidence is long and involved (but not, it seems, where the document is an unsigned record of an accused's confession). See:

R v *Sekhon* (1987) 85 Cr App R 19, CA *cf. R* v *Dillon* (1983) 85 Cr App R 29.

As to the use of copies of the original document, see:

Attorney-General's Reference (No. 3 of 1979) (1979) 68 Cr App R 411.

R v *Simmonds* (1967) 51 Cr App R 316, CA.

R v *Mills* [1962] 1 WLR 1152, CA.

R v *Cheng* (1976) 63 Cr App R 20, CA.

Doe d Church & Phillips v *Perkins* (1790) 3 TR 749.

The best summary of the effect of inspecting and cross-examining on a memory-refreshing document is that of Sir Jocelyn Simon P in *Senat* v *Senat* (1965) P 172 at p. 177:

> Where a document is used to refresh a witness's memory, cross-examining counsel may inspect that document in order to check it, without making it evidence. Moreover he may cross-examine upon it without making it evidence provided that his cross-examination does not go further than the parts which are used for refreshing the memory of the witness.

The meaning of 'making it evidence', for these purposes, varies according to whether proceedings are civil or criminal. In civil proceedings, see Civil Evidence Act 1968, s. 3(2):

Nothing in this Act shall affect any of the rules of law relating to the circumstances in which, where a person called as a witness in any civil proceedings is cross-examined on a document used by him to refresh his memory, that document may be made evidence in those proceedings; and where a document or any part of a document is received in evidence in any such proceedings by virtue of any such rule of law, any statement made in that document or part by the person using the document to refresh his memory shall by virtue of this subsection be admissible as evidence of any fact stated therein of which direct oral evidence by him would be admissible.

In criminal proceedings, however, the document can only be used as evidence of consistency or inconsistency affecting the credibility of the witness. See *R* v *Virgo* (1978) 67 Cr App R 323, CA; and *R* v *Britton* [1987] 1 WLR 539, CA.

5.2.2.2 Out of court

A witness may also refresh his or her memory from a document outside the court room and before giving evidence. The pre-conditions which apply in the case of memory-refreshing documents in court have no application. However, concerning inspection and cross-examination upon a document used to refresh the memory outside court, the rules are the same as those applying to the use of memory-refreshing documents in the witness-box. See *R* v *Richardson* [1971] 2 QB 484, CA; *R* v *Westwell* [1976] 2 All ER 812, CA; and *Owen* v *Edwards* (1984) 77 Cr App R 191, DC.

A witness may likewise refresh his memory from a document outside the court room after he or she has begun to give evidence: *R* v *Da Silva* [1990] 1 All ER 29. See *per* Stuart-Smith LJ at p. 33:

> In our judgment, therefore, it should be open to the judge, in the exercise of his discretion and in the interests of justice, to permit a witness who has begun to give evidence to refresh his memory from a statement made near to the time of events in question, even though it does not come within the definition of contemporaneous, provided he is satisfied (1) that the witness indicates that he cannot now recall the details of events because of the lapse of time since they took place, (2) that he made a statement much nearer the time of the events and that the contents of the statement represented his recollection at the time he made it, (3) that he had not read the statement before coming into the witness box and (4) that he wished to have an opportunity to read the statement before he continued to give evidence.

> We do not think that it matters whether the witness withdraws from the witness box and reads his statement, as he would do if he had had the opportunity before entering the witness box, or whether he reads it in the witness box. What is important is that, if the former course is adopted, no communication must be had with the witness, other than to see that he can read the statement in peace. Moreover, if either course is adopted, the statement must be removed from him when he comes to give his evidence and he should not be permitted to refer to it again, unlike a contemparaneous statement which may be used to refresh memory while giving evidence.

In this case the initiative came from the judge, but it is clear that it is no ground of objection if the judge thinks it is in the interests of justice that he intervene: see *R* v *Fotheringham* [1975] Crim LR 710 and *R* v *Tyagi* (1986) *The Times*, 21 July 1986.

5.2.3 UNFAVOURABLE AND HOSTILE WITNESSES

The general rule at common law is that the credit of a party's own witnesses may not be impeached by that party, whether by:

(a)   asking leading questions, or
(b)   asking about or calling evidence to prove prior inconsistent statements, prior discreditable conduct, bad character, previous convictions or bias.

*An unfavourable witness = a witness who, called by a party to prove a certain matter(s), simply fails to do so or proves the opposite.

*A hostile witness = a witness who, in the opinion of the judge, displays a hostile animus to the party who called the witness or who shows no desire to tell the truth at the instance of the party calling him.

See *R* v *Prefas and Pryce* (1988) 86 Cr App R 111, CA; *R* v *Fraser* (1956) 40 Cr App R 160, CCA; and *Price* v *Manning* (1980) 42 ChD 372, CA.

In deciding whether a witness is hostile, the witness should not be questioned in the absence of the jury: *R* v *Darby* [1989] Crim LR 817, CA.

If a witness is merely unfavourable, the general rule holds good. See *Ewer* v *Ambrose* (1825) 3 B & C 746.

If the judge grants leave to treat a witness as hostile, the party calling the witness may, at common law, ask leading questions. That party may also ask the witness about, and prove, previous inconsistent statements.

Criminal Procedure Act 1865, s. 3:

> *A party producing a witness shall not be allowed to impeach his credit by general evidence of bad character; but he may, in case the witness shall in the opinion of the judge prove adverse, contradict him by other evidence, or, by leave of the judge, prove that he has made at other times a statement inconsistent with his present testimony; but before such last-mentioned proof can be given the circumstances of the supposed statement, sufficient to designate the particular occasion, must be mentioned to the witness, and he must be asked whether or not he has made such statement.*

Greenough v *Eccles* (1859) 5 CB (NS) 786.

The effect of proving a previous inconsistent statement in this way varies according to whether the proceedings are civil or criminal.

In civil proceedings, see Civil Evidence Act 1968, s. 3(1):

> *Where in any civil proceedings—*
>
> *(a)   a previous inconsistent or contradictory statement made by a person called as a witness in those proceedings is proved by virtue of section 3 . . . of the Criminal Procedure Act 1865; . . .*
>
> *that statement shall by virtue of this subsection be admissible as evidence of any fact stated therein of which direct oral evidence by him would be admissible.*

In criminal proceedings, however, a previous statement can only be treated as evidence of inconsistency going to the witness's credit. See *R* v *White* (1922) 17 Cr App R 60; and *R* v *Golder* [1960] 1 WLR 1169, CCA. Because the statement is only relevant to credit, the jury should not be given copies of it: *R* v *Darby* [1989] Crim LR 817, CA.

See also:

R v *Thomas* [1985] Crim LR 445, CA.

R v *Thompson* (1976) 64 Cr App R 96, CA.

R v *Pitt* [1983] QB 25, CA.

R v *Powell* [1985] Crim LR 592, CA.

5.2.4 **PREVIOUS CONSISTENT STATEMENTS**

5.2.4.1 **The general rule**

In both civil and criminal cases, a witness may not be asked in chief whether formerly the witness has made a statement consistent with his or her testimony. What is banned is proof of the prior statement as evidence of the witness's consistency (cf. the rule against hearsay whereby the prior statement is not admissible as evidence of the facts contained in it). This would appear to be the reason why truth drug evidence is inadmissible (*Fennell* v *Jerome Property Maintenance Ltd* (1986) *The Times*, 26 November 1986). See:

R v *Roberts* [1942] 1 All ER 187.

Corke v *Corke* [1958] P 93, CA.

5.2.4.2 **The exceptions**

(a) *Civil Evidence Act 1968.* In civil cases, previous consistent statements of a witness are, with the leave of the court, admissible under the 1968 Act. See further **Chapter 9**.

(b) *Memory-refreshing documents.* See **5.2.1**.

(c) *Complaints in sexual cases* (or 'a perverted survival of the ancient requirement that a woman should make hue and cry as a preliminary to an appeal of rape': *per* Oliver Wendell Holmes J in *Commonwealth* v *Cleary* (1898) 172 Mass 175).

In sexual cases, whether or not consent is in issue, evidence of a complaint made voluntarily and at the first opportunity reasonably afforded may be given by the complainant and by any person to whom the complaint was made, as evidence of the complainant's consistency and, if consent is in issue, as evidence to disprove such consent. The exception is now confined to sexual cases: *R* v *Jarvis and Jarvis* [1991] Crim LR 374, CA. See also *R* v *Wink* (1834) 6 C & P 397 and *R* v *Lillyman* [1896] 2 QB 167.

R v *Osborne* [1905] 1 KB 551, CCR, *per* Ridley J:

> . . . the mere fact that the statement is made in answer to a question in such cases is not of itself sufficient to make it inadmissible as a complaint. Questions of a suggestive or leading character will, indeed, have that effect but a question such as this, put by the mother or other person, 'What is the matter?' or 'Why are you crying?' will not do so. These are questions which a person in charge will be likely to put; on the other hand, if she were asked, 'Did So-and-So (naming the prisoner) assault you?' 'Did he do this and that to you?' then the result would be different.

See also:

R v *Camelleri* [1922] 2 KB 122, CCA: the exception applies in the case of sexual offences against males as well as females.

Where the exception applies, evidence may be given not only of the fact that a complaint has been made but also of the details of what was actually said by way of complaint. The complaint, however, is not evidence of the facts contained in it but only goes to consistency. Thus if consent is not in issue and the complainant does not give evidence, the complaint is inadmissible; because there is no evidence with which it can be consistent: see *R* v *Wallwork* (1958) 42 Cr App R 153. Likewise, if the terms of the complaint are not ostensibly consistent with the terms of the complainant's testimony, the introduction of the complaint has no legitimate purpose and should be excluded: *R* v *Wright and Ormerod* (1990) 90 Cr App R 91, CA. See also: *Kilby* v *R* (1973) 129 CLR 460, High Court of Australia.

(d) *Statements made on accusation.* A statement made by an accused when taxed with incriminating facts is admissible as evidence of attitude and reaction. See:

R v *Storey* (1968) 52 Cr App R 334.

R v *Pearce* (1979) 69 Cr App R 365: the principle is not limited to a statement made on the first encounter with the police (or anyone else). However, the longer the time that has elapsed after the first encounter, the less weight to be attached to the denial. If an accused produces a carefully written statement to the police with a view to it being made part of the prosecution evidence, the trial judge may rule it inadmissible: see *R* v *Newsome* (1980) 71 Cr App R 325.

See also *R* v *Tooke* (1990) 90 Cr App R 417, CA: the statement must be relevant as well as spontaneous and it is a matter for the judge's discretion where the dividing line falls. A statement will not be relevant if it does not add anything to the evidence already before the jury about the accused's reaction (e.g. evidence of an earlier statement, in similar terms, made by the accused at the scene of the alleged crime).

Where the accused makes a statement which is partly inculpatory, should the judge direct the jury that the inculpatory parts are evidence of the facts they state (by way of exception to the hearsay rule) but that the exculpatory parts are only evidence of the accused's attitude and reaction? No. See *R* v *Duncan* (1981) 73 Cr App R 359, *per* Lord Lane CJ:

It is, to say the least, not helpful to try to explain to the jury that the exculpatory parts of the statement are something less than evidence of the facts they state. Equally, where appropriate, as it usually will be, the judge may, and should, point out that the incriminatory parts are likely to be true (otherwise why say them?), whereas the excuses do not have the same weight.

See also, applying *R* v *Duncan* (1981) 73 Cr App R 359; *R* v *Hamand* (1985) 82 Cr App R 65, CA; and *R* v *Sharp* [1988] 1 WLR 7, HL.

The principle established in *Duncan* and endorsed by the House of Lords in *Sharp* applies whether the 'mixed statement' is a written statement or a record of questions and answers at an interview, as between which there is no sensible distinction on grounds of logic or policy: *R* v *Polin* [1991] Crim LR 293, CA.

(e) *Previous identification*. Evidence is admissible of a former identification of the accused by a witness out of court. It may be given either by that witness or by some other person present at the identification and may include the words declaratory of the identification, e.g. 'That's him!' See:

R v *Christie* [1914] AC 545.

Moreover, it is, in general, improper to identify the accused for the first time when he is in the dock: *R* v *Cartwright* (1914) 10 Cr App R 219. An obvious exception to this is when the accused refuses to take part in an identification parade: *R* v *John* [1973] Crim LR 113, CA. See also:

R v *Eatough* [1989] Crim LR 289, CC.

Evidence of previous identification may be excluded under the Police and Criminal Evidence Act 1984, s. 78, especially if there have been serious and substantial breaches of the Code of Practice on Identification: see generally **Chapter 12**. Another important limitation on the adducing of evidence of previous identification arises out of cases in which the identification involved the use of police photographs. If the witness is shown in court a police photograph used by him to identify the accused, it is almost impossible for the jury not to be prejudiced by the fact that the accused was known to the police, i.e. previously convicted: *R* v *Varley* (1914) 10 Cr App R 125. See also:

R v *Dwyer* [1925] 2 KB 799.

R v *Kingsland* (1979) 14 Cr App R 8.

R v *Governor of Pentonville Prison, ex parte Voets* [1986] 1 WLR 470, DC.

(f)   *Statements in rebuttal of allegations of recent fabrication.* Where, in cross-examination, it is suggested that a witness has recently fabricated his or her evidence, evidence is admissible in rebuttal to show that on an earlier occasion the witness made a statement consistent with that testimony. See:

Flanagan v *Fahy* [1918] 2 IR 361.

R v *Oyesiku* (1971) 56 Cr App R 240, CA.

Fox v *General Medical Council* [1960] 1 WLR 1017, PC.

In criminal cases, a statement in rebuttal is admitted merely to bolster the witness's credibility by negativing the allegation of invention or reconstruction. In civil cases, however, the statement is also admitted for the truth of its contents. See Civil Evidence Act 1968, s. 3(1)(b), which provides that:

Where in any civil proceedings—

(b)   a previous statement made by a person called as [a witness in those proceedings] is proved for the purpose of rebutting a suggestion that this evidence has been fabricated.

that statement shall by virtue of this subsection be admissible as evidence of any fact stated therein of which direct oral evidence by him would be admissible.

(g)   *Res gestae statements.* Under the doctrine of *res gestae*, evidence is admissible of any act or statement so closely associated in time, place and circumstances with some matter in issue that it can be said to be a part of the same transaction. See *R* v *Fowkes* (1856) *The Times*, 8 March 1856 (Assizes) and generally, **Chapter 9** at **9.2.1.1**.

5.3   Cross-Examination

5.3.1   LIABILITY TO CROSS-EXAMINATION

Where a witness has been intentionally called by a party and taken the oath, then whether or not examination-in-chief takes place, the other party has the right to cross-examine.

Some witnesses, however, are totally or partially exempt from cross-examintion:

*A witness called merely to produce a document under a *subpoena duces tecum.*

*A witness genuinely unable to give evidence on the matter in question, sworn by mistake, examination-in-chief having barely commenced.

See also:

Hobbs v *C.T. Tinling & Co. Ltd* [1929] 2 KB 1, CA.

R v *Doolin* (1832) Jebb CC 123, CCR, Ireland (death prior to cross-examination).

R v *Stretton* (1988) 86 Cr App R 7, CA (illness before or during cross-examination).

R v *Wyatt* [1990] Crim LR 343, CA (extreme distress during cross-examination).

A witness called by one party to the proceedings and liable to cross-examination, may be cross-examined by counsel for the other party or, if that party is not represented, by that other party in person. However, note that in criminal proceedings, there is an exception to cross-examination by the accused in person in the case of witnesses who are alleged child victims: see Criminal Justice Act 1988, s. 34A (inserted by Criminal Justice Act 1991, s. 55(7)).

5.3.2 THE OBJECT AND SCOPE OF CROSS-EXAMINATION

The object of cross-examination is to qualify, weaken or destroy your opponent's case and, if you can, to establish your own case.

The cross-examining party must put to his opponent's witnesses every part of his own case as to which those witnesses can speak — if not he will be treated as having accepted their version and in his closing speech will not be allowed to attack their version or to put forward explanations which he did not put to the witnesses. See:

R v *Bircham* [1977] Crim LR 430, CA.

Browne v *Dunn* (1893) 6 R 67, HL.

In cases tried by lay justices, however, the rule (that evidence unchallenged in cross-examination cannot be attacked in a closing speech and must be accepted by the tribunal of fact) does not apply: *O'Connell* v *Adams* [1973] Crim LR 113. See also:

R v *Wilson* [1977] Crim LR 553, CA.

Evidence which is inadmissible in chief remains inadmissible in cross-examination. See:

R v *Treacy* [1944] 2 All ER 229, CCA (inadmissible confession).

R v *Gillespie* (1967) 51 Cr App R 172, CA (inadmissible hearsay).

R v *Windass* (1989) 89 Cr App R 258, CA: highly damaging statements contained in a document written by one co-accused may be admissible against that co-accused, if accompanied by a proper warning to the jury as to their status, but it is improper for the prosecution, during cross-examination of another co-accused, to ask him to explain such damaging statements when they are *inadmissible* against that other co-accused.

Re P [1989] Crim LR 897: it is improper to cross-examine an accused in a sexual case on a complaint which is otherwise inadmissible because not a 'recent' complaint (see **5.2.3.2**).

The rule obtains in favour of any co-accused of the maker of a confession: *R* v *Rice* [1963] 1 QB 857, CCA. But if co-D1's inadmissible confession statement is relevant to the defence of a co-D2 and co-D1 gives evidence inconsistent with the statement, co-D2 can cross-examine him on it, provided that the judge makes clear to the jury that it is no evidence of co-D1's guilt: *R* v *Rowson* [1986] QB 174, CA; *Lui Mei Lin* v *R* [1989] 1 All ER 359, PC.

However, counsel may produce a document, the contents of which are inadmissible hearsay, hand it to a witness, ask the witness to read it to himself, and then ask him if the contents are true. If the witness says that the contents are true, then they become the witness's evidence and can be revealed. See *R* v *Cooper (Warwick)* (1985) 82 Cr App R 74, CA and *R* v *Cross* (1990) 91 Cr App R 115, CA.

Counsel should not add to costs and waste time by protracted and irrelevant cross-examination but should cross-examine with restraint and the courtesy and consideration which witnesses are entitled to expect in a court of law. See *Mechanical & General Inventions Co. Ltd* v *Austin* [1935] AC 346.

See also paras 5.10(e), 5.10(h) and 5.11 of Annexe H to the Code of Conduct of the Bar of England and Wales.

5.3.3 CROSS-EXAMINATION ON DOCUMENTS

Where a party calls for and inspects a document, other than a memory-refreshing document, in the possession of another party, the other party can require the first party to put it in evidence. See *Stroud* v *Stroud* [1963] 1 WLR 1080.

5.3.4   CROSS-EXAMINATION AS TO CREDIT

The limits to cross-examination on the bad character of one's opponent's witnesses are best summarised by Sankey LJ in *Hobbs* v *C.T. Tinling & Co. Ltd* [1929] 2 KB 1, CA:

> questions on bad character are only proper when the answer would seriously impair the credibility of the witness and are improper if either:
>
> (a) they relate to matters so remote in time or of such a character that, if true, they could not seriously impair the credibility of the witness, or
> (b) there is a substantial disproportion between the importance of the implication against the witness's character and the importance of his evidence to the issue to be decided.

In *R* v *Edwards* [1991] 1 WLR 207, CA it was held that police officers may be cross-examined as to any relevant criminal offences or disciplinary charges found proved against them but may not be questioned about (i) complaints by members of the public about behaviour on other occasions not yet adjudicated upon by the Police Complaints Authority or (ii) discreditable conduct by other officers in the same squad. It was further held that where an officer, who has allegedly fabricated an admission in case B, has also given evidence of an admission in case A, where there was an acquittal by virtue of which his evidence is demonstrated to have been disbelieved, the jury in case B should be made aware of that fact.

However, where the acquittal in case A does not necessarily indicate that the jury disbelieved the officer, such cross-examination should not be allowed.

See also *R* v *H* (1990) 90 Cr App R 440, CA.

5.3.4.1   The character of the complainant on charges of rape etc.

At common law, on a charge of rape, the complainant may be cross-examined on previous acts of sexual intercourse with *the accused* and, if she denies such acts, they can be proved. See *R* v *Riley* (1887) 18 QBD 481, CCR.

Concerning acts of intercourse with *men other than the accused*, see, at common law:

R v *Holmes* (1871) LR 1 CCR 334.

R v *Bashir* [1969] 1 WLR 1303.

R v *Krausz* (1973) 57 Cr App R 466.

The common law position concerning acts of intercourse with men other than the accused has now been modified by Sexual Offences (Amendment) Act 1976, ss. 2 and 7(2):

> 2.—(1)   *If at a trial any person is for the time being charged with a rape offence to which he pleads not guilty, then except with the leave of the judge, no evidence and no question in cross-examination shall be adduced or asked at the trial, by or on behalf of any defendant at the trial, about any sexual experience of a complainant with a person other than that defendant.*
>
> (2)   *The judge shall not give leave in pursuance of the preceding subsection for any evidence or question except on an application made to him in the absence of the jury by or on behalf of a defendant: and on such an application the judge shall give leave if and only if he is satisfied that it would be unfair to that defendant to refuse to allow the evidence to be adduced or the question to be asked.*
>
> (3)   *In subsection (1) of this section 'complainant' means a woman upon whom, in a charge for a rape offence to which the trial in question relates, it is alleged that rape was committed, attempted or proposed.*

(4)   Nothing in this section authorises evidence to be adduced or a question to be asked which cannot be adduced or asked apart from this section.

7.—(2)   In this Act—

'a rape offence' means any of the following, namely rape, attempted rape, aiding, abetting, counselling and procuring rape or attempted rape [incitement to rape, conspiracy to rape and burglary with intent to rape]. (Amended by the Criminal Justice Act 1988, s. 158(b).)

Note that s. 7(2) does not include all offences involving unlawful sexual intercourse, for example, unlawful sexual intercourse with a girl under the age of 16 is not included. However, in *R* v *Funderburk* [1990] 2 All ER 482, the Court of Appeal held that although cross-examination in such a case is not governed by the restrictions imposed by s. 2, the court will be astute to see that such cross-examination is not abused or unnecessarily extended.

The phrase 'sexual experience' has been given a very wide interpretation. See:

R v *Hinds* [1979] Crim LR 111.

R v *Viola* [1982] 1 WLR 1138, CA.

When is it 'unfair' to the accused not to allow him to bring in such evidence? The test is whether the evidence might reasonably lead the jury to take a different view of the complainant's evidence from that which they might take if the evidence were not let in: *R* v *Lawrence* [1977] Crim LR 492, approved by the Court of Appeal in *R* v *Mills* (1978) 68 Cr App R 327. The evidence must be relevant to the facts in issue. See:

R v *Hinds* [1979] Crim LR 111.

R v *Viola* [1982] 1 WLR 1138, CA.

R v *Cox* (1987) 84 Cr App R 132, CA.

R v *Brown (Uriah)* (1989) 89 Cr App R 97, CA.

R v *Redguard* [1991] Crim LR 213.

In *R* v *Ellis* [1990] Crim LR 717, CA, a rape case, the sole issue was consent. In her evidence C, the complainant, said that after the rape she had bathed more than once because she felt dirty as a result of being raped. The defence were granted leave to cross-examine her about alleged previous consensual sexual intercourse with another man, S, after which she was reported to have said to a girlfriend, G, that she had felt dirty and had a bath. C denied the sexual encounter with S. *Held*: the defence had been improperly refused leave to call G.

See also *R* v *Riley* [1991] Crim LR 460, CA: evidence in rebuttal of a denial by the complainant that she would not have consensual sexual intercourse with a child present, was held to be in the same sort of category as the evidence which should have been admitted in *R* v *Ellis*.

In *R* v *S.M.S.* [1992] Crim LR 310, CA, a rape case, the sole issue was whether the complainant, aged 14, had consented. Medical evidence elicited by the defence in cross-examination indicated that the complainant may have had sexual intercourse previously, but was not conclusive. The defence wished to cross-examine the complainant about this (but not about the details or circumstances of prior intercourse). It was submitted that the jury might have believed that the complainant was a virgin and, on hearing the sordid circumstances of the instant case, might have found it impossible to believe that she would have consented to her first act of sexual intercourse in such circumstances. Leave was refused. The Court of Appeal quashed the conviction on the basis that if the jury had been told that the complainant had engaged in prior voluntary intercourse, their verdict might have been different.

The courts have expressed conflicting views on the question whether, in deciding 'unfairness' to the accused, the court may also consider unfairness to the complainant and take into account such factors as her age and feelings. See:

R v *Fenlon* (1980) 71 Cr App R 307, CA.

R v *Barton* (1987) 85 Cr App R 5, CA.

Cf. R v *Bogie* [1992] Crim LR 301, CA: the material matter is whether exclusion of the evidence will be unfair to the accused; it matters not that it may be unfortunate for the complainant.

5.3.4.2 Previous inconsistent statements

Proof of previous inconsistent statements is now governed by Criminal Procedure Act 1865, ss. 4 and 5. Section 4 seems to apply to both oral and written statements whereas s. 5 is confined to written statements only:

> 4. *If a witness, upon cross-examination as to a former statement made by him relative to the subject-matter of the indictment or proceeding, and inconsistent with his present testimony, does not distinctly admit that he has made such statement, proof may be given that he did in fact make it; but before such proof can be given the circumstances of the supposed statement, sufficient to designate the particular occasion, must be mentioned to the witness, and he must be asked whether or not he has made such statement.*

> 5. *A witness may be cross-examined as to previous statements made by him in writing, or reduced into writing, relative to the subject-matter of the indictment or proceeding, without such writing being shown to him; but if it is intended to contradict such witness by the writing, his attention must, before such contradictory proof can be given, be called to those parts of the writing which are to be used for the purpose of so contradicting him: Provided always, that it shall be competent for the judge, at any time during the trial, to require the production of the writing for his inspection, and he may thereupon make such use of it for the purposes of the trial as he may think fit.*

The phrase 'relative to the subject-matter of the indictment or proceeding', which is used in both s. 4 and s. 5, means relevant to the facts in issue as opposed to some collateral matter (typically, e.g. a matter simply going to credit): *R* v *Funderburk* [1990] 2 All ER 482, CA. In that case, it was held that if the inconsistent statement is not 'relative to the subject matter of the indictment . . .', s. 4 does not apply — whether counsel may cross-examine on the statement at all is determined by the common law, the test being whether the inconsistency relates to the witness' likely standing, after cross-examination, with the tribunal trying him or listening to his evidence (*R* v *Sweet-Escott* (1971) 55 Cr App R 316). The importance of this distinction is that if the cross-examination is permitted *under the common-law rule*, and the witness denies the earlier statement, then because the issue goes to credit only (a collateral matter), *the cross-examining party cannot proceed to proof of the making of the statement* with a view to impeaching the witness's credit — see the rule of finality of answers to collateral questions, **5.3.4.3**. However, *if the cross-examination falls within s. 4,* it explicitly states that if the witness does not distinctly admit that he has made the statement, *proof may be given that he did in fact make it.*

Where, in the course of a trial of a sexual charge, the issue is whether sexual intercourse has taken place between two persons in private, the difference between questions going to credibility and questions going to an issue is reduced to vanishing point: *Funderburk*, ibid.

Counsel cross-examining under s. 5, even if he does not intend to show the writing to the witness with a view to contradicting him, must have the document with him in court: *R* v *Anderson* (1930) 21 Cr App R 178.

Where a witness has been cross-examined on a previous inconsistent statement, then (i) the judge may allow the whole of the statement to go before the jury but has a discretion to allow the jury to see only those parts of the statement on which the cross-examination was based; and (ii) the party calling the witness is *not* entitled, merely by reason of such cross-examination, to re-examine the witness on a previous statement consistent with the witness's testimony; and the consistent statement, if in written form, should not be put before the jury: *R* v *Beattie* (1989) 89 Cr App R 303, CA.

Example (W = witness; C = cross-examining counsel; J = judge)

W. Her fingers were smeared with a red substance.

C. Do you remember making a statement about this incident to the police on April 1st, 1990?

W. Yes, I made such a statement.

C. And in that statement did you refer to her fingers being smeared with a red substance?

W. Yes, I think I did, but to be honest I can't remember now.

C. Your honour, may the witness be shown the statement.

J. Of course.

C. I'm much obliged.

[The usher hands the statement to the witness].

C. Is that the statement that you made?

W. Yes.

C. And does it bear your signature?

W. Yes

C. When you signed it you were doubtless aware of the declaration at the top of that document of the consequences of wilfully stating in it anything that you knew to be false or did not believe to be true?

W. I guess so.

C. Would you look at the first line of the second page, please.

[Counsel waits for a moment or two].

Now that you have read that, do you still say that her fingers were smeared with a red substance?

W. Yes.

C. You made that statement some two hours after you saw her, didn't you?

W. That's right.

C. While the matter was doubtless fresh in your mind?

W. Yeah, but I was a bit shook up.

C.   In your statement you say, and I quote: 'She was dressed in black, black dress, black hat, even black tights. All black, except for her gloves. They were white, bright white.' Why did you just tell the jury that you saw red-smeared fingers?

W.   I dunno . . . I should have said red-smeared gloves.

C.   But there's no mention of red-smeared anything in your statement. Can you explain that to the jury?

W.   I must have forgot in all the excitement.

C.   The truth is that she was wearing bright white gloves and there were no smears of any kind or any colour. That's the truth, isn't it?

W.   I must have been very confused.

C.   Your honour, may the witness's statement be shown to the jury at this stage?

In criminal proceedings, the prior statement only goes to the witness's credibility. See *R* v *Askew* [1981] Crim LR 398.

In civil proceedings, the prior statement comes in for the truth of its contents as well as to attack the witness's credibility. See Civil Evidence Act 1968, s. 3:

(1)   *Where in any civil proceedings—*

(a)   a previous inconsistent or contradictory statement made by a person called as a witness in those proceedings is proved by virtue of section . . . 4 or 5 of the Criminal Procedure Act 1865 . . .

that statement shall by virtue of this subsection be admissible as evidence of any fact stated therein of which direct oral evidence by him would be admissible.

5.3.4.3   The rule of finality of answers to collateral questions and four exceptions

The rule is that where a witness, during cross-examination, answers questions on collateral matters, the answers are conclusive: the cross-examining party cannot then proceed to impeach the credit of the witness by calling other witnesses to contradict that witness.

What are 'collateral matters'? See *Attorney-General* v *Hitchcock* (1847) 1 Exch 91 *per* Pollock CB:

If the answer of a witness is a matter which you would be allowed on your own part to prove in evidence — if it had such a connection with the issues, that you would be allowed to give it in evidence — then it is a matter on which you may contradict him.

See also:

R v *Burke* (1858) 8 Cox CC 44.

R v *Marsh* [1986] Crim LR 120, CA.

In *R* v *Busby* (1981) 75 Cr App R 79, CA, two officers were cross-examined with a view to showing that they had fabricated statements alleged to have been made by the accused and threatened a potential defence witness to stop him giving evidence. They denied these allegations. The Court of Appeal held that the trial judge had improperly prevented the defence from calling the witness to rebut the police denials bcause the evidence was relevant to an issue in the case, namely whether the police were 'prepared to go to improper lengths to secure a conviction'. The decision in *Busby* has provoked considerable judicial comment in subsequent cases. In *R* v *Funderburk* [1990] 2 All ER 482,

CA, it was taken to add a further exception to the rule of finality. In *R* v *Edwards* [1991] 1 WLR 207, however, Lord Lane CJ was of the opinion that the fact that the police were allegedly prepared to prevent a potential defence witness from testifying fell within the exception of bias or partiality (see below). Compare *Edwards* itself where it was held that: (i) although officers could be cross-examined about other cases which had resulted in acquittal in circumstances which tended to cast doubt on their reliability (e.g. that in those other cases interview notes were inaccurate or had been rewritten to include admissions which did not exist in the originals), (ii) such allegations, if denied, could not be proved by evidence in rebuttal.

In *R* v *S* [1992] Crim LR 307, CA, it seems to be suggested that whether the rule of finality applies may turn on whether the matter which the cross-examining party seeks to prove is a single and distinct fact and therefore easy to prove as opposed to a broad and complex issue which it would be difficult to prove. *Sed quaere.*

(a)   *Bias or partiality.* If a party in cross-examination denies being biased or partial in relation to the parties or the cause, evidence in rebuttal is admissible to prove such bias or partiality. See:

Thomas v *David* (1836) 7 C & P 350.

R v *Philips* (1936) 26 Cr App R 17.

R v *Mendy* (1976) 64 C App R 4, CA.

(b)   *Previous convictions.* Criminal Procedure Act 1865, s. 6:

A witness may be questioned as to whether he has been convicted of any felony or misdemeanour, and upon being so questioned, if he either denies or does not admit the fact, or refuses to answer, it shall be lawful for the cross-examining party to prove such conviction.

This rule is subject to the provisions of the Rehabilitation of Offenders Act, 1974. Section 4(1) of the Act forbids the questioning of a 'rehabilitated' person about 'spent' convictions. Although s. 7(2)(a) says that s. 4(1) does not apply to criminal cases, in a Practice Direction issued by the Lord Chief Justice in June 1975 (1975) 61 Cr App R 260 it is recommended that in criminal cases no reference to a spent conviction should be made if it can reasonably be avoided and no reference should be made in open court to a spent conviction without the authority of the judge, which authority should only be given if the interests of justice so require.

In *R* v *Evans* [1992] Crim LR 125, CA, on a charge of wounding, the defence being self-defence, it was held that the defence should have been allowed to cross-examine the victim on her previous spent convictions for dishonesty and violence because there was a 'head-on' collision between her evidence and that of the accused. A retrial was ordered.

(c)   *Evidence of reputation for untruthfulness.* Evidence is admissible that a witness called by one's opponent bears such a general reputation for untruthfulness that he is unworthy of belief. See *R* v *Richardson* (1968) 52 Cr App R 317; and *R* v *Whelan* (1881) 14 Cox CC 595.

(d)   *Evidence of disability affecting reliability.* Lord Pearce in *Toohey* v *Metropolitan Police Commissioner* [1965] AC 595, HL, at p. 609.

Medical evidence is admissible to show that a witness suffers from some disease or defect or abnormality of mind that affects the reliability of his evidence. Such evidence is not confined to a general opinion of the unreliability of the witness but may give all the matters necessary to show, not only the foundation of and reasons for the diagnosis, but also the extent to which the credibility of the witness is affected. See:

R v *Eades* [1972] Crim LR 99, Assizes.

R v *Turner* [1975] QB 834, CA.

R v *MacKenney* (1983) 76 Cr App R 271.

5.4   Re-Examination

After cross-examination a witness may be re-examined by the party calling him. Re-examination must be confined to the explanation of matters which arose on cross-examination: it is an exercise in repairing damage done. See *Prince* v *Samo* (1838) 7 A & E 627.

As in examination-in-chief, leading questions may not be asked in re-examination.

Questions

OBJECTIVES

By the conclusion of this chapter, you should be able:

(a)   to understand the procedural issues relating to witnesses and analyse the questioning of witnesses during the course of the trial; and

(b)   to understand and apply the rules (and exceptions) relating to leading questions; refreshing memory; previous consistent or self-serving statements; unfavourable and hostile witnesses; cross-examination on documents; cross-examination as to credit; previous inconsistent statements; and the finality of answers to collateral matters.

RESEARCH

(a)   Read the materials contained in **Chapter 5** of this Manual.

(b)   Read:

Keane, *The Modern Law of Evidence* (2nd ed., 1989), ch. 5 and 6, OR

Murphy, *A Practical Approach to Evidence* (4th ed., 1992), ch. 13 and 14; AND

Carter, *Cases and Statutes on Evidence* (2nd ed., 1990), ch. 9 and the Supplement (1992), OR

Heydon, *Evidence Cases & Materials* (3rd ed., 1991).

(c)   On the basis of this research, answer the following questions.

Question 1
Harry is charged with theft. PC Ings carried out most of the investigation, contemporaneously recording all his findings in his notebook. He then used his notebook to refresh his memory while he wrote out his witness statement, which was used at the committal proceedings. PC Ings lost the notebook before the trial, and now has no independent recollection of the investigation. May he refresh his memory from the witness statement?

[A]   No, because the document used to refresh his memory must be the original.
[B]   No, because it would amount to relying on hearsay evidence.
[C]   Yes, if the court is satisfied that the witness statement was a true copy of the notebook.
[D]   Yes, if the court exercised its discretion in favour of PC Ings.

Question 2
Norman is charged with robbing Olivia. The facts alleged by the Prosecution are that Olivia was walking down a lonely road when Norman ran up behind, grabbed her handbag and ran off. Olivia continued her journey home. When her flatmate, Phillipa, arrived home about two hours later, Olivia

told her what had happened. During examination-in-chief at Norman's trial, Olivia now wishes to refer to her conversation with Phillipa. Olivia's statement to Phillipa is:

[A]   Admissible as part of the *res gestae*.
[B]   Admissible as a previous consistent statement.
[C]   Inadmissible as a previous consistent statement.
[D]   Admissible as a recent complaint.

Question 3
Colin is charged with murder and Dennis is called as a witness for the Prosecution. The defence has evidence to suggest that Dennis is suffering from such disease of the mind as to be unable to distinguish between truth and fiction. In these circumstances, psychiatric evidence may be called to show:

[A]   That Dennis is unable to distinguish between truth and fiction.
[B]   That Dennis was in fact telling the truth.
[C]   Neither [A] nor [B].
[D]   Both [A] and [B].

Question 4
Read the following witness statements. Then read the trial manuscript and as you do so, identify any procedural and evidential errors that ocurred during the course of the hearing. Prepare skeleton arguments on any points of objection or other submissions that you would have made if appearing at this trial:

(a)   For the prosecution; *and*
(b)   for the defence.

STATEMENT OF WITNESS
(MCA 1980, s. 102; CJA 1967, s. 9; MCR 1981, r. 70)

Statement of: Stephen WELHAM
Age of witness: Over 21
Occupation of witness: Financial Services Manager
Address and telephone number: 187 St John's Avenue, Friern Barnet

This statement, consisting of two pages, each signed by me, is true to the best of my knowledge and belief and I make it knowing that, if it is tendered in evidence, I shall be liable to prosecution if I have wilfully stated in it anything which I know to be false or do not believe to be true.

Dated the 9th day of September 1992

Signed: S. Welham

Signature witnessed by: J. Osborn

On Tuesday 8 September 1992 I was returning from work at about 8 p.m., and left the Underground at Highgate. It is a short walk round the corner to the bus stop for the bus home. I must have ben thinking about work, because the next thing I knew a young fellow had stepped in front of me barring my path. He was in his early 20s, casually dressed with a waist-length dark cotton coat. He must have been about 5'10", and well-built. He asked if I had a fiver. I started to say it was none of his business, when I noticed another youth standing against the railings a couple of yards away looking on casually. The man in front pulled me forward with one hand. I tried to push him away, but suddenly felt a sharp pain in my shin, followed by a blow to the side of my face. I lost my balance and fell to the ground. He then ran off in the direction of Muswell Hill. The other man simply disappeared — he must have gone in the other direction.

I picked myself up and went back to the main road. I saw a police car waiting at the lights. I flagged it down and explained to the driver that I had just been attacked by two muggers, and that one of them had run off towards Muswell Hill. I was told to get into the car and the other officer asked for a description. We went down a side road and stopped alongside some parked cars. The officers jumped out, and when I looked out of the side window I saw them with the man who had hit me.

I have a 2 inch long bruise on my left shin and am rather tender where I was hit in front of my right ear.

Signed: S. Welham

Signature witnesed by: J. Osborn

STATEMENT OF WITNESS
(MCA 1980, s. 102: CJA 1967, s. 9; MCR 1981, r. 70)

Statement of:	John WOOD
Age of witness:	Over 21
Occupation of witness:	Joiner
Address and telephone number:	157 Granville Avenue, London N22

This statement consisting of one page, each signed by me, is true to the best of my knowledge and belief and I make it knowing that, if it is tendered in evidence, I shall be liable to prosecution if I have wilfully stated in it anything which I know to be false or do not believe to be true.

Dated the 9th day of September 1992

Signed: J. Wood

Signature witnessed by: J. Osborn

Yesterday evening Alan LYNCH and myself went out for a drink. We are both unemployed at the moment. When we got to Highgate we both realised we didn't have any money. We stood talking outside the pub for a couple of minutes, a bit fed up. A City gent came round the corner, and Alan bumped into him. Alan asked for a fiver; it was all a piece of fun. I saw a police car coming up Archway Road, so decided to make myself scarce.

Signed: J. Wood

Signature witnessed: J. Osborn

STATEMENT OF WITNESS
(MCA 1980, s. 102; CJA 1967, s. 9; MCR 1981, r. 70)

Statement of:	D. Sgt William CRANSTOUN
Age of witness:	Over 21
Occupation of witness:	Detective Sergeant
Address and telephone number:	Muswell Hill Police Station

This statement consisting of two pages, each signed by me, is true to the best of my knowledge and belief and I make it knowing that, if it is tendered in evidence, I shall be liable to prosecution if I have wilfully stated in it anything which I know to be false or do not believe to be true.

Dated the 9th day of September 1992

Signed: W. Cranstoun

Signature witnessed by: J. Osborn

On 8 September 1992 at 20.00 acting on information received I went with D.C. Henson and Stephen WELHAM towards Muswell Hill via Queen's Wood Road. I noticed a young man who I now know to be Alan LYNCH walking along the pavement. He looked over his shoulder and then ducked behind a parked car. I pulled up, and D.C. HENSON and I got out. I introduced myself. Stephen WELHAM called out 'He is the one'. I asked LYNCH where he was going. LYNCH replied, 'I am meeting some friends in Hornsey'. 'I asked him whereabouts, to which he replied, 'The Nightingale'. I asked, 'Where do you live?' Lynch said 'Lymington Avenue'. D. C. HENSON said 'Wood Green?' LYNCH said 'Yes'. I said, 'But that's in the opposite direction'. LYNCH replied, 'Yeah, but I've not come from home'. I said, 'Where have you come from?' LYNCH said, 'I don't have to answer these questions, do I?' D. C. HENSON said, 'Why did you try to hide from us?' LYNCH said, 'I was doing up my shoelace'. I said, 'Have you been near Highgate Underground station this evening?' LYNCH replied, 'What's it to you?' I said, 'I have a reason to believe you assaulted this gentleman', indicating Stephen WELHAM, 'and I am arresting you on suspicion of assault'. I then cautioned him, to which he said, 'You've got the wrong man. You are making a big mistake'. LYNCH was then taken to the police station.

Later, I saw LYNCH at the police station with D. C. HENSON. I reminded LYNCH of the caution. D. C. HENSON said, 'The man in the car was punched and kicked this evening near Highgate tube a couple of minutes before we stopped you. He has positively identified you. You tried to hide from us when you saw our car. Do you want to tell us about it?' LYNCH looked into the corner of the room for a couple of minutes, then said, 'All right, I might have asked for money. It was a bit of a lark. It wasn't nothing serious. Give us a break'. I asked if he wanted to make a written statement, to which LYNCH replied, 'No. Nothing in writing'.

On 8 September 1992 at 22.15 LYNCH was charged, the charge was read over, and he was cautioned. LYNCH made no reply.

Acting on local knowledge, on 9 September in company with D. C. HENSON, I attended at 157 Granville Avenue N22 where I saw John WOOD. As a result of our conversation John WOOD made a statement under caution at Muswell Hill Police Station.

Signed: W. Cranstoun

Signature witnessed by: J. Osborne

D. C. Henson made a statement in the same terms, with necessary changes.

Alan Lynch of 298 Lymington Avenue, Wood Green, N22 will say:

I am aged 22 and live at home with my parents, a brother and a sister. I am a car mechanic, but lost my job four months ago for bad timekeeping. I have several previous convictions for petty offences going back a long time. My most recent conviction was for fighting outside a pub when I was 20, I was fined £75.

On Tuesday 8 September I was arrestd by the police. I was on my way to meet some friends at the Nightingale pub in Hornsey. We had nothing planned. We often meet for a drink and a game of pool. I had been to see a friend's car in Mill Hill, and decided to get off the tube at Highgate and walk through the woods and then across to the pub. I would say it was about a 1.5-mile walk.

The bloke in Mill Hill is really a friend of a friend. I had agreed with Trevor Jones, one of my friends, to look over a car one of Trevor's friends was going to buy. The car was in Oakhampton Road but I didn't go into the house so don't know the full address. I had been given a tenner for doing it, so didn't want to say anything to the police.

As I was coming up to the woods my shoelace came undone. I stopped to do it up. Then a car pulled up, and next thing I knew there were two policemen asking me a lot of questions about where I was going, where I had been and where I lived. They accused me of thumping a bloke they had in the car, arrested me and took me to Muswell Hill Police Station.

When I was seen by the police at the station I did not admit I had hit anybody. I did not do it and I never said that I did to the police. I might have said that I had asked for money to look over the car, and that I hadn't done anything seriously wrong, but those comments were not about hitting anybody.

Trevor moved to Borehamwood a couple of years ago. I don't have his address, he just meets us every so often. I haven't seen him since I was arrested.

A. Lynch

1st October 1992

POLICE V ALAN LYNCH
Trial Transcript

Clerk: The next case is Alan Lynch, sir, number 16 in the list. (*Lynch is brought into the court and enters the dock*).
Clerk: Are you Alan Lynch?
Lynch: Yes
Clerk: Alan Lynch, you are charged with assault occasioning actual bodily harm contrary to section 47 of the Offences Against the Person Act 1861 in that you, on the 8th day of September 1992, did assault one Stephen Welham thereby occasioning unto him actual bodily harm. Do you plead guilty or not guilty?
Lynch: Not guilty.
Clerk: You may sit down.
Prosecution Counsel: May it please you, sir, I appear on behalf of the prosecution and my learned friend Miss Lucy Davies appears for the defence. It is the prosecution's case that the defendant assaulted his victim outside the Three Tuns public house in Highgate, which as I am sure you are aware is somewhat notorious. However, this case is not one in which alcohol is a factor. It is more in the nature of a mugging. The prosecution's first witness is the victim, Mr Stephen Welham, who will tell you about the circumstances of the assault on his way home from work and the extent of his injuries. The second witness will be Mr John Wood, an identification witness. He will be followed by Detective Sergeant Cranstoun, the arresting officer. I should at this stage mention that the arrest occurred a matter of just a few minutes after the incident. The fourth witness will be Detective Constable Henson, who was also present at the time of the arrest. Without further ado, and with your permission, sir, I will call Stephen Welham.
Usher: Mr Welham, please hold the Testament in your right hand and read the words on the card.
Welham: I swear by Almighty God that the evidence I shall give shall be the truth, the whole truth and nothing but the truth.
Pros: Is your full name Stephen Welham and do you live at 187 St John's Avenue, Barnet?
Welham: Yes
Pros: Are you a financial services manager?
Welham: That's right.
Pros: And who is your employer?
Welham: Barclays International, in the City.
Pros: How do you get to work?
Welham: I catch the bus on Colney Hatch Lane down to Highgate tube on Archway Road, then change from the Northern Line at Tottenham Court Road on to the Central Line to Bank.
Pros: And the reverse on the way home?
Welham: Yes.
Pros: Do you remember your journey home on Tuesday, 8th September?
Welham: I think so — I'm not sure of the date.
Pros: Was there an occasion when your usual routine was broken?

Welham: Yes, a couple of months ago I was threatened in the street by him (*points to defendant in the dock*).

Pros: Could you tell us where this happened?

Welham: I was leaving the Underground and walking round the corner to catch the bus. As I turned the corner I was confronted by the defendant.

Pros: What did he do?

Welham: He demanded money. Ten pounds, as I remember. Of course I refused. He had an accomplice with him. He grabbed me by the throat and started kicking me and punching — he was really wild. I managed to push him away and they ran off.

Pros: Could you tell us what your injuries were?

Welham: I had a large bruise on my shin and the side of my face became puffed up.

Pros: Were you cut at all?

Welham: No.

Pros: How clearly did you see your attacker?

Welham: He was facing me the whole time. He was a young man in his early 20s wearing a dark cotton jacket. It was still light and I remember the lights in the Three Tuns were still on. I had a good look at him.

Pros: What did you do after the attack?

Welham: I went back to the main road, where there was a police car. We went off towards Muswell Hill. We caught up with him and he was arrested.

Pros: When the police car stopped, what did you do?

Welham: I remained in it until I was asked to move into the front passenger seat.

Pros: When the police officers left the car, did you see what they did?

Welham: They arrested the defendant.

Pros: Did anyone say anything at that stage?

Welham: Yes, the police asked the defendant a lot of questions.

Pros: Did anyone else say anything?

Welham: The defendant gave them his name, and . . .

Pros: I had better stop you there. Did anyone apart from the police officers and the defendant say anything?

Welham: No.

Pros: Was anyone else present?

Welham: No. Only myself.

Pros: Did you say anything.

Welham: No. The policemen asked all the questions.

Pros: After the car stopped, did you identify anyone to the police officers?

Welham: Yes. When I looked out of the window I saw that they had caught my attacker, and I shouted something like 'That's him!'

Pros: Thank you Mr Welham. Please wait here in case there are any further questions.

Def: Mr Welham, at what time do you finish work of an evening?

Welham: About 6 p.m.

Def: Do you work overtime?

Welham: No. I am not in a grade that gets paid overtime.

Def: Do you ever work late?

Welham: Not normally, it depends on how much work we have on.

Def: How long does it take to get to Highgate from your office?

Welham: About 45 minutes.

Def: You seem unsure about the date of the alleged assault. How can you be sure it was the 8th September?

Welham: I think I was working late that night.

Def: At what time did you arrive at Highgate?

Welham: About 8 p.m.

Def: That's after lighting-up time at that time of year?

Welham: I don't know.

Def: Do you remember if the street lights were on?

Welham: I didn't notice. It was quite light.

Def: Did you make a statement to the police after the incident?

Welham: Yes.

Def: Have you recently read that statement?

Welham: Why?

Def: I put it to you that you read your statement this morning before coming into court.

Welham: Well, I did, I wanted to get the facts straight.

Def: Do you drink, Mr Welham?

Welham: A little. Sometimes.

Def: Did you have a drink that evening?

Welham: No.

Def: I put it to you that the reason you were late that evening was that you had had a drink or two before leaving for home.

Welham: I have told you I was working late.

Def: You said you were confronted by your attacker, and after a brief exchange of words, he punched and kicked you, then ran off.

Welham: That's right.

Def: It would all have been over very quickly.

Welham: Yes, that must be right.

Def: He demanded ten pounds, Mr Welham?

Welham: Yes.

Def: But that is not right, is it?

Welham: Yes, I have already said he demanded money.

Def: You said ten pounds.

Welham: He demanded ten pounds.

Def: I put it to you, Mr Welham, that the man you saw did not demand ten pounds.

Welham: He demanded ten pounds.

Def: I put it to you, Mr Welham, that the man you saw did not demand ten pounds.

Welham: Yes, he did.

Def: I put it to you that when you described the attack to the police you did not mention a demand for ten pounds.

Welham: I did.

Def: It is true, is it not, that you told the police the day after the incident that the man who attacked you demanded five pounds not ten?

Welham: All right, it may have been five.

Def: May, or was, five pounds?

Welham: It was five pounds.

Def: After your attacker grabbed hold of you, would I be right in thinking you would have been watching his hands?

Welham: I don't recall — but I did get a good look at his face.

Def: It's only a natural reaction to look at what his hands were doing, isn't it?

Welham: I'm not sure.

Def: You have already told this court that you were repeatedly kicked and punched.

Welham: That's right.

Def: The assault you mentioned to the police wasn't at all wild, was it?

Welham: I don't know what you mean.

Def: I am referring to the statement you made to the police after the attack. The account of the attack contained in your statement is rather different from what you have told the court today, isn't it?

Welham: Not so far as I remember.

Def: Sir, perhaps the witness could be shown his statement. Mr Welham do you recognise this statement?

Welham: Yes.

Def: And is it your signature at the bottom?

Welham: Yes.

Def: And have you signed a declaration to say that the statement is true to the best of your knowledge and belief?

Welham: I did.

Def: Would you look at the second half of the first paragraph of the statement. (*Witness reads statement to himself.*)

Def: Do you now wish to tell the justices again about the nature of the attack?

Welham: No.

Def: Very well. About half-way down the first page, the ninth sentence begins, 'I tried to push him away'. Could you read that sentence?

Welham: I tried to push him away, but suddenly felt a sharp pain in my shin, followed by a . . . This is rather underhand.

Def: Could you please continue.

Welham: Followed by a blow to the side of my face. It is rather immaterial how many times he hit me. The fact is he hit me, and nothing can take that away.

Def: Will you accept that at the time of the incident you said you were only kicked once and punched once?

Welham: Of course, I have to.

Def: Tell me, Mr Welham, have you yourself ever been in trouble?

Welham: What do you mean?

Def: Trouble with the police?

Welham: Er . . . no.

Def: Is it not the case that you have a criminal record?

Welham: In a manner of speaking, but it was a long time ago.

Def: Is it true that you have a record for indecent exposure?

Welham: It was while I was a student. I was fined.

Chairman: Mr Welham, what was the date of that conviction?

Welham: It was when I was about 20. It must have been 1975, or thereabouts.

Def: Thank you, Mr Welham.

Pros: Mr Welham, I have one or two further questions to ask you. You were working late on the evening in question.

Welham: Yes.

Pros: At about what time did you leave the office?

Welham: Let me see. It must have been about 7.15 p.m.

Pros: Did you stop off anywhere either before catching the Underground or *en route*?

Welham: No.

Pros: Can you remind the Court how long it took to get to Highgate?

Welham: 45 minutes.

Pros: And the time of the attack?

Welham: 8 p.m.

Pros: You were asked a number of questions by the defence about the lighting conditions and the period over which you saw your attacker. How well did you see him?

Welham: Very well. We were face to face for some time, and I got a very good look at him.

Pros: Mr Welham, you have already described him as a man in his early twenties wearing a dark cotton jacket. How tall was he?

Welham: About 5' 10".

Pros: At the time of the attack, did you notice anyone else present?

Welham: There was an accomplice lounging against the railings.

Pros: Thank you, Mr Welham. Unless you have any questions, sir.

Chairman: Mr Welham, you go home via Highgate every day?

Welham: Yes

Chairman: Then you will appreciate that Muswell Hill Road slopes very steeply down towards Muswell Hill?

Welham: It does.

Chairman: Which way were you facing when you were attacked?

Welham: Towards Muswell Hill.

Chairman: So you were uphill of your attacker?

Welham: Yes.

Chairman: When you described your attacker as 5' 10" did you take into account that you were uphill of him, and that he would therefore appear shorter than if you were at the same level as him?

Welham: I hadn't really thought about it. My impression was that he was about 5' 10". Bearing in mind what you say, it may be that he was a little taller than that.

Chairman: I have no further questions.

Pros: Sir, may the witness be released?

Def: I have no objection.

Chairman: Very well, thank you Mr Welham. You have been very helpful. (*J. Wood is called and sworn*).

Pros: Are you John Woods of 157 Granville Avenue, London N22?

Wood: I am.

Pros: Are you an unemployed joiner?

Wood: No. I got a job.

Pros: Who are you employed by, Mr Wood?

Wood: I've been taken on by me uncle.

Pros: Do you remember the events of the evening of 8th September?

Wood: No.

Pros: Do you remember an arrangement to visit a public house in Highgate?

Wood: Nope.

Pros: Have you every visited a public house called the Three Tuns in Highgate? It's located at the corner of Archway Road and Muswell Hill Road. Do you know the public house I am referring to?

Wood: I don't live in Highgate.

Pros: It's not very far from Wood Green. Have you ever been to Highgate?

Wood: I may have passed through.

Pros: Have you every stopped off at the Three Tuns?

Wood: I can't remember.

Pros: Do you recognise anyone in court today?

Wood: No.

Pros: Mr Wood, please look around the room, and think carefully before answering. Is there anyone here that you know?

Wood: No.

Pros: I have no further questions of this witness.

Def: No cross-examination, sir.

(*D. S. Cranstoun is called and sworn.*)

Pros: Are you Detective Sergeant William Cranstoun, attached to Muswell Hill Police Station?

Cranstoun: I am.

Pros: Were you on patrol with Detective Henson on the evening of 8th September this year?

Cranstoun: I was.

(*At this point D. S. Cranstoun produces a notebook from his top pocket and starts flicking through it.*)

Cranstoun: Do you mind if I refer to my notes, your worship?

Pros: If I may help, sir.

Chairman: Please do.

Pros: Could you help us, Sergeant, by telling the court when the notes were written up?

Cranstoun: Contemporaneously, while the events were fresh in my memory.

Pros: In the circumstances I would ask that the witness be permitted to refresh his memory.

Chairman: Yes, please continue.

Pros: I think you were given a description of a person who was alleged to have committed an assault?

Cranstoun: Yes, I was driving towards Muswell Hill along Queen's Wood Road.

Pros: Why did you choose that route?

Cranstoun: The main road to Muswell Hill is very long with only one turning off for some distance that leads anywhere. I guessed that the suspect would leave Muswell Hill Road as soon as he could, so I did the same.

Pros: As you were driving, did you notice anything suspicious?

Cranstoun: I noticed a young man walking along the pavement. He looked over his shoulder and then ducked behind a parked car.

Pros: Why was he looking over his shoulder?

Cranstoun: He must have been looking to see if he was being followed.

Pros: Then what did you do?

Cranstoun: I stopped the car and got out. Detective Constable Henson did likewise.

Pros: Did you speak to the gentleman in the street?

Cranstoun: Yes, sir.

Pros: What did you say?

Cranstoun: I introduced myself. Mr Welham called out, 'He is the one'. At that time I ascertained that the man we had stopped was the defendant, Alan Lynch.

Pros: What did you say?

Cranstoun: I asked the defendant where he was going. He replied, 'I am meeting some friends in Hornsey'. I asked him whereabouts, to which he replied, 'The Nightingale'.

Pros: Where is that?

Cranstoun: It is about 2 miles from there, cutting through the side roads, on the corner of Nightingale Road and Hornsey High Street.

Pros: What did you say after that?

Cranstoun: I asked, 'Where do you live?' The defendant said, 'Lymington Avenue'. Detective Constable Henson asked if that was in Wood Green. The defendant said, 'Yes'. I said, 'But that's in the opposite direction'. The defendant said, 'Yeah, but I've not come from home'. I said, 'Where have you come from?' The defendant said, 'I don't have to answer these questions, do I?' Detective Constable Henson said, 'Why did you try to hide from us?' The defendant said, 'I was doing up my shoelace'. I said 'Have you been near Highgate Underground station this evening?' The defendant replied, 'What's it to you?'

Pros: I think you then told the defendant that you were arresting him for the assault on Mr Welham, and gave him the caution.

Cranstoun: That is right.

Pros: Did the defendant say anything in reply to the caution?

Cranstoun: Yes. He said, 'You've got the wrong man. You are making a big mistake'.

Pros: Was the accused then taken to Muswell Hill Police Station?

Cranstoun: Yes, sir.

Pros: Did you speak to the defendant at the station?

Cranstoun: Yes, together with Detective Constable Henson. I started by reminding Lynch of the caution.

Pros: Did Detective Constable Henson remind the accused of the facts of the incident?

Cranstoun: He did. The defendant looked into space for a while, then said, let me see, 'All right, I might have asked for money. It was a bit of a lark. It wasn't nothing serious. Give us a break'.

Pros: I think you then asked the defendant if he wanted to make a written statement.

Cranstoun: But he refused.

Pros: I understand the defendant was then charged.

Cranstoun: Yes, sir.

Pros: At what time was that?

Cranstoun: 10.15 p.m., sir.

Pros: Did he make any reply?

Cranstoun: No. None.

Pros: Thank you Sergeant.

6   Similar Fact Evidence

May evidence be adduced to show that an accused is disposed to misconduct of the kind alleged in the instant proceedings (similar fact evidence)?

6.1   Criminal Cases

6.1.1   THE PRINCIPLES

The best starting-point to this complex and controversial area of the law of evidence is the dictum of Lord Herschell LC giving the judgment of the Privy Council in *Makin* v *Attorney-General for New South Wales* [1894] AC 57, PC at p. 65:

> In their Lordships' opinion the principles which must govern the decision of the case are clear, though the application of them is by no means free from difficulty. It is undoubtedly not competent for the prosecution to adduce evidence tending to show that the accused has been guilty of criminal acts other than those covered by the indictment, for the purpose of leading to the conclusion that the accused is a person likely from his criminal conduct or character to have committed the offence for which he is being tried. [THE FIRST PROPOSITION.] On the other hand, the mere fact that the evidence adduced tends to show the commission of other crimes does not render it inadmissible if it be relevant to an issue before the jury, and it may be so relevant if it bears upon the question whether the acts alleged to constitute the crime charged in the indictment were designed or accidental, or to rebut a defence which would otherwise be open to the accused. [THE SECOND PROPOSITION.] The statement of these general principles is easy, but it is obvious that it may often be very difficult to draw the line and to decide whether a particular piece of evidence is on the one side or the other.

6.1.1.1   Lord Herschell's first proposition or 'Leopards that change their spots'
The first proposition means that prosecution evidence which shows *only* that the accused is disposed to crime in general, or to commit certain types of crime in particular, is not admissible to prove that he is guilty of the crime charged. The reason for the first proposition is probably best explained in *R* v *Boardman* [1975] AC 421 by Lord Cross of Chelsea at p. 456:

> ... the reason for this general rule is not that the law regards such evidence as inherently irrelevant but that it is believed that if it were generally admitted jurors would in many cases think that it was more relevant than it was, so that, as it is put, its prejudicial effect would outweigh its probative value.

For examples of the first proposition, see: *Noor Mohamed* v *R* [1949] AC 182, PC (and *cf R* v *Armstrong* [1949] AC 182, PC); *R* v *Marshall* [1989] Crim LR 819, CA.

6.1.1.2 **Lord Herschell's second proposition or 'Leopards that don't change their spots' (or 'Baby farming and brides in the bath')**
The second proposition is also probably best explained in *R* v *Boardman* by Lord Cross at p. 456:

> Circumstances, however, may arise in which such evidence is so very relevant that to exclude it would be an affront to common sense.

Consider the following examples:

Makin v *Attorney-General for New South Wales* [1894] AC 57, PC: the Crown, in seeking to prove deliberate killing were entitled to rely on evidence which negatived the possibility that the child in question died accidentally or from natural causes. (In fact, this was not the defence — the accused simply denied all connection with both the mother and the baby.) In other words, to find so many bodies of children in the back-yards of so many sets of premises all of which were occupied by the accused, rendered quite ludicrously incredible any suggestion that this had nothing to do with the accused but must have been accidental or coincidental.

R v *Smith* (1915) 11 Cr App R 229, CCA: if what had happened in this case had happened once only, an explanation based on accident might have been plausible. But when it happened three times, in remarkably similar circumstances and on each occasion to the benefit of the accused, it gave rise to a very strong inference that the events were so very coincidental that they must have been brought about by design and not by accident.

R v *Sims* [1946] KB 531, CCA: if strikingly similar allegations are made by different persons about the behaviour of the accused on different occasions, each allegation may be admitted on the basis that whereas the jury might think that one man might be telling an untruth, three or four, unless conspiring together, are hardly likely to tell the same untruth.

R v *Ball* [1911] AC 47, HL: it might well be thought to be passing odd if a brother and sister who had practised sexual intercourse in the past now lived together as man and wife and shared the same bed but did not have sexual intercourse.

R v *Straffen* [1952] 2 QB 911, CCA: a resemblance so striking to the offence charged as to be inexplicable on the basis of coincidence.

R v *Wilmot* (1989) 89 Cr App R 341, CA: there are circumstances in which, where it is proved or admitted that a man has had sexual intercourse with a number of young women, the question whether it is proved that one of them did not consent may in part be answered by proving that another of the women did not consent if the cirumstances bear a striking resemblance.

For an example of Lord Herschell's second proposition in which the evidence, although not evidence of facts which were strikingly similar to the facts of the offence charged, nevertheless did go to 'rebut a defence which would otherwise be open to the accused', see *R* v *Anderson* [1988] QB 678, CA. See also *R* v *Williams* (1987) 84 Cr App R 299, CA and *cf R* v *Carrington* [1990] Crim LR 330, CA.

See also *R* v *Lunt* (1987) 85 Cr App R 241, CA (applied in *R* v *Shore* (1989) 89 Cr App R 32, CA) *per* Neill LJ at p. 244:

> evidence is admissible as 'similar fact' evidence if, but only if, it goes beyond showing a tendency to commit crimes of the kind charged and is positively probative in regard to the crime charged... In order to decide whether the evidence is positively probative . . . it is first necessary to identify the issue to which the evidence is directed. Thus the evidence may be put forward, e.g. to support an identification (where unusual points of similarity of appearance or method can be relevant and positively probative) or to prove intention, or to rebut a possible defence of accident or innocent association. In these several examples the answer to the question of what is positively probative

may vary. Once the issue has been identified the question will be: will the 'similar fact' evidence be positively probative, in the sense of assisting the jury to reach a conclusion on that issue on some ground other than the accused's bad character or disposition to commit the sort of crime with which he is charged? If the evidence of similar facts will not assist the jury to this end, it is irrelevant and inadmissible.

6.1.1.3   The abandonment of categories of relevance (e.g. 'Proof of system', 'Proof of identity', 'Rebuttal of accident', 'Rebuttal of mistake' or 'Rebuttal of innocent association')

Although at one time it was thought that there were categories of relevance comprising a closed list of the cases in which similar fact evidence is admissible, such a view has now been repudiated. See:

R v *Bond* [1906] 2 KB 389.

DPP v *Boardman* [1975] AC 421, HL.

Harris v *DPP* [1952] AC 694, HL: it is erroneous to draw up a closed list because it can only provide instances of a principle of general application — what matters is the principle itself and its proper application to the particular circumstances of the charge in question.

6.1.1.4   Cogency

(a)   The cogency of the evidence of the commission by the accused of the offence charged.

Similar fact evidence would appear to be admissible in cases where the other prosecution evidence, i.e. the evidence connecting the accused with the offence charged, is so weak that a submission of no case to answer would succeed. See *Harris* v *DPP* [1952] AC 694, HL. See also *R* v *Strafen* [1952] 2 QB 911, CCA.

(b)   The cogency of the 'similar fact' evidence or 'a visit to Bradford Market'.

It is no bar to the admission of similar fact evidence that the defence disputes the facts that it seeks to prove. See *R* v *Rance* (1975) 62 Cr App R 462, CA.

However, there must be sufficient evidence to justify, as a possibility, a finding by the tribunal of fact, that the accused was guilty of the misconduct alleged to have occurred on another occasion. See:

Harris v *DPP* [1952] AC 694, HL.

R v *Mansfield* (1977) 65 Cr App R 276, CA.

R v *Lunt* (1987) 85 Cr App R 241, CA.

Moreover, in cases where identity is in issue, it seems that there has to be some evidence to make the jury *sure* that the accused is the offender, because the similar facts go to show that the same man committed both offences, not that the accused was that man: *R* v *McGranaghan* (1991) *The Times*, 1 November 1991. McG was convicted of three separate aggravated burglaries of homes and rapes or grossly indecent assaults on women in those homes. McG denied having anything to do with any of the offences. The Court of Appeal held that the similarities in the features of all the alleged offences rendered the evidence on one admissible in relation to the others, but allowed the appeal on the grounds that the jury should have been directed to consider first whether, disregarding the similarity of the facts, the other evidence in the case was sufficient to make them sure that the accused committed at least one of the offences. Only if they were so sure, was evidence of similarity then admissible to prove that the accused committed the second offence. An identification about which the jury were not sure could not support another identification of which they were also not sure, however similar the facts of the two offences might be. The *McGranaghan* principle is, it seems, limited to case of alleged mistaken identification: see, *R* v *S* [1993] Crim LR 293.

6.1.1.5   'Similar facts' subsequent to the offence charged

Evidence may be given of misconduct alleged to have occurred on another occasion either before or after the crime with which the accused is charged. See *R* v *Smith* (1915) 11 Cr App R 229, CA and *R* v *Geering* (1849) 18 LJ MC 215.

6.1.1.6   Convictions

If the accused was convicted of an offence in respect of his conduct on some other occasion and evidence of that conduct is admissible under the similar fact evidence doctrine, is the prosecution also entitled to prove the fact of the conviction? The position is not clear. See *R* v *Shepherd* (1980) 71 Cr App R 120.

See also Police and Criminal Evidence Act 1984, s. 74(3) in **Chapter 11** of this Manual.

6.1.1.7   Discretion

There are numerous dicta to the effect that the trial judge does have a discretion to exclude otherwise admissible similar fact evidence if its prejudicial effect outweighs its probative value: see, e.g. *Noor Mohamed* v *R; Harris* v *DPP; DPP* v *Boardman*; and *R* v *Lunt*.

6.1.1.8   Crimes committed in a strikingly similar manner to other crimes committed by the accused

The leading authority in relation to crimes committed in a strikingly similar manner to other crimes committed by the accused is *DPP* v *Boardman* [1975] AC 421, HL.

Per Lord Morris of Borth-y-Gest at p. 441:

> . . . there may be cases where a judge, having both limbs of Lord Herschell's famous proposition in mind, considers that the interests of justice (of which the interests of fairness form so fundamental a component) make it proper that he should permit a jury when considering one fact or set of facts also to consider the evidence concerning another fact or set of facts if between the two there is such close or striking similarity or such an underlying unity that probative force could fairly be yielded.

Per Lord Wilberforce at p. 444 dealing with the probative force of admissible similar fact evidence:

> This probative force is derived, if at all, from the circumstances that the facts testified to by the several witnesses bear to each other such a striking similarity that they must, when judged by experience and common sense, either all be true, or have arisen from a cause common to the witnesses or from pure coincidence. The jury may, therefore, properly be asked to judge whether the right conclusion is that all are true, so that each story is supported by the other(s).

Per Lord Cross of Chelsea at p. 456:

> Circumstances, however, may arise in which such evidence is so very relevant that to exclude it would be an affront to common sense. . . The question must always be whether the similar fact evidence taken together with the other evidence would do no more than raise or strengthen a suspicion that the accused committed the offence with which he is charged or would point so strongly to his guilt that only an ultra-cautious jury, if they accepted it as true, would acquit in face of it.

Per Lord Salmon at p. 462:

> It has . . . never been doubted that if the crime charged is committed in a uniquely or strikingly similar manner to other crimes committed by the accused the manner in which the other crimes were committed may be evidence on which a jury could reasonably conclude that the accused was guilty of the crime charged. The similarity would have to be so unique or striking that common sense makes it inexplicable on the basis of coincidence.

Per Lord Hailsham at p. 453:

A mere succession of facts is not normally enough . . . There must be something more than mere repetition. The test is whether there is such an underlying unity between the offences as to make coincidence an affront to common sense.

For a recent illustration of the point made by Lord Hailsham, see *R* v *Wells* (1991) 92 Cr App R 24, CA. The accused's home was raided twice, resulting in two sets of charges for possession of cocaine with intent to supply. As to the similarities between the items recovered on each of the two raids, paperfolds, scales and cocaine in 1 and ½ gramme units were found — but these are all commonplace for drug suppliers; the cutting agent Mannitol was found — the most common in use; and the percentage purity of cocaine was 21% on the first raid, 15–23% on the second raid — this was hardly striking. Compare *R* v *Mullen* [1992] Crim LR 735.

See also *R* v *Beggs* (1990) 90 Cr App R 430, CA and *R* v *Bedford* (1991) 93 Cr App R 113, CA.

In *R* v *P* [1991] 3 All ER 337, an important decision of the House of Lords, it was made clear that in cases where the evidence sought to be adduced comes from another alleged victim or victims, striking similarity is *not* an essential element except in cases where the identity of the offender is in issue. The accused was convicted on two counts of rape and eight counts of incest. One of the rapes and four of the incest counts related to daughter B. The other rape count and the other four incest counts related to daughter S. The trial judge found the following to be strikingly similar: (a) the extreme discipline and almost dictatorial power exercised over the female children of the family; (b) the abortions undergone by each girl paid for by P; (c) the apparent acquiescence of the mother in his sexual attentions to his daughters. The Court of Appeal held that these features (with the possible exception of (b)) did not relate to P's *modus operandi* and could not be described as unusual features such as to make the account of one girl more credible because they were mirrored in the statement of the other. As to (a), the discipline was applied to all the family, not just the girls. As to (b), P's financial commitment was limited, his wife was also involved and the fact that he might have arranged and paid for the abortion did not necessarily point to his being responsible for the pregnancy. As to (c), the acquiescence related principally to the eldest girl and might have been due to fear of P. Moreover, it would be unusual if a third party's reaction to offences could ever operate as a striking similarity. The Court of Appeal allowed the appeal, therefore, because, as it understood the law, there was a requirement of similarity going beyond what was described as 'the incestuous father's stock-in-trade', and that feature was lacking. However, leave to appeal to the House of Lords was granted and the following point was certified:

Where a father/step-father is charged with sexually abusing a young daughter of the family, is evidence that he has also similarly abused other young children of the family admissible (assuming there to be no collusion) in support of such charge in the absence of any other 'striking similarities?'

The House of Lords held that the true test of admissibility is whether the evidence in question has a probative force sufficiently great to make it just to admit it, notwithstanding that it is prejudicial in tending to show that the accused is guilty of another crime. There was no requirement, as the Court of Appeal believed, of some feature of similarity beyond the incestuous father's stock-in-trade. Lord Mackay LC, giving the judgment of the House, answered the certified question as follows:

When a question of the kind raised in this case arises I consider that the judge must first decide whether there is material upon which the jury would be entitled to conclude that the evidence of one victim, about what occurred to that victim, is so related to the evidence given by another victim, about what happened to that other victim, that the evidence of the first victim provides strong enough support for the evidence of the second victim to make it just to admit it, notwithstanding the prejudicial effect of admitting the evidence. This relationship, from which support is derived, may take many forms and while these forms may include 'striking similarity' in the manner in which the crime is committed, consisting of unusual characteristics in its execution the necessary relationship is by no means confined to such circumstances. Relationships in time and circumstances other than these may well be important relationships in this connection. Where the identity of the perpetrator is in issue, and evidence of this kind is important in that connection, obviously something in the nature of what has been called in the course of the argument a signature or other special feature will be necessary. To transpose this requirement to other situations where the question is whether a crime has been committed, rather than who did commit it, is to impose an unnecessary and improper restriction upon the application of the principle.

For these reasons, the appeal was allowed and the conviction restored.

Three propositions may still be derived from *DPP* v *Boardman*:

(a)   The admission of similar fact evidence is exceptional and requires a strong degree of probative force.

(b)   Sufficient probative force may be gained where the evidence as to the similar facts and as to the facts in issue display such a close or striking similarity or such an underlying unity that, if accepted, it would be inexplicable, in common sense, on grounds of coincidence (but this is not an essential element unless identity is in issue — see *R* v *P*).

(c)   If there is a real possibility that the several witnesses to the strikingly similar facts have concocted false evidence by conspiracy or collaboration, the similar fact evidence should be excluded: *per* Lords Wilberforce and Cross. (On this point see now *R* v *Ryder* (1993) *The Times*, 16 March 1993.)

6.1.2   CRIMES COMMITTED WHERE THE CIRCUMSTANCES SURROUNDING THE COMMISSION OF THE OFFENCE ARE STRIKINGLY SIMILAR (A) TO THE CIRCUMSTANCES SURROUNDING OTHER CRIMES COMMITTED BY THE ACCUSED OR (B) TO OTHER NON-CRIMINAL BEHAVIOUR OF THE ACCUSED

6.1.2.1   Other crimes or 'amusement arcades and beaches'

Evidence of the circumstances surrounding other crimes committed by the accused is admissible under the similar fact evidence doctrine if those circumstances have a sufficient degree of probative force derived from a striking similarity between those circumstances and the circumstances surrounding the commission of the offence charged. See:

R v *Novac* (1976) 65 Cr App R 107, CA.

R v *Johannsen* (1977) 65 Cr App R 101, CA.

R v *Scarrott* [1978] QB 1016, CA *per* Scarman LJ:

Plainly some matters, some circumstances may be so distant in time or place from the commission of an offence as not to be properly considered when deciding whether the subject-matter of similar fact evidence displays striking similarities with the offence charged. On the other hand, equally plainly, one cannot isolate, as a sort of laboratory specimen, the bare bones of a criminal offence from its surrounding circumstances and say that it is only within the confines of that specimen, microscopically considered, that admissibility is to be determined.

See also *R* v *Smith* (1915) 11 Cr App R 229, CCA; and *Lanford* v *GMC* [1989] 2 All ER 921, PC, in which a doctor was charged with using obscene and indecent language and behaving improperly to two female patients in the course of professional consultations and examinations. The argument advanced for the appellant was that the admitted similarity in what the doctor allegedly said to Mrs A and Mrs B respectively could not properly be relied on by the prosecution when there was no striking similarity in what he allegedly did to them. The argument was rejected: the evidence of each patient was that the contact was indecent and improper; the evidence of what the doctor said before and after his examination tended, if believed to prove that the contact was indecent; and the evidence of what the doctor allegedly said in one case, provided a striking similarity was found between the two cases, was capable of corroborating the evidence of indecency in the other.

6.1.2.2 **Other non-criminal behaviour or the 'nude baby-sitters'**
Evidence of non-criminal behaviour of the accused is admissible under the similar fact evidence doctrine if such behaviour has a sufficient degree of probative force derived from a striking similarity between that behaviour and the circumstances surrounding the commission of the offence charged. See:

R v *Barrington* [1981] 1 WLR 419, CA.

R v *Rodley* [1913] 3 KB 468, CCA.

R v *Butler* (1987) 84 Cr App R 12, CA.

R v *Tricoglus* (1976) 65 Cr App R 16, CA.

6.1.3 **PROBATIVE VALUE WITHOUT STRIKING SIMILARITY**

The test of striking similarity is not appropriate in every case; what the law requires is positive probative value (albeit that in some cases such probative value is derived from striking similarity). See: *R* v *Rance* (1975) 62 Cr App R 462, CA; *R* v *Scarrott* [1978] QB 1016, CA; and *R* v *P* [1991] 3 All ER 337, HL.

The cases show that evidence of disposition may possess a sufficient degree of probative value which is derived not from any unique or striking similarity between the various facts testified to, but from (a) the other prosecution evidence in the case, taken together with (b) the nature of the actual or likely defence.

6.1.3.1 **The relevance of the actual or likely defence**
Similar fact evidence is admissible to rebut a defence which, even if not raised, is fairly open to the accused. See:

Thompson v *R* [1918] AC 221, HL.

Noor Mohamed v *R* [1949] AC 182, PC.

Harris v *DPP* [1952] AC 694, HL.

The nature of the defence, whether actually raised or fairly open to the accused, is a highly relevant factor in determining admissibility. See:

R v *Chandor* [1959] 1 QB 545, CCA.

R v *Flack* [1969] 1 WLR 937, CA.

DPP v *Boardman* [1975] AC 421, HL; Lord Hailsham said he failed to see the logical distinction between a case of innocent association and a case of complete denial. See also Lord Cross, who said that he failed to see the distinction, in the case of a sexual offence, between a defence that the meeting at which the offence is said to have been committed never took place and a defence that the meeting did take place but that no offence was committed in the course of it. In both cases, said Lord Cross, the accused would be saying that the accuser is lying. Subsequent case law, however, maintains the validity of exactly these distinctions. See, for example, *R* v *Lewis* (1983) 76 Cr App R 33, CA.

6.1.3.2 **Some examples**
Examples of probative value without striking similarity include cases involving homosexual misconduct and incriminating articles. In some of these cases, the evidence has probative value in identifying the accused. In others, such as *R* v *Lewis*, it has probative value in rebutting a defence of innocent association. It should be stressed, however, that this is not to return to the repudiated view

that admissibility is restricted to evidence falling within a closed list of categories of relevance — the sole test is probative value; each case turns on its own facts; and all the examples which follow are nothing more than instances of a doctrine of general application.

(a) Cases involving homosexual misconduct. See:

Thompson v *R* [1918] AC 221, HL.

DPP v *Boardman* [1975] AC 421, HL.

R v *King* [1967] 2 QB 358, CA.

R v *Horwood* [1970] 1 QB 133, CA.

(b) Incriminating articles.

Evidence of the accused's possession of incriminating articles may show nothing more than the accused's criminal disposition, in which case it will be inadmissible pursuant to the first of Lord Herschell's propositions in *Makin* v *Attorney-General for New South Wales* (see **6.1.1**). See *R* v *Taylor* (1923) 17 Cr App R 109.

However, evidence of the possession of incriminating articles may be admitted under the similar fact evidence doctrine to identify the accused as the offender where the articles in question could have been used, even if they are not proved to have been used, in committing the offence charged. See *R* v *Reading* [1966] 1 WLR 836, CCA; and *R* v *Mustafa* (1976) 65 Cr App R 26, CA.

(c) Other cases.

Evidence of misconduct may be admitted not to show that the accused is more likely to have committed the offence by reason of his disposition, but in order to establish a particular and essential part of the prosecution case. Consider the following examples:

R v *Straffen* [1952] 2 QB 911, CCA.

R v *Ducsharm* [1956] 1 DLR 732, Canada.

R v *Salisbury* (1831) 5 C & P 155. A postman, A, is charged with stealing a letter belonging to B and containing bank-notes. There is evidence that the accused has also opened a letter, also containing bank-notes, belonging to C, and that the accused has put the notes from B's letter into C's letter, and taken notes from C's letter to the same amount, which notes are found in A's possession. Such evidence is admissible to establish a link in the chain of events relating to the offence charged. See also:

R v *Ellis* (1826) 6 B & C 145.

R v *Mackie* (1973) 57 Cr App R 463, CA.

6.1.4 'SIMILAR FACT' EVIDENCE FOR THE DEFENCE

It is not normally permissible for one co-accused to give evidence showing the misconduct of another co-accused on some other occasion. However, such evidence may be admissible, notwithstanding that it prejudices the other co-accused, if it be relevant to the defence of the first co-accused. See *R* v *Miller* [1952] 2 All ER 667, Assizes; and *R* v *Neale* (1977) 65 Cr App R 304, CA. See also *Lowery* v *R* [1974] AC 85 and *R* v *Bracewell* (1978) 68 Cr App R 44. In *R* v *Douglass* (1989) 89 Cr App R 264, CA, D and P were charged with causing death by reckless driving. A van driven by P collided head-on with another car. D and P were allegedly vying together before the accident, D having pulled out into the centre of the road several times to prevent P from overtaking. Their vehicles collided and this caused P's van to hit the oncoming car. P gave no evidence but his counsel, in cross-examination of P's girlfriend, elicited evidence that P had never drunk alcohol in the two years that she had known him. The prosecution suggested that D had been drinking before the accident. Evidence of P's previous convictions, which included offences involving drink, was ruled inadmissible. P was acquitted. D was convicted.

Held, the fact that joint enterprise was not alleged was no basis for excluding evidence of character if it became relevant to the issue of guilt of one of the accused. The evidence elicited on behalf of P as to his lack of propensity to have driven as alleged became relevant to the issue of D's guilt. In such a case contradictory evidence as to propensity could be called by D. D should have been allowed to adduce evidence of P's criminal record.

6.1.5 STATUTORY PROVISIONS

Theft Act 1968, s. 27(3):

> *Where a person is being proceeded against for handling stolen goods (but not for any offence other than handling stolen goods), then at any stage of the proceedings, if evidence has been given of his having or arranging to have in his possession the goods the subject of the charge, or of his undertaking or assisting in, or arranging to undertake or assist in, their retention, removal, disposal or realisation, the following evidence shall be admissible for the purpose of proving that he knew or believed the goods to be stolen goods:—*
>
> *(a) evidence that he has had in his possession, or has undertaken or assisted in the retention, removal, disposal or realisation of, stolen goods from any theft taking place not earlier than 12 months before the offence charged; and*
>
> *(b) (provided that seven days' notice in writing has been given to him of the intention to prove the conviction) evidence that he has within the five years preceding the date of the offence charged been convicted of theft or of handling stolen goods.*

See generally:

R v *Wilkins* [1975] 2 AllER 734, CA: the evidence is only relevant to those counts in which guilty knowledge is in issue.

R v *Bradley* (1980) 70 Cr App R 200, CA (applied in *R* v *Wood* [1987] 1 WLR 799, CA): under sub-paragraph (a) the only evidence admissible is that which the sub-paragraph describes.

R v *Fowler* (1987) 86 Cr App R 219, CA: sub-paragraph (b) only permits the prosecution to relate the fact of a previous conviction for handling, where and when. The sub-paragraph should only be used where the interests of justice so demand and not as a matter of course: *R* v *Rasini* (1986) *The Times*, 20 March 1986, CA.

The judge has a discretion to exclude the evidence where its prejudicial effect is such as to make it virtually impossible for a jury thereafter to take a dispassionate view of the crucial facts of the case. See:

R v *List* [1966] 1 WLR 9.

R v *Knott* [1973] Crim LR 36, CA.

R v *Perry* [1984] Crim LR 680, CA.

6.2 Civil Cases

In civil cases, the emphasis is not so much on prejudicial effect but on probative force, i.e. the relevance of the evidence to the facts in issue. For this reason, in civil cases, similar fact evidence tends to be much more readily admissible than in criminal cases. See:

Hollingham v *Head* (1858) 27 LJCP 241.

Joy v *Phillips Mills & Co. Ltd* [1916] 1 KB 849, CA.

Sattin v *National Union Bank* (1978) 122 SJ 367, CA.

Mood Music Publishing Co. Ltd v *De Wolfe Ltd* [1976] Ch 119, CA; per Lord Denning MR:

> The criminal courts have been very careful not to admit such evidence unless its probative value is so strong that it should be received in the interests of justice; and its admission will not operate unfairly to the accused ... In civil cases the courts will admit evidence of similar facts if it is logically probative, that is, if it is logically relevant in determining the matter which is in issue: provided that it is not oppressive or unfair to the other side; and also that the other side has fair notice of it and is able to deal with it.

Berger v *Raymond Sun Ltd* [1984] 1 WLR 625.

Questions

OBJECTIVES

This chapter is designed to assist you:

(a) to understand the rationale for the admission of evidence of disposition and behaviour on other occasions to prove commission of the offence by the accused despite the general rule to the contrary; and

(b) to relate the rules discussed in this Chapter to the concepts of relevance, admissibility and weight discussed in **Chapter 2** of this Manual.

RESEARCH

(a) Read the materials contained in **Chapter 6** of this Manual.

(b) Read:

Keane, *The Modern Law of Evidence* (2nd ed., 1989), ch. 14, OR

Murphy, *A Practical Approach to Evidence* (4th ed., 1992), ch. 5; AND

Carter, *Cases & Statutes on Evidence* (2nd ed., 1990), ch. 20 and the Supplement (1992), OR

Heydon, *Evidence Cases & Materials* (3rd ed, 1991).

(c) On the basis of this research, answer the following questions.

Question 1

Herbert, a bank manager, is charged with committing an act of bestiality with a sheep while on a walking tour of the Lake District. The prosecution wishes to adduce evidence that when the police (lawfully) searched the lodgings where he was staying they discovered in his possession a quantity of farming magazines containing photographs of sheep. Such evidence would be:

[A]   Admissible to rebut a defence of innocent association.
[B]   Admissible to establish a propensity for a particular form of unnatural behaviour.
[C]   Inadmissible because the law does not recognise a separate category of people who commit bestiality.
[D]   Inadmissible because irrelevant.

Question 2

Joe is charged with obtaining money by deception from Arthur. The prosecution allege that Joe sold Arthur a fake diamond ring having represented that it was genuine. Joe puts forward the defence that he mistakenly believed the ring was genuine. The prosecution wish to prove that on five previous occasions over a period of several years Joe had sold fake diamond rings to different people having represented that the rings were genuine.

Such evidence is
[A]   Admissible to show that Frank was not mistaken about the genuiness of the ring he sold to Arthur.
[B]   Admissible because all the transactions constitute a connected series of events.
[C]   Inadmissible because irrelevant.
[D]   Inadmissible in the absence of previous convictions for obtaining money by deception in relation to the other incidents.

Question 3

Unattended handbags were stolen within a four-week period from four separate open-plan offices in the same vicinity. On each occasion the staff had just received their pay and the thefts occurred when the staff were at lunch in a staff canteen. On the fourth occasion Veronica, returning to her office, passed a young woman with bright red hair and wearing a leather jacket leaving the office. Veronica found her handbag missing and chased after the young woman who was found to have her handbag. In explanation, the young woman, Dorothea, said she came to the office to clean typewriters and had picked up Veronica's handbag by mistake. Indeed, a handbag very similar to Veronica's was found on the floor behind Veronica's desk and Dorothea claimed that it was hers. Office workers in three other offices recalled seeing Dorothea there on pay-days, but could not recall the time. In one of these three offices Dorothea had been questioned about a missing handbag but her explanation that it had been knocked off the desk into her bucket of cleaning materials was accepted at the time. Dorothea was charged with theft on counts relating to these three occasions, and a fourth relating to the theft of Veronica's handbag. The judge directed the jury that, although the evidence on the first counts of theft was flimsy, it might be considered as supporting the fourth count. Dorothea was convicted on the fourth count only. You are counsel for Dorothea who wishes to appeal. Prepare the grounds of appeal.

Question 4

Mark is charged with causing grievous bodily harm with intent contrary to the Offences Against the Person Act 1861, s. 18. The case is that on 23 December Mark was involved in a loud argument with a publican whom he hit with a billiard cue. Mark claims that it was an accident. The police have evidence that a few weeks earlier Mark had threatened the publican because he suspected that he was having an affair with Mark's former girlfriend. Advise the prosecution as to the admissibility of the evidence of the threats.

Question 5

David has been convicted of indecently assaulting Elaine. Elaine, a girl of 12, gave sworn evidence that when she was exercising her puppy at dusk in a public park she was approached by a man who said that he had a puppy exactly like hers, and invited her to his home, which he said was two minutes away, to see it. On the way he talked obscenities to her and pulled her behind some bushes, where he committed an indecent assault on her. She was not confident in her identification of the accused as the man involved. Despite the objection of defence counsel, Fay, a girl of 15, was allowed to give sworn evidence of an almost identical approach to her in a public park three miles away about the same date, and also at dusk. She said she had run away when the man started talking obscenities and that no assault had been committed on her. She identified the accused confidently as the man. The defence bring out that Elaine and Fay attend the same school, though they hardly know each other, and that there have been rumours circulating there about a man molesting young girls. Should Fay's evidence have been admitted?

Question 6
Alan is charged on two counts of handling stolen goods. On count 1 he denies that the goods were ever in his possession; on count 2 he admits that the goods were in his possession but denies that he knew they were stolen. Two years ago Alan was convicted of theft arising out of shoplifting and the police found three stolen video cassettes in a lock-up garage of which Alan had the use. Advise the prosecution as to the use which may be made of this evidence.

Question 7
Alfred is charged with assault with intent to rob, after Bernard was found unconscious in his caravan at a holiday site. Alfred has admitted that he was staying at the same caravan site at the time but denies the charge and states that he got drunk, entered a caravan he thought was his own and finding Bernard there attacked him in the belief that he was an unauthorised intruder. The prosecution has evidence (a) that two days earlier Connie discovered Alfred in her caravan at the site, and that Alfred had then offered the explanation that he was so drunk that he had entered the wrong caravan by mistake; (b) that Alfred had in his possession property stolen from Donald's caravan a week earlier; (c) that Alfred has previous convictions for theft of a motor vehicle, shoplifting and assault; and (d) that property was stolen from several other caravans during Alfred's stay at the site.

Advise the prosecution as to the admissibility of the above evidence.

7 Character Evidence

May evidence be adduced to show the good character of a party or of a party's witnesses?

May you adduce evidence to show the bad character of your opponent or of the opponent's witnesses?

7.1 Civil Cases

7.1.1 CHARACTER AS A FACT IN ISSUE

Evidence of a person's good or bad character is admissible, in civil proceedings, if among the facts in issue in the case or of direct relevance to the facts in issue. See *Scott* v *Sampson* [1882] 8 QBD 491.

7.1.2 CHARACTER RELEVANT TO A FACT IN ISSUE

Evidence of a person's good or bad character, if not among, or of direct relevance to, the facts in issue and not being relevant to credit (see below at **7.1.3**) is generally excluded even though it may have some relevance to the facts in issue. See *Narracott* v *Narracott* (1864) 3 Sw & Tr 408 and *Attorney-General* v *Bowman* (1791) 2 Bos & P 532.

7.1.3 CHARACTER RELEVANT TO CREDIT

Evidence of the character of a party to civil proceedings (or a witness called by him) may be adduced because of its relevance to his credibility. See generally **Chapter 5** of this Manual and *Mechanical & General Inventions Co. Ltd* v *Austin* [1935] AC 346 and *Hobbs* v *C.T. Tinling & Co. Ltd* [1929] 2 KB 1, CA.

7.2 Criminal Cases

7.2.1 CHARACTER AS A FACT IN ISSUE

In criminal cases, evidence of a person's character is admissible if it is among the facts in issue in the case or of direct relevance to the facts in issue. See *R* v *B* [1979] 1 WLR 1185, CA.

7.2.2 CHARACTER RELEVANT TO A FACT IN ISSUE OR TO CREDIT

7.2.2.1 The prosecutor and witnesses other than the accused
In the absence of authority to the contrary, it would appear that evidence of the character of the prosecutor or any witness other than the accused is admissible to the extent that it is relevant to the facts in issue in the case. Evidence of the character of such persons may also be adduced because of its relevance to their credibility. See generally **Chapter 5** of this Manual.

7.2.2.2   The accused: good character
The accused is allowed to call evidence of his good character provided that it is confined to evidence of his general reputation amongst those to whom he is known: evidence of a witness's opinion as to his good character and evidence of particular creditable acts is inadmissible. See *R* v *Rowton* (1865) Le & CA 520, CCR; and *R* v *Redgrave* (1982) 74 Cr App R 10, CA.

There has always been some confusion as to the precise purpose for which evidence of the good character of the accused is adduced i.e. whether it is relevant to the accused's credibility only (first limb) or whether it is also relevant to the accused's propensity not to act in the way alleged by the prosecution (second limb): see, e.g. *R* v *Stannard* (1837) 7 C & P 673, *R* v *Bellis* [1966] 1 WLR 234, CA, *R* v *Falconer-Atlee* (1973) 58 Cr App R 348, CA and *R* v *Bryant* [1979] QB 108, CA. As regards the judge's direction to the jury on good character, in *R* v *Berrada* (1990) 91 Cr App R 131, CA, it was held that the modern *practice* is that if good character is raised by the accused, it *should* be dealt with in the summing-up.

As to the first limb there is no doubt that where there is an issue as to the accused's credibility the judge should clearly direct the jury that good character supports credibility. It is a serious misdirection to direct the jury that they may put good character 'in the scales' when considering the accused's credibility — the judge should say that good character *is* relevant to credibility: *R* v *Boyson* [1991] Crim LR 274, CA.

Even if the accused elects not to give evidence, the judge may be justified in directing the jury that his good character is relevant to his credibility. The credibility of the accused may be important, for example, with regard to whether he was truthful in his exculpatory statement to the police: see *R* v *Chapman* [1989] Crim LR 60, CA and *cf R* v *Briley* [1991] Crim LR 444, CA.

As to the second limb (relevance to guilt) in *R* v *Marr* (1990) 90 Cr App R 154, CA, Lord Lane suggested that the second limb direction may be essential. In *R* v *Thanki* (1991) 93 Cr App R 12, however, Lord Lane said that the second limb direction was not obligatory in every case. Fortunately a spate of conflicting decisions on this matter (see *R* v *Cohen* (1990) 91 Cr App R 125, CA, *R* v *Anderson* [1990] Crim LR 862, CA, *R* v *Bravery* [1991] Crim LR 443, CA and *R* v *Kabariti* (1991) 92 Cr App R 362, CA) has resulted in the Court of Appeal laying down the following general guidelines in *R* v *Vye*; *R* v *Wise*; R v *Stephenson* (1933) *The Times*, 22 February 1993:

1.   A direction as to the relevance of the defendants' good character to his credibility was to be given where he had testified or made pre-trial answers to statements.
2.   A direction as to the relevance of his good character to the likelihood of his having committed the offence charged *was to be given, whether or not he had testified, or made pre-trial answers or statements.*
3.   Where a defendant of good character was jointly tried with a defendant of bad character, *1 and 2* still applied.

Having stated these general principles the Court of Appeal recognised that it had to be for trial judges in each case to decide how they tailored their directions to the particular circumstances. They would probably wish to indicate, as was commonly done, that good character could not amount to a defence.

Previous good character does not mean merely an absence of previous convictions. Thus where an accused has no previous convictions but evidence is properly admitted of his previous dishonesty, it may be appropriate to give the normal direction and then to qualify it by inviting the jury to balance against previous good reputation the revealed dishonesty: see *R* v *Buzalek* [1991] Crim LR 116.

7.2.2.3   The accused: bad character: at common law
The general rule is that the prosecution may not adduce evidence of the accused's bad character nor cross-examine the accused or any defence witness with a view to eliciting such evidence. At common law, there are only two exceptions:

(a)   Where the evidence is admissible under the similar facts doctrine; and
(b)   where the defence adduces evidences of the accused's good character.

If the accused puts his character in issue by giving or calling evidence of his good character or cross-examining witnesses to that effect, then at common law the prosecution may call evidence of his bad character in rebuttal: *R* v *Rowton* (1865) Le & Ca 520, CCR. See also *R* v *Waldman* (1934) 24 Cr App R 204, CCA.

The evidence in rebuttal need not be confined to the character trait under consideration but may refer to any character trait of the accused. See *R* v *Winfield* (1939) 27 Cr App R 139, CCA. See also *R* v *Butterwasser* [1948] 1 KB 4, CCA.

Of course the accused himself may choose to introduce evidence of his previous convictions to show that he pleaded guilty on the previous occasions and ought therefore to be believed now when he denies his guilt. In the case of convictions for offences of dishonesty, the judge must then direct the jury that the previous convictions are relevant to the defendant's credibility and that the jury *may* take such evidence into account: *R* v *Prince* [1990] Crim LR 49, CA.

7.2.2.4   The accused: bad character: by statute

The general rule at common law that the prosecution may not adduce evidence of the accused's bad character applies equally to questions asked in cross-examination of the accused. See, e.g. *R* v *Weekes* (1983) 77 Cr App R 207, CA. However, with regard to cross-examination of the accused, the primary issue is to apply the important statutory rules set out in Criminal Evidence Act 1898, s. 1:

(e)   A person charged and being a witness in pursuance of this Act may be asked any question in cross-examination notwithstanding that it would tend to criminate him as to the offence charged:

(f)   A person charged and called as a witness in pursuance of this Act shall not be asked, and if asked shall not be required to answer, any question tending to show that he has committed or been convicted of or been charged with any offence other than that wherewith he is then charged, or is of bad character, unless—

(i)   the proof that he has committed or been convicted of such other offence is admissible evidence to show that he is guilty of the offence wherewith he is then charged; or

(ii)   he has personally or by his advocate asked questions of the witnesses for the prosecution with a view to establish his own good character, or has given evidence of his good character, or the nature or conduct of the defence is such as to involve imputations on the character of the prosecutor or the witnesses for the prosecution; or

(iii)   he has given evidence against any other person charged in the same proceedings.

(a)   *The relationship between proviso (e) and proviso (f). Jones* v *DPP* [1962] AC 635, HL. Three propositions:

1.   Proviso (e) permits questions which tend directly to incriminate the accused.
2.   Proviso (f) prohibits questions which tend indirectly to incriminate the accused by reference to his misconduct on other occasions or his commission of other offences or his bad character generally unless f(i), f(ii) or f(iii) applies.
3.   'Tending to show' means 'tending to show for the first time' or 'tending to reveal'.

(b)   *Proviso (f): the prohibition.* 'Any question tending to show' means 'tending to show for the first time'. Thus if the prosecution has already adduced evidence of the accused's misconduct on other occasions under the similar facts doctrine, or the accused himself has given evidence of his previous misconduct or convictions, then the accused may be cross-examined on the matter. See *R* v *Anderson* [1988] QB 678, CA; and *R* v *Ellis* [1910] 2 KB 746, CCA.
Stirland v *DPP* [1944] AC 315, HL: 'charged with any offence' means 'accused before a criminal court'.

R v *Dunkley* [1927] 1 KB 323, CCA: evidence of 'bad character' is not confined to evidence of general reputation.

Where cross-examination on offences is permitted under s. 1(f) because the accused has lost his shield, the accused may be asked about an offence whether it was committed before or after commission of the offence with which he is charged. See:

R v *Wood* [1920] 2 KB 179, CCA.

R v *Coltress* (1978) 68 Cr App R 193, CA.

Maxwell v *DPP* [1935] AC 309, HL: where the shield is lost, cross-examination is still subject to the requirement of relevance; questions about a previous acquittal will usually be inadmissible because irrelevant both to the charge and the credibility of the accused.

(c)   *Section 1(f)(i)*. If evidence of the accused's commission of another offence is admissible under the similar fact evidence doctrine because of its probative value in relation to the accused's guilt, the accused can be cross-examined about such matters under s. 1(f)(i). Such cross-examination is relevant to the issue of the accused's guilt.

However s. 1(f)(i) cannot be used to cross-examine an accused about a charge in respect of which he has been acquitted: *R* v *Cokar* [1960] 2 QB 207, CCA. See also:

Jones v *DPP* [1962] AC 635, HL.

R v *Coombes* (1960) 45 Cr App R 36.

R v *Anderson* [1988] QB 678, CA.

(d)   *Section 1(f)(ii): attempts to establish good character*. The accused will lose his shield if he puts his good character in issue either (i) by cross examination of the prosecution witnesses or (ii) by giving evidence about himself; or also, presumably, (iii) by calling defence witnesses to give evidence about it. However, the shield is not lost when a defence witness volunteers a statement as to the good character of the accused which he has not been asked to make. See *R* v *Redd* [1923] 1 KB 104.

Consider the following examples:

R v *Ferguson* (1909) 2 Cr App R 250: a religious man who had attended church services for a number of years.

R v *Baker* (1912) 7 Cr App R 252: earning an honest living for a number of years.

R v *Coulman* [1927] 20 Cr App R 106: a married man with a family and in regular work.

R v *Samuel* (1956) 40 Cr App R 8, CCA.

Contrast:

R v *Lee* [1976] 1 WLR 71, CA: 'it is not implicit in an accusation of dishonesty that the accuser himself is an honest man'.

R v *Beecham* [1921] 3 KB 464: defendant led into making assertions of good character by prosecution counsel in cross-examination.

R v *Hamilton* [1969] Crim LR 486, CA: the wearing of a regimental blazer!

Malindi v *R* [1967] AC 439; see also *R* v *Stronach* [1988] Crim LR 48.

Once an accused puts his character in issue, he puts his whole character in, character for these purposes being indivisible. See *Stirland* v *DPP* [1944] AC 315, HL, *per* Viscount Simon p. 324:

He cannot assert his good character in certain respects without exposing himself to inquiry as to the rest of his record.

The primary purpose of cross-examination under this part of s. 1(f)(ii) is, apparently, to show that the accused should not be believed on his oath. See *R* v *Richardson* [1969] 1 QB 299, CA; and *Maxwell* v *DPP* [1935] AC 309, HL.

(e) *Section 1(f)(ii): imputations on the character of prosecution witnesses.* This part of the subparagraph operates on a tit-for-tat principle: where the defence makes an attack on the character of the prosecutor or a prosecution witness, e.g. by imputing misconduct or bad character, the accused renders himself liable to cross-examination on his own bad character and previous convictions. See *R* v *Biggin* [1920] KB 213.

The shield will be lost even if the imputation is a necessary part of the defence. In these circumstances, however, the judge has a *discretion* to refuse to permit cross-examination. See generally:

R v *Hudson* [1912] 2 KB 464, CCA: the accused claimed that a prosecution witness had committed the offence.

R v *Bishop* [1975] QB 274, CA: the accused claimed that he had had a homosexual relationship with a prosecution witness. See also:

R v *Flynn* [1963] 1 QB 729, CCA.

Selvey v *DPP* [1970] AC 304, HL.

The accused will not lose the shield if he merely asserts his innocence or denies his guilt, albeit in emphatic terms. See:

R v *Rouse* [1904] 1 KB 184, CCR: it was alleged that the evidence of the prosecution witness was 'a lie' and the witness 'a liar'. *Held*: an emphatic denial of guilt. See also *R* v *St Louis* (1984) 79 Cr App R 53 and *R* v *Wignall* [1993] Crim LR 62.

R v *Rappolt* (1911) 6 Cr App R 156, CCA: it was alleged that the prosecution witness was 'such a horrible liar that his brother would not speak to him'. *Held*: an imputation. See also *R* v *Owen* (1986) 83 Cr App R 100, CA.

R v *Lasseur* [1991] Crim LR 53, CA: it was put to an accomplice who had turned Queen's evidence that he was lying and that he was implicating the accused so that he would get a lenient sentence. *Held*: an imputation.

In rape cases, the accused may allege consent without thereby placing himself in danger of cross-examination on his bad character. See *R* v *Sheean* (1908) 21 Cox CC 56 and *R* v *Turner* [1944] KB 463.

The following examples should be considered:

R v *Wright* (1910) 5 Cr App R 131: it was alleged that a confession was obtained by bribes. Held: an imputation.

R v *Jones* (1923) 17 Cr App R 117: it was alleged that the accused was deliberately held on four remands in order to manufacture a confession. Held: an imputation.

R v *Cook* [1959] 2 QB 340: it was alleged that an admission was extorted by threatening to charge the accused's wife. Held: an imputation.

R v *Westfall* (1912) 7 Cr App R 176: it was alleged that the prosecutor was a habitual drunkard. Held: no imputation.

R v *MacLean* [1988] Crim LR 430.

One area of particular complexity concerns cases in which the defence challenge the evidence of police officers about alleged confession statements. See:

R v *Nelson* (1978) 68 Cr App R 12.

R v *Tanner* (1977) 66 Cr App R 56.

R v *McGee* (1979) 70 Cr App R 247.

R v *Britzman* [1983] 1 WLR 350.

Three guidelines:

(i) Exercise the discretion if the accused merely denies, however emphatically or offensively, an incident or the contents of a short interview (as opposed to a long period of detailed observation or a long conversation).

(ii) Allow the cross-examination where there is no chance of mistake, misunderstanding or confusion and the jury will have to decide whether the prosecution witness has fabricated evidence. In the case of an accused making wild allegations, allowance should be made for the strain of being in the witness box and the exaggerated use of language resulting from that or from lack of education or mental stability. Allowance should also be made for an accused led into making allegations during cross-examination.

(iii) Disallow the cross-examination where the evidence against the accused is overwhelming.

The sole purpose of cross-examination under this part of s. 1(f)(ii) is to show that the accused should not be believed on his oath. See:

R v *Jenkins* (1945) 31 Cr App R 1.

R v *Inder* (1977) 67 Cr App R 143, CA.

R v *Cook* [1959] 2 QB 340.

If there is any risk that cross-examination will lead the jury to infer that the accused is guilty of the offence charged, should the trial judge, in the exercise of his discretion, disallow the cross-examination? See *R* v *Watts* [1983] 3 All ER 101, CA; and *Maxwell* v *DPP* [1935] AC 309, HL *per* Viscount Sankey LC: cross-examination should not be permitted 'if there is any risk of the jury being misled into thinking that it goes not to credibility but to the probability of (the accused) having committed the offence with which he is charged'. See also *R* v *Braithwaite*, 24 November 1983, CA (unreported).

Compare these cases, however, with *R* v *Burke* (1985) 82 Cr App R 156, CA; and *R* v *Powell* [1985] 1 WLR 1364, CA, *per* Lord Lane CJ at p. 1370:

> ... if there is a deliberate attack being made upon the conduct of a prosecution witness calculated to discredit him wholly, if there is a real issue about the conduct of an important witness which the jury will have to settle in order to reach their verdict, the judge is entitled to let the jury know the previous convictions of the man who is making the attack. The fact that the defendant's convictions are not for offences of dishonesty, the fact that they are for offences bearing a close resemblance to the offences charged, are matters for the judge to take into consideration when exercising his discretion, but they certainly do not oblige the judge to disallow the proposed cross-examination.

Selvey v *DPP* [1970] AC 304, HL.

See also *R v Lasseur* [1991] Crim LR 53, CA.

Given that the sole purpose of cross-examination under this part of s. 1(f)(ii) is to attack the accused's credibility as a witness, does it follow that cross-examination, where allowed, should be confined to the fact of the previous convictions and should not extend to the factual details of the offences in question? See *R v France* [1979] Crim LR 48, CA; and *R v Duncalf* [1979] 1 WLR 918, CA. In *R v Khan* [1991] Crim LR 51, CA, at K's trial for affray and assault, including assault on the police, his defence involved an imputation on the character of the prosecution's witnesses; anticipating a loss of shield, his counsel elicited in chief a previous conviction for assault on the police. K was then cross-examined at length about the detailed facts of the previous incident. It was held, allowing the appeal, that evidence of previous convictions must only relate to the issue of credibility and therefore any evidence, no matter what the manner of its introduction, whch tended to go beyond that and into the territory of disposition was inadmissible. Note that the court referred to neither *France* nor *Duncalf*.

Nothing in the wording of s. 1(f)(ii) prohibits the cross-examination from being conducted by counsel for a co-accused. With the leave of the judge, co-defendant 1 may cross-examine co-defendant 2 if co-defendant 2 has cast imputations on the character of a prosecution witness: *R v Lovett* [1973] 1 WLR 241, CA.

If an accused, charged in one indictment with two offences and convicted of one but acquitted of the other, faces a subsequent trial at which the prosecution cross-examines him under s. 1(f)(ii) on the previous conviction, then in appropriate circumstances the defence may be allowed to re-examine him on the acquittal. See e.g. *R v Doosti* [1985] 82 Cr App R 181, CA in which at the subsequent trial, evidence of the acquittal was likely to throw doubt on the reliability of a prosecution witness, and *cf* *R v Henri* [1990] Crim LR 51, CA.

(f)   *Section 1(f)(iii); evidence against a co-accused.* The justification given for this subparagraph is that if one co-accused gives evidence against another, the other should be entitled to treat the first as if he were a witness appearing for the prosecution and, accordingly, liable to cross-examination on his character.

Murdoch v Taylor [1965] AC 574, HL.

Eight propositions which emerge:
    (i)   'Evidence against' means evidence which supports the prosecution case in a material respect or which undermines the defence of the co-accused.
    (ii)   One test is to ask whether the evidence would be included in a summary of the evidence in the case which, if accepted, would lead to the conviction of the co-accused.
    (iii)   Evidence which only contradicts something which a co-accused has said without further advancing the prosecution case in any significant degree is not 'evidence against'.
    (iv)   'Evidence against' may be given either in examination-in-chief or in cross-examination.
    (v)   Section 1(f)(iii) is not confined to cases where the 'evidence against' is given with hostile intent. The intention or state of mind of the person giving the 'evidence against' is irrelevant. What is material is the effect of the evidence on the minds of the jury. The test is objective, not subjective.
    (vi)   The purpose of cross-examination is to show that the person giving 'evidence against' is not to be believed on his oath.
    (vii)   Where cross-examination is permissible, the judge has no discretion to exclude it: an accused, in seeking to defend himself, should not be fettered in any way.
    (viii)   The prosecution may cross-examine under s. 1(f)(iii) but the court does have a discretion to prevent it as part of its function to exclude any prosecution evidence the prejudicial effect of which outweighs its probative value.

On the meaning of 'undermining the defence of the co-accused' see *R v Bruce* [1975] 1 WLR 1252, CA; and *R v Hatton* (1976) 64 Cr App R 88, CA.

It is possible to undermine the defence of the co-accused even if the co-accused, although pleading not guilty, gives evidence in which he appears to be confessing to the offence charged. He remains in the jury's charge and even if he only has a scintilla of a defence (because the jury may miraculously and inexplicably come to his rescue) there is still the possibility of undermining it and the judge has no discretion in the matter, see *R* v *Mir* [1989] Crim LR 894, CA.

Where the evidence in question appears to be no more than a mere contradiction of the evidence given by a co-accused or a mere denial of participation in a venture alleged to be joint, it may amount to evidence against the co-accused, depending upon the precise circumstances of the case. See *R* v *Davies* [1975] 1 WLR 345, CA; and *R* v *Varley* [1982] 2 All ER 519, CA.

In appropriate circumstances, cross-examination on previous convictions under s. 1(f)(iii) may go beyond the fact of the conviction and elicit the facts underlying the previous conviction. See *R* v *Reid* [1989] Crim LR 719, CA in which the co-accused, charged with robbery, was cross-examined on a previous conviction for robbery. There was a real issue of credibility arising from consideration of the detailed circumstances of both robberies. The evidence went to two questions. First, did the co-accused seek to run the same lying defence when charged with robbery (leaving before the robbery occurred)?

The second and more directly relevant question was did that lying defence involve the co-accused seeking falsely to incriminate others?

7.3 Inadmissible Evidence of Previous Convictions

There are two further restrictions on the admissibility of evidence of previous convictions over and above the common law and statutory restrictions already considered:

(a)   Rehabilitation of Offenders Act 1974. See **5.3.4.3**. *R* v *Nye* (1982) 75 Cr App R 247, CA: the Act does not confer on an accused who is a rehabilitated person the right to put himself forward as being of good character. In order to do so, the defence should apply to the trial judge at the outset of the trial. The judge's ruling is an exercise of discretion. See also *R* v *Bailey* [1989] Crim LR 723, CA.

(b)   Children and Young Persons Act 1963, s. 16(2):

In any proceedings for an offence committed or alleged to have been committed by a person of or over 21, any offence of which he was found guilty while under the age of 14 shall be disregarded for the purposes of any evidence relating to his previous convictions; and he shall not be asked, and if asked shall not be required to answer, any question relating to such an offence, notwithstanding that the question would otherwise be admissible under section 1 of the Criminal Evidence Act 1898.

Questions

OBJECTIVES

This chapter is designed to ensure that you:

(a)   understand the reasons for the prohibition of cross-examination of the accused as to character in cases where the accused gives evidence;

(b)   understand the nature of the exceptions contained in s. 1(f)(i), (ii) and (iii) of the Criminal Evidence Act 1898;

(c)   relate s. 1(f) to the rules regarding examination of witnesses discussed in **Chapter 5** of this Manual; and

(d)   develop a sense of the tactical use of character evidence.

RESEARCH

(a)   Read the materials contained in **Chapter 7** of this Manual.

(b)   Read:

Keane, *The Modern Law of Evidence* (2nd ed., 1989), ch. 13, OR

Murphy, *A Practical Approach to Evidence* (4th ed., 1992), ch. 4; AND

Carter, *Cases and Statutes on Evidence* (2nd ed., 1990), ch. 21 to 23 and the Supplement (1992), OR

Heydon, *Evidence Cases & Materials* (3rd ed., 1991).

(c)   On the basis of this research, answer the following questions.

Question 1
Some months ago, James was charged with possession of drugs and obstruction under the Misuse of Drugs Act 1971. The principal prosecution witness was Sergeant Wolf. James was convicted of obstruction, but acquitted on the charge of possession. James is now charged with conspiracy to supply heroin. His defence is that the chief prosecution witness, Sergeant Wolf, has fabricated the evidence against him. Prosecution counsel is given leave to cross-examine James on his previous conviction for obstruction. James' counsel now wishes to re-examine James to show that, on the same occasion, he was acquitted on the charge of possession, in respect of which evidence had also been given against him by Sergeant Wolf. Will leave be granted?

[A]   Yes, because the acquittal is relevant and likely to throw doubt on the reliability of Sergeant Wolf.
[B]   No, because the fact of the acquittal was not raised in examination-in-chief or cross-examination.
[C]   No, because the conviction for obstruction is merely evidence attacking James' credibility and, therefore, the answer given in cross-examination must be regarded as final.
[D]   Yes, because it is open to defence counsel as of right to re-examine on issues not raised in either examination-in-chief or cross-examination.

Question 2
Adam and Ben are jointly charged with indecently assaulting Jane, aged 12 years. During examination-in-chief Adam gives evidence against Ben alleging that it was Ben who masterminded the plan and in fact carried out the assault single-handed. Adam has two previous convictions for similar offences. Can the prosecution cross-examine Adam in relation to his previous convictions?

[A]   Yes, but only with the leave of the judge.
[B]   Yes, as of right.
[C]   No, because Adam has not cast imputations on a prosecution witness.
[D]   No, because the previous convictions are irrelevant.

Question 3
Henry, James and Albert are jointly charged with burglary of a shop. They each have a number of previous convictions for the same offence. The only evidence which connects them with the crime is that of Sam, who claims to have driven their get-away car and has now turned Queen's evidence.

(a)   Henry gives no evidence but his counsel puts to Sam in cross-examination that he has 14 previous convictions for offences involving dishonesty and Sam admits this to be true. Can the prosecution lead evidence of Henry's previous convictions?
(b)   James says in evidence that Sam is a liar. Can the prosecution cross-examine James on his previous convictions?
(c)   Albert says in evidence that Henry, James and Sam invited him to help with the break-in but he refused and did not take part. Can Henry's counsel cross-examine Albert on his previous convictions?
(d)   Assuming Henry's counsel does not cross-examine Albert on his previous convictions, can the prosecution cross-examine Albert on them?

Question 4

Philip is charged with burglary of a flat belonging to Anita. Philip's counsel cross-examines Anita and puts to her that she had given Philip permission to enter her flat at any time because they were at the material time lovers. Anita denies this. Philip's counsel also cross-examines a police officer and suggests that Philip is a man of good character and excellent reputation which the officer is then unable to dispute.

(a) May the prosecution cross-examine Philip, if he gives evidence, as to his previous convictions for burglary and causing death by reckless driving, which the officer has now discovered?

(b) Would it make any difference if the conviction for burglary related to an offence committed on a date subsequent to that of the offence now charged?

(c) Assuming that the previous offence of burglary can be put to Philip in cross-examination, may he also be asked in detail about the manner in which it was committed?

(d) If Philip elects not to give evidence, what, if anything, can the prosecution do in the light of the cross-examination by Philip's counsel?

Question 5

Oliver, Peter and Quentin are jointly charged with the theft of equipment from their employer. All three plead not guilty. In evidence, Oliver denies his guilt and says that he has worked for the employer for 11 years in a position of trust, that he feels loyalty and gratitude to the employer for giving him a job which has allowed him to go straight, and would not have done anything to injure the company. Peter testifies that he knew of Oliver and Quentin's plans to steal the equipment but he took no part in it. Quentin claims in his evidence that a policeman who testified that he had confessed to the offence was being 'terminologically inexact'.

All three accused have previous convictions, although Oliver's are spent. May these convictions be put to them in cross-examination?

8   Hearsay: The Exclusionary Rule

May a party prove facts by adducing evidence that such facts were asserted by persons — whether orally, in writing, or by conduct — prior to the instant in–court proceedings (the rule against hearsay and the exceptions thereto)?

8.1   An Attempt at Definition

Myers v *DPP* [1965] AC 1001, HL, *per* Lord Reid: 'it is difficult to make any general statement about the law of hearsay which is entirely accurate'.

Any statement other than one made by a witness while giving testimony in the proceedings in question is inadmissible as evidence of the facts stated.

The rule applies to cross-examination as well as examination-in-chief: see *R* v *Gillespie* (1967) 51 Cr App R 172, CA.

Note that the rule applies:

(a)   to both examination in chief and cross-examination;
(b)   whether the statement was made by the witness personally or by some other person;
(c)   where the statement was made by some other person, irrespective of whether that other person is called as a witness in the proceedings;
(d)   to *any* 'out-of-court' statement, whether oral, written, by gesture, on oath or unsworn;
(e)   whether or not the maker of the statement intended to communicate thereby;
(f)   only if the statement is tendered as evidence of the truth of its contents — the statement, if tendered for any other purpose which is relevant to the facts in issue in the case, is admissible as original evidence.

Two devices used by counsel to try to evade the rule are improper. The first is to ask not what was actually said in a conversation but what that conversation was about. The second is to ask about what was done but not said, using questions to which the answer can only be either 'yes' or 'no', with a view to enabling the tribunal of fact to infer what was said. See *Glinski* v *McIver* [1962] AC 726, HL. For example, assuming that Mr B makes an out-of-court statement to Mr A that 'X killed Y' (inadmissible hearsay), consider the impropriety of the following series of questions put by counsel for the prosecution to A during the course of his examination-in-chief at X's trial for the murder of Y:

Q.   You say that you came across Mr B. What happened then?
A.   We held a conversation. He said that . . .
Q.   Sorry to interrupt, Mr A. I don't want you to tell the court what Mr B said but, if you can, to answer this question 'yes' or 'no': as a result of that conversation with Mr B, did you do anything?
A.   Yes.

Q.   What was that?
A.   Well of course I instantly used my citizen's rights and arrested X.

8.2   Examples

In the case of oral statements, consider the following examples (and note the potential for injustice).

Sparks v *R* [1964] AC 964, PC: the trial of a white man for indecent assault at which the following out-of-court statement of the girl complainant was ruled inadmissible: 'It was a coloured boy'.

R v *Turner* (1975) 61 Cr App R 67, CA: evidence that a third party, not called as a witness, had admitted that he had committed the robbery with which the accused was charged. Milmo J. stated:

> The idea, which may be gaining prevalence in some quarters, that in a criminal trial the defence is entitled to adduce hearsay evidence to establish facts which if proved would be relevant and would assist the defence, is wholly erroneous.

In the case of documentary statements, consider:

Myers v *DPP* [1965] AC 1001, HL (microfilm of cards completed by employees at Austins and showing the numbers stamped on the cylinder blocks of cars manufactured).

Patel v *Comptroller of Customs* [1966] AC 356, PC (bags of coriander seed inscribed with the words: 'produce of Morocco'). See also *R* v *Brown* [1991] Crim LR 835, CA.

Jones v *Metcalfe* [1967] 1 WLR 1286, DC (a record of the registration number of a vehicle).

R v *McLean* (1968) 52 Cr App R 80, CA (a dictated note of the registration number of a vehicle).

In the case of statements made by signs or gestures, consider:

R v *Gibson* [1887] 18 QBD 539, CCR (the act of pointing accompanied by the statement, 'The man who threw the stone went in there'). See also:

Chandrasekera v *R* [1937] AC 220, PC.

R v *Rothwell* (1993) *The Times* 27 April 1993.

As to the use of interpreters in the interrogation of suspects, see *R* v *Attard* (1958) 43 Cr App R 90: the translated answers, if admissible, can be given in evidence by the interpreter but not the police.

8.3   Rationale

Eight reasons may be advanced to justify the exclusion of hearsay evidence:

(a)   To admit hearsay is often to admit superfluous material and raise side-issues, both of which result in an undue protraction of the trial.

(b)   Juries find it difficult to evaluate hearsay properly.

(c)   To admit hearsay is to increase the opportunities for fraud or the deliberate manufacture of evidence and to enable a party to achieve a tactical advantage of surprise.

(d)   Hearsay statements are only occasionally made on oath and usually not in the solemn and serious circumstances which surround the giving of evidence in court.

(e)   The tribunal of fact has no opportunity to observe the speaker's demeanour, inflection, tone of voice etc.

(f)   The opponent has no opportunity to cross-examine the speaker to probe his veracity, sincerity, powers of perception, means of knowledge etc.

(g)   There is a danger of mistake resulting from repetition, especially in the case of multiple oral hearsay.

(h)   The admission of hearsay encourages the substitution of weaker evidence for stronger evidence.

(i)   It is not the best evidence.

8.4   Scope

8.4.1   ORIGINAL EVIDENCE

Original evidence is evidence of an 'out-of-court' statement adduced for any relevant purpose other than that of proving the truth of the facts it contains. Original evidence is admissible.

The relevant purpose (other than proving the truth of the facts contained in the statement) may be, for instance:

(a)   simply to show that the statement was made, e.g. in a contract case in which the formation of the contract is disputed, to show that an offer was made and accepted; or

(b)   to show the state of mind or knowledge of the maker of the statement; e.g. to show that the victim of a crime was in a state of emotion or fear because of an existing or impending emergency; or

(c)   to show the state of mind of the person who heard the statement, e.g. a case of misrepresentation in which the plaintiff gives evidence of a statement made to him by the defendant to show that he was misled by the defendant, i.e. to show what the plaintiff, on hearing the statement, thought or believed.

Consider the following examples:

R v *Chapman* [1969] 2 QB 436, CA (the evidence of a police officer that a doctor had *not* objected, on the grounds of prejudice to the proper care or treatment of the patient, to the provision of a breath specimen).

Woodhouse v *Hall* (1981) 72 Cr App R 39, DC (evidence that employees of a sauna and massage parlour had offered 'sexual services').

Ratten v *R* [1972] AC 378, PC (evidence of a telephone call made by a woman who in an hysterical and sobbing voice had said, 'Get me the police, please' — admitted because it allowed the jury to infer that the woman, at that time, was in a state of emotion or fear because of an existing or impending emergency). *Cf R* v *Harry* (1988) 86 Cr App R 105, CA (evidence of telephone calls made to P's flat asking for a man called Sacha, P's nickname, and enquiring whether drugs were for sale, *inadmissible* to prove that P was running a drug-dealing business from the flat); *R* v *Blastland* [1986] AC 41, HL in which the state of mind of the maker of the statement was held to be irrelevant to the facts in issue; and *R* v *Kearley* [1992] 2 All ER 345, HL.

Subramaniam v *Public Prosecutor* [1956] 1 WLR 965, PC (evidence of what terrorists had said to the accused, after they had captured him, should have been admitted in order to show whether they might reasonably have induced in him an apprehension of immediate death if he failed to comply with their wishes, which was of direct relevance to the issue of duress).

Attorney-General v *Good* (1825) M'Cle & Yo 286 (evidence of a wife's demonstrably untrue statement that her husband was away from home in order to show the husband's intention to defraud his creditors). See also *Mawaz Khan* v *R* [1967] 1 AC 454, PC and *R* v *Binham* [1991] Crim LR 774, CA.

8.4.2 IMPLIED ASSERTIONS

Does the hearsay rule apply to implied assertions, i.e. statements or conduct resting on some assumption of fact which can be inferred by the court? Until recently, the English authorities were not entirely clear. The authorities suggesting that the rule does *not* apply to implied assertions include *Ratten* v *R* (*supra*), *Woodhouse* v *Hall* (*supra*), and *Manchester Brewery Co. Ltd* v *Coombs* (1901) 82 LT 347. Authorities to suggest that the hearsay rule *does* operate to exclude implied assertions include, in the case of oral statements, *Teper* v *R* [1952] AC 480, PC and *R* v *Harry* (*supra*) and, in the case of written statements, *Wright* v *Doe d Tatham* (1837) 7 A & E 313.

The question came before the House of Lords in *R* v *Kearley* [1992] 2 All ER 345. K's flat was raided by the police who found drugs there, but not in sufficient quantities to raise the inference that he was a dealer. After the search, the police remained there for several hours and intercepted ten telephone calls in which the caller asked to speak to K and asked for drugs. Later, while the police were still on the premises, seven persons arrived at the flat, some with money, also asking for K and asking to be supplied with drugs. At the relevant times, K was either not present or not within earshot. K denied a charge of possession with intent to supply. At the trial, the prosecution were allowed to call the police officers who had intercepted the calls or received the visitors at the flat to give evidence of the conversations they had had with the callers or visitors. The Court of Appeal dismissed the appeal against conviction but certified the following question as raising a point of law of general public importance:

> Whether evidence may be adduced at a trial of words spoken (namely a request for drugs to be supplied by K), not spoken in the presence or hearing of the defendant, by a person not called as a witness, for the purpose not of establishing the truth of any fact narrated by the words, but of inviting the jury to draw an inference from the fact that the words were spoken (namely that K was a supplier of drugs).

The House of Lords, by a majority of three to two, held that evidence of such a request was irrelevant because it could only be evidence of the state of mind of the person making the request, which was not a relevant issue at the trial — the issue at the trial was whether or not K intended to supply drugs, and in so far as evidence of a request was relevant to that issue (as an implied assertion that K was a supplier of drugs), it was inadmissible hearsay in the same way that an express out-of-court assertion to the same effect would be inadmissible hearsay, and it made no difference that there was a large number of such requests all made at the same place on the same day. Accordingly, the appeal was allowed.

In reaching this decision, the majority applied *R* v *Blastland* [1986] AC 41 and *Wright* v *Doe d Tatham* (*supra*) and cited with approval *R* v *Harry* (*supra*). *Woodhouse* v *Hall* (*supra*) was distinguished on the basis that in order to establish that premises are being used as a brothel, it is sufficient to prove that at the premises more than one woman *offers* herself as a participant in physical acts of indecency for the sexual gratification of men; and the evidence of the conversations in that case provided direct evidence of these offers — it was original and not hearsay evidence. *Ratten* v *R* (*supra*) was distinguished on the basis that:

(a) the fact that a call was made from the premises at all at the relevant time was directly in issue;
(b) the fact that it was made by a woman who was both frightened and hysterical was relevant to the accused's defence of accident; and
(c) in so far as the evidence was admitted for the truth of the inference that the victim was under attack from her husband, that could only have been justified by treating the contents of the call as part of the *res gestae*.

8.4.3 NEGATIVE HEARSAY

In principle, it is clear that the hearsay rule should apply not only to positive statements but also to negative statements, i.e. statements concerning the non-existence as opposed to the existence of certain facts. Proving a negative by direct rather than hearsay evidence, however, can be a notoriously difficult matter, and some authorities indicate that the non-existence of a fact may be proved by evidence of the absence of a recording of that fact in a record in which, having regard to its compilation and custody, one might have expected that fact, had it existed, to have been recorded. See:

R v *Patel* [1981] 3 All ER 94, CA (evidence of an appropriate officer that the name of a particular person did not appear in the Home Office records of persons entitled to a certificate of registration in the UK).

R v *Shone* (1983) 76 Cr App R 72, CA (evidence of company employees responsible for stock record cards that certain cards bore no marks to indicate that the stock in question had been sold or used). See also *R* v *Muir* (1984) 79 Cr App R 153, CA.

8.4.4 STATEMENTS PRODUCED BY CALCULATORS AND OTHER ELECTRONIC OR MECHANICAL DEVICES

Where a computer or other electronic or mechanical device is used as a calculator, that is, as a tool which does not contribute its own knowledge but merely does a calculation, albeit a sophisticated one, which could have been done manually, the resulting print-out, reading or other information produced by the device is not hearsay but admissible as a variety of real evidence.

The proof and relevance of such evidence, however, depends upon the testimony of the person or persons in charge of the computer or other device, such as the computer programmer and operator. See:

R v *Wood* (1982) 76 Cr App R 23, CA, (the print-out of a computer programmed to carry out calculations relating to the analysis of the chemical composition of certain metal alleged to be part of a stolen consignment).

Castle v *Cross* [1984] 1 WLR 1372, DC, (the print-out of an Intoximeter 3000 breath-test machine recording that it did not have a sufficient sample to perform an analysis).

In *R* v *Spiby* (1990) 91 Cr App R 186, the Court of Appeal held that the print-out from a computerised machine used to monitor telephone calls and record such information as the numbers from which and to which the calls were made and the duration of the calls, is not hearsay but real evidence. Compare *R* v *Neville* [1991] Crim LR 288, CA. See also *Garner* v *DPP* [1989] NLJ 548, DC. The principle under discussion is probably the best way to approach the case of *Taylor* v *Chief Constable of Cheshire* [1986] 1 WLR 1479, DC.

8.4.5 CABBAGES AND KINGS

The common theme of the following cases is that in all of them identification was in issue and in many of them there appears to have been evasion (or a 'side-stepping') of the hearsay rule. Consider first the following clear statement of principle in *Sparks* v *R* [1964] AC 964, PC, *per* Lord Morris of Borth-y-Gest at p. 981: 'There is no rule which permits the giving of hearsay evidence merely because it relates to identity'. Then consider *R* v *Burke* (1847) 2 Cox CC 295.

R v *Osbourne* [1973] QB 678, CA, *per* Lawton LJ: 'It would be wrong, in the judgment of this court, to set up artificial rules of evidence which hinder the administration of justice'. See also *R* v *McCay* [1990] 1 WLR 645, CA.

R v *Percy Smith* [1976] Crim LR 511, CA: at the direction of a witness a police officer made a sketch which was admitted in evidence.

R v *Okorudu* [1982] Crim LR 747: a witness made a photofit which was admitted in evidence.

The difficulty of reconciling cases such as *Sparks* v *R* with cases such as *R* v *Percy Smith* and *R* v *Okorudu* has now been side-stepped. See *R* v *Cook* [1987] QB 417, CA: a photofit and a sketch made by a police officer are, like photographs taken when a suspect is actually committing an offence, in a class of evidence of their own to which neither the rule against hearsay nor the rule against the admission of an earlier consistent statement applies. *R* v *Cook* was applied in *R* v *Constantinou* (1990) 91 Cr App R 74, CA.

Consider finally *R* v *Rice* [1963] 1 QB 857, CCA. A used airline ticket bearing a name is inadmissible hearsay if tendered to show that the booking was effected by any person of that name; but, *per* Winn J at p. 871:

> The relevance of that ticket in logic and its legal admissibility as a piece of real evidence both stem from the same root, viz., the balance of probability recognised by common sense and common knowledge that an air ticket which has been used on a flight and which had a name upon it has more likely than not been used by a man of that name or by one of two men whose names are upon it.

See also *R* v *Lydon* (1987) 85 Cr App R 221, CA: Sean Lydon, charged with robbery, ran a defence of alibi. On the verge of the road on the route taken by the getaway car, about a mile from the place of the robbery, the police found a gun and, nearby, two pieces of rolled paper containing the written messages, 'Sean rules' and 'Sean rules 85'. There was ink on the gun barrel and it was of similar appearance and composition to that on the bits of paper. The Court of Appeal held that this evidence had been properly admitted: if the jury concluded that the gun had been used in the robbery and that the gun was linked to the bits of paper, then the words 'Sean' on the bits of paper would be consistent with the allegation that Sean Lydon had committed the robbery.

Cf R v *Horne* [1992] Crim LR 304, CA. See also *R* v *Van Vreden* (1973) 57 Cr App R 818, CA; and see again *Myers* v *DPP* [1965] AC 1001, HL.

Questions

OBJECTIVES

The aim of this chapter is to ensure that you have a thorough grasp of:

    (a)   what constitutes hearsay;

    (b)   the difference between hearsay and original evidence;

    (c)   the difference between hearsay and real evidence (including statements produced by mechanical and other devices); and

    (d)   the particular problems associated with implied assertions and the non-existence of facts (or negative hearsay).

RESEARCH

    (a)   Read the materials contained in **Chapter 7** of this Manual.

    (b)   Read:

Keane, *The Modern Law of Evidence* (2nd ed., 1989), ch. 9, OR

Murphy, *A Practical Approach to Evidence* (4th ed., 1992), ch. 6; AND

Carter, *Cases and Statutes on Evidence* (2nd ed., 1990), ch. 13 and the Supplement (1992), OR

Heydon, *Evidence Cases & Materials* (3rd ed., 1991).

    (c)   On the basis of this research, answer the following questions.

Question 1
In an action for the specific performance of a contract for the sale of a car, the plaintiff, in order to prove the contract, wishes to call Stephen to give evidence that he heard the defendant offer the car for sale to the plaintiff for £2,500. This evidence is: —

[A]   Not hearsay.
[B]   Hearsay and comes within no exception to the rule against hearsay.
[C]   Hearsay, but admissible, with the leave of the court, under Civil Evidence Act, 1968, s. 2.
[D]   Hearsay, but admissible as an informal admission under Civil Evidence Act, 1968, s. 9.

Question 2
Keith and Leonard are charged with the murder of Martin. In their statements to the police, they both say that on the evening of the murder they met for a drink in The Lamb public house, then went to the Jewel in the Crown Indian restaurant for a meal. They are each able to state precisely what dishes they ordered. Further, they both state that they had not seen Martin on that evening, and know nothing about the circumstances of his death. The police have evidence to show that though they did meet in The Lamb public house they had stayed there for only 15 minutes and not 2 hours as they had stated, and that they did not visit the Jewel in the Crown Indian restaurant at all. The prosecution wishes to adduce in evidence the statements made by Keith and Leonard. The judge should rule these statements: —

[A]   Inadmissible, because hearsay.
[B]   Admissible as an exception to the hearsay rule, because they are completely exculpatory statements.
[C]   Inadmissible, because previous consistent statements.
[D]   Admissible, in order to show that they had fabricated a joint story after the offence.

Question 3
Peter is charged with indecently assaulting Ruth, a 14-year-old girl, who gives evidence of the assault. In his defence, Peter wishes to say that he had been standing at a bus-stop with Ruth and an elderly woman, Mrs Owen; that Mrs Owen had suddenly called out, 'This child tried to pick my pocket. Catch the thief!'; and that he had therefore grabbed hold of Ruth and held her tightly to prevent her escape. Mrs Owen cannot be called as a witness because, Peter says, he has been unable to trace her. Peter has a previous conviction for indecent exposure, and was dismissed from his last job after complaints by female colleagues that he pestered them with indecent suggestions.

Advise Peter on the admissibility in evidence of his version of the alleged incident, and of the likely consequences (if any) should he choose to testify.

Question 4
Robert Smith is being prosecuted for causing death by reckless driving and for failing to stop after an accident in Kensington, London. Robert says that on the night in question he was driving his car (registration number NFC 62P) in Bristol. Immediately after the accident, Mary saw a car disappearing and memorised the number, which she quickly wrote down with lipstick on the back of her hand. Later she showed her hand to a police officer, who wrote down the number in his notebook. Mary cannot remember the number any more but says she wrote the correct number on her hand, while the police officer says that he saw 'NFC 62P' written on her hand. May the *police officer* be called to give evidence to this effect?

Question 5
Duncan Jones, a director of a public company, is charged with conspiracy to defraud. It is alleged that at a meeting of directors on 5 June 1992, Duncan and others agreed to produce and publish false accounts in order to deceive investors and creditors. Duncan's defence is that on 5 June 1992 he could not have been at the meeting because he was in France. Duncan wants to know whether a used ticket, which he has in his possession, for a journey from Calais to Ramsgate dated 6 June 1992, and bearing the names 'Jones', is admissible, *at common law*, in support of his defence.

Question 6

Edward has been charged with selling food unfit for human consumption. May Fred give evidence for the prosecution that while visiting Edward's restaurant he saw a number of customers leave their food unfinished and, clutching their stomachs, rush to the lavatories?

Question 7

Freda, a student at the Inns of Court School of Law, is charged with taking a conveyance without authority. Her defence is one of alibi, that at the relevant time she was attending a tutorial. A register kept by the tutor who conducted the tutorial in question contains a number of tick marks alongside the names of those students who attended the tutorial. No such mark has been made alongside Freda's name. At *common law*, may the prosecution put the register in evidence?

9   Hearsay Exceptions

When is hearsay admissible?

9.1   General Points

A hearsay statement which falls within any of the hearsay exceptions considered in this chapter is admissible as evidence of the truth of the facts it contains.

There are many common law and statutory hearsay exceptions and it is not easy to draw up useful general classifications but probably the most important is between criminal and civil cases.

The position in civil cases is now, technically speaking, covered exclusively by statute (or by agreement of the parties). This follows from Civil Evidence Act 1968, s. 1:

(1)   In any civil proceedings a statement other than one made by a person while giving oral evidence in those proceedings shall be admissible as evidence of any fact stated therein to the extent that it is so admissible by virtue of any provision of this Part of this Act or by virtue of any other statutory provision or by agreement of the parties, but not otherwise.

(2)   In this section 'statutory provision' means any provision contained in, or in an instrument made under, this or any other Act, including any Act passed after this Act.

Section 1 creates no new exceptions to the hearsay rule. However, the Act goes on, notably in ss. 2, 4 and 5, to create 'new', wide exceptions to the hearsay rule. Although s. 1 appears to abolish *common law* exceptions in civil cases, s. 9 'preserves' some of them — notably the exceptions relating to (a) informal admissions by a party to proceedings and (b) public documents. As will be seen in **9.3** (below), it is important in civil cases to maintain the distinction between the 'new' exceptions and the 'preserved' exceptions.

The position in criminal cases is covered partly by common law exceptions and partly by statutory exceptions. However, whilst there is a much greater variety of hearsay exceptions in criminal cases their scope is generally narrower than the scope of the exceptions created by Civil Evidence Act 1968. Moreover the courts have set their face against the creation of new common law (judge-made) exceptions to the hearsay rule — see *Myers* v *DPP* [1965] AC 1001, HL. The overall effect is that hearsay is less likely to be admissible in criminal cases than in civil cases.

9.2   Hearsay Exceptions in Criminal Cases

9.2.1   COMMON LAW EXCEPTIONS

(It should be assumed that the exception was not preserved by Civil Evidence Act 1968, s. 9, and has no application in civil cases unless the contrary is stated.)

9.2.1.1 *Res gestae*

A preliminary difficulty about the heading *res gestae* in this context is that it has been employed in relation to the admissibility of facts (as opposed to statements) where the problem does not relate to hearsay but to some other exclusionary rule; see, for example, *R* v *Ellis* (1826) 6 B & C 145. You should consult the texts on this aspect of *res gestae*. Here we are concerned exclusively with *res gestae* as it relates to hearsay statements.

The phrase '*res gestae*' has been used to describe an out-of-court statement which relates to and is closely associated in time and place with a state of affairs or 'event' (res) as it arises or occurs (*gestae*). The broad theory is that such statements should generally be admitted since the 'events' in question are likely to monopolise the thoughts of the maker of the statement to an extent where the chances of concoction (arguably the main risk with hearsay statements) can be safely discounted. The formation of more specific principles of admissibility has depended upon the type of 'event' which the statement relates to. There are essentially four main categories of statement which fall under the umbrella heading *res gestae*.

(a) *Statements relating to a specific event (usually a crime).*

The 'usual' examples of this aspect of *res gestae* are cases where the victim of an assault makes a statement identifying the assailant shortly after the assault. The leading case now is *R* v *Andrews* [1987] AC 281 where, at pp. 300–1, Lord Ackner stated the general test of admissibility:

1.   The primary question which the judge must ask himself is — can the possibility of concoction or distortion be disregarded?

2.   To answer that question the judge must first consider the circumstances in which the particular statement was made, in order to satisfy himself that the event was so unusual or startling or dramatic as to dominate the thoughts of the victim, so that his utterance was an instinctive reaction to that event, thus giving no real opportunity for reasoned reflection. In such a situation the judge would be entitled to conclude that the involvement or the pressure of the event would exclude the possibility of concoction or distortion, providing that the statement was made in conditions of approximate but not exact contemporaneity.

3.   In order for the statement to be sufficiently 'spontaneous' it must be so closely associated with the event which has excited the statement, that it can be fairly stated that the mind of the declarant was still dominated by the event. Thus the judge must be satisfied that the event, which provided the trigger mechanism for the statement, was still operative. The fact that the statement was made in answer to a question is but one factor to consider under this heading.

4.   As to the possibility of error in the facts narrated in the statement, if only the ordinary fallibility of human recollection is relied on, this goes to the weight to be attached to and not the admissibility of the statement ... However ... there may be special features that may give rise to the possibility of error [e.g. when the defendant had drunk to excess or suffered from defective eyesight]. In such circumstances the trial judge must consider whether he can exclude the possibility of error.

R v *Bedingfield* (1879) 14 Cox CC 341, *Teper* v *R* [1952] AC 480, PC, *Ratten* v *R* [1972] AC 378, PC, *R* v *Turnbull* (1985) 80 Cr App R 104. For further examples and points of controversy, see *R* v *Glover* [1991] Crim LR 48 and *Edwards & Osakwe* v *DPP* [1992] Crim LR 576.

It seems that the exception should not be relied upon where the maker of the statement is available as a witness. See *Tobi* v *Nicholas* (1988) 86 Cr App R 323, but *cf. R* v *Nye* (1977) 66 Cr App R 252.

(b) *Statements relating to the maker's state of mind or emotion.*

There is sometimes a dispute about whether such statements are truly categorised as hearsay. See: *Lloyd* v *Powell Duffryn Steam Co. Ltd* [1914] AC 73 (a man's statement of intention to set up a household with a pregnant woman taken as non-hearsay evidence of paternity); and see *Thomas* v *Connell* (1838) 4 M & W 267 on statements indicative of knowledge. But in *R* v *Blastland* [1986] AC 41, HL the House of Lords made it clear that courts should scrutinise the argument that such statements are not hearsay with great care. An express assertion of a state of mind or emotion does seem to be properly classified as hearsay.

On the assumption that the statement in question is hearsay, what is the scope of this exception?

The statement is admissible to prove the mental/emotional state of the maker of the statement at the time when the statement was made — i.e. the statement should be in the present tense. The statement is not admissible to prove the *cause* of the mental/emotional state. Statements of intention are sometimes proved to support the inference that the intention was acted upon — see *R* v *Buckley* (1873) 13 Cox CC 293; *R* v *Moghal* (1977) 65 Cr App R 56; but *cf R* v *Wainwright* (1875) 13 Cox CC 171; *R* v *Thomson* [1912] 3 KB 19.

(c)   *Statements relating to the maker's physical state.*
The statement must be approximately contemporaneous with the physical state. See *Aveson* v *Kinnaird* (1805) 6 East 188, and *R* v *Black* (1922) 16 Cr App R 118.

The statement can prove the existence of the physical state but not its cause. See *Gilbey* v *G.W.R.* (1910) 102 LT 202, and *R* v *Gloster* (1888) 16 Cox CC 471.

(d)   *Statements relating to the maker's performance of an act.*
The statement must be approximately contemporaneous with the act, and, the maker of the statement and the performer of the act must be the same person. See *Peacock* v *Harris* (1886) 5 Ad & El 449 and *Howe* v *Malkin* (1878) 40 LT 196.

The act should in itself, be relevant to an issue before the court (i.e. the act should not be simply an excuse for admitting the statement). See *R* v *Bliss* (1837) 7 A & E 550 *cf R* v *McCay* [1990] 1 WLR 645.

In *Skinner* v *Shew & Co.* [1894] 2 Ch 581, the exception was relied upon to prove a letter which explained the reason for termination of contractual negotiations.

9.2.1.2   Informal admissions by a party to the proceedings
(This exception was expressly preserved by Civil Evidence Act 1968, s. 9, and is of continuing importance in civil cases. In criminal cases the basic common law exception has been considerably overlaid by Police and Criminal Evidence Act 1984, s. 76. This creates a statutory regime for controlling the admissibility of confessions made by an accused (the statutory definition of a confession is virtually identical to the common law definition of an informal admission). These rules are of such practical importance and raise issues which are so far removed from the hearsay problem that confessions (and related topics) will form the basis for the whole of **Chapter 10** of this Manual. However, s. 76 does not abolish the common law exception; it simply adds (considerably) to the conditions attaching to it where the informal admission in question is a confession by an accused.)

An informal admission is a statement which is or turns out to be adverse to the case of the person who makes it. Such a statement is generally admissible to prove the truth of the facts it contains so long as the statement was made by a person who is a party to the proceedings in which it is to be proved. The theory behind this exception is that parties are unlikely to run the risk of stating something against their own case unless it is true, because it is in their (selfish) interests to make statements which will favour their case. Clearly, if the admission is made as a result of an inducement it is less likely to be reliable. This explains (to an extent) why it is necessary in criminal cases to impose special restrictions on the admissibility of confessions by an accused — see **Chapter 10**.

General points about the nature and scope of the exception:

(a)   *Informal and formal admissions distinguished.*

For formal admissions see **Chapter 2** of this Manual. An informal admission (unlike a formal admission) is proved against the maker without his agreement. The word 'admission' in this section means 'informal admission'.

(b)   *Implied admissions.*
An admission may be implied by conduct see *Moriarty* v *London, Chatham and Dover Railway* (1870) LR 5 QB 314. Occasionally a party's silence or demeanour in the face of an accusation *may* be taken to imply acceptance of it. See: *Bessela* v *Stern* (1877) 2 CPD 265; *Wiedmann* v *Walpole* [1891] 2 QB 534.

The position in criminal cases is complicated by the impact of the, so called, right to silence and the circumstances in which acceptance can properly be inferred are limited.

See *R* v *Norton* [1910] 2 KB 496; *R* v *Christie* [1914] AC 545; *Hall* v *R* [1971] 1 WLR 298.

For examples of cases where acceptance might properly be inferred see:

Parkes v *R* [1976] 1 WLR 1251.

R v *Chandler* [1976] 1 WLR 585.

R v *Horne* [1990] Crim LR 188.

(c)   *Admissions not based on known facts.*
The admission must generally be based on facts which are known to the party making it. See: *R* v *Hulbert* (1979) 69 Cr App R 243, *Attorney-General's Reference (No. 4 of 1979)* [1981] 1 WLR 667, and *Comptroller of Customs* v *Western Lectric Co. Ltd* [1966] AC 367, PC.

However where the party making the admission might reasonably be expected to know, in a general sense, what he is talking about, the admission may be admitted. See *R* v *Chatwood* [1980] 1 WLR 874; *R* v *Turner* [1910] 1 KB 346.

(d)   *Vicarious admissions.*
The admission must generally be made by the party against whom it is to be proved. But an admission made with the authority of a party will be admissible against that party.

Kirkstall Brewery Co. v *Furness Railway Co.* (1874) LR 9 QB 468.

Woolway v *Rowe* (1834) 1 A & E 114.

On the question whether parties are bound by admissions of their lawyers see *Ellis* v *Allen* [1914] 1 Ch 904 and *R* v *Turner* (1975) 61 Cr App R 67, CA.

An admission by one defendant is generally no evidence against co-defendants i.e. defendant X is *not* the agent of defendant Y for the purpose of making admissions. This, of course, leads to difficulties in joint trials where the admission of one defendant contains statements which are adverse to another. See *R* v *Pearce* (1979) 69 Cr App R 365, and *R* v *Silcott* [1987] Crim LR 765 (as to the possibility of editing); *R* v *Gunewardene* [1951] 2 KB 600 and *R* v *Lake* (1977) 64 Cr App R 172 (as to the possibility of separate trials).

For the special difficulties of admissions by co-conspirators see:

R v *Blake & Tye* (1844) 6 QB 126.

R v *Donat* (1985) 82 Cr App R 173.

R v *Governor of Pentonville Prison, ex parte Osman* [1989] 3 All ER 701, QBD.

(e) *Mixed statements (statements which are partly adverse and partly favourable to the maker)*. Theoretically only the adverse parts of such statements fall within this exception, but see:

R v *Duncan* (1981) 73 Cr App R 359.

R v *Hamand* (1985) 82 Cr App R 65, CA.

R v *Sharp* [1988] 1 WLR 7, HL.

9.2.1.3 **Statements by persons since deceased (persons who are dead at the time of the trial)**
This heading embraces several distinct exceptions each with its own set of rules. The feature which is common to all is that the maker of the statement (M) is dead (a fact which needs to be proved as a pre-condition of reliance on these exceptions). Clearly there is no question of calling M as a witness! There is no general common law exception relating to statements by persons since deceased. If the statement by the person since deceased was made in documentary form it may well be admissible under Criminal Justice Act 1988, s. 23 or s. 24, (see below at **9.2.2.1**) however, if the statement was made orally, in criminal cases reliance must still be placed on the following exceptions.

(a) *Dying declarations.*
A dying person's statement of the cause of his or her death is admissible in trials for that person's murder or manslaughter if, when it was made, M had a settled, hopeless expectation of impending death (*R* v *Perry* [1909] 2 KB 697). *The exception is very narrow — it does not* apply to all deathbed statements — only those relating to the causes of M's death in trials for M's murder or manslaughter. The rationale seems to be that M will know that he has little to gain from lying when making such a statement. The main difficulty in relying on the exception will be to establish M's state of mind (again see *R* v *Perry*). The statement will only be admitted if M would have been able to give direct oral evidence of the facts (if alive), see *R* v *Pike* (1829) 3 C & P 598. It seems that if the statement is incomplete it may not be admitted (*Waugh* v *R* [1950] AC 203). For a recent application of the exception see *Nembhard* v *R* (1982) 74 Cr App R 144, PC.

(b) *Statements in the course of duty.*
Statements about acts made by the person who performed them in the course of duty are generally admitted (on M's death) to prove the performance of the act in question (see *Price* v *Torrington* (1703) 1 Salk 285). The statement should be contemporaneous with the act and the act in question should be M's. In *The Henry Coxon* (1878) 3 PD 156 a ship's log was not admitted because it was made two days after the acts in question and it referred to acts other than M's. The exception does not apply to a record of opinions see *R* v *McGuire* (1985) 81 Cr App R 323. The practical value of this exception has been greatly diminished by Criminal Justice Act 1988, s. 23 and s. 24, since most statements falling within the exception will be in documentary form.

(c) *Statements against proprietary or pecuniary interest.*
Statements against the proprietary or pecuniary interest of M are generally admitted (on M's death). The exception does *not* extend to statements which tend to incriminate M unless they are also against his proprietary or pecuniary interests (see the *Sussex Peerage Case* (1844) 11 Cl & F 85 and *B* v *Attorney-General* [1965] P 278). M must have known the facts on which the statement was based and that it was against his proprietary or pecuniary interests (see *Ward* v *Pitt & Co.* [1913] 2 KB 130). But it does not matter how significant the interest in question. Thus it seems any statement conceding indebtedness or the satisfaction of a debt owed to M would suffice. Where this exception applies it can be used to admit facts which were incidental to the statement against interest. Thus in *Higham* v *Ridgway* (1808) 10 East 109 a midwife's statement recording a payment for assisting at the birth of a child on a particular day was received as evidence of the date of birth of the child.

(d) *Statements as to public or general rights.*
(This exception may still apply in civil cases but only if it is not possible to admit the statement under the Civil Evidence Act 1968, s. 2 or s. 4.) A public right applies to the whole population. A general right applies to a particular section of it. The statement should assert the right in question directly and

should have been made prior to the dispute in question (see *Mercer* v *Denne* [1905] 2 Ch 538 and *Knight* v *David* [1971] 1 WLR 1671).

(e)   *Statements as to pedigree.*
(The exception may still apply in civil cases but only if it is not possible to admit the statement under Civil Evidence Act 1968, s. 2 or s. 4.) Pedigree means the relationship between persons by blood or marriage. A statement about the pedigree of another person alleged to be related to M by blood or marriage is admissible (on M's death). The dispute in question must relate to a matter of pedigree and the statement must have been made before the dispute arose. See *Haines* v *Guthrie* (1884) 13 QBD 818.

9.2.1.4   Evidence given in former proceedings

At common law statements made by witnesses in former proceedings are generally inadmissible (despite their being made on oath). However, such statements are admissible if they were subject to cross-examination by the party against whom the statement is to be proved (X) so long as the witness is dead or unable to attend or give evidence or is kept out of the way by X. This exception is likely to be of diminishing importance as the evidence will probably be recorded in documentary form and should therefore be admissible under Criminal Justice Act 1988, *infra*. See *R* v *Thompson* [1982] QB 647.

9.2.1.5   Public documents

(This exception was specifically preserved by Civil Evidence Act 1968, s. 9.) For a document to qualify as a public document the facts recorded in it must be of public interest and concern and the person recording the fact must be under a public duty to do so and to satisfy himself of the truth of the facts. In *R* v *Halpin* (1975) QB 907, it was held that the exception applied to extracts from documents which had to be filed at the Companies Registry. However this exception would not generally apply to the 'internal' records of a company. Further examples of public documents are given in the recommended texts.

9.2.2   STATUTORY EXCEPTIONS

(Again it should be assumed that these exceptions have no application in civil cases unless the contrary is stated.)

9.2.2.1   Criminal Justice Act 1988, sections 23 and 24

These sections create the most important statutory exceptions in criminal cases. However, they only apply to documentary hearsay (that is, the statement which is to be proved must be made in or contained in a document). The words 'statement' and 'document' which appear frequently in ss. 23 and 24 are defined for the purposes of the Act by references to Civil Evidence Act 1968, s. 10 (see sch. 2, para. 5 of the 1988 Act). 'Statement' includes any representation of fact by words or otherwise. 'Document' is very widely defined to include maps, photographs, discs, tapes and films as well as 'ordinary' documents.

Even though the requirements of s. 23 and s. 24 are satisfied the court is given a specific discretion to exclude the statement in question by s. 25. Moreover by virtue of s. 26 if the document in question is prepared for the purposes of either pending or contemplated criminal proceedings or a criminal investigation it cannot be admitted under s. 23 or s. 24 without the leave of the court (see below at **9.2.2.2**).

(a)   Criminal Justice Act 1988, section 23.

(1)   Subject—

(a)   to subsection (4) below;
(b)   to paragraph 1A of Schedule 2 to the Criminal Appeal Act 1968 (evidence given orally at original trial to be given orally at retrial); and
(c)   to section 69 of the Police and Criminal Evidence Act 1984 (evidence from computer records).

a statement made by a person in a document shall be admissible in criminal proceedings as evidence of any fact of which direct oral evidence by him would be admissible if—

(i)   the requirements of one of the paragraphs of subsection (2) below are satisfied; or

(ii)   the requirements of subsection (3) below are satisfied.

(2)   The requirements mentioned in subsection (1)(i) above are—

(a)   that the person who made the statement is dead or by reason of his bodily or mental condition unfit to attend as a witness;
(b)   that—

(i)   the person who made the statement is outside the United Kingdom; and
(ii)   it is not reasonably practicable to secure his attendance; or

(c)   that all reasonable steps have been taken to find the person who made the statement, but that he cannot be found.

(3)   The requirements mentioned in subsection (1)(ii) above are—

(a)   that the statement was made to a police officer or some other person charged with the duty of investigating offences or charging offenders; and
(b)   that the person who made it does not give oral evidence through fear or because he is kept out of the way.

(4)   Subsection 1 above does not render admissible a confession made by an accused person that would not be admissible under s. 76 of the Police and Criminal Evidence Act 1984.

The following is a preliminary guide to s. 23. In cases of doubt reference should be made to the exact wording of the section. Before a hearsay statement in a document can be admitted under s. 23 three main questions must be answered in the affirmative:

(i)   Was the hearsay statement made in a document? The document in question should be in such form as, 'I saw X punch Y', or 'I heard a gunshot at 11 p.m.' or 'Fred hit me', i.e. the 'eye-witness' (or, to be more exact, the person who claims any form of direct perception of the facts) should be the creator or author of the document. (But remember that a tape is a document so that an eye-witness who records his own statement of fact on a tape thereby makes a statement in a document. Also the concept of agency would apply, e.g. if the eye-witness acknowledges (e.g. by signing) a document which is written at his dictation by another person. As to other forms of acknowledgment see *R* v *McGillivray* [1993] Crim LR 530.)
(ii)   Could the eye-witness/author have given direct oral evidence of the *facts* contained in the statement? If, for example, he would not have been a competent witness or the facts are themselves inadmissible, s. 23 will not overcome the problem.
(iii)   Does the eye-witness/author not give evidence for one of the reasons specified in s. 23? The s. 23 reasons for not giving evidence are (1) he is dead or unfit (by reason of his bodily or mental condition) (s. 23(2)(a)); or (2) he is outside the UK and it is not reasonably practicable to secure his attendance (s. 23(2)(b)) (see *R* v *Bray* (1989) 88 Cr App R 354, *R* v *Case* [1991] Crim LR 192, and *R* v *French* (1993) *The Times*, 25 March 1993); or (3) all reasonable steps have been taken to find him but he cannot be found (s. 23(2)(c)); or (4) through fear or because he is kept out of the way (s. 23(3)) (this remarkably vague reason only applies when the statement was made to a police officer or some other person charged with the duty of investigating offences or charging offenders).

Section 23(3) 'does not give oral evidence through ear' has already spawned a considerable amount of case law: see generally *R* v *Acton Justices, ex parte McMullen* (1990) 92 Cr App R 98; *R* v *Ashford Justices, ex parte Hilden* (1993) 96 Cr App R 92; *Neill* v *N. Antrim Magistrates' Court* [1992] 4 All ER 846 and *R* v *Churchill* [1993] Crim LR 285.

Even if these conditions are satisfied the court may still exclude the statement under s. 25 or s. 26. (See **9.2.2.2**, below.)

(b)   Criminal Justice Act 1988, section 24.

(1)   Subject—

    (a)   to subsections (3) and (4) below;
    (b)   to paragraph 1A of Schedule 2 to the Criminal Appeal Act 1968, and
    (c)   to section 69 of the Police and Criminal Evidence Act 1984.

a statement in a document shall be admissible in criminal proceedings as evidence of any fact of which direct oral evidence would be admissible, if the following conditions are satisfied—

    (i)   the document was created or received by a person in the course of a trade, business, profession or other occupation, or as the holder of a paid or unpaid office; and
    (ii)   the information contained in the document was supplied by a person (whether or not the maker of the statement) who had, or may reasonably be supposed to have had, personal knowledge of the matters dealt with.

(2)   Subsection (1) above applies whether the information contained in the document was supplied directly or indirectly but, if it was supplied indirectly, only if each person through whom it was supplied received it—

    (a)   in the course of a trade, business, profession or other occupation; or
    (b)   as the holder of a paid or unpaid office.

(3)   Subsection (1) above does not render admissible a confession made by an accused person that would not be admissible under section 76 of the Police and Criminal Evidence Act 1984.

(4)   A statement prepared otherwise than in accordance with section 3 of the Criminal Justice (International Cooperation) Act 1990 or an order under paragraph 6 of Schedule 13 to this Act or under section 30 or 31 below for the purposes—

    (a)   of pending or contemplated criminal proceedings; or
    (b)   of a criminal investigation.

shall not be admissible by virtue of subsection (1) above unless—

    (i)   the requirements of one of the paragraphs of subsection (2) of section 23 above are satisfied; or
    (ii)   the requirements of subsection (3) of that section are satisfied; or
    (iii)   the person who made the statement cannot reasonably be expected (having regard to the time which has elapsed since he made the statement and to all the circumstances) to have any recollection of the matters dealt with in the statement.

The following is a preliminary guide to s. 24. In cases of doubt reference should be made to the exact wording of the section. In general s. 24 lets in (subject to s. 25 or s. 26) any stage of hearsay if:

(i)   the document containing the statement which is to be proved was either *created* by a person in the course of a trade, business etc. (see s. 24(1)(c)(i)) or *received* by such person;
and

(ii)   any intermediaries between the eye-witness and the creator of the document were acting in the course of a trade, business etc.;
and

(iii)   it is a reasonable inference that the person claiming to be the eye-witness did indeed have personal knowledge of the facts in question (s. 24(1)(c)(ii)). (See cases concerning the similar requirement in Civil Evidence Act 1968, s. 4: *Knight* v *David* [1971] 1 WLR 1671 and *Re Koscot Interplanetary (UK) Ltd* [1972] 3 All ER 829.)

There is no general requirement under s. 24 to show why the eye-witness does not give evidence (*cf.* s. 23). Thus, a document admitted under s. 24 could be in the form, 'E told A who told B who told me, C, that he (E) had seen X punch Y' (C is the creator of the document). So long as it is reasonable to infer that E had the personal knowledge he claimed and A, B and C acted in the course of trade etc. the document *may* be admitted under s. 24 to prove that X punched Y (subject to s. 25) even though E is available. However, if the document was prepared for the purposes of either pending or contemplated criminal proceedings *or* a criminal investigation (which may well apply to the example just given) then it must be shown either that one of the s. 23 reasons for the eye-witness not giving evidence exists *or* that he cannot reasonably be expected to have any recollection of the matters dealt with in the statement. (This reason is added by s. 24(4)(b)(iii).) Moreover leave would be required under s. 26 (see below). As to the meaning of 'prepared for the purposes of criminal proceedings etc' see *R* v *Bedi* (1992) 95 Cr App R 21.

9.2.2.2   Provisions ancillary to sections 23 and 24

(a)   Criminal Justice Act 1988, s. 25 and 26.

25.—*(1)   If, having regard to all the circumstances—*

(a)   the Crown Court—

(i)   on a trial on indictment;
(ii)   on an appeal from a magistrates' court; or
(iii)   on the hearing of an application under section 6 of the Criminal Justice Act 1987 (applications for dismissal of charges of fraud transferred from magistrates' court to Crown Court); or

(b)   the criminal division of the Court of Appeal; or
(c)   a magistrates' court on a trial of an information,
is of the opinion that in the interests of justice a statement which is admissible by virtue of section 23 or 24 above nevertheless ought not to be admitted, it may direct that the statement shall not be admitted.

(2)   Without prejudice to the generality of subsection (1) above, it shall be the duty of the court to have regard—

(a)   to the nature and source of the document containing the statement and to whether or not, having regard to its nature and source and to any other circumstances that appear to the court to be relevant, it is likely that the document is authentic;
(b)   to the extent to which the statement appears to supply evidence which would otherwise not be readily available;
(c)   to the relevance of the evidence that it appears to supply to any issue which is likely to have to be determined in the proceedings; and
(d)   to any risk, having regard in particular to whether it is likely to be possible to controvert the statement if the person making it does not attend to give oral evidence in the proceedings, that its admission or exclusion will result in unfairness to the accused or, if there is more than one, to any of them.

26.   *Where a statement which is admissible in criminal proceedings by virtue of section 23 or 24 above appears to the court to have been prepared, otherwise than in accordance with section 3 of the Criminal Justice (International Cooperation) Act 1990 or an order under paragraph 6 of Schedule 13 to this Act or under section 30 or 31 below, for the purposes—*

(a) of pending or contemplated criminal proceedings; or
(b) of a criminal investigation,

the statement shall not be given in evidence in any criminal proceedings without the leave of the court, and the court shall not give leave unless it is of the opinion that the statement ought to be admitted in the interests of justice; and in considering whether its admission would be in the interests of justice, it shall be the duty of the court to have regard—

(i) to the contents of the statement;
(ii) to any risk, having regard in particular to whether it is likely to be possible to controvert the statement if the person making it does not attend to give oral evidence in the proceedings, that its admission or exclusion will result in unfairness to the accused or, if there is more than one, to any of them; and
(iii) to any other circumstances that appear to the court to be relevant.

The difference between s. 25 and s. 26 was explained in *R* v *Cole* [1990] 2 All ER 108. 'By s. 25 if, having regard to all the circumstances, the court is of the opinion that a statement, admissible by virtue of ss. 23 or 24, in the interests of justice ought not to be admitted, it may direct that it be not admitted. In short, the court must be made to hold the opinion that the statement ought not to be admitted.

By contrast, under s. 26, when a statement is admissible by virtue of ss. 23 and 24 and was prepared for the purposes of criminal proceedings, the statement shall not be given in evidence unless the court is of the opinion that the statement ought to be admitted in the interests of justice. The court is not to admit the statement unless made to hold the opinion that it ought to be admitted.'

As to how these sections have been/should be applied see *R* v *Cole (supra)*, *R* v *Acton Justices, ex parte McMullen* (1990) 92 Cr App R 98, *R* v *Price* [1991] Crim LR 706, and the Privy Council decision in *Scott* v *R* [1989] AC 1242 which contains useful dicta (albeit interpreting a different statutory provision) and *R* v *Patel* [1993] Crim LR 291. The s. 25 discretion does not apply in committal proceedings: see *R* v *Acton Justices (supra)*.

(b) Criminal Justice Act 1988, s. 27.

Where a statement contained in a document is admissible as evidence in criminal proceedings, it may be proved—

(a) by the production of that document; or
(b) (whether or not that document is still in existence) by the production of a copy of that document, or of the material part of it.

authenticated in such manner as the court may approve; and it is immaterial for the purposes of this subsection how many removes there are between a copy and the original.

(c) Criminal Justice Act, s. 28.

(1) Nothing in this Part of this Act shall prejudice—

(a) the admissibility of a statement not made by a person while giving oral evidence in court which is admissible otherwise than by virtue of this Part of this Act; or
(b) any power of a court to exclude at its discretion a statement admissible by virtue of this Part of this Act.

(2) Schedule 2 to this Act shall have effect for the purpose of supplementing this Part of this Act.

SCHEDULE 2

Documentary Evidence — Supplementary

1.   Where a statement is admitted as evidence in criminal proceedings by virtue of Part II of this Act—

(a)   any evidence which, if the person making the statement had been called as a witness, would have ben admissible as relevant to his credibility as a witness shall be admissible for that purpose in those proceedings;

(b)   evidence may, with the leave of the court, be given of any matter which, if that person had been called as a witness, could have been put to him in cross-examination as relevant to his credibility as a witness but of which evidence could not have been adduced by the cross-examining party; and

(c)   evidence tending to prove that that person, whether before or after making the statement, made (whether orally or not) some other statement which is inconsistent with it shall be admissible for the purpose of showing that he has contradicted himself.

2.   A statement which is given in evidence by virtue of Part II of this Act shall not be capable of corroborating evidence given by the person making it.

3.   In estimating the weight, if any, to be attached to such a statement regard shall be had to all the circumstances from which any inference can reasonably be drawn as to its accuracy or otherwise.

4.   Without prejudice to the generality of any enactment conferring power to make them—

(a)   Crown Court Rules;
(b)   Criminal Appeal Rules; and
(c)   rules under section 144 of the Magistrates' Courts Act 1980,

may make such provision as appears to the authority making any of them to be necessary or expedient for the purposes of Part II of this Act.

5.   Expressions used in Part II of this Act and in Part I of the Civil Evidence Act 1968 are to be construed in Part II of this Act in accordance with section 10 of that Act.

6.   In Part II of this Act 'confession' has the meaning assigned to it by section 82 of the Police and Criminal Evidence Act 1984.

(d)   Criminal Justice Act 1988, ss. 30 and 31 and Criminal Justice (International Cooperation) Act 1990 s. 3.

These sections deal with a variety of specific forms of documentary evidence, i.e. evidence obtained from expert reports (s. 30), glossaries (s. 31) a foreign authority on the issue of a letter of request (s. 3). For further details on s. 30 see **Chapter 11** of this Manual.

(e)   Police and Criminal Evidence Act 1984, s. 69(1).

(See Criminal Justice Act 1988, ss. 23(1)(c) and 24(1)(c).)

In any proceedings, a statement in a document produced by a computer shall not be admissible as evidence of any fact stated therein unless it is shown—

(a)   that there are no reasonable grounds for believing that the statement is inaccurate because of improper use of the computer;

(b)   that at all material times the computer was operating properly, or if not, that any respect in which it was not operating properly or was out of operation was not such as to affect the production of the document or the accuracy of its contents; and

> *(c)   that any relevant conditions specified in rules of court under subsection (2) are satisfied.*

See also PCEA 1984, sch. 3, Part II and *R* v *Minors* [1989] 2 All ER 208 and *R* v *Shephard* (1993) 96 Cr App R 345.

(f)   Criminal Appeal Act 1968, sch. 2, para. 1A.

(See Criminal Justice Act 1988, ss. 23(1)(b) and 24(1)(b).) This makes separate provision for documentary evidence at re-trials ordered by the Court of Appeal.

9.2.2.3   Banker's Books Evidence Act 1879, sections 3 and 4
(This exception also applies in civil cases.)

Banker's Books Evidence Act 1879, s. 3, provides that:

> *a copy of any entry in a banker's book shall in all legal proceedings be received as prima facie evidence of such entry, and of the matters, transactions, and accounts therein recorded.*

Section 4 adds that the book in question must have been one of the ordinary books of the bank, that the entry was made in the usual and ordinary course of business and that the book is in the custody or control of the bank. Important considerations are what is meant by 'bank' and what is meant by 'bankers' book'. As originally enacted the definitions restricted the utility of the exception given the development of the banking system (especially in recent years). Schedule 6 to the Banking Act 1979 therefore amended the 1897 Act to provide that 'bank' refers to an institution authorised under the Banking Act 1979 or a municipal bank within the meaning of that Act, a trustee savings bank, the National Savings Bank and the Post Office in the exercise of its powers to provide banking services.

'Bankers' books' include ledgers, day books, cash books, account books and other records used in the ordinary business of the bank, whether these records are in written form or are kept on microfilm, magnetic tape or any other form of mechanical or electronic data retrieval mechanism.

Even these extended definitions cause some problems. In *Williams* v *Williams* [1988] QB 161 it was held that paying-in slips and paid cheques were not entries in bankers' books for the purposes of the 1879 Act. This case actually related to another aspect of the Act, namely, the very wide powers given in s. 7 for the court to order that a party to legal proceedings be at liberty to inspect and take copies of bankers' books for the purposes of such proceedings.

9.2.2.4   Criminal Justice Act 1925, section 13(3)
Depositions taken at committal proceedings where, for specified reasons, W does not attend at trial. For a recent review of the law on this see *R* v *O'Loughlin* (1987) 85 Cr App R 157 and *R* v *Neshet* [1990] Crim LR 578, CA. (This provision will probably be superseded in practice by CJA 1988, ss. 23 and 24 which are much broader in their effect.)

9.2.2.5   Children and Young Persons Act 1933, sections 42 and 43
Depositions from a child witness where testifying in court would involve serious danger to the child's health. (The importance of this exception may be diminished by: (i) Criminal Justice Act 1988, s. 32(2), allowing for evidence to be given by children through a live television link in trials for offences involving an assault on any person and offences under Children and Young Persons Act 1933, s. 1 (ss. 32(2)(a) and (b)) and offences under the Sexual Offences Acts 1956 and 1967, Indecency with Children Act 1960, Protection of Children Act 1978 and Criminal Law Act 1977, s. 54 (s. 32(2)(c)) see **Chapter 5** at **5.1(g)**; and (ii) the effect of the Criminal Justice Act 1988, s. 32A — see below at **9.2.2.7**).

9.2.2.6   Magistrates' Courts Act 1980, section 105 and Criminal Law Amendment Act 1867, section 6
Depositions from witnesses who are dangerously ill.

9.2.2.7   Criminal Justice Act 1988, section 32A (created by Criminal Justice Act 1991, section 54)

(1)   This section applies in relation to the following proceedings, namely—

(a)   trials on indictment for any offence to which section 32(2) above* applies;
(b)   appeals to the criminal division of the Court of Appeal and hearings of references under section 17 of the Criminal Appeal Act 1968 in respect of any such offence; and
(c)   proceedings in youth courts for any such offence and appeals to the Crown Court arising out of such proceedings.

(2)   In any such proceedings a video recording of an interview which—

(a)   is conducted between an adult and a child who is not the accused or one of the accused ('the child witness'); and
(b)   relates to any matter in issue in the proceedings,

may, with the leave of the court, be given in evidence in so far as it is not excluded by the court under subsection (3) below.

(3)   Where a video recording is tendered in evidence under this section, the court shall (subject to the exercise of any power of the court to exclude evidence which is otherwise admissible) give leave under subsection (2) above unless—

(a)   it appears that the child witness will not be available for cross-examination;
(b)   any rules of court requiring disclosure of the circumstances in which the recording was made have not been complied with to the satisfaction of the court; or
(c)   the court is of the opinion, having regard to all the circumstances of the case, that in the interests of justice the recording ought not to be admitted;

and where the court gives such leave it may, if it is of the opinion that in the interests of justice any part of the recording ought not to be admitted, direct that that part shall be excluded.

(4)   In considering whether any part of a recording ought to be excluded under subsection (3) above, the court shall consider whether any prejudice to the accused, or one of the accused, which might result from the admission of that part is outweighed by the desirability of showing the whole, or substantially the whole, of the recorded interview.

(5)   Where a video recording is admitted under this section—

(a)   the child witness shall be called by the party who tendered it in evidence;
(b)   that witness shall not be examined in chief on any matter which, in the opinion of the court, has been dealt with in his recorded testimony.

(6)   Where a video recording is given in evidence under this section, any statement made by the child witness which is disclosed by the recording shall be treated as if given by that witness in direct oral testimony; and accordingly—

(a)   any such statement shall be admissible evidence of any fact of which such testimony from him would be admissible;
(b)   no such statement shall be capable of corroborating any other evidence given by him;

and in estimating the weight, if any, to be attached to such a statement, regard shall be had to all the circumstances from which any inference can reasonably be drawn (as to its accuracy or otherwise).

(7)   In this section child means a person who—

(a)   in the case of an offence falling within section 32(2)(a) or (b) above*, is under fourteen years of age, or if he was under that age when the video recording was made under fifteen years of age; or

(b)   in the case of an offence falling within section 32(2)(c) above*, is under seventeen years of age or, if he was under that age when the video recording was made is under eighteen years of age.

(8)   Any reference in subsection (7) above to an offence falling within paragraph (a), (b) or (c) of section 32(2) above includes a reference to an offence which consists of attempting or conspiring to commit, or of aiding, abetting, counselling, procuring or inciting the commission of, an offence falling within that paragraph.

(9)   In this section—
'statement' includes any representation of fact, whether made in words or otherwise;
'video recording' means any recording, on any medium, from which a moving image may by any means be produced and includes the accompanying sound-track.

(10)   A magistrates' court inquiring into an offence as examining justices under section 6 of the Magistrates' Courts Act 1980 may consider any video recording as respects which leave under subsection (2) above is to be sought at the trial, notwithstanding that the child witness is not called at the committal proceedings.

(11)   Without prejudice to the generality of any enactment conferring power to make rules of court, such rules may make such provision as appears to the authority making them to be necessary or expedient for the purpose of this section.

(12)   Nothing in this section shall prejudice the admissibility of any video recording which would be admissible apart from this section.

[*The offences are those listed at **9.2.2.5**, supra, including attempting or conspiring to commit such offences and being a secondary party to such offences. (For the full text of s. 32(2) see **Chapter 5** at **5.1(g)**).]

The procedure for applying for leave to adduce a s. 32A video recording is laid down in r. 23C, Crown Court Rules 1982 (as inserted by the Crown Court (Amendment) Rules 1992). See also the *Practice Note* [1992] 3 All ER 909.

9.2.2.8   Miscellaneous statutory exceptions depending on the consent of the parties

(a)   Criminal Justice Act 1967, s. 9 (as amended by the Children and Young Persons Act 1969).

(1)   In any criminal proceedings, other than committal proceedings, a written statement by any person shall, if such of the conditions mentioned in the next following subsection as are applicable are satisfied, be admissable as evidence to the like extent as oral evidence to the like effect by that person.

(2)   The said conditions are—

(a)   the statement purports to be signed by the person who made it;
(b)   the statement contains a declaration by that person to the effect that it is true to the best of his knowledge and belief and that he made the statement knowing that, if it were tendered in evidence, he would be liable to prosecution, if he wilfully stated in it anything which he knew to be false or did not believe to be true;
(c)   before the hearing at which the statement is tendered in evidence, a copy of the statement is served, by or on behalf of the party proposing to tender it, on each of the other parties to the proceedings; and

(d)   none of the other parties or their solicitors, within seven days from the service of the copy of the statement, serves a notice on the party so proposing objecting to the statement being tendered in evidence under this section:

Provided that the conditions mentioned in paragraphs (c) and (d) of this subsection shall not apply if the parties agree before or during the hearing that the statement shall be so tendered.

(3)   The following provisions shall also have effect in relation to any written statement tendered in evidence under this section, that is to say—

(a)   if the statement is made by a person under the age of 21, it shall give his age;
(b)   if it is made by a person who cannot read it, it shall be read to him before he signs it and shall be accompanied by a declaration by the person who so read the statement to the effect that it was so read; and
(c)   if it refers to any other document as an exhibit, the copy served on any other party to the proceedings under paragraph (c) of the last foregoing subsection shall be accompanied by a copy of that document or by such information as may be necessary in order to enable the party on whom it is served to inspect that document or a copy thereof.

(3A)   In the case of a statement which indicates in pursuance of subsection (3)(a) of this subsection that the person making it has not attained the age of 14, subsection (2)(b) of this section shall have effect as if for the words from 'made' onwards there were substituted the word 'understands the importance of telling the truth in it'.

(b)   Theft Act 1968, s. 27(4). Statutory declarations relating to goods in transmission (whether by post or otherwise) e.g. that a particular parcel did not arrive.

(c)   Magistrates' Courts Act 1980, s. 103 (as substituted by the Criminal Justice Act 1988, s. 33). Any statement (not necessarily written: see *R* v *H* (1990) 90 Cr App R 440) made by or taken from a person under 14 may be admissible in *committal proceedings* relating to charges involving assault on, or injury or threat of injury to, a person, cruelty contrary to the Children and Young Persons Act 1933, s. 1 and various sexual offences.

9.3   Hearsay Exceptions in Civil Cases

9.3.1   GENERAL POINTS

As already noted in **9.1** (above), by virtue of Civil Evidence Act 1968, s. 1, in civil proceedings (which are widely defined in s. 18 *but which do not include civil proceedings in magistrates' courts*) hearsay evidence may be admitted (i) under the other sections of the Act; or (ii) under any other statute not repealed by the Act; or (iii) by agreement of the parties; *but not otherwise.*

As to (ii) most of the relevant provisions contained in *other* statutes were repealed for the purposes of proceedings in the High Court and county court by the 1968 Act (an important exception is the Bankers' Books Evidence Act 1879; see **9.2.2.3**). However an important recent addition to 'other statutory exceptions' has been the Children Act 1989, s. 96 (see **9.3.2**). The Evidence Act 1938, which still applies to civil proceedings in Magistrates' Courts, was held to be incapable of rendering admissible a computer print-out recording the names of persons who had not paid their community charge, see *R* v *Coventry Justices ex parte Bullard* [1992] NLJ 383.

As to (iii) the agreement of the parties would not generally be forthcoming where the evidence is disputed (also agreement is defined fairly narrowly — disclosure of a hearsay statement in a document during the disclosure of documents procedure does not amount to an implied agreement to allow it to be admitted as evidence, see *Follows* v *Peabody Trust* (1983) 10 HLR 62). It should be noted, in this context, that in most forms of civil proceedings the court is unlikely to allow evidence by affidavit if the evidence is contested (interlocutory proceedings in family matters are a major exception). As to affidavits generally see RSC Ord. 38, rr. 2 and 2A and CCR Ord. 20, r. 6 and the **Civil Litigation Manual**.

The exceptions created by Civil Evidence Act 1968, ss. 2, 3, 4 and 5 (the 'new' exceptions) are so wide that a large proportion of hearsay statements do fall within them. However, a party who seeks to rely on these new exceptions to the hearsay rule (apart from s. 3) is required to comply with the 'notice procedures' set out in rules made under s. 8 of the Act. The relevant rules are to be found in RSC Ord. 38, rr. 20–34 and CCR Ord. 20, rr. 14 to 26 (see **9.3.3.1** and **9.3.5.5** below).

Certain common law exceptions were preserved by Civil Evidence Act 1968, s. 9. The most important for practical purposes is the informal admissions exception. If a statement falls within one of these preserved common law exceptions it is preferable to rely on that exception (rather than the new exceptions) because the notice procedures do not apply to them (see **9.3.8**).

The Civil Evidence Act 1968 exceptions apply to hearsay statements of fact. However, by virtue of Civil Evidence Act 1972, s. 1, the exceptions under ss. 2 and 4 of the 1968 Act are extended to statements of opinion which would otherwise (i.e. apart from the hearsay problem) be admissible, see generally **Chapter 11** of this Manual.

As regards civil proceedings in the magistrates' courts, hearsay evidence may be admitted by virtue of the common law exceptions (see **9.2.1**) and various statutory exceptions including the Evidence Act 1938 (which was repealed as regards High Court and county court proceedings by the Civil Evidence Act 1968).

As these general points will have revealed, the position regarding hearsay in civil proceedings is not straightforward. An attempt to summarise the position by way of a flow chart can be found at **9.3.9**, below.

9.3.2 CHILDREN ACT 1989/CHILD SUPPORT ACT 1991

The Children (Admissibility of Hearsay Evidence) Order 1993 (made under the Children Act 1989, s. 96 and effective on 5 April 1993) provides that in civil proceedings before the High Court or a County Court and in family proceedings and civil proceedings under the Child Support Act 1991 in a magistrates' court, evidence may be given in connection with the upbringing, maintenance or welfare of a child notwithstanding that the evidence in question would otherwise be inadmissible because of the 'hearsay rule' in the law of evidence.

See, as to the effect of this Order and the question of compellability of the child who has made the statement, *R* v *B — County Council, ex parte P* [1991] 2 All ER 65.

9.3.3 CIVIL EVIDENCE ACT 1968, SECTION 2

(1) In any civil proceedings a statement made, whether orally or in a document or otherwise, by any person, whether called as a witness in those proceedings or not, shall, subject to this section and to rules of court, be admissible as evidence of any fact stated therein of which direct oral evidence by him would be admissible.

(2) Where in any civil proceedings a party desiring to give a statement in evidence by virtue of this section has called or intends to call as a witness in the proceedings the person by whom the statement was made, the statement—

(a) shall not be given in evidence by virtue of this section on behalf of that party without the leave of the court; and
(b) without prejudice to paragraph (a) above, shall not be given in evidence by virtue of this section on behalf of that party before the conclusion of the examination-in-chief of the person by whom it was made, except

(i)   where before that person is called the court allows evidence of the making of the statement to be given on behalf of that party by some other person; or

(ii)   insofar as the court allows the person by whom the statement was made to narrate it in the course of his examination-in-chief on the ground that to prevent him from doing so would adversely affect the intelligibility of his evidence.

(3)   Where in any civil proceedings a statement which was made otherwise than in a document is admissible by virtue of this section, no evidence other than direct oral evidence by the person who made the statement or any person who heard or otherwise perceived it being made shall be admissible for the purpose of proving it:

Provided that if the statement in question was made by a person while giving oral evidence in some other legal proceedings (whether civil or criminal), it may be proved in any manner authorised by the court.

The words 'statement' and 'document' are defined in precisely the same way as they are in the Criminal Justice Act 1988 (in relation to ss. 23 and 24) because the 1988 Act borrowed the definitions contained in Civil Evidence Act 1968, s. 10.

Section 2(1) has the general effect of letting in first-hand hearsay. If the maker of the statement (M) could have given direct oral evidence of the *facts* contained in the statement then (subject to the rest of the section and rules of court) the statement is admissible notwithstanding that it is hearsay. It is therefore necessary that M would have been a competent witness and that the facts stated would not have been excluded under some other exclusionary rule.

In relation to *documentary* hearsay s. 2 is broadly similar to Criminal Justice Act 1988, s. 23 (see **9.2.2.1**). The statement must be *made in a document* in the sense defined in *Re D* [1986] 2 FLR 189 — i.e. the 'author' of the document must be the person whose statement you wish to prove (although it should be remembered that the definition of document includes a tape-recording — a statement *deliberately* recorded on tape could therefore be said to be a statement 'made in a document': see on this point *Ventuoris* v *Mountain (No. 2)* [1992] 3 All ER 414 where the Court of Appeal held that a statement whose maker was unaware that his statement was being taped was *not* a statement made in a document). It seems that if the author *could* have given evidence of another's statement, e.g. because it was an informal admission, such statement is admissible under s. 2, see *Compagnie Générale Maritime* v *Diakan Spirit SA* [1981] 1 Lloyd's Rep 550 sed quaere.

However, s. 2 is *much* wider than Criminal Justice Act 1988, s. 23, in that it also applies to oral statements and it *may* apply even though the maker of the statement is available as a witness. Regarding oral hearsay, s. 2(3) provides that if the hearsay statement is an oral statement the only persons who can prove it in court are those who heard or otherwise perceived it being made (out of court) or the maker of the statement himself (i.e. it must be first-hand hearsay). There is an exception in relation to statements made in previous legal proceedings. Such statements can be proved under s. 2 in any manner authorised by the court — see *Taylor* v *Taylor* [1970] 1 WLR 1148.

Although the maker of the statement *can* give evidence of his own out-of-court statement (whether documentary or oral), since he could give direct evidence of the facts there is generally no obvious reason why he should be allowed to make any reference to his out-of-court statement. Section 2(2) therefore provides that it will not be possible to rely on s. 2 unless the court gives leave and even if it does give leave the hearsay statement should only be proved after the maker of the statement has given evidence-in-chief. A case illustrating the type of situation in which it may be appropriate to give leave is *Morris* v *Stratford-on-Avon Rural District Council* [1973] 1 WLR 1059. However, s. 2(2) must now be read in the light of the provisions of RSC Ord. 38, r. 2A (see **5.1**).

9.3.3.1   The notice procedures

The Civil Evidence Act 1968, s. 2(1), refers to rules of court. Section 8 made provision for the rules which are now contained in RSC Ord. 38. rr. 20 to 34, and CCR Ord. 20, rr. 14–26 (the rules are usually referred to as the notice procedures). They are quite detailed and what follows is an outline of the rules as they apply to s. 2. However, they also apply *mutatis mutandis* to ss. 4 and 5. (See **9.3.5.5** and **9.3.6.**)

(a) *Notice*.

A party intending to rely on s. 2 should give notice to the other parties of such intention within 21 days of setting down for trial (within 14 days of the hearing in the county court). The notice should contain: (a) the time, place and circumstances at or in which the statement was made; (b) the person by whom and the person to whom the statement was made; and (c) the substance of the statement or, if material, the words used (documentary statements or a copy thereof should be enclosed with the notice).

If it is alleged that one of the 'reasons' for not calling the eye-witness (specified in s. 8) exists the notice must state that reason. The s. 8 reasons are that he is (a) dead, (b) beyond the seas, (c) unfit, (d) cannot with due diligence be identified or found, (e) cannot reasonably be expected to have any recollection of the matters in question. The list is disjunctive (*Rasool* v *West Midland Passenger Transport Executive* [1974] 3 All ER 638). The 'reasons' will be referred to as the s. 8 reasons.

The s. 8 reasons are similar to the list of reasons in Criminal Justice Act 1988, ss. 23 and 24 (see **9.2.2.1**). However, there are significant differences:

(i)   Whereas under Criminal Justice Act 1988, ss. 23 and 24, the unavailability reasons are *conditions of admissibility* (i.e. unless the reason can be established the statement *cannot* be proved), under Civil Evidence Act 1968, s. 2 (and, for that matter, ss. 4 and 5), the reasons simply form part (albeit an important part) of the notice procedure and, as we shall see, the non-existence of a reason will not *necessarily* result in the exclusion of the statement.

(ii)   There is no distinction based upon the purpose of creating the document — whatever the purpose the list of reasons is always the same.

(iii)   There is no equivalent in Civil Evidence Act 1968 to the Criminal Justice Act 1988, s. 23, reason that the witness does not give evidence 'through fear' (whatever this means).

(iv)   It is not necessary to establish that it is not reasonably practicable to secure the attendance of a person who is beyond the seas (which is a poetic way of saying 'outside the UK' — see *Rover International Ltd* v *Cannon Film Sales Ltd* [1987] 3 All ER 986).

(v)   It is sufficient to prove that the witness cannot be identified. There is no equivalent under Criminal Justice Act 1988, ss. 23 and 24 (but it *may* be that this distinction is not of major significance because under ss. 23 and 24 there is the 'cannot be traced' reason).

(b) *Counter-notice*. If a notice is served but no s. 8 reason is given the other side can then within 21 days (seven days in the county court) serve a counter-notice challenging the admissibility of the statement and requiring the original witness to be called (r. 26). The statement *may* still be put in evidence but only at the court's discretion (under r. 29). Where the notice relates to a statement made in previous legal proceedings a counter-notice should not be served but directions should be sought — see Ord. 38, r. 28.

If a s. 8 reason *is* stated in the notice, a counter-notice should not be served unles it is to challenge the existence of the reason: if such challenge is made the existence of the s. 8 reason will be determined by a master or registrar prior to the trial.

(c) *Results of complying with the procedures*. If a proper notice is served and a s. 8 reason is stated in it (which is not challenged or, having been challenged, is proved to exist) then the s. 2 statement can be proved as of right (*Piermay Shipping Co. SA* v *Chester* [1978] 1 WLR 411).

Where the notice does not state a s. 8 reason, if no counter-notice is served it will be inferred that there is no objection to proving the s. 2 statement.

When no s. 8 reason is stated and a counter-notice *is* served the usual result will be that the s. 2 statement is inadmissible. However, the court has a discretion to admit a s. 2 statement even where the procedures have not been complied with (see (d) below) and the court may exercise the same discretion if there is no s. 8 reason and a counter-notice has been served, especially where (if the s. 2 statement is excluded) a party might be obliged to call an opposing party (or his servant or agent) as a witness. See:

Tremelbye (Selangor) Rubber Co. Ltd v *Stekel* [1971] 1 WLR 226;

Greenaway v *Homelea Fittings (London) Ltd* [1985] 1 WLR 234.

(d)   *Non-compliance with the procedures.* The usual result of non-compliance with the notice procedures (even if there is a valid s. 8 reason) is that the s. 2 statement is excluded. Although the court has a discretion to waive non-compliance with the rules (Ord. 38, r. 29), the cases indicate that non-compliance with the rules is not a matter that can be lightly overlooked (see *Ford* v *Lewis* [1971] 1 WLR 623). For cases where the discretion was exercised see:

Follows v *Peabody Trust* (1983) 10 HLR 62.

Morris v *Stratford-on-Avon Rural District Council* [1973] 1 WLR 1059.

(The notice procedures are affected by the new rules regarding the exchange of witness statements: see **Chapter 5** at **5.1(g)**).

9.3.4   CIVIL EVIDENCE ACT 1968, SECTION 3

(1)   Where in any civil proceedings—

(a)   a previous inconsistent or contradictory statement made by a person called as a witness in those proceedings is proved by virtue of section 3, 4 or 5 of the Criminal Procedure Act 1865; or
(b)   a previous statement made by a person called as aforesaid is proved for the purpose of rebutting a suggestion that his evidence has been fabricated,

that statement shall by virtue of this subsection be admissible as evidence of any fact stated therein of which direct oral evidence by him would be admissible.

(2)   Nothing in this Act shall affect any of the rules of law relating to the circumstances in which, where a person called as a witness in any civil proceedings is cross-examined on a document used by him to refresh his memory, that document may be made evidence in those proceedings; and where a document or any part of a document is received in evidence in any such proceedings by virtue of any such rule of law, any statement made in that document or part by the person using the document to refresh hs memory shall by virtue of this subsection be admissible as evidence of any fact stated therein of which direct oral evidence by him would be admissible.

It may be somewhat misleading to describe this as a 'new' exception because as a matter of common law (in combination with the Criminal Procedure Act 1865) it is, in several circumstances, possible to prove a prior consistent or inconsistent statement by a witness who is being examined in chief or cross-examined (see **Chapter 5** of this Manual). However, in criminal cases the hearsay problem raised by these statements is overcome by the expedient of treating them simply as evidence of consistency or inconsistency *not* as evidence of the truth of the facts they contain (whilst the distinction is rigorously maintained by the judges it may be lost on the jury!). By virtue of s. 3, in civil cases this distinction no longer needs to be maintained. When the rules for examining witnesses permit a consistent or inconsistent statement to be put to a witness they may be treated as evidence of the truth of the facts they contain, hence the description of s. 3 as a 'new' exception. The notice procedures, for obvious reasons, do *not* apply.

9.3.5   CIVIL EVIDENCE ACT 1968, SECTION 4

(1)   Without prejudice to section 5 of this Act, in any civil proceedings a statement contained in a document shall, subject to this section and to rules of court, be admissible as evidence of any fact stated therein of which direct oral evidence would be admissible, if the document is, or forms part of, a record compiled by a person acting under a duty from information which was supplied by a person (whether acting under a duty or not) who had, or may reasonably be supposed to have had, personal knowledge of the matters dealt with in that information and which, if not supplied by that person to the compiler of the record directly, was supplied by him to the compiler of the record indirectly through one or more intermediaries each acting under a duty.

(2)   Where in any civil proceedings a party desiring to give a statement in evidence by virtue of this section has called or intends to call as a witness in the proceedings the person who originally supplied the information from which the record containing the statement was compiled, the statement—

(a)   shall not be given in evidence by virtue of this section on behalf of that party without the leave of the court; and

(b)   without prejudice to paragraph (a) above, shall not without the leave of the court be given in evidence by virtue of this section on behalf of that party before the conclusion of the examination-in-chief of the person who originally supplied the said information.

(3)   Any reference in this section to a person acting under a duty includes a reference to a person acting in the course of any trade, business, profession or other occupation in which he is engaged or employed or for the purposes of any paid or unpaid office held by him.

Section 4 effectively lets in any stage of documentary hearsay so long as (a) the document in question is or forms part of a record; (b) compiled by a person acting under a duty; (c) from information supplied by a person (whether acting under a duty or not) who had or may reasonably be supposed to have had personal knowledge of the facts contained in the statement; (d) any intermediary, I, between the supplier, S, and the compiler, C, must also have been acting under a duty; (e) the notice procedures (*mutatis mutandis*) are complied with and the court's leave is obtained if it is also proposed to call S as a witness. These elements will be considered in turn.

9.3.5.1   The document is or forms part of a record

The word 'record' is not defined in Civil Evidence Act 1968 and it has given the courts some difficulty. See *H* v *Schering Chemicals Ltd* [1983] 1 WLR 143, in which Bingham J defined records for the purposes of s. 4 as:

documents which either (1) give effect to a transaction itself or (2) which contain a contemporaneous register of information supplied by those with direct knowledge of the facts (alternatively, 'records which a historian would regard as original or primary sources').

This is a fairly restrictive definition (which may explain why the word was not used in Criminal Justice Act 1988, s. 24). It seems that, certainly in relation to (2), if 'registering the information' was not the primary intention of the author of the document in question the document may not be a record for the purpose of s. 4. Thus a file containing letters of complaint would not qualify because it seems the primary purpose of the author of the letters was to make a complaint not to record or register (for future reference by others) the facts contained therein. See *R* v *Tirado* (1974) 59 Cr App R 80.

Moreover a selective summary of facts does not qualify as a record. See *H* v *Schering Chemicals Ltd* and *Savings and Investment Bank Ltd* v *Gasco Investments (Netherlands) BV* [1984] 1 WLR 271 in which Peter Gibson J rejected a report prepared by Board of Trade inspectors because 'it falls short of simply compiling the information supplied to them in the sense that some information will not be included in the report'. See also *Re D* [1986] 2 FLR 189.

9.3.5.2 Compiled by a person acting under a duty

This concept should give no real difficulty. It is 'defined' in s. 4(3) in such a way as to be indistinguishable from the requirement under Criminal Justice Act 1988, s. 24(1)(c)(i) (see **9.2.2.1**).

9.3.5.3 From information supplied by a person (whether acting under a duty or not) etc.

Again this is similar to the requirement in Criminal Justice Act 1988, s. 24(1)(c)(ii). Indeed the cases mentioned in that context — *Knight* v *David* [1971] 1 WLR 1671 and *Re Koscot Interplanetary (UK) Ltd* [1972] 3 All ER 829 — were civil cases dealing with this aspect of s. 4. In the former Goulding J was prepared to infer personal knowledge on the part of S (even though he could not be identified). If S is also the compiler (C), he must be acting under a duty.

9.3.5.4 Any intermediary etc.

This element makes clear that there can be intermediaries (I) between S and C as long as I acts under a duty. However, it is not necessary that the chain linking S with C be in any specific form, i.e. the communication can be oral or documentary. (But the wording would clearly suggest a deliberate transfer of information from S to I to C.)

Example 1. X is suing Y for negligence as a result of an accident in which a car driven by Y knocked X down on a pelican crossing. Steve, a bystander, tells Ian (I), a friend of X, that he (S) saw that the light was on red to traffic when Y's car hit X. I relays the information to Charles (C), a police officer, who records it.

Stage 1   S observes the crossing light on red to traffic.

Stage 2   S tells (supplies information to) I.

Stage 3   I relays information to C.

Stage 4   C records the information.

The record compiled by C would not be admissible under s. 4 (even assuming compliance with the procedures) because I was not (apparently) acting under a duty.

Example 2.   Same as example 1, except that Ian is a police officer who reports the matter to Charles (also a police officer) who records it. Since both I and C would have been acting under a duty the note of S's statement would be admissible under s. 4 (subject to the notice procedures).

9.3.5.5 The notice procedures (as regards section 4) and the need for leave to prove the record (if it is also intended to call the supplier of the information)

It is not necessary to repeat in detail the notice procedures which were considered in relation to s. 2 (see **9.3.3.1** above). The notice for a s. 4 statement should include details of the supplier, the compiler and any intermediary. Moreover s. 8 reasons should be stated, if applicable, not only in relation to S, but also in relation to C and I. The counter-notice provisions apply *mutatis mutandis*. Since a s. 4 statement must be in documentary form a copy of it should be attached to the notice. If it is proposed to call S as a witness in addition to proving the s. 4 statement it is necessary to obtain the leave of the court (s. 4(2)(a)). As with s. 2 statements the court will presumably need a good reason for granting leave. Moreover even if leave is granted the s. 4 statement cannot (without leave) be proved until the conclusion of the examination-in-chief of S.

9.3.6 CIVIL EVIDENCE ACT 1968, SECTION 5

The precise wording of s. 5 will not be set out here as it is unduly complicated. Its basic effect is to render admissible statements contained in documents produced by computers (widely defined in s. 5(6) as any device for storing and processing information) so long as:

(a)   The facts stated would otherwise be admissible (apart from any hearsay problem).

(b) The documents were produced by the computer during a period over which the computer was used regularly.

(c) Information of the kind which is contained in the document was regularly supplied to the computer in the ordinary course of the activities in relation to which the computer was being used.

(d) Throughout the material period (see (b)) the computer was operating properly.

All these requirements are aimed (presumably) at ensuring the reliability of the computer (and can be proved by certificate s. 5(4)). However, there seems to be nothing in s. 5 aimed directly at ensuring the reliability of the information which is supplied to the computer (e.g. there is no requirement that anyone should have had personal knowledge of it). This would not matter if (like Police and Criminal Evidence Act 1984, s. 69) the wording of the section was negative in form because then the original statements in which the relevant information is supplied would need to fall within a distinct exception to the hearsay rule (such as s. 4). But s. 5(1) is positive in form so that, in theory, if scurrilous rumours were regularly fed into a computer and repeated in a print-out from that computer (so long as the computer was operating properly) they would magically become admissible under s. 5. However, the position is probably redeemed by the notice procedures which apply to s. 5. (See Ord. 38, r. 24 and Ord. 20, r. 16). The notice of any s. 5 statement should specify the persons who occupied a responsible position in relation to the management of the relevant activities, supply of the relevant information and operation of the computer and any s. 8 reason which applies to them. In the absence of s. 8 reasons a counter-notice may be served. The net effect of these procedures may therefore be to close or reduce the apparent gap in the regime created by s. 5.

9.3.7 GENERAL MATTERS RELATING TO SECTIONS 2, 3, 4 AND 5

Section 6(1) provides that a document admissible under s. 2, 4 or 5 can be proved by production of a copy authenticated in such manner as the court may approve. Section 6(3) provides that, in estimating the weight to be attached to a statement proved under s. 2, 3, 4 and 5, regard should be had in particular to whether the maker of the statement or supplier of the information had any motive to misrepresent the facts and whether the statement was contemporaneous with the occurrence of the facts in question. Section 7 provides that where the statement of an absent witness is proved under s. 2 or s. 4 his credibility can be challenged notwithstanding that he is absent. A previous inconsistent statement proved under s. 7 will attract the effect of s. 3 (i.e. it is admissible as evidence of the truth of the facts it contains). The main exception to s. 7 arises when the notice of intention to prove the s. 2 or s. 4 statement does not include a s. 8 reason and the party on whom it was served failed to serve a counter-notice — such party cannot then rely on s. 7 to challenge the credibility of the absent witness (see Ord. 38, r. 30). The aim here is to prevent the failure to serve a counter-notice being used as a tactical device to enable a party to challenge a witness's credibility in his absence. Indeed any party seeking to prove a previous inconsistent statement under s. 7 must give notice of his intention to do so (see Ord. 38, r. 31).

9.3.8 CIVIL EVIDENCE ACT 1968, SECTION 9

Preserved Common Law Exceptions

(1) In any civil proceedings a statement which, if this Part of this Act had not been passed, would by virtue of any rule of law mentioned in subsection (2) below have been admissible as evidence of any fact stated therein shall be admissible as evidence of that fact by virtue of this subsection.

(2) The rules of law referred to in subsection (1) above are the following, that is to say any rule of law—

(a) whereby in any civil proceedings an admission adverse to a party to the proceedings, whether made by that party or by another person, may be given in evidence against that party for the purpose of proving any fact stated in the admission;

(b) whereby in any civil proceedings published works dealing with matters of a public nature (for example, histories, scientific works, dictionaries and maps) are admissible as evidence of facts of a public nature stated therein;

(c)   whereby in any civil proceedings public documents (for example, public registers and returns made under public authority with respect to matters of public interest) are admissible as evidence of facts stated therein; or

(d)   whereby in any civil proceedings records (for example, the records of certain courts, treaties, Crown grants, pardons and commissions) are admissible as evidence of facts stated therein.

In this subsection 'admission' includes any representation of fact, whether made in words or otherwise.

Subsections (1) and (2) are of considerable practical importance because a hearsay statement falling within the informal admissions and public documents exceptions can be proved as of right (without compliance with any notice procedures).

Section 9(3) provides that a statement which tends to establish reputation or family tradition may be admitted under the common law exception relating to a deceased person's statements as to public or general rights or as to pedigree — see **9.2.1.3(e)**.

9.3.9   CIVIL HEARSAY IN CHART FORM

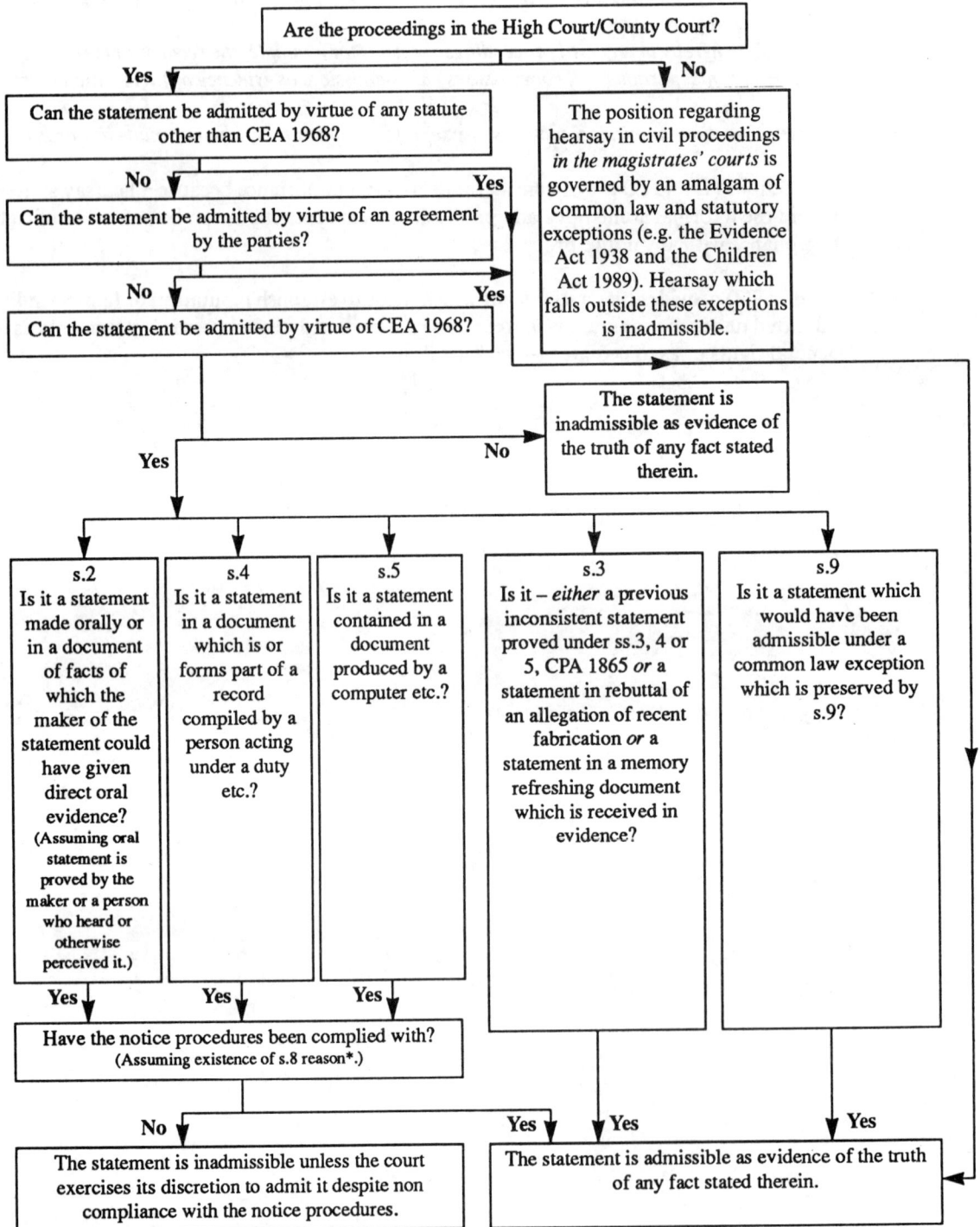

Are the proceedings in the High Court/County Court?

Yes → Can the statement be admitted by virtue of any statute other than CEA 1968?

No ↓   **Yes** →

Can the statement be admitted by virtue of an agreement by the parties?

No ↓   **Yes** →

Can the statement be admitted by virtue of CEA 1968?

No (top right) → The position regarding hearsay in civil proceedings *in the magistrates' courts* is governed by an amalgam of common law and statutory exceptions (e.g. the Evidence Act 1938 and the Children Act 1989). Hearsay which falls outside these exceptions is inadmissible.

No → The statement is inadmissible as evidence of the truth of any fact stated therein.

Yes ↓

s.2	s.4	s.5	s.3	s.9
Is it a statement made orally or in a document of facts of which the maker of the statement could have given direct oral evidence? (Assuming oral statement is proved by the maker or a person who heard or otherwise perceived it.)	Is it a statement in a document which is or forms part of a record compiled by a person acting under a duty etc.?	Is it a statement contained in a document produced by a computer etc.?	Is it – *either* a previous inconsistent statement proved under ss.3, 4 or 5, CPA 1865 *or* a statement in rebuttal of an allegation of recent fabrication *or* a statement in a memory refreshing document which is received in evidence?	Is it a statement which would have been admissible under a common law exception which is preserved by s.9?

Yes ↓ (s.2)   **Yes** ↓ (s.4)   **Yes** ↓ (s.5)

Have the notice procedures been complied with? (Assuming existence of s.8 reason*.)

No ↓

The statement is inadmissible unless the court exercises its discretion to admit it despite non compliance with the notice procedures.

Yes (s.3) / **Yes** / **Yes** (s.9) →

The statement is admissible as evidence of the truth of any fact stated therein.

Notes

Although statements of fact are referred to in this chart the Civil Evidence Act 1972 extends the effect of ss. 2 and 4, CEA 1968 to statements of opinion (see **Chapter 11, 11.1.4.1**).

*The asumption that there is a s. 8 reason (see **9.3.3.1(a)**) with respect to statements falling within ss. 2, 4 or 5 is necessary to justify the suggestion that if the notice procedures are complied with such statements are admissible. If there is no s. 8 reason the statement may only be admissible at the court's discretion even if the procedures are complied with.

Questions

OBJECTIVES

This chapter is designed to ensure that you can:

(a) demonstrate a sound understanding of the principles underlying the exceptions to the hearsay rule (other than the special provision relating to confessions which will be dealt with in **Chapter 10** of this Manual);

(b) identify the circumstances in which the exceptions may apply;

(c) identify which preliminary facts need to be proved and (when applicable) which procedural steps need to be taken; and

(d) raise and/or counter an objection to hearsay evidence.

RESEARCH

(a) Read the materials contained in **Chapter 9** of this Manual.

(b) Read:

Keane, *The Modern Law of Evidence* (2nd ed., 1989), ch. 10 and 11, and ch. 12, pt A and C, OR

Murphy, *A Practical Approach to Evidence* (4th ed., 1992), ch. 6, pt B, ch. 7, pt A and C, and ch. 8; AND

Carter, *Cases and Statutes on Evidence* (2nd ed., 1990 and Supplement (1992)), ch. 14, 15 and 16, OR

Heydon, *Evidence Cases and Materials* (3rd ed., 1991);

On the topic of hearsay in civil proceedings you should cross-refer to the **Civil Litigation Manual**.

(c) On the basis of this research answer the following questions.

Question 1
Ian is charged with the theft from a shop (E.T. Electrics) of a TV set which was found at Ian's house. Ian denies theft claiming that he has had the TV set for some time. In order to prove that the TV set is the one which was stolen from E.T. Electrics, the prosecution wish to adduce evidence of records obtained from the manufacturers of the TV set, (Tosh Ltd) which show that the 'unit' number printed on the inside of the TV set found in Ian's house corresponds to the number on the TV set which was delivered to E.T. Electrics. The records were compiled by clerks at Tosh Ltd's factory on the basis of information given to them by employees on the production line. The records are:—

[A] Inadmissible hearsay.
[B] Admissible in principle under CJA 1988, s. 23.
[C] Admissible in principle under CJA 1988, s. 24.
[D] Admissible at common law under the public records exception.

Question 2
In a defamation trial in which Peter is suing David for damages, David wishes to call Edward to give evidence that he overheard Peter offering a bribe to Quentin if Quentin would commit perjury and give false evidence in support of his (Peter's) claim. Edward's evidence of this conversation is:—

[A] Inadmissible because hearsay.
[B] Inadmissible because irrelevant.
[C] Admissible as an informal admission by Peter of the weakness and falsity of his claim.
[D] Admissible as an exception to the rule against prior consistent or self-serving statements.

Question 3
Arthur is charged with murdering his ex-lover Edith in June 1993. He has pleaded not guilty and has given notice of an alibi defence.

(a)   Advise the prosecution whether it will be possible to adduce the following items of evidence:

(i)   Testimony by a police officer that as he was approaching the place where Edith was found dying from stab wounds he heard an unknown person shout, 'Hello Arthur, where are you rushing off to?'
(ii)   A letter in Arthur's handwriting (dated May 1993) found in a waste bin at Arthurs' home which reads 'Love has turned to hate. So help me, Edith, I'll finish you for good'.
(iii) Testimony by a doctor that just before she died Edith said, 'I have a terrible pain in my back where Arthur stabbed me'.
(iv)   Testimony by Oliver, a friend of Edith's, that several days before she was stabbed she told him that Arthur had threatened to kill her.

(b)   Advise Arthur whether he can adduce evidence of a deathbed confession by Judas that he (not Arthur) had murdered Edith.

Question 4

(a)   Alvin is being prosecuted for causing death by reckless driving. The prosecution case is that Alvin ran down Bert as he was crossing the road at a pelican crossing when the lights were on red to traffic. The prosecution alleges that Alvin was driving at excessive speed for the conditions (it was dark and raining), that he was aware his brakes were defective and that he failed to keep a proper look out.

Alvin's case is that he was driving at a reasonable speed, was unaware of the defective condition of his brakes and that Bert ran across the road in front of his car when the crossing lights were on green to traffic.

PC Trotter was on the scene soon after the accident and spoke to a bystander who claimed to have seen 'everything' and stated that the crossing lights were on red to traffic at the time of the accident. He added that just after the accident Alvin had told him that he (Alvin) had simply not seen the crossing lights. PC Trotter noted down the bystander's statement. Unfortunately it has not been possible to trace this bystander since the accident.

Although he did not sustain any head injury Bert died in hospital several days after the accident. Whilst he was being taken to the hospital he told an ambulanceman that he had waited until the crossing lights changed in his favour before starting to walk across the road.

The police have been contacted by Laura who claims that, on the day before the accident, her boyfriend Tommy, a part-time car mechanic, told her that he had promised Alvin a refund on a payment for servicing Alvin's car because he had been unable to fix the brakes. Tommy was killed in a stock-car race shortly after this conversation.

The prosecution proposes to call PC Trotter to prove the note and to call the ambulanceman and Laura to give evidence. Leaving aside any tactical considerations, prepare an objection to this evidence and, in each case, prepare an argument to support the overruling of the objection.

(b)   Assume that the case described above was the subject of a civil action brought by Bert's dependants. Advise them whether at the trial of the civil action they may rely on the evidence of PC Trotter and his note, the ambulanceman and Laura and if so which, if any procedural requirements should be complied with.

Question 5

After negotiations for the assignment of the benefits of a lease by Vendors Ltd to Purchasers Ltd have broken down, Purchasers Ltd brings proceedings against White, an estate agent, for the recovery of £20,000 paid to him, it alleges, as a stakeholder. White, who has paid the money over to Vendors Ltd, pleads in his defence that he received it as agent for Vendors Ltd and not as a stakeholder. During the negotiations Arthur, who as company secretary to Purchasers Ltd was concerned in the negotiations on its behalf, telephoned the managing director, Bryan, in New York. In reporting to him on the transaction Arthur stated that it has been agreed with White and Vendors Ltd that the sum should be paid to White to be held until the formal documents were drawn up. Arthur also dictated a memo to the same effect into a recording machine, from which it was transcribed by a temporary typist who can no longer be identified. Arthur has since died. Peter, a former colleague of White, can testify that he overheard White saying in a public house after receiving the £20,000 that 'he did not know what he should do with it, whether to hold it or pay it to Vendors Ltd'.

Advise Purchasers Ltd whether and how the telephone conversation, the memo and Peter's story can be put in evidence.

[A suggested answer outline to Question 5 can be found in **Appendix 1** to this Manual.]

10 Confessions and Illegally or Improperly Obtained Evidence in Criminal Cases

When is a confession, made by an accused person prior to a criminal trial, admissible in the trial to prove that the accused is guilty of the offence?

In a criminal trial when, if at all, may the prosecution adduce evidence obtained improperly or illegally?

The position in relation to a confession by an accused is now governed by Police and Criminal Evidence Act 1984 (PCEA 1984).

PCEA 1984, s. 82(1), provides:

'confession' includes any statement wholly or partly adverse to the person who made it, whether made to a person in authority or not and whether made in words or otherwise.

As noted in para **9.2.1.2** this statutory definition is virtually identical to the common law definition of an informal admission (but see *R v Sat-Bhambra* (1988) 88 Cr App R 55, where the Court of Appeal restricted the definition of 'confessions' to statements which were adverse *when made*. Statements which were favourable when made, but which later proved to be adverse are not, it seems, confessions). It is important to stress that there is no requirement in the definition that the confession should be in any particular form. Very often an entire interview between a police officer and a suspect will be proved by the prosecution as a confession so long as some of the accused's answers were incriminating. For a recent example see *R v Welch* [1992] Crim LR 368. For a good example of this see the interview of Heath in the **Advocacy, Negotiation and Conference Skills Manual, Chapter 57**. It seems that a video re-enactment of a crime by an accused qualifies as a confession (see *Li Shu-Ling v R* [1989] AC 270).

An accused's confession was generally admissible at common law as an exception to the hearsay rule and this general rule is confirmed by PCEA 1984, s. 76(1) which provides:

In any proceedings a confession made by an accused person may be given in evidence against him in so far as it is relevant to any matter in issue in the proceedings and is not excluded by the court in pursuance of this section.

However, the general rule admitting confessions is and always has been subject to exception, for example, where the confession was obtained by threats or violence on the part of the interrogator. Accordingly, s. 76(1) is subject to s. 76(2) (see **10.1.1**) which provides two grounds on which such confessions *will* be excluded. Moreover the confession *may* be excluded by virtue of the discretions provided for in s. 78(1) and s. 82(3) which apply to prosecution evidence generally (including confessions — See *R v Mason* [1988] 1 WLR 139).

131

The main barrier to the admissibility of confessions is s. 76(2) for the reason that it operates as a matter of law whereas the other barrier (ss. 78 and 82(3)) operates as a matter of discretion.

Since ss. 78 and 82(3) apply to other forms of evidence (i.e. apart from confessions), it is appropriate to deal also in this chapter with the effect which these provisions may have on evidence other than confessions which have been obtained illegally or improperly (see **10.2**). However, it should be stressed that the discretion to exclude evidence is not solely concerned with evidence which is illegally or improperly obtained; evidence which has been obtained with perfect propriety may be excluded at the court's discretion if its probative value is outweighed by its prejudicial effect (see **Chapters 2, 11 and 12** of this Manual).

The Codes of Practice provided for under PCEA 1984, s. 66, have become a very important factor in relation to this topic. Section 67(11) provides that the court *shall* take account of the codes in determining any question (to which the codes might be relevant) arising in any proceedings. The codes are expressed as applying to police officers, however s. 67(9) provides that

> *persons other than police officers who are charged with the duty of investigating offences or charging offenders shall in the discharge of that duty have regard to any relevant provision of [the] Codes.*

In *R* v *Seelig & Spens* (1992) 94 Cr App R 17, the Court of Appeal accepted a narrow interpretation of the words 'charged with the duty of investigating offences' when upholding a decision, on the facts, that Department of Trade inspectors were not persons who were 'charged with the duty of investigating offences'. As to investigations by the SFO see *R* v *Director of Serious Fraud Office ex parte Smith* [1992] 3 All ER 456. Cf. *R* v *Twaites* (1991) 92 Cr App R 106.

The codes which are important in this context are those relating to the detention, treatment and questioning of suspects (Code C), the tape recording of interviews (Code E), the search of premises and the seizure of property (Code B). There are extracts from Code C in **Appendix 2** to this Manual.

By virtue of the Police and Criminal Evidence Act 1984 (Tape Recording of Interviews) Order 1991 (SI 1991 No. 2687), in most police areas of England and South Wales (for the full list of areas see the schedule to SI 1991 No. 2686, set out in **Appendix 2**) most interviews in police stations of persons suspected of the commission of indictable offences commenced after midnight on 31 December 1991 shall be tape-recorded in accordance with Code E (the exceptions relate to cases involving 'terrorist' offences). As a result of this order the Practice Direction issued by the Lord Chief Justice on 26 May 1989 is of considerable importance. (The Practice Direction, reported in (1989) 89 Cr App R 132, is set out in full in **Appendix 2** after the excerpts from Code C.)

The general effect of Code E and the Practice Direction will be that even though an interview is tape-recorded, it will normally be proved at trial in the form of a transcript. However, in *R* v *Riaz*; *R* v *Burke* [1992] Crim LR 366, the Court of Appeal held that, even after the jury retired, the jury was entitled to hear the tape of the interview which had been proved in the first instance by transcript. As the Court of Appeal said, the evidence was the tape itself — the transcript is merely a convenient means of presenting it. See also *R* v *Aitken* (1992) 94 Cr App R 85.

Many of the provisions of Code C only apply to 'interviews'. An interview for these purposes is defined in Notes for Guidance-11A. See also *DPP* v *D* (1992) 94 Cr App R 185 and *R* v *Cox* (1993) 96 Cr App R 464.

10.1   Confessions: The Barriers to Admissibility

10.1.1   THE FIRST BARRIER—POLICE AND CRIMINAL EVIDENCE ACT 1984, SECTION 76(2)-(3)

> *(2)   If, in any proceedings where the prosecution proposes to give in evidence a confession made by an accused person, it is represented to the court that the confession was or may have been obtained—*

(a) by oppression of the person who made it; or

(b) in consequence of anything said or done which was likely, in the circumstances existing at the time, to render unreliable any confession which might be made by him in consequence thereof.

the court shall not allow the confession to be given in evidence against him except insofar as the prosecution proves to the court beyond reasonable doubt that the confession (notwithstanding that it may be true) was not obtained as aforesaid.

(3) In any proceedings where the prosecution proposes to give in evidence a confession made by an accused person, the court may of its own motion require the prosecution, as a condition of allowing it to do so, to prove that the confession was not obtained as mentioned in subsection (2) above.

10.1.1.1 Procedural and preliminary points

Section 76(2) comes into operation where the prosecution proposes to prove the confession (see *R v Sat-Bhambra* (1988) 88 Cr App R 55) and representations about s. 76(2) are made (see *R v Liverpool Juvenile Court, ex parte R* [1988] QB 1) or the court raises the issue of its own motion (s. 76(3)). Once the admissibility issue is raised it seems it *must* be determined on the *voir dire* (see *R v Oxford City Justices, ex parte Berry* [1988] QB 507). The following general statements on the procedure to be adopted where the admissibility of a confession is in issue were made in *Ajodha v The State* [1982] AC 204 at p. 223 (*per* Lord Bridge):

(1)   In the normal situation which arises at the vast majority of trials where the admissibility of a confession statement is to be challenged, defending counsel will notify prosecuting counsel that an objection to admissibility is to be raised, prosecuting counsel will not mention the statement in his opening to the jury, and at the appropriate time the judge will conduct a trial on the voir dire to decide on the admissibility of the statement; this will normally be in the absence of the jury, but only at the request or with the consent of the defence: *R v Anderson* (1929) 21 Cr App R 178. [But regarding the last point see now *R v Hendry* [1988] Crim LR 766.]

(2)   Though the case for the defence raises an issue as to the voluntariness of a statement in accordance with the principles indicated earlier in this judgment, defending counsel may for tactical reasons prefer that the evidence bearing on that issue be heard before the jury, with a single cross-examination of the witnesses on both sides, even though this means that the jury hear the impugned statement whether admissible or not. If the defence adopts this tactic, it will be open to defending counsel to submit at the close of the evidence that, if the judge doubts the voluntariness of the statement, he should direct the jury to disregard it, or, if the statement is essential to sustain the prosecution case, direct an acquittal. Even in the absence of such a submission, if the judge himself forms the view that the voluntariness of the statement is in doubt, he should take the like action *proprio motu*. [But regarding the second point made here, see now *R v Sat-Bhambra* (1988) 88 Cr App R 55.]

(3)   It may sometimes happen that the accused himself will raise for the first time when giving evidence an issue as to the voluntariness of a statement already put in evidence by the prosecution. Here it will be a matter in the discretion of the trial judge whether to require relevant prosecution witnesses to be recalled for further cross-examination. If he does so, the issue of voluntariness should be dealt with in the same manner as indicated in paragraph (2) above.

(4)   Particular difficulties may arise in the trial of an unrepresented defendant, when the judge must, of course, be especially vigilant to ensure a fair trial. No rules can be laid down, but it may be prudent, if the judge has any reason to suppose that the voluntary character of a statement proposed to be put in evidence by the prosecution is likely to be in issue, that he should speak to the defendant before the trial begins and explain his rights in the matter. [And see now s. 76(3).]

(a)   *Voir dire* not required unless admissibility issue raised; see:

Ajodha v The State [1982] AC 204.

R v *Flemming* (1987) 86 Cr App R 32.

R v *Keenan* [1989] 3 All ER 598.

    (b)   Evidence given by the accused on the *voir dire*; see:

Wong Kam-Ming v *R* [1980] AC 247.

R v *Brophy* [1982] AC 476.

    (c)   Proving the confession — documentary or oral evidence; see:

R v *Todd* (1980) 72 Cr App R 299.

R v *Dillon* (1983) 85 Cr App R 29. Cf. *R* v *Sekhon* (1987) 85 Cr App R 19, CA.

10.1.1.2   Oppression (section 76(2)(a))
By s. 76(8):

> *In this section 'oppression' includes torture, inhuman or degrading treatment, and the use or threat of violence (whether or not amounting to torture).*

For more specific guidance see *R* v *Fulling* [1987] QB 426 *per* Lord Lane CJ at p. 432:

'Oppression' in s. 76(2)(a) should be given its ordinary dictionary meaning. The *Oxford English Dictionary* as its third definition of the word runs as follows: 'Exercise of authority of power in a burdensome, harsh, or wrongful manner; unjust or cruel treatment of subjects, inferiors etc., the imposition of unreasonable or unjust burdens.' One of the quotations given under that paragraph runs as follows: 'There is not a word in our language which expresses more detestable wickedness than oppression'. . . We find it hard to envisage any circumstances in which such oppression would not entail some impropriety on the part of the interrogator.

See also *R* v *Hughes* [1988] Crim LR 519 and *R* v *Ismail* [1990] Crim LR 109.

10.1.1.3   Unreliability (section 76(2)(b))

This element is so widely drafted that it leaves a good deal of latitude to the court. However, some guidelines are to be found in *R* v *Fulling* [1987] QB 426 and the following Court of Appeal decisions.

R v *Everett* [1988] Crim LR 826.

R v *Delaney* (1988) 88 Cr App R 338.

R v *Goldenberg* (1989) 88 Cr App 285.

R v *Tyrer* (1989) 90 Cr App R 446.

R v *Crampton* (1991) 92 Cr App R 369 but cf. *R* v *Barry* (1992), 95 Cr App R 384.

R v *Chung* (1991) 92 Cr App R 314.

10.1.1.4   'The fruits of the poisoned tree'
PCEA 1984, s. 76(4), (5) and (6) provides:

> *(4)   The fact that a confession is wholly or partly excluded in pursuance of this section shall not affect the admissibility in evidence—*

> *(a)   of any facts discovered as a result of the confession: or*
>
> *(b)   where the confession is relevant as showing that the accused speaks, writes or expresses himself in a particular way, of so much of the confession as is necessary to show that he does so.*
>
> *(5)   Evidence that a fact to which this subsection applies was discovered as a result of a statement made by an accused person shall not be admissible unless evidence of how it was discovered is given by him or on his behalf.*
>
> *(6)   Subsection (5) above applies—*
>
> *(a)   to any fact discovered as a result of a confession which is wholly excluded in pursuance of this section: and*
>
> *(b)   to any fact discovered as a result of a confession which is partly so excluded, if the fact is discovered as a result of the excluded part of the confession.*

The basic effect of this part of s. 76 is that when a confession is excluded under s. 76(2) any *facts* discovered as a result of the confession can be proved (s. 76(4)(a)) but it cannot be proved that the facts were discovered as a result of something said by the accused (s. 76(5)). Section 76(5) cannot be avoided by reference to a video re-enactment by the accused of the crime (see *Lam Chi-Ming v R* [1991] 3 All ER 172).

Example: A, who is charged with the theft of some gold coins, confesses (as a result of oppression) and in his confession informs the police that the coins are buried at a particular spot in Epping Forest. This is confirmed by a police search. Assuming that the confession is excluded under s. 76(2), the prosecution may nevertheless prove that the coins were found buried in Epping Forest (s. 76(4)(a)) but *not* that this resulted from something said by the accused (s. 76(5)). It hardly needs saying that the effect of s. 76(5) in such a case is that the evidential impact against A of the discovery of the coins is nil (unless, of couse, the coins can be linked to A *factually*, e.g. by the presence of his fingerprints).

For an illustration of the potential application of s. 76(4)(b) see *R v Voisin* [1918] 1 KB 531.

Documents are both facts and statements. It would seem that if incriminating documents are part and parcel of an inadmissible confession the documents also will be excluded. See *R v Barker* [1941] 2 KB 381.

10.1.2   THE SECOND BARRIER — THE DISCRETION(S) TO EXCLUDE

Police and Criminal Evidence Act 1984, s. 78:

> *(1)   In any proceedings the court may refuse to allow evidence on which the prosecution proposes to rely to be given if it appears to the court that, having regard to all the circumstances, including the circumstances in which the evidence was obtained, the admission of the evidence would have such an adverse effect on the fairness of the proceedings that the court ought not to admit it.*
>
> *(2)   Nothing in this section shall prejudice any rule of law requiring a court to exclude evidence.*

Police and Criminal Evidence Act 1984, s. 82(3):

> *Nothing in this Part of this Act shall prejudice any power of a court to exclude evidence (whether by preventing questions from being put or otherwise) at its discretion.*

Section 82(3) basically preserves any common law discretion to exclude evidence which existed prior to PCEA 1984.

10.1.2.1   General points
There is little doubt that the discretion to exclude a confession will be exercised when the confession has been obtained by deliberate impropriety or bad faith. See: *R v Mason* [1988] 1 WLR 139.

However, cases which do not fall clearly into this category are more problematical: see *R* v *Jelen* (1989) 90 Cr App R 456; *R* v *Christou* (1992) 95 Cr App R 264; *R* v *Bryce* (1992) 95 Cr App R 320; *R* v *Bailey* (1993) *The Times*, 22 March.

On the crucial question of the effect of breaches of the Code of Practice for Detention, Treatment and Questioning (excerpts from the Code are in **Appendix 2**) see:

R v *Delaney* (1988) 88 Cr App R 338, 341 per Lord Lane, 'It is no part of the duty of the court to rule a statement inadmissible simply in order to punish the police for failure to observe the codes of practice'.

R v *Keenan* [1989] 3 All ER 598, 609 per Hodgson J, 'But if the breaches are significant and substantial we think it makes good sense to exclude . . .'.

R v *Walsh* (1990) 91 Cr App R 161, 163 per Saville J, 'Although bad faith may make substantial or significant that which might not otherwise be so, the contrary does not follow. Breaches which are in themselves significant and substantial are not rendered otherwise by the good faith of the officers concerned'.

R v *Canale* [1990] 2 All ER 187.

R v *Oliphant* [1992] Crim LR 40.

R v *Purcell* [1992] Crim LR 806.

On the question whether a *voir dire* is necessary see *R* v *Manji* [1990] Crim LR 512.

10.1.2.2   **Confessions obtained after an unjustified refusal of access to legal advice**
PCEA 1984, s. 58:

58.—*(1)   A person arrested and held in custody in a police station or other premises shall be entitled, if he so requests, to consult a solicitor privately at any time.*

(2)   Subject to subsection (3) below, a request under subsection (1) above and the time at which it was made shall be recorded in the custody record.

(3)   Such a request need not be recorded in the custody record of a person who makes it at a time while he is at a court after being charged with an offence.

(4)   If a person makes such a request, he must be permitted to consult a solicitor as soon as is practicable except to the extent that delay is permitted by this section.

(5)   In any case he must be permitted to consult a solicitor within 36 hours from the relevant time, as defined in section 41(2) above.

(6)   Delay in compliance with a request is only permitted—
    (a)   in the case of a person who is in police detention for a serious arrestable offence; and
    (b)   if an officer of at least the rank of superintendent authorises it.

(7)   An officer may give an authorisation under subsection (6) above orally or in writing but, if he gives it orally, he shall confirm it in writing as soon as is practicable.

(8)   An officer may only authorise delay where he has reasonable grounds for believing that the exercise of the right conferred by subsection (1) above at the time when the person detained desires to exercise it—
    (a)   will lead to interference with or harm to evidence connected with a serious arrestable offence or interference with or physical injury to other persons; or

    (b)   will lead to the alerting of other persons suspected of having committed such an offence but not yet arrested for it; or

    (c)   will hinder the recovery of any property obtained as a result of such an offence.

(9)   If delay is authorised—

    (a)   the detained person shall be told the reason for it; and

    (b)   the reason shall be noted on his custody record.

(10)   The duties imposed by subsection (9) above shall be performed as soon as is practicable.

(11)   There may be no further delay in permitting the exercise of the right conferred by subsection (1) above once the reason for authorising delay ceases to subsist.

(12)   The reference in subsection (1) above to a person arrested includes a reference to a person who has been detained under the terrorism provisions.

(13)   In the application of this section to a person who has been arrested or detained under the terrorism provisions—

    (a)   subsection (5) above shall have effect as if for the words from 'within' onwards there were substituted the words 'before the end of the period beyond which he may no longer be detained without the authority of the Secretary of State';

    (b)   subsection (6)(a) above shall have effect as if for the words 'for a serious arrestable offence' there were substituted the words 'under the terrorism provisions'; and

    (c)   subsection (8) above shall have effect as if at the end there were added 'or

    (d)   will lead to interference with the gathering of information about the commission, preparation or instigation of acts of terrorism; or

    (e)   by alerting any person, will make it more difficult—

        (i)   to prevent an act of terrorism; or

        (ii)   to secure the apprehension, prosecution or conviction of any person in connection with the commission, preparation or instigation of an act of terrorism.'

(14)   If an officer of appropriate rank has reasonable grounds for believing that, unless he gives a direction under subsection (15) below, the exercise by a person arrested or detained under the terrorism provisions of the right conferred by subsection (1) above will have any of the consequences specified in subsection (8) above (as it has effect by virtue of subsection (13) above), he may give a direction under that subsection.

(15)   A direction under this subsection is a direction that a person desiring to exercise the right conferred by subsection (1) above may only consult a solicitor in the sight and hearing of a qualified officer of the uniformed branch of the force of which the officer giving the direction is a member.

(16)   An officer is qualified for the purpose of subsection (15) above if—

    (a)   he is of at least the rank of inspector; and

    (b)   in the opinion of the officer giving the direction he has no connection with the case.

(17)   An officer is of appropriate rank to give a direction under subsection (15) above if he is of at least the rank of Commander or Assistant Chief Constable.

(18)   A direction under subsection (15) above shall cease to have effect once the reason for giving it ceases to subsist.

(a)   Breach of s. 58 — confession should have been excluded under s. 78, see:

R v *Samuel* [1988] QB 615.

R v *Parris* (1989) 89 Cr App R 68.

(b)   Breach of s. 58 — confession not excluded under s. 78, decision upheld, see:

R v *Alladice* (1988) 87 Cr App R 380.

R v *Dunford* (1990) 91 Cr App R 150.

(c)   Miscellaneous points about s. 58, see:

R v *Beycan* [1990] Crim LR 185.

R v *Chief Constable of Avon & Somerset, ex parte Robinson* [1989] 2 All ER 15.

R v *Dunn* [1990] NLJ 592.

10.2   Illegally or Improperly Obtained Evidence other than Confessions

Again see PCEA 1984, ss. 78 and 82(3) in **10.1.2**.

In *R* v *Sang* [1980] AC 402 the House of Lords seemed to suggest that *at common law* a court did not have a discretion to exclude illegally or improperly obtained evidence (*other than confessions and evidence analogous to confessions*) unless its probative value was outweighed by its prejudicial effect. For examples of evidence analogous to a confession see *R* v *Payne* [1963] 1 WLR 637 and *R* v *Apicella* (1986) 82 Cr App R 295.

The effect of *R* v *Sang* is therefore that PCEA 1984, s. 82(3) (which preserves the common law position), would have no effect on, for example, an illegal search which produces relevant evidence.

However, s. 78, which applies to *all* prosecution evidence, makes specific reference to 'the circumstances in which the evidence was obtained'. It now seems clear that, under s. 78, evidence other than confessions may be excluded at the court's discretion by reason of the fact that it has been obtained illegally or improperly. In *R* v *Quinn* [1990] Crim LR 581, Lord Lane stated 'Proceedings may become unfair . . . where there has been an abuse of process, for example, because evidence has been obtained in deliberate breach of procedures laid down in an official code of practice'. See also:

Matto v *DPP* [1987] Crim LR 641.

However, evidence obtained by police 'undercover operations' is generally admitted, see:

DPP v *Marshall* [1988] 3 All ER 683.

R v *Edwards* [1991] Crim LR 45.

R v *Christou* [1992] NLJ 823.

Williams v *DPP* (1983) *The Times*, 9 March 1993.

Obviously if the illegality or impropriety affects the probative value/prejudicial effect of the evidence it may be excluded under s. 78 or s. 82(3). See the cases relating to the admissibility of identification evidence and the Code of Practice on Identification in **Chapter 12** of this Manual and **Appendix 3**.

Questions

OBJECTIVES

This chapter is designed to ensure that you can:

(a)   demonstrate a sound understanding of the principles governing the admissibility of confessions (with particular reference to Police and Criminal Evidence Act 1984, ss. 76 and 78);

(b)   apply the principles to specific factual situations;

(c)   describe the procedural requirements when the admissibility of a confession is challenged;

(d)   demonstrate a sound understanding of the basis upon which a judge might exclude evidence *other than* confessions on the ground that it is illegally or improperly obtained (including any procedural requirements); and

(e)   raise and/or counter an objection to the admissibility of confessions and illegally or improperly obtained evidence.

RESEARCH

(a)   Read the materials contained in **Chapter 10** of this Manual (and see **Chapter 9** in relation to informal admissions).

(b)   Read:

Keane, *The Modern Law of Evidence* (2nd ed., 1989), ch. 12, pt. B, OR

Murphy, *A Practical Approach to Evidence* (4th ed., 1992), ch. 7, pt. B; AND

Carter, *Cases and Statutes on Evidence* (2nd ed., 1990), ch. 17 and Supplement (1992), OR

Heydon, *Evidence Cases and Materials* (3rd ed., 1991).

See also articles in [1988] Crim LR 722, [1989] Crim LR 95 and [1990] Crim LR 452.

(c)   On the basis of this research answer the following questions.

Question 1
After being arrested and detained for questioning in respect of the theft of a painting, Nick made a confession in which he informed the police that the painting was hidden in the gardening shed at his allotment. The police found the painting hidden there. Nick's confession was obtained by oppression and counsel for Nick takes objection to its admissibility. Subject to any discretion the judge may have to exclude it, which of the following items of evidence is admissible:

[A]   The whole of the confession (because the successful search for the painting confirms its reliability).

[B]   Evidence that the painting was recovered as a result of something said by Nick.

[C]   Evidence that the painting was found in the gardening shed at Nick's allotment.

[D]   Evidence that the painting has been recovered but not where it was found.

Question 2
Adam is suspected of committing arson. He is arrested and detained for questioning. During ths period there are several breaches of The Code of Practice — namely, failure to give adequate breaks for refreshment, failure to take a note of the interview and an unjustified refusal of access to legal advice. Adam eventually makes a full confession. At his trial his counsel represents to the court that the confession should be excluded. The judge rules that although there were breaches of the Code they did not amount to oppression nor were they likely to render any confession made by Adam unreliable. He nevertheless decides to exclude the confession. On what legal basis could this have been?

[A]   Under PCEA 1984, s. 76(2)(a).

[B]   Because it is hearsay.

[C]   Under PCEA 1984, s. 76(2)(b).

[D]   Under PCEA 1984, s. 78.

Question 3

You are defending Ambrose (who has several previous convictions for theft) on a charge of burglary, to which he has pleaded not guilty. He tells you that after he was arrested and detained for questioning he asked on several occasions to speak to his solicitor, but this was refused. After eight hours in custody, during which he was interviewed several times, he is alleged to have made two separate statements admitting his guilt, which were recorded in the interviewing officer's notebook. He was then charged and allowed to see his solicitor. Ambrose tells you that he made one of the statements after a police inspector told him that one of his alleged associates had made a statement incriminating him. In fact the associate made no such statement. Ambrose denies making the other alleged statement. The prosecution intends to tender both statements in evidence.

Advise Ambrose as to (a) the law, and (b) the procedure for determining the admissibility of the two statements at the trial.

Question 4

Smith and Jones are indicted for robbery and attempted murder. The case arises from an armed robbery during which a security guard was shot and seriously wounded. Both men are denying the offences and have put forward alibis. Assuming that they are tried jointly consider the admissibility of the evidence obtained in the following circumstances.

(a) Smith made a taped confession after he was subjected to a series of violent assaults by a police officer (who has since been disciplined and has left the force). As a result of detailed information given in the confession the police went to a derelict farmhouse where they found a suitcase containing most of the money stolen in the robbery and a sawn-off shotgun which was used in the robbery. Smith's fingerprints are discovered both on the suitcase and on the sawn-off shotgun.

(b) Jones made a taped confession shortly after a police officer had informed him that Smith had been having an affair with his (Jones's) wife. Although he asserted that he had accompanied Smith on the robbery he claimed that he had only done so because he was frightened of Smith and that he had not been involved in the planning of the robbery nor in the shooting. Shortly before this confession was made the police had conducted an illegal search of Jones's country mansion and had discovered there several shotguns which were of a similar type to that used in the robbery and maps and plans in Jones's handwriting of the area where the robbery occurred.

Question 5

Steve and Dave were arrested on suspicion of committing a burglary in which £10,000 of used notes was stolen. They were taken to the local police station where they were interviewed separately.

Steve claims that he asked to see his solicitor but that his request was refused on the ground that waiting for his solicitor would cause unreasonable delay to the investigation. He further claims that it was only when the police told him that Dave had confessed (and had implicated Steve) that he decided to confess. Steve then made a taped statement in which he admitted his part in the burglary but claimed that it had been master-minded by Dave. In fact Dave had not made any confession and he maintained his silence throughout his interrogation. However, whilst Dave was in custody, the police searched his house (without a warrant and despite his wife's protestations) and discovered hidden there £5,000 in used notes. Both men now stand jointly charged with burglary. During the trial a *voir dire* is held to determine the admissibility of Steve's confession and the search of Dave's house.

(a) On the assumption that the trial judge accepts in substance Steve's account of what took place during his interrogation, prepare an argument to support the exclusion of his confession:

(i) under PCEA 1984, s. 76(2), and
(ii) under PCEA 1984, s. 78.

(b) On the assumption that the trial judge rejects Steve's account of his interrogation prepare an argument on Dave's behalf to support the editing of Steve's confession to exclude any reference to Dave.

(c)   Prepare an argument to support the exclusion of the evidence of the discovery of the £5,000 at Dave's house.

[A suggested answer outline to Question 3 can be found in **Appendix 1** to this Manual.]

11 Opinion Evidence and Judgments as Evidence of the Facts on Which They are Based

When may a party call a witness to give evidence of opinion (as opposed to evidence of fact)?

May a party adduce evidence of an earlier judgment or verdict to prove the facts on which that judgment or verdict was based (assuming such facts are relevant to the instant proceedings)?

11.1 Opinion Evidence

11.1.1 THE GENERAL RULE

Both in civil and criminal cases the opinions of witnesses are not, in general, admissible. Witnesses should normally be confined to stating the facts. The basic rationale of this exclusionary rule is that it is the task of the *court* (tribunals of fact and law) to form any opinions which need to be formed in any particular case (obviously the court must form some opinions in *every* case). There is a risk either that the court might be unduly influenced by the opinion of a person who will not necessarily share the court's impartiality, or that the court will be unaware of the factual basis (or lack of it) on which the opinion is founded. Alternatively, it may be thought that, when the court is perfectly capable of forming an opinion on the matter in issue, allowing a witness to state his opinion would waste the court's time.

The following list of cases, in which opinion evidence has been excluded, is merely intended to give a general impression of the impact of the rule.

R v *Chard* (1971) 56 Cr App R 268;

R v *Turner* [1975] QB 834, CA;

R v *Camplin* [1978] AC 705;

R v *Roberts* [1990] Crim LR 122

(murder cases — provocation defence — expert witness not allowed to state opinion that in the light of the accused's personality he lacked the intent to commit murder);

R v *Stamford* [1972] 2 QB 391;

R v *Anderson* [1972] 1 QB 304

(obscenity cases — expert witness not allowed to state opinion as to whether a particular article/publication had a tendency to deprave or corrupt);

143

R v *MacKenney* (1983) 76 Cr App R 271;

R v *Turner* [1975] QB 834, CA

(murder cases — expert witness not allowed to state opinion as to whether another witness was telling the truth);

R v *Wood* [1990] Crim LR 264
(murder case — defence of unsuccessful suicide pact — likelihood of D's participation, psychiatric evidence inadmissible);

R v *Weightman* [1991] Crim LR 204
(murder case — D not suffering from mental illness — psychiatric evidence describing personality disorder inadmissible);

Haynes v *Doman* [1899] 2 Ch 13
(reasonableness of restraint of trade — affidavits from traders expressing opinions on the reasonableness of the clause in question inadmissible);

Rabin v *Gerson Berger Association Ltd* [1986] 1 WLR 526
(effect of trust deed — opinion evidence of barrister who had drafted the deed inadmissible);

North Cheshire & Manchester Brewery Co. Ltd v *Manchester Brewery Co. Ltd* [1899] AC 83
(passing-off action — witness not allowed to state opinion as to whether defendant company intended to pass itself off as plaintiff company).

Any textual description of the rule against opinion evidence, even if it is supported with examples, fails to give a true impression of the impact of the rule upon the day to day practice of an advocate. There are many occasions on which an objection to a particular question is made (and sustained) on the basis that the witness is being invited to state his opinion — despite there being no express reference to the rule against opinion evidence. Sometimes the objection is based on the ground that the question itself is really nothing more than comment on the witness's evidence.

The general rule excluding opinion evidence is subject to two important exceptions. These arise in cases where the court lacks the witness's competence to form an opinion on a particular issue whether through lack of the necessary direct knowledge or through lack of the necessary expertise.

11.1.2 EYE-WITNESS OPINIONS OR OPINIONS AS SHORTHAND FOR FACTS

Statements of opinion by an eye-witness (E) to the facts in issue are often in essence a convenient way of stating several facts. Thus an assertion by E that the defendant was drunk is a convenient way of stating the various facts which E saw (heard or smelt) which led him to form that opinion. See *R* v *Davies* [1962] 1 WLR 1111. Such a statement will generally be admissible as long as a proper appraisal of the facts does not call for any special expertise (see below).

In a case concerning a road accident it will often be necessary to consider the speed at which the vehicles involved were travelling — again E will be allowed to state his opinion on this issue.

A very important issue in many cases is the *identification* of persons, animals, places or things. Statements of identification might seem to be factual but they are, technically speaking, statements of opinion. Clearly it is often necessary for the courts to have regard to such statements and they would generally be admissible under this exception. See *Fryer* v *Gathercole* (1849) 4 Exch 262 (but special rules apply to the identification of an accused — see **Chapter 12** of this Manual). If it is necessary to identify handwriting (as it often is — especially in relation to signatures) it may be possible to call the alleged writer or a person who saw the alleged writer doing the writing or a person who is well acquainted with the writing in question. However, if it is not possible to prove the document in this way and comparison between different samples of handwriting is necessary, the court should seek assistance from a handwriting expert (see below).

In civil cases this exception has been put into statutory form — Civil Evidence Act 1972, s. 3(2):

It is hereby declared that where a person is called as a witness in any civil proceedings, a statement of opinion by him on any relevant matter on which he is not qualified to give expert evidence, if made as a way of conveying relevant facts personally perceived by him, is admissible evidence of what he perceived.

11.1.3   EXPERT OPINIONS

11.1.3.1   General points

There are many situations in which the issues the court is required to determine are so far removed from the court's experience that it needs to obtain the opinions of experts to help it determine the issue in question. See generally *Folkes* v *Chadd* (1782) 3 Doug KB 157. When such need arises the opinion of an expert *is* admissible. (If an issue does call for expert evidence, the evidence of a non-expert should not be admitted; see *R* v *Inch* (1989) *The Times*, 28 November 1989.) It is not possible to list all the matters in respect of which expert evidence is required; some matters (e.g. medical and scientific) obviously call for the opinions of experts. However, the line between matters which do call for expert evidence and matters which do not is often extremely fine (especially in relation to psychiatric evidence) and the courts consider the question most carefully. In *R* v *Turner* [1975] QB 834, CA at p. 841 Lawton LJ put the point very effectively in this way:

The fact that an expert witness has impressive scientific qualifications does not by that fact alone make his opinion on matters of human nature and behaviour *within the limits of normality* any more helpful than that of the jurors themselves; but there is a danger that they may think it does. [Emphasis supplied.]

But this sometimes begs the question, What is normality? In *R* v *Masih* [1986] Crim LR 395 the Court of Appeal kept faith with Lawton LJ in deciding that psychiatric evidence in respect of an accused who had an intelligence quotient of 72 (2 points *above* the subnormal level) was inadmissible — see further M. Beaumont, 'Psychiatric evidence: over-rationalising the abnormal' [1988] Crim LR 290.

The following list is intended to give a general guide to the sort of questions which have been held to call for expert evidence (and should be compared with the list of cases *excluding* opinion given in **11.1.1**).

R v *Holmes* [1953] 1 WLR 686
(whether an accused (A) is suffering from a disease of the mind within the M'Naghten rules).

R v *Bailey* (1977) 66 Cr App R 31
(whether A is suffering from diminished responsibility — but note the distinction drawn between diminished responsibility and other forms of incapacity e.g. drunkenness in *R* v *Tandy* [1989] 1 Al ER 267).

R v *Smith* [1979] 1 WLR 1445
(whether A, who had put forward a defence of non-insane automatism, was sleep-walking).

Toohey v *Metropolitan Police Commissioner* [1965] AC 595, HL; cf. *R* v *MacKenney* (1983) 76 Cr App R 271
(whether a witness is suffering from a mental disability such as to render him incapable of giving reliable evidence — but expert evidence will not be admitted on the question whether a witness who has a normal capacity for reliability is actually giving reliable evidence — this is always a matter for the tribunal of fact; see *R* v *MacKenney*).

R v *Tilley* [1961] 1 WLR 1309
(whether two samples of handwriting were written by the same person).

Pugsley v *Hunter* [1973] 1 WLR 578
(as to the effect on the level of blood alcohol of 'spiked' drinks).

Lowery v *R* [1974] AC 85 but cf. *R* v *Turner* [1975] QB 834, CA
(as to the relative likelihood of one accused having committed a sadistic murder rather than another).

DPP v *A & BC Chewing Gum Ltd* [1968] 1 QB 159 but cf. *R* v *Stamford* [1972] 2 QB 391 and *R* v *Anderson* [1972] 1 QB 304
(as to the psychological effect on children of cards depicting, in graphic detail, the horrors of war and, thus, whether the cards had a tendency to deprave or corrupt).

R v *Skirving* [1985] QB 819
(as to the various ways of using cocaine and the effects thereof and, thus, whether an article describing these matters had a tendency to deprave or corrupt).

R v *Oakley* (1979) 70 Cr App R 7
(as to the probable circumstances and causes of a fatal accident).

R v *Toner* (1991) 93 Cr App R 382
(as to the possible effects of a medical condition on a person's mental processes and ability to form an intent).

R v *Silcott, Braithwaite and Raghip* (1991), *The Times*, 9 December 1991
(as to the reliability of a confession made by a person who was abnormally susceptible to suggestion).

R v *Stockwell* (1993) *The Times*, 11 March 1993
(as to whether the face on a video taken by a security camera was that of the accused (evidence of facial mapping expert)).

This list has been drawn exclusively from criminal cases but this does not mean that expert evidence is less common in civil cases, indeed, in general, it is probably encountered more frequently in civil cases.

11.1.3.2 The ultimate issue rule

The rule that an expert should not be asked to state his opinon on the ultimate issue in a case has been noticed more in its breach than in its observance even in criminal cases see *R* v *Holmes* (1953) 1 WLR 686. It has ben abolished in civil cases by Civil Evidence Act 1972, s. 3(1):

> *Subject to any rules of court made in pursuance of Part 1 of the Civil Evidence Act 1968 or this Act, where a person is called as a witness in any civil proceedings, his opinion on any relevant matter on which he is qualified to give expert evidence shall be admissible in evidence.*

11.1.3.3 Who is an expert?

Where a matter does call for expert evidence only a suitably qualified expert can give it. Indeed the starting-point in examining in chief an expert witness is to establish his or her expertise. But this does not necessarily mean that there must be formal qualifications — see e.g. *R* v *Silverlock* [1894] 2 QB 766 — solicitor who had for many years studied handwriting as a hobby (handwriting expert); *Ajami* v *Comptroller of Customs* [1954] 1 WLR 1405 — banker with 24 years experience of Nigerian banking law (foreign law expert). (Matters of *foreign* law are generally treated as calling for expert evidence: obviously matters of English law are for the judge to determine.) However, it will not be easy to satisfy a judge that a witness is an expert in a field if he lacks formal qualifications.

11.1.3.4 The 'status' of expert evidence

As Diplock LJ said in *R* v *Lanfear* [1968] 2 QB 77:

> Expert evidence should be treated like the evidence of any other witness and it will be a misdirection to the jury that they must accept it.

However, in *R* v *Anderson* [1972] 1 QB 304 it was held that it would equally be a misdirection to tell a jury that it could disregard expert evidence which had been given by only one witnes and which, if accepted, dictated one answer. See also, to the same effect, *R* v *Bailey* (1977) 66 Cr App R 31.

11.1.3.5 Nature and content of expert evidence

An expert opinion will be based upon much more than the facts of the particular case he is considering. It will be based on the expert's experience and any information that he has obtained from extraneous sources such as textbooks, articles and journals. Such information (often referred to as secondary facts) is not treated as hearsay but simply as part of the basis for the expert opinion. Obviously the facts of the particular case on which the opinion is given (the primary facts) should be proved by admissible evidence (whether or not by the expert). See generally *English Exporters (London) Ltd* v *Eldonwall Ltd* [1973] Ch 415 and *H* v *Schering Chemicals Ltd* [1983] 1 WLR 143 cf. *R* v *Bradshaw* (1986) Cr App R 79 — 'as a concession to the defence' a psychiatrist was allowed to base his opinion on the accused's mental state upon statements made out of court by the accused (i.e. hearsay).

A good example of the difference between primary and secondary facts is *R* v *Abadom* (1983) 76 Cr App R 48. A was charged with robbery. A forensic expert gave opinion evidence that glass found on A's shoes came from a window which had been broken during the robbery. Samples of glass from both locations had the same refractive index. The expert stated that according to statistics produced by the Home Office Research Establishment the chances of the glass being from two distinct sources were minimal. A was convicted and appealed on the grounds that the HORE statistics were hearsay. The Court of Appeal held that the statistics were secondary facts supporting the expert's opinion. So long as the primary facts (i.e. that the glass compared was (a) the glass on A's shoes and (b) the glass from the robbery scene) were proved by admissible evidence the expert could (indeed should) state why he arrived at his opinion on those facts.

Secondary facts are essentially parasitic in that they cannot be stated in the absence of an expert's opinion. Thus in *Dawson* v *Lunn* [1986] RTR 234 the Divisional Court held that a defendant on a drink-driving charge could not make reference to a medical journal to support his defence. The defendant was not a medical expert.

11.1.3.6 Advance notice of expert evidence in civil cases

Civil Evidence Act 1972, s. 2(3), made provision for rules of court to be made in relation to advance notice of expert evidence in civil cases. By virtue of RSC Ord. 38, r. 36 (see also CCR Ord. 20, r. 27), a party seeking to adduce such evidence without the leave of the court or without agreement must apply to the court for directions to determine whether he will be required to disclose the substance of the expert's evidence (give advance notice) to the other parties. This application will generally result in a direction to give advance notice in the form of a report. In personal injury actions there is an automatic direction to give advance notice under RSC Ord. 25, r. 8. (For further details on this see the **Civil Litigation Manual**.)

A party should be sure that he wishes to use the expert's opinion as part of his case *before* seeking directions because RSC Ord. 38, r. 42, provides that any party to whom such a report is disclosed can put it in evidence. In general an expert's report which is commissioned by a party for the purposes of pending or contemplated litigation would be protected from disclosure (at any stage of the proceedings) by legal professional privilege (se **Chapter 13** of this Manual) but r. 42 makes it clear that the privilege cannot be relied on once the report has been disclosed under the advance notice procedure. Even where a party does rely on privilege in respect of an expert's report it should be remembered that there is no property in a witness. This means that although a party who chooses not to use an expert's evidence is not bound by the advance notice procedures (and can claim privilege in respect of any report prepared, for that party, by the expert) he cannot muzzle the expert and other parties are entitled to subpoena the expert — see *Harmony Shipping Co. SA* v *Saudi Europe Line Ltd* [1979] 1 WLR 1380, CA.

11.1.3.7 Advance notice of expert evidence in criminal cases

The prosecution is obliged to disclose expert evidence to the defence on general principles (see the **Criminal Litigation and Sentencing Manual**). However, there used to be no obligation on the defence to disclose expert evidence even in cases where the defence carried a legal burden of proving a matter calling for expert evidence, e.g. insanity or diminished responsibility. This has been changed, as regards Crown Court cases, by the Crown Court (Advance Notice of Expert Evidence) Rules 1987 (SI 1987 No. 716) made pursuant to PCEA 1984, s. 81, which require any party proposing to adduce expert evidence to furnish the other parties with a statement in writing of the expert finding or opinion. Such party then, *on request* in writing by any other party, must provide a copy of the record of any observation, test or calculation on which the finding or opinion is based.

If the rules are not complied with the expert evidence can only be admitted with the leave of the court but a party may elect not to comply with the rules if that party has reasonable grounds for believing that compliance might lead to intimidation or attempted intimidation of an expert witness or to interference with the course of justice (but such party must give notice of the grounds for non-compliance to the other parties).

For recent cases on the extent of the prosecution's duty of disclosure, see *R* v *Maguire* [1992] 2 All ER 433 and *R* v *Ward* [1992] NLJ 859.

11.1.4 OPINION EVIDENCE AND THE HEARSAY RULE

11.1.4.1 In civil cases

Civil Evidence Act 1972, s. 1(1):

> *Subject to the provisions of this section, Part I (hearsay evidence) of the Civil Evidence Act 1968, except section 5 (statements produced by computers), shall apply in relation to statements of opinion as it applies in relation to statements of fact, subject to the necessary modifications and in particular the modification that any reference to a fact stated in a statement shall be construed as a reference to a matter dealt with therein.*

This provision makes it clear that, in general, a hearsay (out-of-court) statement of opinion is admissible to the same extent as a hearsay statement of fact is admissible under the provisions of Civil Evidence Act 1968 (except s. 5).

Of course s. 1(1) cannot make a statement of opinion admissible if the opinion *itself* would not have been admissible under the principles considered earlier in this chapter.

The notice procedures applicable to Civil Evidence Act 1968, ss. 2 and 4, apply with equal force to hearsay statements of opinion which are essentially a shorthand for facts directly perceived (see **11.1.2** above).

Regarding expert opinions, it has been stated already that these are subject to a separate regime of 'advance notice' procedures. It is therefore generally inappropriate to subject such opinions to the Civil Evidence Act 1968 notice procedures and this is confirmed by Civil Evidence Act 1972, s. 2(2). (However, where it is claimed that the expert in question cannot or should not be called as a witness the court may direct that the Civil Evidence Act 1968 notice procedures shall apply (with such modifications as the court thinks fit) (see RSC Ord. 38, r. 41)). Civil Evidence Act 1972, s. 1(2), makes it clear that where Civil Evidence Act 1968, s. 4, is relied on to admit expert opinion there is no requirement of personal knowledge of the facts on which the opinion is based (as already noted such a requirement is inappropriate in the case of expert opinion evidence).

The net effect is that most experts' reports (disclosed under the advance notice procedures) would be admissible *in court* due to the combined effects of Civil Evidence Act 1968, s. 2 or s. 4, and Civil Evidence Act 1972, s. 1(1). Where a party intends to prove the expert's report *and* to call him as a witness (as is often the case) there is no special requirement for leave and the report can be put in at the commencement of the expert's evidence-in-chief (see RSC Ord. 38, r. 43: cf. Civil Evidence Act 1968, s. 2(2) and s. 4(2)).

11.1.4.2   In criminal cases
By Criminal Justice Act 1988, s. 30:

> *(1)   An expert report shall be admissible as evidence in criminal proceedings, whether or not the person making it attends to give oral evidence in those proceedings.*
>
> *(2)   If it is proposed that the person making the report shall not give oral evidence, the report shall only be admissible with the leave of the court.*
>
> *(3)   For the purpose of determining whether to give leave the court shall have regard—*
>
> *(a)   to the contents of the report;*
> *(b)   to the reasons why it is proposed that the person making the report shall not give oral evidence;*
> *(c)   to any risk, having regard in particular to whether it is likely to be possible to controvert statements in the report if the person making it does not attend to give oral evidence in the proceedings, that its admission or exclusion will result in unfairness to the accused or, if there is more than one, to any of them; and*
> *(d)   to any other circumstances that appear to the court to be relevant.*
>
> *(4)   An expert report, when admitted, shall be evidence of any fact or opinion of which the person making it could have given oral evidence.*
>
> *In this section 'expert report' means a written report by a person dealing wholly or mainly with matters on which he is (or would if living be) qualified to give expert evidence.*

The effect of this section (which applies to statements of fact *and* opinion) is clear. It creates a hearsay exception specifically directed at expert reports. However, it represents a significant change in the law and it remains to be seen how strictly the courts apply it, particularly where the expert is not available as a witness (and the court's leave to admit the report is required). There is no specific provision applicable in criminal cases to out-of-court statements of opinion which are essentially a shorthand for facts. However, insofar as such statements would be admissible if made in court by a witness, it is at least arguable that they *may* be admissible if made or contained in a document falling within Criminal Justice Act 1988, ss. 23 and 24.

11.2   Judgments as Evidence of the Facts on Which They are Based

It is appropriate to deal with this topic in the same section as Opinion Evidence because judgments (i.e. findings on matters of fact, e.g. a guilty verdict) are themselves statements of opinion. The general rule (known as the rule in *Hollington* v *Hewthorn*) has been to regard them as inadmissible. Thus in a civil suit alleging negligent driving it was not possible to prove the defendant's conviction for driving without due care and attention to prove the facts on which the conviction was based — see *Hollington* v *F. Hewthorn & Co. Ltd* [1943] KB 587. The inconvenience of this general rule was obvious. (It often led to lengthy proceedings in the civil courts being used as a means of re-opening issues which had already been the subject of lengthy criminal proceedings see *Hinds* v *Sparks* [1964] Crim LR 717) and there are now several major exceptions to it both in civil and criminal proceedings.

[A final judgment may have the effect of barring any parties to that judgment from relitigating any issues *between them* which were determined in that judgment. Where this principle (often referred to under the heading '*res judicata*') applies, the judgment is not used as *evidence* in the subsequent proceedings it simply operates to bar the subsequent proceedings (or the reopening of an issue decided in the earlier proceedings). Moreover the principle only affects the *same* parties; accordingly it would not generally transcend the division between criminal and civil proceedings. ('Res judicata' is not dealt with in this Manual; you should consult the sections of the recommended textbooks concerned with cause of action estoppel or issue estoppel in civil cases and autrefois convict or autrefois acquit in criminal cases.)]

11.2.1 EXCEPTIONS TO THE RULE IN *HOLLINGTON* v *HEWTHORN* IN CIVIL CASES

11.2.1.1 Civil Evidence Act 1968, section 11

(1)   In any civil proceedings the fact that a person has been convicted of an offence by or before any court in the United Kingdom or by a court-martial there or elsewhere shall (subject to subsection (3) below) be admissible in evidence for the purpose of proving, where to do so is relevant to any issue in those proceedings, that he committed that offence, whether he was so convicted upon a plea of guilty or otherwise and whether or not he is a party to the civil proceedings; but no conviction other than a subsisting one shall be admissible in evidence by virtue of this section.

(2)   In any civil proceedings in which by virtue of this section a person is proved to have been convicted of an offence by or before any court in the United Kingdom or by a court-martial there or elsewhere—

(a)   he shall be taken to have committed that offence unless the contrary is proved; and
(b)   without prejudice to the reception of any other admissible evidence for the purpose of identifying the facts on which the conviction was based, the contents of any document which is admissible as evidence of the conviction, and the contents of the information, complaint, indictment or charge-sheet on which the person in question was convicted, shall be admissible in evidence for that purpose.

(3)   Nothing in this section shall prejudice the operation of section 13 of this Act or any other enactment whereby a conviction or a finding of fact in any criminal proceedings is for the purposes of any other proceedings made conclusive evidence of any fact.

(4)   Where in any civil proceedings the contents of any document are admissible in evidence by virtue of subsection (2) above, a copy of that document, or of the material part thereof, purporting to be certified or otherwise authenticated by or on behalf of the court or authority having custody of that document shall be admissible in evidence and shall be taken to be a true copy of that document or part unless the contrary is shown.

Civil Evidence Act 1968, s. 11, reverses the actual decision in *Hollington* v *F. Hewthorn & Co. Ltd* [1943] KB 587 (i.e. the conviction for driving without due care would now be admissible in the civil case to prove negligence) and, of course, creates a major exception to the general rule. However, although it puts the legal burden of proof on the party who denies that the person convicted of the offence in question committed it, s. 11 does *not* create a *conclusive presumption* (i.e., the presumption is rebuttable). Although the basic effect of s. 11 is relatively clear there has been some dispute (largely theoretical and, as yet, unresolved) about the way in which the party upon whom the burden of proof falls might properly set about discharging it (see *Stupple* v *Royal Insurance Co. Ltd* [1971] 1 QB 50, *Taylor* v *Taylor* [1970] 1 WLR 1148 and *Wauchope* v *Mordechai* [1970] 1 WLR 317).

In practice s. 11 has made it extremely difficult for a party to challenge successfully the conclusion that the person convicted did in fact commit the offence in question. Section 11 only applies to subsisting convictions. When a conviction (which is to be proved under s. 11) is being appealed the civil proceedings should be adjourned until the appeal has been heard — see *Re Raphael* [1973] 1 WLR

998. A party seeking to rely on s. 11 should state this in the appropriate pleadings including details of the conviction and the issue to which it is relevant (see RSC Ord. 18, r. 7A). Section 11(4) allows a certified copy of the conviction, indictment etc. to be used to prove the facts on which the conviction was based.

11.2.1.2   Civil Evidence Act 1968, section 13

Section 11, would not prevent a party from seeking to use libel proceedings to reopen a criminal case which resulted in his conviction (because it only creates a rebuttable presumption). This specific difficulty is confronted by s. 13 of the Act:

(1)   In an action for libel or slander in which the question whether a person did or did not commit a criminal offence is relevant to an issue arising in the action, proof that, at the time when that issue falls to be determined, that person stands convicted of that offence shall be conclusive evidence that he committed that offence; and his conviction thereof shall be admissible in evidence accordingly.

(2)   In any such action as aforesaid in which by virtue of this section a person is proved to have been convicted of an offence the contents of any document which is admissible as evidence of the conviction, and the contents of the information, complaint, indictment or charge-sheet on which that person was convicted, shall, without prejudice to the reception of any other admissible evidence for the purpose of identifying the facts on which the conviction was based, be admissible in evidence for the purpose of identifying those facts.

(3)   For the purposes of this section a person shall be taken to stand convicted of an offence if but only if there subsists against him a conviction of that offence by or before a court in the United Kingdom or by a court-martial there or elsewhere.

The effect of s. 13 is such that an action in defamation based on the defendant's assertion that the plaintiff committed an offence for which he has been convicted would be struck out, i.e. in defamation cases a person convicted of an offence is *conclusively* presumed to have committed it. However, s. 13 does not give publishers *carte blanche* to make general attacks on the character of convicts (see *Levene v Roxhan* [1970] 1 WLR 1322).

Sections 11 and 13 apply only to convictions (in respect of which the standard proof is at its highest). Previous acquittals are almost certainly *not* admissible in civil proceedings to establish innocence of the offences charged. Also there is no *general* provision allowing for previous civil judgments to be used as evidence of the facts on which they were based. However, Civil Evidence Act 1968, s. 12, allows a very limited range of civil judgments to be used as evidence of the facts on which they are based.

11.2.1.3   Civil Evidence Act 1968, section 12

(1)   In any civil proceedings—

(a)   the fact that a person has been found guilty of adultery in any matrimonial proceedings;
(b)   the fact that a person has been adjudged to be the father of a child in affiliation proceedings before any court in the United Kingdom.

shall be . . . admissible in evidence for the purpose of proving, where to do so is relevant to any issue in those civil proceedings, that he committed the adultery to which the findings relates or, as the case may be, is (or was) the father of that child, whether or not he offered any defence to the allegation of adultery or paternity and whether or not he is a party to the civil proceedings; but no finding or adjudication other than a subsisting one shall be admissible in evidence by virtue of this section.

(2)   In any civil proceedings in which by virtue of this section a person is proved to have been found guilty of adultery as mentioned in subsection (1)(a) above or to have been adjudged to be the father of a child as mentioned in subsection (1)(b) above—

> *(a)* he shall be taken to have committed the adultery to which the finding relates or, as the case may be, to be (or have been) the father of that child, unless the contrary is proved; and
>
> *(b)* without prejudice to the reception of any other admissible evidence for the purpose of identifying the facts on which the finding or adjudication was based, the contents of any document which was before the court, or which contains any pronouncement of the court, in the matrimonial or affiliation proceedings in question shall be admissible in evidence for that purpose.

The effect of s. 12(2) is very similar to the effect of s. 11(2), i.e. the legal burden is put on the party denying the facts on which the finding is based but the *scope* of s. 12 is very narrow. Section 12(5) provides that the phrase 'matrimonial proceedings' (used in s. 12(1)(a)) only includes matrimonial proceedings in the High Court and county court (not the magistrates' court). Moreover affiliation proceedings were abolished by Family Law Reform Act 1987, s. 17. RSC Ord. 18, r. 7A, applies to s. 12 as it applies to s. 11.

11.2.2 EXCEPTIONS TO THE RULE IN *HOLLINGTON* v *HEWTHORN* IN CRIMINAL CASES

Until relatively recently the rule excluding judgments as evidence of the facts on which they are based was of general application in criminal cases. For example, where A was charged with handling stolen goods, it was not permissible to prove that B was convicted of the theft of the goods in question to show that the goods were stolen. The rule as regards convictions has been changed by PCEA 1984, s. 74. A distinction needs to be drawn between (a) convictions of persons other than the accused and (b) convictions of the accused.

11.2.2.1 Convictions of persons other than the accused
PCEA 1984, s. 74(1) and (2) provides:

> *(1)* In any proceedings the fact that a person other than the accused has been convicted of an offence by or before any court in the United Kingdom or by a Service court outside the United Kingdom shall be admissible in evidence for the purpose of proving, where to do so is relevant to any issue in those proceedings, that that person committed that offence, whether or not any other evidence of his having committed that offence is given.
>
> *(2)* In any proceedings in which by virtue of this section a person other than the accused is proved to have been convicted of an offence by or before any court in the United Kingdom or by a Service court outside the United Kingdom, he shall be taken to have committed that offence unless the contrary is proved.

By s. 75(1):

> Where evidence that a person has been convicted of an offence is admissible by virtue of section 74 above, then without prejudice to the reception of any other admissible evidence for the purpose of identifying the facts on which the conviction was based
>
> *(a)* the contents of any document which is admissible as evidence of the conviction; and
>
> *(b)* the contents of the . . . indictment . . . on which the person in question was convicted, shall be admissible in evidence for that purpose.

The effect of s. 74(1) and (2) is very similar to the effect of Civil Evidence Act 1968, s. 11, in civil cases, i.e. it puts the legal burden of proof on the party who denies that the person convicted committed the offence in question (of course the *standard* of proof in a criminal case will vary according to whether that party is the prosecution or the defence).

Few can have anticipated the difficulties which s. 74(1) and (2) have caused in practice. These arise in cases where it is alleged that the accused was very closely involved in the offence (of which another person has been convicted) *and* the conviction of the other person clearly *and of itself* implies that the accused is also guilty. The Court of Appeal has in such cases held that although a conviction was admissible according to the terms of s. 74(1) and (2), to admit it would nevertheless be unfair to the accused and it should be excluded under s. 78. To understand how the courts deal with this problem consider the following cases:

(a)   *R* v *O'Connor* (1986) 85 Cr App R 298, CA.

By the Police and Criminal Evidence Act 1984, s. 74(1):

> *In any proceedings the fact that a person other than the accused has been convicted of an offence by or before any court in the United Kingdom . . . shall be admissible evidence for the purpose of proving, where to do so is relevant to any issue in those proceedings, that that person committed that offence, whether or not any other evidence of his having commited that offence is given.*

The appellant was charged with conspiracy to obtain property by deception, the relevant count in the indictment by its particulars alleging that he and his co-accused B conspired together to obtain by deception insurance moneys from two insurance companies by falsely reporting and claiming that a vehicle was stolen. The appellant initially confessed to the offence but later retracted that confession. B pleaded guilty to conspiracy to defraud before the appellant's trial, and evidence of that admission was admitted under the Police and Criminal Evidence Act 1984, s. 74(1), at the trial, although the judge in effect invited the jury to disregard it. The appellant was convicted and appealed on the ground that that evidence was inadmissible: alternatively, that it should have been excluded under s. 78 of that Act as unfair to the appellant. It was submitted that (i) if s. 74 applied in the present case it enabled the prosecution to put before the jury a statement made by a co-accused in the absence of the defendant; and (ii) the evidential effect of the co-accused's plea of guilty was only that he had conspired with the appellant and not that the appellant had necessarily conspired with him.

Held, that the object of the Police and Criminal Evidence Act 1984, s. 74, was to deal with cases where it was necessary to prove the conviction of another as a condition precedent to the conviction of the defendant of the charge laid against him. In the present case the conviction of B, the co-defendant, which was proved before the court, related to the very charge which was also levelled at the appellant. As s. 75 of the Act made clear, where the conviction was admitted in evidence, it was not admitted as a mere plea of guilty, but with all the detail that was contained in the relevant count in the indictment. Once that was done it was difficult to contend realistically that the jury would not be entitled to draw the inference from that admission and those details that not only had B conspired with the appellant but also that the converse had taken place — a most unfair state of affairs. Thus, in the court's opinion s. 78 of the Act ought to have been brought into play by the trial judge, and that evidence not admitted. Thus to that extent there had been an irregularity in the course of the trial. However, the remainder of the evidence against the appellant was so overwhelming — the explanation why he made the admissions when he was withdrawing them was one which the jury would have been certain to reject — that, coupled with the fact that in his summing-up the judge effectively told the jury to disregard evidence of B's conviction, had that evidence not been admitted the result of the case would have been the same.

Accordingly, the court applied the proviso to s. 2(1) of the Criminal Appeal Act 1968, and dismissed the appeal.

(b)   *R* v *Curry* [1988] Crim LR 527, CA.

The appellant was convicted of conspiracy to obtain property by deception. She was charged with two others, one of whom, H, pleaded guilty upon arraignment. It was the prosecution case that the appellant, with H's knowledge, had used H's credit card to obtain goods and H then intended to report the card as stolen and not be held liable to pay for the goods. The other co-defendant, W, had driven the women to the shops. The judge allowed the prosecution to adduce evidence of H's conviction to establish the existence of an unlawful agreement to deceive.

Held, allowing the appeal and quashing the conviction, the conviction of H was relevant in the trial of the appellant to the issue of whether the conspiracy existed (*R* v *Robertson* [1987] QB 920 and *R* v *Lunnon* [1988] Crim LR 456, CA). The present case differed in that the adduction of the evidence clearly implied as a matter of fact that the appellant had been party to the conspiracy, even though it did not have the effect as a matter of law. The judge accepted that W could not be convicted if the appellant were acquitted. It was therefore necessary to consider whether the admission of the evidence would have such an adverse effect on the fairness of the proceedings that the court should not admit it, by virtue of s. 78 of the 1984 Act. There was only one answer — the effect was such that the jury would be bound to use it as showing not only that there had been a conspiracy but also that the appellant was party to it. The evidence should not have been admitted; it weighted the case unfairly against the appellant. (*R* v *O'Connor* (1986) 85 Cr App R 298, CA followed.) The court endorsed the observations in *R* v *Robertson* [1987] QB 920 that s. 74 should be sparingly used; particularly so in relation to joint offences such as conspiracy and affray. Where the evidence sought to be placed before the jury by virtue of s. 74 expressly or by necessary inference imported the complicity of the person on trial it should not be used.

(c)   *R* v *Lunnon* [1988] Crim LR 456, CA.

The appellant was charged, jointly with three others, with conspiracy to steal from retail outlets. One of the co-accused, Lake, pleaded guilty to that conspiracy and the prosecution applied to adduce his plea of guilty, under the Police and Criminal Evidence Act 1984, s. 74, in the trial of the others. The judge admitted evidence of the plea and the appellant was convicted. On appeal his counsel argued that it was unfair, in the exercise of the judge's discretion under s. 78 of the 1984 Act, to admit the plea because the appellant in order to be acquitted had to prove that Lake, despite his plea, was not guilty of the conspiracy.

Held, the appeal would be dismissed. The plea of guilty was clearly relevant to an issue in the proceedings (*R* v *Robertson* [1987] QB 920 followed). The judge in his summing-up separated for the jury's consideration two questions, first whether there was a conspiracy to steal and secondly who was a party to the conspiracy; and he made it clear that despite Lake's plea the jury could acquit all the others of conspiracy. The plea of guilty was adduced only for the purpose of proving the existence of the conspiracy and the judge did not suggest to the jury that any defendant had the burden of disproving membership of any conspiracy found to exist. The judge was entitled to look for the purpose for which it was sought to adduce the evidence and it was not unfair to admit it. If there had been only two defendants jointly charged with conspiracy, the situation would have been different. (*R* v *Robertson* [1987] QB 920 considered; *R* v *O'Connor* (1986) 85 Cr App R 298, CA distinguished.)

See also *R* v *Chapman* [1991] Crim LR 44, CA.

(d)   *R* v *Bennett* [1988] Crim LR 686, CA.

B was charged with theft. Her co-accused, a supermarket cashier, pleaded guilty to theft, the allegation being that she passed goods to B for less than their true price. The trial judge admitted evidence of the co-accused's plea of guilty pursuant to the Police and Criminal Evidence Act 1984, s. 74. B was convicted and appealed, contending that the judge was wrong to admit the evidence under s. 74 of the Act or, alternatively, should in the exercise of his discretion have excluded the evidence as unfair under s. 78.

Held, the appeal would be dismissed. Cases where it was sought to adduce evidence of a co-accused's plea of guilty varied from one such as *R* v *O'Connor* (1986) 85 Cr App R 298, CA, where two accused were charged with conspiracy with each other and to have admitted the plea of guilty of one accused would have made the defence of the other accused very difficult, to one such as *R* v *Robertson* [1987] QB 920, where the pleas of guilty were not directly on the count of conspiracy faced by the accused. In the present case, a decision not to have admitted evidence of the co-accused's plea, and thus the fact of a theft, would have bewildered the jury. The issue, which was whether B was a party to the theft, had been left fairly with the jury and the judge had properly exercised his discretion under s. 78, bearing in mind that the purpose of adducing the evidence was to establish that there had been a theft. (*R* v *Lunnon* [1988] Crim LR 456, CA considered.)

See also *R* v *Turner* [1991] Crim LR 57, CA.

(e)　*R* v *Kempster* (1990) 90 Cr App R 14, CA.

The appellant stood trial on four counts of burglary and one count of robbery, having been jointly charged on one or more of the counts with three other co-accused, all of whom had pleaded guilty and implicated the appellant in interviews with the police. The prosecution led evidence that the appellant had been seen in the company of the co-accused before or immediately after the offences had been committed. There was other evidence, such as cars owned by the appellant, lies which he told to the police and the descriptions given by victims of the robberies and a witness of the burglary. Those descriptions were consistent with the appearance of the appellant and his three co-accused; but not more than consistent. It was not submitted that the descriptions were in themselves sufficient to identify any of the robbers or burglars. The prosecutor sought a ruling to adduce in opening and in evidence the pleas of guilty of the co-accused. Defence counsel submitted that he would object if anything further than the pleas were tendered. The trial judge ruled that evidence of the pleas could be given; but no details. He left to the jury the possibility that the pleas of others might assist them in deciding on the guilt of the appellant. The appellant was convicted on all five counts and appealed on the grounds, *inter alia*, that the judge was wrong to admit evidence of the guilty pleas without imposing and enforcing some limit on the purpose for which those pleas could be used by the prosecution and he also failed to explain to the jury the evidential effect of those pleas.

Held, that (1) if it was intended to rely on the pleas of others as evidence of guilt of the appellant, and not merely to prevent mystification of the jury, that should have been said in express terms when the application was first made under s. 74 of the Police and Criminal Evidence Act 1984. (2) If that had been said, and if the defence had referred to s. 78 of the 1984 Act, the judge might well have excluded the evidence by virtue of that section. (3) The equivocal argument for the prosecution in answer to the defence submission at the close of the prosecution case had demanded clarification. If it had emerged that the prosecution were in fact relying on the evidence of the convictions in the process of proving the guilt of the appellant, the judge might even then have ruled that their use for that purpose should be excluded by virtue of s. 78, without ordering a re-trial. (4) In the result the jury were encouraged to rely on the evidence for that purpose, without a clear and informed decision by the judge as to any adverse effects it might have had on the fairness of the proceedings. (5) Thus, as the evidence against the appellant certainly could not have been called overwhelming without the pleas of the other co-accused, the Court considered that the case was not one for the application of the proviso to s. 2(1) of the Criminal Appeal Act 1968; therefore the appeal would be allowed and the convictions quashed.

(f)　*R* v *Mattison* [1990] Crim LR 117, CA.

M was charged in one count with gross indecency with D; in another count D was charged with gross indecency with M in a public place. D pleaded guilty but M pleaded not guilty. At M's trial the judge admitted in evidence the guilty plea of D but in summing-up directed the jury that D's plea of guilty did not mean that M was guilty; but the plea was before the jury to make the background accurate. After retiring, the jury asked in a note whether D was charged with M alone, to which the trial judge answered in the affirmative (as was the case). M was convicted and appealed, submitting that the judge was wrong in law to admit D's plea of guilty in evidence.

Held, allowing the appeal, it was obvious that D's plea of guilty was relevant in proceedings against M and therefore admissible under s. 74 of the Police and Criminal Evidence Act 1984. (*Robertson & Golder* (1987) 85 Cr Ap R 304.) However, bearing in mind M's defence, which was one of complete denial, the judge should have exercised the discretion under s. 78(1) of the Act to exclude the evidence. From their question it was clear that the jury did not treat the evidence as background only, but as going to proof of M's guilt. It was impossible to say what the verdict would have been without the evidence being admitted and the conviction must be quashed. (*O'Connor* (1987) 85 Cr App R 298, CA considered).

For more recent examples see *R* v *Warner* (1993) 96 Cr App R 324 and *R* v *Humphreys* [1993] Crim LR 288.

11.2.2.2   Convictions of the accused
PCEA 1984, s. 74(3) provides:

> *In any proceedings where evidence is admissible of the fact that the accused has committed an offence, insofar as that evidence is relevant to any matter in issue in the proceedings for a reason other than a tendency to show in the accused a disposition to commit the kind of offence with which he is charged, if the accused is proved to have been convicted of the offence—*
>
>> *(a)   by or before any court in the United Kingdom; or*
>> *(b)   by a Service court outside the United Kingdom,*
>
> *he shall be taken to have committed that offence unless the contrary is proved.*

This subsection has no effect on the general rule that the accused's previous convictions are generally inadmissible at his trial. Where, exceptionally, such convictions *are* admissible s. 74(3) will apply. The only real problem in this context is created by s. 75(1) which deals with the way in which the facts on which a conviction is based can be established (for s. 75(1), see **11.2.2.1**).

Section 75(1)(b) provides that the contents of the indictment (information, complaint or charge-sheet) on which the accused was convicted 'shall be admissible' for this purpose. However, where a conviction is admissible to challenge the accused's credibility (e.g. where he is in breach of Criminal Evidence Act 1898, s. 1(f)(ii): see **7.2.2.4**) it is not generally permissible to prove the particulars of the conviction (because these are not relevant to the issue of credibility and may be prejudicial). It is assumed that despite the wording of s. 75 this approach will still apply.

Questions

OBJECTIVES

This chapter is designed to ensure that you can:

(a)   demonstrate a sound understanding of the principles underlying the general exclusionary rule in relation to evidence of opinion and the main exceptions to that rule, i.e. (i) where an opinion is a shorthand for several factual observations and (ii) where it is necessary to seek the opinion of experts;

(b)   demonstrate a sound understanding of the special rules relating to the opinion evidence of experts — including the definition of an expert, the general form and content of expert evidence (secondary facts etc.), the status of such evidence, the requirements for advance notice (and the procedures to be complied with); and

(c)   demonstrate a sound understanding of the rule in *Hollington* v *F. Hewthorn & Co. Ltd* and the exceptions to the rule created by Civil Evidence Act 1968, ss. 11 to 13 and PCEA 1984, s. 74.

RESEARCH

(a)   Read the materials contained in **Chapter 11** of this Manual.
(b)   Read:

Keane, *The Modern Law of Evidence* (2nd ed., 1989) ch. 15 and 19, OR

Murphy, *A Practical Approach to Evidence* (4th ed., 1992) ch. 9 and 10; AND

Carter, *Cases and Statutes on Evidence* (2nd ed., 1990), ch. 18 and 19 and the Supplement 1992, OR

Heydon, *Evidence: Cases and Materials* (3rd ed., 1991).

For further reading see R. Munday, 'Excluding the expert witness' [1981] Crim LR 688 and Jackson, 'The ultimate issue rule: one rule too many' [1984] Crim LR 75.

(c) On the topic of expert witnesses you should cross-refer to the **Civil Litigation Manual**. The topics dealt with in this Chapter will *not* form the basis of any Evidence tutorials. Opnion evidence will be dealt with in a Civil Litigation tutorial. The following questions on judgments as evidence of the facts on which they are based are for self-assessment purposes only. You should attempt these in your own time and the check the answers in Appendix 1.

Question 1
Len was convicted of stealing certain items of jewellery. The jewellery was returned to the alleged owner Oswald. Len then commences a civil action for conversion against Oswald alleging that he (Len) is and always has been the owner of the jewellery. Oswald defends the action and proves Len's conviction.

Evidence of Len's conviction:

[A]   is inadmissible and should not have been proved.
[B]   is admissible but only on the issue of credibility.
[C]   is conclusive evidence tht Len stole the jewellery.
[D]   creates a rebuttable presumption that Len stole the jewellery.

Question 2
Sally pleaded guilty to conspiring with Theresa to defraud Una. Theresa pleaded not guilty. At her (Theresa's) trial the prosecution seek to prove Sally's conviction by producing a certificate of conviction and proving that Sally is the person named in that certificate but the trial judge refuses to allow this. The best explanation for this is:—

[A]   That the conviction is caught by the rule in *Hollington* v *Hewthorn*.
[B]   That the conviction is irrelevant.
[C]   That the judge exercised the discretion provided by the Police and Criminal Evidence Act 1984, s. 78.
[D]   That the conviction is inadmissible hearsay.

Question 3
Tom is charged with mudering Wilf by stabbing him. Dick is charged separately with assisting Tom by concealing his (Tom's) knife with intent to impede the arrest of a person who had committed an arrestable offence.

Assuming that Tom is convicted of murder will his conviction be admissible (to prove that Tom committed the murder) at the trial of Dick for assisting Tom by concealing his knife 'with intent to impede the arrest of a person who had committed an arrestable offence?'

Question 4
T entered hospital for what should have been a routine minor operation. He was seen by Dr J, an inexperienced and overworked houseman, who gave him an overdose of a drug which caused his death.

If in a civil action T's widow wishes to prove that Dr J has been convicted of T's manslaughter what procedural steps must be taken?

Question 5

Brian Laird and his brother Charles, together with three other named persons, have been jointly charged with conspiracy to obtain property by deception. Charles Laird will plead guilty but Brian and all the other co-accused will plead not guilty. Defence counsel are aware that at the trial, the prosecution, in reliance upon s. 74(1) and (2) of the Police and Criminal Evidence Act, 1984, will seek to admit in evidence Charles' conviction (of the offence charged).

(a)   You are counsel for Brian Laird — what action will you take before the prosecution opens its case?

Make a note of the submissions you will make to the trial judge on the question of the admissibility of this evidence.

(b)   You are counsel for the prosecution — make a note of the submissions you will make to the trial judge on the question of the admissibility of this evidence.

(Answers to these Questions can be found in **Appendix 1** to this section of the Manual.)

12 Corroboration and Identification

When should the tribunal of fact be told that it cannot act on evidence *unless* it is corroborated?

When should the tribunal of fact be *warned* of the danger of acting upon uncorroborated evidence? What is the nature of the warning to be given in such cases?

How should the judge direct the jury in a criminal trial in which the case against the accused depends wholly or mainly on the correctness of one or more identifications which the defence alleges to be mistaken?

In English law the general rule is that a court's decision (verdict) can properly be based on the evidence of *one* witness, i.e. there is usually no legal requirement as to the amount of evidence which should be called or the proper weight to attach to it.

This chapter is concerned with cases where this general rule is abandoned or qualified and there *is* a legal requirement to search for additional evidence (corroboration). In general terms such a requirement is imposed where the case depends predominantly on categories of evidence, e.g. an accomplice's evidence or identification evidence, which, though admissible, are thought to be potentially suspect for a variety of reasons. Such requirements are mainly confined to criminal cases (and the terminology used here will reflect this).

However, as will soon be apparent, generalisations in this context are dangerous. First, corroboration is sometimes required for reasons other than suspicion of a category of witness. Secondly, it is misleading to think that there is one form of requirement. Sometimes corroboration of an item of evidence is required as a matter of law before any conviction can be based on that item (such a requirement will be referred to here as a category 1 requirement). Sometimes an item of evidence calls for a mandatory warning of the dangers of convicting in the absence of corroboration but so long as the warning is properly given there can still be a conviction in the absence of corroboration (category 2). Thirdly the word 'corroboration' may be used in a technical or non-technical sense, e.g. although the evidence of a witness as to identification should generally be supported by other evidence this need not be corroboration in the technical sense. Whether corroboration is required, the nature of the requirement and whether evidence is capable in law of being corroborative are questions for the judge. The effect of a corroboration warning and the effect of corroborative evidence are matters for the jury to determine when considering their verdict.

12.1 Corroboration

12.1.1 CATEGORY 1: CORROBORATION REQUIRED AS A MATTER OF LAW

12.1.1.1 Treason
Treason Act 1795, s. 1: the oaths of two 'lawful and credible' witnesses are necessary for a conviction under the section.

12.1.1.2 Perjury

Perjury Act 1911, s. 13: a person cannot be convicted of an offence of perjury 'solely upon the evidence of one witness as to the falsity of any statement alleged to be false' (see *R* v *Threlfall* (1914) 10 Cr App R 112, *R* v *Rider* (1986) 83 Cr App R 207 and *R* v *Peach* [1990] 2 All ER 966).

12.1.1.3 Speeding

Road Traffic Regulation Act 1984, s. 89: a person cannot be convicted of speeding solely on the opinion evidence (as to the speed of the vehicle) of one witness:

Swain v *Gillet* [1974] Crim LR 433.

Burton v *Gilbert* [1984] RTR 162.

Crossland v *DPP* [1988] 3 All ER 712.

12.1.1.4 Procuration

Sexual Offences Act 1956, ss. 2 to 4, 22 and 23: a person cannot be convicted of an offence under these sections 'on the evidence of one witness only, unless the witness is corroborated in some material particular by evidence implicating the accused'. The offences are procuring a woman by threats (s. 2) or false pretences (s. 3) to have sexual intercourse with the offender; administering drugs to obtain or facilitate sexual intercourse (s. 4); causing prostitution and procuring girls under 21 (s. 23).

12.1.2 CATEGORY 2: FULL CORROBORATION WARNING REQUIRED AS A MATTER OF LAW (BUT CONVICTION STILL POSSIBLE IN THE ABSENCE OF CORROBORATION)

12.1.2.1 Accomplices giving evidence for the prosecution

The reason for the accomplice rule is 'The danger that the accomplice may be giving false evidence against the accused in order to minimise his own part in the offence or out of spite against the accused (Criminal Law Revision Committee, 11th Report, 1972, para. 183).

Davies v *DPP* [1954] AC 378 confirmed the mandatory warning requirement in the case of any witness *for the prosecution* who is:

    (a)   a participant in the offence charged whether as principal or aider and abettor;
    (b)   a handler of stolen goods (at the trial of the alleged thief of the goods in question);
    (c)   a participant in an offence which is admissible at the trial in question as an exception to the similar fact rule.

It is for the judge to decide on the basis of the available evidence whether the witness is capable of falling within this definition (and to warn the jury accordingly). Often the evidence on this issue will not be disputed but, if it is, the *jury* must decide whether the witness is *in fact* an accomplice.

For specific points on the definition of accomplice see:

R v *Vernon* [1962] Crim LR 35.

R v *Sidhu* (1976) 63 Cr App R 24. Cf. *R* v *Williams* [1992] Archbold News No. 13.

R v *Royce-Bentley* [1974] 1 WLR 535.

12.1.2.2 Complainants in sexual cases

The reason for the rule is 'the danger that the complainant may have made a false accusation owing to sexual neurosis, jealousy, fantasy, spite or a girl's (sic) refusal to admit that she consented to an act of which she is now ashamed' (Criminal Law Revision Committee, 11th Report, 1972, para. 186).

R v *Trigg* [1963] 1 WLR 305 confirmed the mandatory warning requirement in the case of complainants.

The requirement applies equally where the complainant is male — see *R* v *Burgess* (1956) 40 Cr App R 144.

The warning is no longer required where there is no dispute that the complainant has been sexually assaulted and the only 'live' issue is whether the accused has been mistakenly identified — see *R* v *Chance* [1988] 3 WLR 661. However in such cases the 'special' warning as to the dangers of identification evidence should be given (see **12.2.1**).

The courts are reluctant to extend the category of complainants by analogy — see *R* v *Simmons* [1987] Crim LR 630.

The warning is still required even though marginal reliance is placed upon the complainant's evidence — see *R* v *Birchall* (1986) 82 Cr App R 208.

12.1.2.3   Nature of the warning: the judge's role
DPP v *Kilbourne* [1973] AC 729.

Attorney-General of Hong Kong v *Wong Muk Ping* (1987) 85 Cr App R 167.

R v *Spencer* [1987] AC 128 per Lord Ackner at p. 140:

> Where there is no corroboration . . . the jury should be warned of the danger of relying upon the sole evidence of an accomplice or of the complainant in the sexual case . . . The warning to be sufficient must explain why it is dangerous so to act, since otherwise the warning will lack significance. The jury are, of course, told that while as a general rule it is dangerous so to act, they are at liberty to do so if they feel sure that the uncorroborated witness is telling the truth. Where, however, there is evidence before the jury which they can properly consider to be corroborative evidence the position becomes less simple. The trial judge has the added obligation of identifying such material, and explaining to the jury that it is for them to decide whether to treat such evidence as corroboration. He should further warn them against treating as potential corroborative evidence, that which may appear to them to be such, but which is not so in law, e.g. evidence of a recent complaint in a sexual offence.

Mere words of caution are generally insufficient — see *R* v *Stewart* (1986) 83 Cr App R 327 and *R* v *Nagy* [1990] Crim LR 187.

The general rule, where there are several accused, is that the warning should be given in respect of each accused — see *R* v *Donat* (1985) 82 Cr App R 173 and *R* v *Webber* [1987] Crim LR 413; but *cf R* v *Olaleye* (1986) 82 Cr App R 337.

12.1.2.4   Is category 2 closed?
See generally:

DPP v *Kilbourne* [1973] AC 729.

For specific examples (which suggest that the answer is 'yes') see:

R v *Beck* [1982] 1 WLR 461.

R v *Bagshaw* [1984] 1 WLR 477.

R v *Spencer* [1987] AC 128.

R v *Lovell* [1990] Crim LR 111.

12.1.3   CATEGORY 3

Miscellaneous cases where (a) simply as a matter of good practice, corroboration is often sought (see **12.1.3.1**) *and* (b) cases where, although there is no requirement for corroboration (or a full corroboration warning), there is a requirement to warn of the need for special caution (see **12.1.3.2**).

12.1.3.1   Corroboration often sought as a matter of practice

(a)   Alli v *Alli* [1965] 3 All ER 480 (claim of adultery).

(b)   *Re Cummins* [1972] Ch 62 (claim against an estate).

(c)   *R* v *Prater* [1960] 2 QB 464 (co-accused gives evidence against the other accused. See also *R* v *Knowlden* (1981) 77 Cr App R 194, but cf. *R* v *Loveridge* (1983) 76 Cr App R 125 and *R* v *Beck* [1982] 1 WLR 461).

(d)   *DPP* v *Hester* [1973] AC 296 (children). Until the passing of the Criminal Justice Act 1988, the sworn evidence of a child fell into category 2 (supra); unsworn evidence of a child of tender years fell into category 1 (by virtue of CYPA 1933, s. 38). These rules were abrogated by CJA 1988, s. 34, which (as amended by CJA 1991) is declaratory of the current position:

(2)   Any requirement whereby at trial on indictment it is obligatory for the court to give the jury a warning about convicting the accused on the uncorroborated evidence of a child is abrogated in relation to cases where such a warning is required by reason only that the evidence is the evidence of a child.

(3)   Unsworn evidence admitted by virtue of section 52 of the Criminal Justice Act 1991 may corroborate evidence (sworn or unsworn) given by any other person.

[S. 52, Criminal Justice Act 1991 created s. 33A, Criminal Justice Act 1988 (see **4.2.2.4**(b)].

However, although there is no longer any technical requirement to seek corroboration of a child's evidence (unless the child is a complainant or accomplice), in many cases corroboration is likely to be sought as a matter of good practice.

See, on the effect of s. 34(2) where the child *is* a complainant or accomplice, *R* v *Pryce* [1991] Crim LR 379.

12.1.3.2   Care warning required

(a)   *R* v *Spencer* [1987] AC 128 (a warning (but not a full corroboration warning) required in respect of prosecution evidence given by inmate of a secure mental institution).

(b)   PCEA 1984, s. 77:

(1)   Without prejudice to the general duty of the court at a trial on indictment to direct the jury on any matter on which it appears to the court appropriate to do so, where at such a trial—

(a)   the case against the accused depends wholly or substantially on a confession by him; and

(b)   the court is satisfied—

(i)   that he is mentally handicapped; and
(ii)   that the confession was not made in the presence of an independent person,

the court shall warn the jury that there is special need for caution before convicting the accused in reliance on the confession, and shall explain that the need arises because of the circumstances mentioned in pararaphs (a) and (b) above.

(2) In any case where at the summary trial of a person for an offence it appears to the court that a warning under subsection (1) above would be required if the trial were on indictment, the court shall treat the case as one in which there is a special need for caution before convicting the accused on his confession.

(3) In this section—

'independent person' does not include a police officer or a person employed for, or engaged on, police purposes;

'mentally handicapped,' in relation to a person, means that he is in a state of arrested or incomplete development of mind which includes significant impairment of intelligence and social functioning; and

'police purposes' has the meaning assigned to it by section 64 of the Police Act 1964.

On the application of s. 77 see *R* v *Lamont* [1989] Crim LR 813, and *R* v *MacKenzie* (1993) 96 Cr App R 98.

(c) For the special warning regarding identification evidence see *R* v *Turnbull* [1977] QB 224, CA in **12.2.1** below.

12.1.4   DEFINITION OF CORROBORATION

R v *Baskerville* [1916] 2 KB 658 per Lord Reading CJ at p. 667:

> We hold that evidence in corroboration must be independent testimony which affects the accused by connecting or tending to connect him with the crime. In other words, it must be evidence which implicates him, that is, which confirms in some material particular not only the evidence that the crime has been committed, but also that the prisoner committed it.

If evidence falls within this definition the judge can (and should) direct the jury that it is capable in law of being corroboration (of course, the weight to attach to it — i.e. its corroborative effect, will always be a matter for the jury). The *Baskerville* definition is of considerable practical importance because (a) lack of such evidence may affect the decision whether to prosecute or form the basis of a submission of 'no case' and (b) a misdirection by the judge on the matter may well form the basis for a successful appeal. The cases listed below deal, first, with general aspects of the definition and secondly with particular types of corroborative evidence.

12.1.4.1   General aspects

(a) *Independence.* A recent complaint is *not* corroboration of the complainant's testimony — see *R* v *Whitehead* [1929] 1 KB 99.

On more complex aspects of the 'independence element' — see *R* v *Chapman* [1973] QB 774; *R* v *Willoughby* (1989) 88 Cr App R 91 and *R* v *McInnes* (1990) 90 Cr App R 99.

(b) *Tendency to connect the accused with the crime.* It is not sufficient for corroborative evidence to support the suspect witness on some of the 'live' issues, it must support on all the 'live' issues. See:

R v *Birkett* (1839) 8 C & P 732.

James v *R* (1971) 55 Cr App 299.

R v *Campbell* [1983] Crim LR 174.

R v *Ensor* [1989] 1 WLR 497.

R v *Beck* [1982] 1 WLR 461.

(c) *The 'standard of proof' for corroborative evidence.* See:

Simpson v *Collinson* [1964] 2 QB 80.

Burbury v *Jackson* [1917] 1 KB 16.

(d) *Cumulative corroboration.* See:

Thomas v *Jones* [1921] 1 KB 22.

R v *Hills* (1987) 86 Cr App R 26.

(e) *Mutual corroboration.* See:

R v *Gay* (1909) 2 Cr App R 327.

12.1.4.2   Particular types of corroborative evidence

(a) *Complainant's distress as corroboration.* Although a recent complaint is not corroboration of the complainant's testimony, his or her distress may be — see:

R v *Redpath* (1962) 46 Cr App R 319.

R v *Knight* (1966) 50 Cr App R 122.

R v *Wilson* (1974) 58 Cr App R 304.

R v *Chauhan* (1981) 73 Cr App R 232.

R v *Dowley* [1983] Crim LR 168.

(b) *Defendant's lies as corroboration.* Lies may be corroborative. See *Credland* v *Knowler* (1951) 35 Cr App R 48 and *R* v *Lucas* [1981] QB 720. However, considerable caution should be exercised by the judge when directing the jury on this matter. *R* v *Lucas* per Lord Lane CJ at p. 724:

> To be capable of amounting to corroboration the lie told out of court must first of all be deliberate. Secondly it must relate to a material issue. Thirdly the motive for the lie must be a realisation of guilt and a fear of the truth. The jury should in appropriate cases be reminded that people sometimes lie, for example, in an attempt to bolster up a just cause, or out of shame or out of a wish to conceal digraceful behaviour from their family. Fourthly the statement must be clearly shown to be a lie by evidence other than that of the accomplice who is to be corroborated, that is to say by admission or by evidence from an independent witness. . . As a matter of good sense it is difficult to see why, subject to the same safeguards, lies proved to have been told in court by a defendant should not equally be capable of providing corroboration.

See:

Jones v *Thomas* [1934] 1 KB 323.

R v *Sutton* [1967] Crim LR 43.

R v *West* [1984] Crim LR 236.

R v *Barber* (1988) *The Times*, 29 July 1988.

R v *Rahmoun* (1986) 82 Cr App R 217.

(c)   *Defendant's silence or evasion as corroboration.* The defendant's silence at any stage of the proceedings is not generally corroborative, see:

R v *Jackson* [1953] WLR 591.

Hall v *R* [1971] 1 WLR 298 cf. *R* v *Cramp* (1880) 14 Cox CC 390.

However, evasion by the defendant or attempts to suppress evidence may be corroborative, see:

R v *Smith* (1985) 81 Cr App R 286.

McVeigh v *Beattie* [1988] Fam 69.

As to the effect of the defendant's refusal to allow samples to be taken from his or her person, a distinction needs to be drawn between intimate and non-intimate samples. These are defined in PCEA 1984, s. 65, as follows:

'intimate sample' means a sample of blood, semen or any other tissue fluid, urine, saliva or pubic hair, or a swab taken from a person's body orifice;

'non-intimate sample' means—

(a)   *a sample of hair other than pubic hair;*
(b)   *a sample taken from a nail or from under a nail;*
(c)   *a swab taken from any part of a person's body other than a body orifice;*
(d)   *a footprint or a similar impression of any part of a person's body other than a part of his hand.*

By virtue of PCEA 1984, s. 62:

62.—*(1)   An intimate sample may be taken from a person in police detention only—*

(a)   *if a police officer of at least the rank of superintendent authorises it to be taken; and*
(b)   *if the appropriate consent is given.*

(2)   An officer may only give an authorisation if he has reasonable grounds—

(a)   *for suspecting the involvement of the person from whom the sample is to be taken in a serious arrestable offence; and*
(b)   *for believing that the sample will tend to confirm or disprove his involvement.*

(3)–(9)...

(10)   Where the appropriate consent to the taking of an intimate sample from a person was refused without good cause, in any proceedings against that person for an offence—

(a)   *the court, in determining—*

(i)   *whether to commit that person for trial; or*
(ii)   *whether there is a case to answer; and*

(b)   *the court or jury, in determining whether that person is guilty of the offence charged, may draw such inferences from the refusal as appear proper; and the refusal may, on the basis of such inferences, be treated as, or as capable of amounting to, corroboration of any evidence against the person in relation to which the refusal is material.*

By virtue of PCEA 1984, s. 63:

63.—*(1)   Except as provided by this section, a non-intimate sample may not be taken from a person without the appropriate consent.*

(2)   Consent to the taking of a non-intimate sample must be given in writing.

(3)   A non-intimate sample may be taken from a person without the appropriate consent if—

(a)   he is in police detention or is being held in custody by the police on the authority of a court; and

(b)   an officer of at least the rank of superintendent authorises it to be taken without the appropriate consent.

(4)   An officer may only give an authorisation under subsection (3) above if he has reasonable grounds—

(a)   for suspecting the involvement of the person from whom the sample is to be taken in a serious arrestable offence; and
(b)   for believing that the sample will tend to confirm or disprove his involvement.

(5)–(9)...

[By s. 65 'appropriate consent' means—

(a)   in relation to a person who has attained the age of 17 years, the consent of that person;
(b)   in relation to a person who has not attained that age but has attained the age of 14 years, the consent of that person and his parent or guardian; and
(c)   in relation to a person who has not attained the age of 14 years, the consent of his parent or guardian;]

12.2   Identification Evidence

12.2.1   THE NEED FOR SPECIAL CAUTION

R v *Turnbull* [1977] QB 224 CA, per Lord Widgery CJ at pp. 228–30:

First, whenever the case against an accused depends wholly or substantially on the correctness of one or more identifications of the accused which the defence alleges to be mistaken, the judge should warn the jury of the special need for caution before convicting the accused in reliance on the correctness of the identification or identifications. In addition he should instruct them as to the reason for the need for such a warning and should make some reference to the possibility that a mistaken witness can be a convincing one and that a number of such witnesses can all be mistaken. Provided this is done in clear terms the judge need not use any particular form of words.

Secondly, the judge should direct the jury to examine closely the circumstances in which the identification by each witness came to be made. How long did the witness have the accused under observation? At what distance? In what light? Was the observation impeded in any way, as for example by passing traffic or a press of people? Had the witness ever seen the accused before? How often? If only occasionally, had he any special reason for remembering the accused? How long elapsed between the original observation and the subsequent identification to the police?

Was there any material discrepancy between the description of the accused given to the police by the witness when first seen by them and his actual appearance?

If in any case, whether it is being dealt with summarily or on indictment, the prosecution have reason to believe that there is such a material discrepancy they should supply the accused or his legal advisers with particulars of the description the police were first given. In all cases if the accused asks to be given particulars of such descriptions, the prosecution should supply them. Finally, he should remind the jury of any specific weakness which had appeared in the identification evidence.

Recognition may be more reliable than identification of a stranger; but even when the witness is purporting to recognise someone whom he knows, the jury should be reminded that mistakes in recognition of close relatives and friends are sometimes made.

When the quality (of the identifying evidence) is good, as for example when the identification is made after a long period of observation, or in satisfactory conditions by a relative, a neighbour, a close friend, a workmate and the like, the jury can safely be left to assess the value of the identifying evidence even though there is no other evidence to support it: provided always, however, that an adequate warning has been given about the special need for caution.

When, in the judgment of the trial judge, the quality of the identifying evidence is poor, as for example when it depends solely on a fleeting glance or on a longer observation made in difficult conditions, the situation is very different. The judge should then withdraw the case from the jury and direct an acquittal unless there is other evidence which goes to support the correctness of the identification. This may be corroboration in the sense lawyers use that word; but it need not be so if its effect is to make the jury sure that there has been no mistaken identification.

The trial judge should identify to the jury the evidence which he adjudges is capable of supporting the evidence of identification. If there is any evidence or circumstances which the jury might think was supporting when it did not have this quality, the judge should say so.

(a) Regarding a failure to observe the *Turnbull* guidelines see:

R v *Hunjan* (1979) 68 Cr App R 99.

Reid v *R* (1990) 90 Cr App R 121.

Scott v *R* [1989] AC 1242.

R v *Bowden* [1993] Crim LR 379.

(b) Regarding 'supporting evidence' see:

R v *Keane* (1977) 65 Cr App R 247.

R v *Weeder* (1980) 71 Cr App R 228.

R v *Breslin* (1985) Cr App R 226.

R v *Penman* (1986) 82 Cr App R 44.

(c) Regarding the limits of the requirement to give a *Turnbull* warning see:

R v *Oakwell* (1978) 66 Cr App R 174.

R v *Courtnell* [1990] Crim LR 115.

R v *Browning* (1992) 94 Cr App R 109.

(d)   Regarding the case where the identification is poor but there is supporting evidence see:

R v *Akaidere* [1990] Crim LR 808.

12.2.2   THE ADMISSIBILITY QUESTION(S)

12.2.2.1   General points
Quite apart from the risks which attach to identification evidence in general (to which the *Turnbull* direction relates) questions arise as to the ways in which identification evidence should be (a) gathered and (b) presented in court. Some methods of gathering and presenting identification evidence, e.g. dock identifications, are thought to carry such a risk of prejudice to the accused that the courts have sometimes excluded such evidence (exclusion has been at the court's discretion either at common law or, now, under PCEA 1984, s. 78). In general the courts have sought to ensure that identification evidence is gathered in 'controlled circumstances' and to this end a code of practice (Code D) has been laid down by virtue of PCEA 1984, s. 66 (for extracts see **Appendix 3**). Recent Court of Appeal decisions illustrate that non-compliance with the Code may be an important factor in deciding the question of admissibility. Some aspects of the admissibility of identification evidence have already been dealt with in **Chapters 5** and **8** of this Manual.

12.2.2.2   Identity parades, confrontations, dock identification, etc.
(See Code of Practice D para. 2 and annex A and B in **Appendix 3** of this Manual.)

(a)   Dock identification. See:

R v *Howick* [1970] Crim LR 403.

R v *John* [1973] Crim LR 113, CA.

R v *Mutch* [1973] 1 All ER 178, CA.

(b)   Breaches of the Code where identification evidence should have been excluded. See:

R v *Leckie* [1983] Crim LR 543.

R v *Gall* (1990) 90 Cr App R 64.

R v *Conway* [1990] Crim LR 402.

R v *Nagah* (1991) 92 Cr App R 344.

(c)   Breaches of the Code not leading to exclusion of identification evidence. See:

R v *Grannell* (1990) 90 Cr App R 149.

R v *Quinn* [1990] Crim LR 581.

R v *Penny* [1992] Crim LR 184.

12.2.2.3   Identification from video, films or photographs
See Code of Practice D para. 4 and annex C in **Appendix 3** of this Manual and:

R v *Fowden* [1982] Crim LR 588.

R v *Grimer* [1982] Crim LR 674.

Kajala v *Noble* (1982) 75 Cr App R 149, DC.

R v *Dodson* [1984] 1 WLR 971.

R v *Smith & Doe* (1987) 85 Cr App R 197.

12.2.2.4   Voice identification

R v *Bentum* (1989) 153 JP 538.

R v *Robb* (1991) 93 Cr App R 161.

12.2.2.5   Procedural matters relating to identification evidence
Note the Attorney-General's guidelines relating to the importance of a full committal when the correctness of identification evidence is likely to be an issue at trial — see the **Criminal Litigation and Sentencing Manual.**

See:

R v *Beveridge* (1987) 85 Cr App R 255.

R v *Flemming* (1987) 86 Cr App R 32.

R v *Horsham Justices, ex parte Bukhari* (1981) 74 Cr App R 291, DC.

R v *Highbury Magistrates' Court, ex parte Boyce* (1984) 79 Cr App R 132.

Questions

OBJECTIVES

This chapter is designed to ensure that, as regards corroboration, you should be able to:

(a)   identify when corroboration, or a corroboration warning or a general warning to exercise caution is required;
(b)   demonstrate a sound understanding of the different roles, in relation to corroboration, of judge and jury and the legal definition of corroboration;
(c)   identify evidence which is capable in law of amounting to corroboration;
(d)   spot a case which is 'weak' in terms of corroboration; and
(e)   spot a misdirection on corroboration.

As regards identification, you should be able to:

(a)   identify the circumstances in which a judge might withdraw from the jury a case based on identification evidence;
(b)   identify the circumstances in which a *Turnbull* warning should be given and display knowledge of the usual terms and content of such a warning;
(c)   display a sound understanding of the basis upon which a judge might exclude an item of identification evidence (including knowledge of the Code of Practice on Identification issued pursuant to PCEA 1984, s. 66); and
(d)   raise and/or counter an objection to identification evidence (including knowledge of appropriate procedural matters).

RESEARCH

(a)   Read the materials contained in **Chapter 12** of this Manual.
(b)   Read:

Keane, *The Modern Law of Evidence* (2nd ed., 1989), ch. 7, OR

Murphy, *A Practical Approach to Evidence* (4th ed., 1992), ch. 15; AND

Carter, *Cases and Statutes on Evidence* (2nd ed., 1990), ch. 10 and the Supplement 1992, OR

Heydon, *Evidence: Cases and Materials* (3rd ed., 1991).

(c)   On the basis of this research, answer the following questions.

Question 1

Lord Simonds LC in *Davies* v *DPP* defined accomplices for the purposes of corroboration warnings. Which of the following persons was included in the definition?

[A]   An agent provocateur.
[B]   A party to another offence committed by the accused in respect of which evidence is admitted under the similar fact evidence doctrine.
[C]   A child victim of a sexual offence.
[D]   A woman upon whose immoral earnings the accused is charged with having lived.

Question 2

Mark was charged with assault and put forward an alibi defence. Norma, the alleged victim, and Oliver were called as identification witnesses and testified that they had observed Mark for several minutes and that they were sure he was the assailant. In his summing up the trial judge told the jury (i) that the identification evidence given by Oliver (if believed) was capable of constituting support for that of Norma and vice versa but that it should be noted that a number of honest witnesses might all be mistaken and (ii) that he would have withdrawn the case from the jury if he had thought that the identification evidence was inadequate. The judge's direction was:—

[A]   Improper because he was wrong to make the first point.
[B]   Improper because he was wrong to make both points.
[C]   Improper because he was wrong to make the second point.
[D]   Perfectly proper.

Question 3

Sam was tried for and convicted of the robbery of a supermarket. His co-accused Delilah pleaded guilty and gave prosecution evidence against Sam. In addition to her evidence of his participation in the robbery the following facts emerged at the trial. On the day after the robbery Sam had gone on holiday but he was found by the police and questioned. At first Sam claimed that he had been ill on the day of the robbery and had spent the day at home in bed. However, when the police proved this to be false he claimed that he had spent the day fishing (he explained his false account to the police by saying that he had told his employer that he was ill). Delilah told the police that the proceeds of the robbery were hidden in a lock-up garage and the police confirmed that this was so. The eye-witnesses to the robbery made a good identification of Delilah but were unable to identify the other robber (who had worn a mask) except to say that he was 'huge' (Sam certainly fell into this category).

Sam elected to give evidence and claimed that Delilah had nurtured a grudge against him ever since he had broken off their engagement. He claimed that she was a liar and a cheat and had the morals of an alley cat. On application by the prosecution the trial judge allowed Sam to be cross-examined about his previous convictions (of which there were a formidable number).

In his summing up on the issue of corroboration the trial judge said:

Members of the jury, I have directed that you should look for corroboration of Delilah's evidence and I have told you what is meant by that term. It is also for me to tell you which items of evidence are capable in law of being corroboration but, of course, it is for you to decide whether such items (if any) do corroborate her. In this case my task is not a difficult one for there are several items which are capable of corroboration. First there is the fact that the police confirmed that Delilah was telling the truth as to the whereabouts of the robbery proceeds. Secondly there is the fact that the defendant was caught out in a blatant lie about his own whereabouts on the day of the robbery. Thirdly there is his conduct in the witness box — if you feel sure that he has lied to you on oath this is capable of corroborating Delilah's evidence. In assessing his credibility you may take account of his previous convictions but of course they do not go to the issue of guilt. Finally, members of the jury, there are several items of circumstantial evidence — the coincidence of the holiday and the fact that all the eye-witnesses state that the second robber was a person of huge stature (which the defendant certainly is). Clearly this evidence by itself could not corroborate but taken together with the other items I have mentioned you may feel that it tips the balance. It is a matter for you.

(a)   Prepare an argument in support of an appeal against conviction on the basis of the judge's directions on corroboration.

(b)   Should the judge have given the jury the *Turnbull* warning in addition to the corroboration warning?

Question 4

Terence is charged with raping his stepdaughter, Una (aged 13), who had been living alone with him following the breakdown of his marriage to her mother. The allegations came to light when on her arrival at school one morning Una was observed by her schoolteacher, Vicki, to be in a very distressed state. She asked her what was the matter and, in reply, Una made the allegation that Terence had raped her.

At the trial Una is allowed to give evidence by way of a live television link. However, her testimony is rather tentative and at times inconsistent. Vicki is allowed to give evidence about the occasion when the allegation came to light including her observations of Una's distress and a detailed report of Una's complaint. Medical evidence is called which shows that Una had had frequent sexual intercourse and the medical examination which was made immediately after her complaint to her teacher shows that such intercourse had occurred recently.

Draft an argument in support of a submission of no case on behalf of Terence. Also draft an argument on behalf of the prosecution in answer to the submission.

Question 5

Mark was tried and convicted on a charge of unlawfully wounding John (contrary to Offences against the Person Act 1861, s. 20). The assault occurred when a fight broke out outside a public house at closing time. John was the only eye-witness called by the prosecution. He was a regular at the pub but his assailant was a stranger. Mark's defence throughout the trial was mistaken identity. John had identified Mark as his assailant shortly after the alleged assault when the police took him to the local bus station where Mark was waiting. He was suffering from a hand injury which was consistent with his being involved in a fight but he explained that he had fallen over when he was running to try to catch a bus. He claimed that he had spent the evening at the cinema but he could not remember the name of the film or the price he had paid to get in.

The police officers who took John to the bus station gave evidence at trial of his confident identification of Mark on that occasion. However, John (whose general confidence had deteriorated since the assault), when called as a witness, was unable to state whom he had identified at the bus station.

In his summing up on the identification issue the trial judge said:

The defendant says that John has identified the wrong man. He says that he went to the cinema on that evening and that he had nothing to do with the events outside the pub. Of course, you should look with great care at the circumstances in which the identification was made. John did not know the defendant and he only had a short time to observe his attacker. Against this it is only fair to point out that only a short time had elapsed between the attack and John's clear identification of the defendant at the bus station. We have also heard how the defendant could remember nothing about the film he had just seen and there was the injury to his hand. Of course in the end, members of the jury, it is a matter for you to decide having heard the evidence of the prosecution witnesses and the defendant.

Draft an argument in support of an appeal against conviction on behalf of Mark. You should also prepare a counter-argument on behalf of the prosecution.

13   Privilege and Public Policy

When is a witness entitled to decline to answer questions put to him/her or to refuse to produce documents or things (privilege)?

When should a judge rule that evidence should be withheld on the grounds that its disclosure would be likely to jeopardise national security, diplomatic relations or other state interests (public policy)?

It is a general principle that evidence which is relevant to the issues in legal proceedings should be admitted. However, this principle may give way where *either* there are doubts as to the reliability or probative value of the evidence in question *or* allowing the evidence to be proved might run counter to some aspect of public policy. In general the emphasis in this Manual has been on the first of these factors (although there are undercurrents of public policy in several of the areas considered already, e.g. competence and compellability of the accused and his spouse and the exclusion of illegally or improperly obtained evidence). This chapter is concerned almost exclusively with the second of these factors and the situations in which a person or body of persons can refuse to disclose information or documents (and, sometimes, prevent others disclosing such evidence) even though the evidence in question is reliable and clearly relevant to the issues in a particular case.

These situations can usefully be divided into two main categories: (a) *privilege* where a person has a specific right (privilege) in respect of non-disclosure, i.e. the public policy justification for upholding the privilege is presumed to exist, and (b) *public policy* where there is no specific right in respect of non-disclosure but it is nevertheless contended that the public policy justification for non-disclosure exists, i.e. the public policy justification is not presumed and a balancing of the conflicting policies is often required. There are significant differences between these categories and they will be dealt with separately.

13.1   Privilege

13.1.1   PRIVILEGE AGAINST SELF-INCRIMINATION

In **Chapter 4** of this Manual it was noted that an accused is (a) incompetent for the prosecution and (b) non-compellable for the defence. These rules are, in a sense, specialised aspects of the privilege against self-incrimination. However, the privilege is of general application and, broadly speaking, may be claimed by any person in any proceedings (civil or criminal). Such persons when called upon to answer questions or disclose documents may refuse to do so on the grounds that they may incriminate themselves. It is the general aspects of the privilege that are considered here.

13.1.1.1   Scope of the privilege
See *Blunt* v *Park Lane Hotel Ltd* [1942] 2 K.B 253 — Goddard LJ at p. 257:

The rule is that no one is bound to answer any question if the answer thereto would, in the opinion of the judge, have a tendency to expose the deponent to any criminal charge, penalty or forfeiture which the judge regards as reasonably likely to be preferred or sued for.

Civil Evidence Act 1968, s. 14(1):

The right of a person in any legal proceedings other than criminal proceedings to refuse to answer any question or produce any document or thing if to do so would tend to expose that person to proceedings for an offence or for the recovery of a penalty—

(a) shall apply only as regards criminal offences under the law of any part of the United Kingdom and penalties provided for by such law; and
(b) shall include a like right to refuse to answer any question or produce any document or thing if to do so would tend to expose the husband or wife of that person to proceedings for any such criminal offence or for the recovery of any such penalty.

Garvin v *Domus Publishing Ltd* [1989] Ch 335.

R v *Boyes* (1861) 1 B & S 311.

A. T. & T. Isted Ltd v *Tully* [1992] 3 All ER 523.

Rio Tinto Zinc Corporation v *Westinghouse Electric Corporation* [1978] AC 547.

Rank Film Distributors Ltd v *Video Information Centre* [1982] AC 380.

R v *Garbett* (1847) 1 Den CC 236.

13.1.1.2 Exceptions to the privilege

(a) Criminal Evidence Act 1898, s. 1(e)

A person charged and being a witness in pursuance of this Act may be asked any question in cross-examination notwithstanding that it would tend to criminate him as to the offence charged.

(b) Theft Act 1968, s. 31

31.—(1) A person shall not be excused, by reason that to do so may incriminate that person or the wife or husband of that person of an offence under this Act—

(a) From answering any question put to that person in proceedings for the recovery or administration of any property, for the execution of any trust or for an account of any property or dealings with property; or
(b) from complying with any order made in any such proceedings;

but no statement or admission made by a person in answering a question put or complying with an order made as aforesaid shall, in proceedings for an offence under this Act, be admissible in evidence against that person or (unless they married after the making of the statement or admission) against the wife or husband of that person.

(2) Notwithstanding any enactment to the contrary, where property has been stolen or obtained by fraud or other wrongful means, the title to that or any other property shall not be affected by reason only of the conviction of the offender.

(c) Criminal Damage Act 1971, s. 9

(d) Supreme Court Act 1981, s. 72

72.—*(1)   In any proceedings to which this subsection applies a person shall not be excused, by reason that to do so would tend to expose that person, or his or her spouse, to proceedings for a related offence or for the recovery of a related penalty—*

(a)   *from answering any question put to that person in the first-mentioned proceedings; or*

(b)   *from complying with any order made in those proceedings.*

(2)   Subsection (1) applies to the following civil proceedings in the High Court, namely—

(a)   *proceedings for infringement of rights pertaining to any intellectual property or for passing off;*

(b)   *proceedings brought to obtain disclosure of information relating to any infringement of such rights or to any passing off; and*

(c)   *proceedings brought to prevent any apprehended infringement of such rights or any apprehended passing off.*

(3)   Subject to subsection (4), no statement or admission made by a person—

(a)   *in answering a question put to him in any proceedings to which subsection (1) applies; or*

(b)   *in complying with any order made in any such proceedings,*

shall, in proceedings for any related offence or for the recovery of any related penalty, be admissible in evidence against that person or (unless they married after the making of the statement or admission) against the spouse of that person.

(4)   Nothing in subsection (3) shall render any statement or admission made by a person as there mentioned inadmissible in evidence against that person in proceedings for perjury or contempt of court.

(5)   In this section—

'intellectual property' means any patent, trade mark, copyright, registered design, technical or commercial information or other intellectual property;

'related offence' in relation to any proceedings to which subsection (1) applies, means—

(a)   *in the case of proceedings within subsection (2)(a) or (b)—*

(i)   *any offence committed by or in the course of the infringement or passing off to which those proceedings relate; or*

(ii)   *any offence not within sub-paragraph (i) committed in connection with that infringement or passing off, being an offence involving fraud or dishonesty;*

(b)   *in the case of proceedings within subsection (2)(c), any offence revealed by the facts on which the plaintiff relies in those proceedings;*

'related penalty', in relation to any proceedings to which subsection (1) applies means—

(a)   *in the case of proceedings within subsection (2)(a) or (b), any penalty incurred in respect of anything done or omitted in connection with the infringement or passing off to which those proceedings relate;*

(b)   *in the case of proceedings within subsection (2)(c), any penalty incurred in respect of any act or omission revealed by the facts on which the plaintiff relies in those proceedings.*

(6)   Any reference in this section to civil proceedings in the High Court of any description includes a reference to proceedings on appeal arising out of civil proceedings in the High Court of that description.

There has been considerable recent development in this context in relation to the investigation of serious commercial fraud. It is not proposed to list here all the statutory provisions involved. The area is helpfully reviewed by Dillon LJ in *Bishopsgate Investment* v *Maxwell* [1992] 2 All ER 856. See also *A. T. & T. Isted* v *Tully* [1992] 3 All ER 523 and *R* v *Kansal* [1992] 3 All ER 844.

13.1.2 LEGAL PROFESSIONAL PRIVILEGE

There is no general privilege in regard to confidential statements made between a professional person and his client. However, legal professional privilege is a major exception to this rule. It attaches (a) to certain communications between lawyer and client and (b) to certain communications relating to pending or contemplated litigation between lawyer and/or client and third parties. The privilege is that of the client. Where the privilege attaches to a particular communication the client can insist on non-disclosure by the lawyer or third party in question.

13.1.2.1 Scope of the privilege

The scope of this privilege was laid down by common law; however, an indication as to its scope is given in PCEA 1984, s. 10 which was stated by Lord Goff in *R* v *Central Criminal Court, ex parte Francis & Francis* [1988] 3 WLR 989, HL, to be intended as a statutory enactment of the common law. Section 10 provides:-

(1)   Subject to subsection (2) below, in this Act 'items subject to legal privilege' means—

(a)   communications between a professional legal adviser and his client or any person representing his client made in connection with the giving of legal advice to the client;

(b)   communications between a professional legal adviser and his client or any person representing his client or between such an adviser or his client or any such representative and any other person made in connection with or in contemplation of legal proceedings and for the purposes of such proceedings; and

(c)   items enclosed with or referred to in such communications and made

(i)   in connection with the giving of legal advice; or

(ii)   in connection with or in contemplation of legal proceedings and for the purposes of such proceedings,

when they are in the possession of a person who is entitled to possession of them.

(2)   Items held with the intention of furthering a criminal purpose are not items subject to legal privilege.

(a)   Communications between lawyer and client for the purpose of giving or receiving legal advice. See PCEA, s. 10(1)(a)(*supra*).

Who is a lawyer for these purposes? — See *Re Duncan* [1968] P 306 and *Alfred Crompton Amusement Machines Ltd* v *Customs & Excise Commissioners* [1974] AC 405.

Which communications are privileged? — See:

Greenhough v *Gaskell* (1833) 1 My & K 98.

Minter v *Priest* [1930] AC 558.

Balabel v *Air India* [1988] Ch 317

On the situation where one lawyer acts for two or more parties — see:

Buttes Gas & Oil Co. v *Hammer (No. 3)* [1981] 1 QB 223.

Re Konigsberg [1989] 3 All ER 289.

(b)   Communications between lawyer and/or client and third parties for the dominant purpose of use in pending or contemplated litigation. See PCEA, s. 10(1)(b) (*supra*) and:

Wheeler v *Le Marchant* (1881) 17 ChD 675.

Waugh v *British Railways Board* [1980] AC 521.

Neilson v *Laugharne* [1981] QB 736.

By virtue of RSC Ord. 38, r. 2A, (and CCR Ord. 20, r. 12A) a party to civil proceedings is required to serve on the other parties written statements of the oral evidence which that party will lead at the trial. This head of privilege would normally attach to such statements and the 'exchange' rules do not affect this (see RSC Ord. 38, r. 2A, para. 6 and CCR Ord. 20, r. 12A, para. 6 i.e., the privilege is preserved if for any reason a party decides not to call the witness whose statement has been 'exchanged'). See **Chapter 5** and the **Civil Litigation Manual** for further treatment of this topic.

(c)   Duration of the privilege. See:

Minet v *Morgan* (1873) 8 Ch App 361.

Schneider v *Leigh* [1955] 2 QB 195.

Lee v *South West Thames Regional Health Authority* [1985] 1 WLR 845.

The Aegis Blaze [1986] Lloyds Rep 203.

13.1.2.2   The nature and effect of the privilege
The privilege allows the client to prevent the lawyer and/or third party disclosing communications made for the purposes mentioned in **13.1.2.1**; it does not prevent the disclosure of all facts discovered as an incident of such communications. This may lead to the drawing of some fine distinctions.

(a)   Whether the lawyer must disclose documents or copies of documents provided by the client. See:

R v *Peterborough Justices, ex parte Hicks* [1977] 1 WLR 1371.

R v *King* [1983] 1 WLR 411.

Dubai Bank v *Galadari* [1989] 3 All ER 769.

Ventuoris v *Mountain* [1991] 3 All ER 472.

(b)   Calling the lawyer or third party as a witness to facts. See:

Harmony Shipping Co. SA v *Saudi Europe Line Ltd* [1979] 1 WLR 1380, CA.

Brown v *Foster* (1857) 1 H & N 736.

Conlon v *Conlons Ltd* [1952] 2 All ER 462.

13.1.2.3   Overriding the privilege

(a)   Disclosing communications made in pursuance of fraud or crime. See generally: PCEA, s. 10(2) at **13.1.2.1** and *R* v *Cox and Railton* (1884) 14 QBD 153.

For the definition of fraud or crime, see:

Crescent Farm (Sidcup) Sports Ltd v *Sterling Offices Ltd* [1972] Ch 553.

As to the meaning of *made in pursuance of* fraud or crime, see:

Butler v *Board of Trade* [1971] Ch 680.

R v *Governor of Pentonville Prison, ex parte Osman* [1989] 3 All ER 701, QBD.

R v *Snaresbrook Crown Court, ex parte DPP* [1988] QB 532.

R v *Central Criminal Court, ex parte Francis & Francis* [1988] 3 WLR 989, HL.

   (b)   Disclosing communications so as to prove the innocence of an accused. See:

R v *Barton* [1973] 1 WLR 115.

R v *Ataou* [1988] 2 WLR 1147, CA.

13.1.2.4   By-passing the privilege (by resorting to secondary evidence)
The privilege prevents facts being proved in a particular way, i.e. through the client or through the lawyer or (where the second head of privilege applies) certain third parties. If a different route for the proof of the facts can be found, the privilege is not, as such, infringed. However, in certain circumstances it may be possible to obtain an injunction to prevent the use of privileged documents by persons who are not bound by the privilege.

   (a)   As to by-passing the privilege see:

Calcraft v *Guest* [1898] 1 QB 759.

R v *Tompkins* (1977) 67 Cr App R 181 but cf. *ITC Film Distributors Ltd* v *Video Exchange Ltd* [1982] Ch 431.

   (b)   On the use of injunctions to prevent by-passing, see:

Lord Ashburton v *Pape* [1913] 2 ChD 469.

Goddard v *Nationwide Building Society* [1987] QB 670.

Re Briamore Manufacturing Ltd [1986] 1 WLR 1429.

Guinness Peat Propeties Ltd v *Fitzroy Robinson Partnership* [1987] 1 WLR 1027.

English & American Insurance Co. Ltd v *Herbert Smith & Co.* [1987] 137 NLJ 148.

Webster v *James Chapman & Co.* [1989] 3 All ER 939.

Derby & Co. v *Weldon (No. 8)* [1990] 3 All ER 762.

Pizzey v *Ford Motor Co. Ltd* (1993) *The Times*, 8 March 1993.

13.1.2.5   Waiving the privilege
The privilege is that of the client and he (but not the lawyer or third party) can waive it. However, he must take care to mark clearly the extent of the waiver. See:

George Doland Ltd v *Blackburn, Robson, Coates & Co.* [1972] 1 WLR 1338.

Great Atlantic Insurance Co. v *Home Insurance Co.* [1981] 1 WLR 529.

General Accident Fire & Life Assurance Corpn Ltd v *Tanter* [1984] 1 WLR 100.

British Coal Corpn v *Dennis Rye Ltd (No. 2)* [1988] 3 All ER 816.

13.1.3 PATENT AND TRADE MARK AGENTS' PRIVILEGE

By virtue of Copyright, Designs and Patents Act 1988, ss. 280 and 284, in civil proceedings, privilege may be claimed in respect of communications between a person and his patent agent or trade mark agent for the purpose of pending or contemplated proceedings.

13.1.4 LIMITED PRIVILEGE IN RESPECT OF A JOURNALIST'S SOURCES

Contempt of Court Act 1981, s. 10:

> *No court may require a person to disclose, nor is any person guilty of contempt of court for refusing to disclose, the source of information contained in a publication for which he is responsible, unless it be established to the satisfaction of the court that disclosure is necessary in the interests of justice or national security or for the prevention of disorder or crime.*

(a) On the meaning of 'is necessary in the interests of justice', see:

X Ltd v *Morgan-Grampian (Publishers) Ltd* [1990] 2 WLR 1000.

Maxwell v *Pressdram Ltd* [1987] 1 WLR 298.

(b) On the meaning of 'is necessary for the prevention of disorder or crime', see:

Re an Inquiry under the Companies Securities (Insider Dealing) Act 1985 [1988] AC 660.

X v *Y* [1988] 1 All ER 648.

13.1.5 'WITHOUT PREJUDICE' STATEMENTS

Generally communications between parties to civil proceedings are not privileged nor would they be 'protected' by legal professional privilege if the lawyers acted as intermediaries. However, it is obviously desirable that litigation should be avoided where possible by way of a negotiated compromise or settlement. In order to facilitate this, statements made as part of such negotiations are generally protected from disclosure (in those proceedings or proceedings relating to the same subject matter) as being 'without prejudice'. It is usual to mark the words 'without prejudice' on the correspondence but the fact that the words do not appear will not affect the position — the important point is whether the correspondence can fairly be said to form part of negotiations genuinely aimed at settlement: see *South Shropshire District Council* v *Amos* [1986] 1 WLR 1271. Once correspondence has fallen into the 'without prejudice' category a party who wishes to revert to open correspondence should signify this clearly: see *Cheddar Valley Engineering* v *Chaddlewood Homes Ltd* [1992] 4 All ER 942 and *Dixons Stores Group Ltd* v *Thames Television* [1993] 1 All ER 349. (If the correspondence does *not* fall into that category any 'without prejudice' heading is nugatory: see *Re Daintrey* [1893] 2 QB 116.)

If the negotiations are successful *the parties to the settlement* may then use the correspondence as evidence of the agreement (see *Tomlin* v *Standard Telephones & Cables Ltd* [1969] 1 WLR 1378). However the correspondence would not generally be made admissible in proceedings relating to the same subject-matter for any other purpose, i.e. the 'without prejudice' protection is not dissolved for all purposes (*Rush & Tompkins Ltd* v *Greater London Council* [1988] 3 WLR 939, HL). The protection can be waived but only if *both* parties to the correspondence agree. An analogous rule applies to communications aimed at the reconciliation of parties to a failing marriage. See:

McTaggart v *McTaggart* [1949] P 94.

Mole v *Mole* [1951] P 21.

Theodoropoulas v *Theodoropoulas* [1964] P 311.

For the rule that an unaccepted offer can be referred to on the matter of costs, see:

Calderbank v *Calderbank* [1976] Fam 93 and the **Civil Litigation Manual**.

13.2 Public Policy

13.2.1 GENERAL POINTS

Even where no private privilege applies there are many situations in which the disclosure of evidence would be damaging in some way to national interests including the effective operation of the public service and the administration of justice. In such cases the evidence may be excluded under the broad heading of public policy. However, it should not be assumed from the breadth of the heading that it is an easy matter to have evidence excluded in this way. The courts have in recent years tended to scrutinise such claims most carefully even when made by a Minister of State.

Although privilege and public policy are related topics there are important differences between them. Whereas privilege is a right which must be exercised by the person(s) claiming it, refusing to disclose evidence on the grounds of public policy is a duty as well as a right (which should, if necessary, be discharged by the court *proprio motu*). It would seem to follow that the 'right' to public policy exclusion cannot be waived — see Lord Simon in *Rogers* v *Home Secretary* [1973] AC 388 (although the fact that the person or institution most obviously affected by disclosure did not seek to resist it might be a factor to weigh in the balance in deciding what was in the public interest). Moreover there can be no question of proving the facts by secondary evidence.

Most of the cases on public policy exclusion relate to the disclosure of documents. Sometimes the objection is based on the contents of the document in question but more frequently the objection is based on the argument that the document falls within a class of documents which should not generally be disclosed. While the issues relating to a 'contents claim' are usually relatively straightforward the issues relating to a 'class claim' tend to be more complex. The leading authority on class claims is *Conway* v *Rimmer* [1968] AC 910. The position is further complicated by the fact that the court retains a discretion in relation to the disclosure of documents procedure — see *Science Research Council* v *Nassé* [1980] AC 1028 and the **Civil Litigation Manual**.

Any attempt to establish separate categories for the cases on public policy exclusion is unlikely to be entirely successful. Even cases involving exactly the same type of document, e.g. statements made pursuant to an inquiry under Police Act 1964, s. 49, may result in different decisions about whether the document in question should be disclosed. However, the general area to which the evidence relates tends to determine the basic principles to be applied and the categorisation adopted here is intended to facilitate an understanding of these principles.

13.2.1.1 National security, affairs of state and the protection of international comity

(a) National security:

Asiatic Petroleum Co. Ltd v *Anglo Persian Oil Co. Ltd* [1916] 1 KB 822.

Duncan v *Cammel Laird & Co. Ltd* [1942] AC 642.

(b) Affairs of state etc.:

Burmah Oil Co. Ltd v *Bank of England* [1980] AC 1090.

Air Canada v *Secretary of State for Trade (No. 2)* [1983] 2 AC 394.

Buttes Gas & Oil Co. v *Hammer (No. 3)* [1981] 1 QB 223.

13.2.1.2 Information in the possession of police and revenue authorities etc. relating to the investigation of crime and revenue fraud

(a) The public policy in not revealing the identity of informants is generally upheld — see:

Marks v *Beyfus* (1890) 25 QBD 494.

Alfred Crompton Amusement Machines Ltd v *Customs & Excise Commissioners* [1974] AC 405.

Rogers v *Home Secretary* [1973] AC 388.

D v *National Society for the Prevention of Cruelty to Children* [1978] AC 171, HL.

(b) But the public policy is not absolute — see:

Norwich Pharmacal Co. v *Customs & Excise Commissioners* [1974] AC 133.

R v *Hennessey* (1979) 68 Cr App R 419.

R v *Agar* (1990) 90 Cr App R 318.

(c) Regarding the extension of informer immunity by analogy (e.g. location of police surveillance) — see:

R v *Rankine* [1986] QB 861.

R v *Brown* (1988) 87 Cr App R 52.

R v *Johnson (Kenneth)* (1989) 88 Cr App R 131.

The following guidelines were given by Watkins LJ at p. 139:

> Clearly a trial judge must be placed by the Crown which seeks to exclude evidence of the identification of places of observation and occupiers of premises, in the best possible position to enable him properly in the interests of justice, which includes of course providing a defendant with a fair trial, to determine whether he will afford to the police the protection sought. At the heart of this problem is the desirability, as far as that can properly be given, of reassuring people who are asked to help the police that their identities will never be disclosed lest they become the victims of reprisals by wrong doers for performing a public service.

> The minimum evidential requirements seem to us to be the following:

> (a) The police officer in charge of the observations to be conducted, one of no lower rank than a sergeant should usually be acceptable for this purpose, must be able to testify that beforehand he visited all observation places to be used and ascertained the attitude of occupiers of premises, not only to the use to be made of them, but to the possible disclosure thereafter of the use made and facts which could lead to the identification of the premises thereafter and of the occupiers. He may of course in addition inform the Court of difficulties, if any, usually encountered in the particular locality of obtaining assistance from the public.
> (b) A police officer of no lower rank than a chief inspector must be able to testify that immediately prior to the trial he visited the places used for observations, the results of which it is proposed to give in evidence, and ascertained whether the occupiers are the same as when the observations took place and whether they are or are not, what the attitude of those occupiers is to the possible disclosure of the use previously made of the premises and of facts which could lead at the trial to identification of premises and occupiers.

> Such evidence will of course be given in the absence of the jury when the application to exclude the material evidence is made. The judge should explain to the jury when summing up or at some appropriate time before that, the effect of his ruling to exclude, if he so rules.

These guidelines were applied and approved in *R* v *Hewitt* [1992] NLJ 160.

13.2.1.3   Confidential/personal statements, especially those made in official reports and inquiries
This is probably the most difficult category of cases to deal with in that it is difficult to identify a dominant head of public policy. For various illustrations of the courts' approach — see:

Conway v *Rimmer* [1968] AC 910 (reports on a probationer police constable — disclosure allowed).

Gaskin v *Liverpool City Council* [1980] 1 WLR 1549 and see *Re M* (1990), *The Times*, 4 January 1990 (social services reports and case notes — disclosure refused).

Science Research Council v *Nassé* [1980] AC 1028 (records and interview notes concerning S.R.C.'s employees not protected from disclosure).

Campbell v *Tameside Metropolitan Borough Council* [1982] QB 1065 (reports in possession of education authority about unruly pupil — disclosure allowed).

Lonrho Ltd v *Shell Petroleum Co. Ltd* [1980] 1 WLR 627 (evidence given in confidence to government enquiry into 'Rhodesian sanctions busting' — disclosure refused).

Brown v *Matthews* [1990] 2 All ER 155 (Court Welfare Officers report could be disclosed at discretion of the court which had ordered the report).

Evans v *Chief Constable of Surrey* [1988] QB 588 (report sent by police to Director of Public Prosecutions — disclosure refused).

Neilson v *Laugharne* [1981] 1 QB 736 (statements in police misconduct inquiry under s. 49 Police Act – disclosure refused).

Peach v *Metropolitan Police Commissioner* [1986] QB 1064 (statement in police misconduct inquiry under s. 49 Police Act — disclosure allowed. Dominant purpose of inquiry was to investigate a matter of public concern: *Neilson* v *Laugharne, supra,* distinguished).

Commissioner of Police of the Metropolis v *Locker* (1993) *The Times,* 16 March 1993 (statements made during the course of the Metropolitan police grievance procedure — disclosure allowed — grievance procedure distinguished from procedure under s. 49, Police Act).

Questions

OBJECTIVES

This chapter is designed to ensure that you have a sound understanding of the principles of privilege and the exclusion of evidence on public policy grounds, and are able to apply them in a number of practical contexts.

RESEARCH

(a)   Read the materials contained in **Chapter 13** of this Manual.
(b)   Read:

Keane, *The Modern Law of Evidence* (2nd ed., 1989), ch. 16 and 17, OR

Murphy, *A Practical Approach to Evidence* (4th ed., 1992), ch. 11; AND

Carter, *Cases and Statutes on Evidence* (2nd ed., 1990) ch. 11 and 12 and the Supplement 1992, OR

Heydon *Evidence: Cases and Materials* (3rd ed., 1991).

See also articles in (1985) 101 LQR 200 and (1989) 105 LQR 608.

(c)   On the basis of this research, answer the following questions.

Question 1
Legal professional privilege covers:—

[A]   All communications between solicitor and client.
[B]   All communications between solicitor and client conducted as part of the firm's ordinary business.
[C]   All communications between solicitor and client for the purpose of obtaining or giving legal advice.
[D]   Only those communications between solicitor and client which are for the purpose of pending or anticipated litigation.

Question 2
Mr and Mrs Chesterton are separated and are thinking of divorce. Mrs Chesterton went to see Father Brown, her priest. She frankly admitted to him certain misconduct on her part and asked Brown to talk to her husband about it to see if he would forgive and forget. Brown did so but Mr Chesterton rejected the approach and went ahead with the divorce petition.

At the defended divorce proceedings Mr Chesterton wants Father Brown to testify as to what his wife said to him. Brown is unwilling to give this evidence:—

[A]   He must give the evidence.
[B]   He cannot give the evidence without Mrs Chesterton's consent, because she was speaking to him as her priest.
[C]   He can give the evidence but cannot be compelled to.
[D]   He cannot give the evidence because it was a without prejudice communication.

Question 3
Consider the correspondence below in conjunction with the information given in the following separate situations and answer the questions posed in each case.

(a)   *Ackroyd* v *Smithson*. In this case, which concerns a claim by the plaintiff for damages for negligence against the defendant arising from a motor car accident, the solicitors for the plaintiff are Adolphus & Ellis, those for the defendant are Carrington & Payne.

From Carrington & Payne

To Adolphus & Ellis

30 September 1992

Dear Sirs

Smithson ats Ackroyd

Further to our telephone conversation of 29 September, we confirm that we have instructions to make an offer on behalf of our client of £17,500 by way of compensation for the physical injuries suffered by your client, without prejudice as to liability. We also confirm that the special damages have been agreed at £377.25.

We look forward to hearing whether this offer is acceptable to your client.

Yours faithfully,

Carrington & Payne

From Adolphus & Ellis

To Carrington & Payne

3 October 1992

Dear Sirs,

<u>Ackroyd v Smithson</u>

We thank you for your letter of 30 September.

We regret that we do not have instructions to accept the offer of £17,500 but an offer of £20,000 would be very favourably considered by our client.

Yours faithfully,

Adolphus & Ellis

From Carrington & Payne

To Adolphus & Ellis

10 October 1992

Dear Sirs,

<u>Smithson ats Ackroyd</u>

We thank you for your letter of 3 October.

Our client is not prepared to offer more than £17,500.

Yours faithfully,

Carrington & Payne

No agreement is reached and the matter proceeds to trial.

    (i)   Is any part of this correspondence admissible in relation to the issue of liability?

    (ii)   Is any part of this correspondence admissible if the plaintiff seeks at trial to adduce evidence to show that the special damages to which he is entitled are in excess of £377.25?

    (b)   *Ball* v *Herbert*. This is a case which involves a claim by the plaintiff for damages for trespass to land and for an injunction restraining the defendant from parking motor cars on a field, the property of the plaintiff, known as Muddock's Square. The solicitors for the plaintiff are Carrington & Kirwan, those for the defendant are Ellis & Blackburn.

From Carrington & Kirwan

To Ellis & Blackburn

1 October 1992

Dear Sirs,

Ball v Herbert: Without Prejudice

We have now taken our client's instructions. The terms upon which he would be prepared to discontinue proceedings against you are as follows:

1. Mr Herbert will forthwith remove any motor vehicles remaining parked on Muddock's Square and will thereafter refrain completely from parking motor vehicles of any description there.

2. Mr Herbert will pay to Mr Ball £25 by way of damages for trespass to land.

3. Mr Herbert will pay to Mr Ball £50 as a contribution towards Mr Ball's costs in this matter.

Are these terms acceptable to your client?

Yours faithfully,

Carrington & Kirwan

From Ellis & Blackburn

To Carrington & Kirwan

10 October 1992

Dear Sirs,

Herbert ats Ball: WITHOUT PREJUDICE

We have taken our client's instructions and confirm that the terms set out in your letter of 1 October, for which we thank you, are acceptable to him.

We understand that no motor vehicles remain parked in Muddock's Square.

We enclose herewith our cheque for £75 in respect of damages and costs.

Yours faithfully,

Ellis & Blackburn

Some months passed without incident but now Mr Herbert has started to park vehicles once more on Muddock's Square. Advise Mr Ball.

   (c)   Explain the effect of 'Without Prejudice' in the following letter.

From Foster & Findlayson, Solicitors

9 Albert Square

London EC23

To Mr T Finkle

Glad Rags
Holborn
London WC1

7 October 1992

Dear Sir,

Re Fruitiboy Enterprises Ltd: WITHOUT PREJUDICE

We act for Fruitiboy Enterprises Ltd who instruct us that in March 1992 they entered into a contract with you for the supply to you of 600 pairs of jeans at a price of £3,000. The goods were delivered to you on 1 April 1992 but despite frequent requests no payment has been made by you.

We are instructed to commence proceedings against you without further notice if the sum of £3,000 is not paid to us within seven days of the date of this letter.

Yours faithfully,

Foster & Findlayson

(d) *Hayward* v *Wilson*. The following letter was written by a partner in the firm of Manning & Grainger (solicitors for the defendant) to a partner in the firm of Espinasse & Co. (solicitors for the plaintiff). The action concerned a claim by the plaintiff against the defendant for damages for wrongful dismissal.

From Manning & Grainger

To Ms Sharon Jackson, Espinasse & Co.

1 October 1992

Dear Sharon,

Wilson ats Hayward: Without Prejudice

Re: our discussions in Dieppe about this matter last weekend. I've taken instructions from Mr Wilson and he would be prepared to offer Mr Hayward £700, each side to pay its own costs.

Yours,

Charlene

From Espinasse & Co.

To Ms Charlene Laidler, Manning & Grainger

10 October 1992

Dear Charlene,

Hayward & Wilson: Without Prejudice

Many thanks for your letter but it looks as if this action will have to remain in an on-going situation at this moment in time. I've been in touch with Mr Hayward but no way will he accept anything less than £5,000.

Yours,

Sharon

Hayward v *Wilson* has not been settled but has not yet come to trial. The original of Ms Laidler's letter of 1 October has come into the hands of her husband. He wishes to use it as evidence in divorce proceedings which he has brought against his wife. He alleges as unreasonable behaviour on her part a lesbian relationship with Ms Jackson and he wishes to put the letter in evidence to establish that she was in Dieppe with Ms Jackson on the weekend referred to. May he do so?

Question 4
Brian claims damages in negligence from Cedric, alleging that Cedric had parked his van negligently on a slope with the result that it had run down the hill and damaged Brian's car and rear wall. Cedric denies negligence, claiming the van's brakes failed to hold it due solely to the exceptionally icy state of the road and its steep camber. Brian has pleaded *res ipsa loquitur*.
A copy of a letter from Donald, Cedric's solicitor, to Cedric, summarising counsel's advice on the claim, was in error included in a bundle of documents made available by Donald for inspection by Brian's solicitors. Advise Cedric.

Question 5
You are instructed for Country Farmers Ltd against Mammon Properties Ltd. Mammon Properties Ltd is the owner and occupier of land on which is constructed an irrigation work which, on 3 December 1992 flooded your lay client's farm. On 7 December 1992, your instructing solicitors intimated to Mammon Properties that their client would look to that company for compensation. Consider and advise whether the following documents can be obtained on discovery from the defendant:

(a)   A report from surveyors, dated 1 January 1992, to Mammon Properties, advising that the irrigation work was prone to flooding and should be altered.
(b)   A report from surveyors, dated 3 September 1978, to a government department, tenants of the land before Mammon Properties. This report together with the document in (c) below passed to Mammon Properties with the land.
(c)   Advice from that government department's legal branch that the irrigation work constituted a nuisance in law.
(d)   Advice from Mammon Properties Ltd's salaried solicitor as to the best method of evading liability for the nuisance by means of a tortious conspiracy with another of the company's servants.

Appendix 1
Suggested Answers

Chapter 2: Preliminary Matters

QUESTION 1

[D]

QUESTION 2

[D]. See *Sparks* v *R* [1964] AC 964, PC.

QUESTION 3, PART 1

(a)   All the elements of theft — see *per* Goddard LCJ in *R* v *Sims* [1946] KB 531: the identity of the accused together with the *actus reus* and *mens rea* of theft.

(b)(i)   The alleged facts that Walter is lying and has defective eyesight: both affect her credibility as a witness.
(b)(ii)   The alleged fact that Smith was subject to oppression.

(c)   The evidence of Walter identifying the property as belonging to her ('property belonging to another') and, arguably, Smith's confession.

(d)(i)(1)   The confession, the till roll(?) (cf. *R* v *Shone* (1983) 76 Cr App R 32, CA) and the price sticker(?) (cf. *Patel* v *Comptroller of Customs* [1966] AC 356, PC). (It is not necessary at this stage of the course to get too involved in the distinction between hearsay and original evidence.)
(d)(i)(2)   The argument about short-changing — comes in as part of the prosecution case, not to show that W did or did not short-change S, but to show that they were on bad terms, which is relevant to motive.
(d)(i)(3)   Virtually all of the prosecution evidence! Note in particular the evidence of motive (the earlier argument), preparatory acts (the sewn-in pocket), opportunity, suspicious behaviour (running away) and identity (the fingerprint evidence).
(d)(ii)   W's suspicions and the lower-than-normal takings.

(e)   The coat and the bottle.

(f)   The confession and the other disputed hearsay.

QUESTION 3, PART 2

R v *Smith & Doe* (1987) 85 Cr App R 197, CA: submission of no case should be in the absence of the jury and if the trial proceeds should not be referred to by the trial judge in his summing-up.

Cozens v *Brutus* [1973] AC 854, *R* v *Feely* [1973] QB 530, CA: 'dishonesty' is an ordinary word in common use and a question of fact for the jury requiring no judicial direction as to its meaning.

R v *Harris* [1986] Crim LR 123, CA: judges should not make comments placing police witnesses in any special category or leading the jury to think that there will be adverse consequences for them if a verdict of not guilty is returned.

Iroegbu (1988) *The Times*, 2 August 1988: a trial judge should never give an indication of his own disbelief in relation to the evidence of a witness (especially that of an accused) even if the evidence warrants incredulity.

QUESTION 4

An exercise which requires you to (a) define relevance (Lord Simon in *DPP* v *Kilbourne* [1973] AC 729 etc.) and (b) appreciate that views differ, that there are varying degrees of relevance and that evidence of insufficient relevance can be excluded.

QUESTION 5

(a)   Within statutory constraints, the magistrates must determine their own procedure: *F* v *Chief Constable of Kent* [1982] Crim LR 682, DC; *R* v *Epping & Ongar Justices, ex parte Manby* (1986) Crim LR 55. Section 78 is not such a statutory constraint: *Vel* v *Chief Constable of North Wales* (1987) Crim LR 496, DC. Section 76 is: *Liverpool Juvenile Court, ex parte R* [1988] QB 1.

(b)   Strictly speaking, this may be necessary, e.g., under s. 76, but failure to hold a *voir dire* will only exceptionally result in an order of *certiorari*: *R* v *Oxford City Justices, ex parte Berry* [1988] QB 507, DC.

Chapter 3: The Burden and Standard of Proof

QUESTION 3

(a)	Fact in issue	Evidential burden	Legal burden	Standard
1.	Existence of contract	Arabian	Arabian	Balance/Prob
2.	Contract terms	Arabian	Arabian	Balance/Prob
3.	Loss of ship (Breach)	Arabian	Arabian	Balance/Prob
4.	Frustration (the explosion)	Bulk Traffic	Bulk Traffic	Balance/Prob
5.	Self-induced	Arabian	Arabian	Balance/Prob

See, e.g., *Joseph Constantine Steamship Line Ltd* v *Imperial Smelting Corpn Ltd* [1942] AC 154, HL.

(b)	Fact in issue	Evidential burden	Legal burden	Standard
1.	Car driven	Pros.	Pros.	B.R. Doubt
2.	Defendant drove without due care	Pros.	Pros.	B.R. Doubt
3.	Non-insane automatism	Defence	Pros.	B.R. Doubt

See *Bratty* v *Attorney General for Northern Ireland* [1963] AC 386, HL

Contrast: *M'Naghten's Case* (1843) 10 Cl & F 200: *Woolmington* v *DPP* [1935] AC 462;
R v *Hennessy* [1989] 2 All ER 9, CA.

(c)	Fact in issue	Evidential burden	Legal burden	Standard
1.	Trust exists	Daphne	Daphne	Balance/Prob.
2.	ID trustee	Daphne	Daphne	Balance/Prob.
3.	Funds mixed deliberately	Daphne	Daphne	Balance/Prob.
4.	Frank spent trust money	Daphne	Daphne	Balance/Prob.

See, e.g., *Hornal* v *Neuberger Products Ltd* [1957] 1 QB 247, CA.

Chapter 9: Hearsay Exceptions

QUESTION 5

The first difficulty is to sort out the facts. Purchasers Ltd is suing White (an estate agent) on the basis that he received its £20,000 as stakeholder (and that he should therefore have returned the £20,000 on the breakdown of the negotiations with Vendors Ltd). White claims in his defence that he held as vendor's agent (and that he is not therefore necessarily bound to return the £20,000 on the breakdown of negotiations).

It then becomes apparent that Purchasers Ltd would wish to prove all the hearsay statements referred to in the question, i.e., the telephone conversation, the memo (on tape, if still available, and typed) and White's statement overheard by Peter. All the section numbers referred to are from Civil Evidence Act 1968.

(a)   Arthur's oral statement in telephone conversation provable by Bryan under s. 2(1) and (3) subject to the notice procedures. (Section 8 reason is that Arthur is dead).

(b)   Recording of memo on tape — also admissible under s. 2 — a statement made in a document — tape = document, by virtue of s. 10 (procedural requirements again). A snag here is that the tape may have been erased — but see (c).

(c)   The memo itself possibly admissible under s. 2, *if* Arthur had verified it (which he may well have done — memos are usually signed) in which case it could be said to be Arthur's statement 'made in a document' — see *Re D* [1986] 2 FLR 189.

Alternatively, it could be argued that the typed memo is a *copy* of the relevant part of the document (the tape) which, as stated in (b), would be admissible under s. 2 (Procedural requirements again.)

It is possible (though probably unnecessary) to argue that the memo may be admissible under s. 4. But can the memo be said to be or form part of a record? See *H* v *Schering Chemicals Ltd* [1983] 1 WLR 143 and *R* v *Tirado* (1974) 59 Cr App R 80. Also it seems odd to think of the information being supplied by Arthur *to* the typist (compiler of the record?). The information is really being supplied by Arthur *to* the addressee(s) of the memo. If these objections could be surmounted — notice procedure for s. 4 includes s. 8 reason for typist.

(d)   White's statement provable by Peter *either* under s. 2 (admittedly no s. 8 reason for not calling witness, but difficulty here expressly recognised in Ord. 38, r. 29(2)) *or*, more sensibly, as an informal admission (the statement is clearly adverse to White's case) by virtue of s. 9 (no procedural requirements). Alternatively the statement could be admitted as a previous inconsistent statement under s. 3 assuming of course that the witness's testimony (if given) is inconsistent.

Chapter 10: Confessions and Illegally or Improperly Obtained Evidence in Criminal Cases

QUESTION 3

PCEA 1984, s. 58, gives a person in custody a right to consult a solicitor privately at any time if he so requests. It is now clear (see *R* v *Samuel* [1988] QB 615 and *R* v *Alladice* (1988) 87 Cr App R 380) that there are very few circumstances in which the police can justify a refusal of access. Must be a serious arrestable offence and probability that the solicitor will wittingly or unwittingly pass information to the suspect's confederates. In *Samuel* the Court of Appeal held that a confession obtained after an (unjustified) refusal of access should have been excluded under PCEA 1984, s. 78 (discretion to exclude evidence which would have such an adverse effect on the fairness of the proceedings that the court ought not to admit it) (and see to the same effect *R* v *Walsh* [1989] Crim LR 822). However in *Alladice* it was held that (except when there was bad faith) an unjustified refusal of access to a solicitor would not always have this effect — it seems that it depends (in part) upon the existence of a causal link between the refusal of access and the making of the confession (i.e., would the accused have confessed in any event even if his solicitor was present). A relevant factor in determining the issue of causation is the experience of the suspect of the process of criminal investigation — see *R* v *Dunford* (1990) 91 Cr App R 150, cf. *R* v *Parris* (1989) 89 Cr App R 68.

Insufficient information given to know whether there are breaches of the Code of Practice (other than the refusal of access) but if the necessary steps were *not* taken and the confession was made in consequence this *may* warrant exclusion under s. 76(2) — see *R* v *Delaney* (1988) 88 Cr App R 338 — but breaches of the code alone, i.e., without bad faith, do not amount to oppression (s. 76(2)(a)) under the *Fulling* definition. See *R* v *Samuel* and *R* v *Hughes* [1988] Crim LR 519.

A further ground for objecting to the admissibility of the confession (which Ambrose admits making) would be the lie told by the police inspector (about an associate's statement incriminating Ambrose). There are clear similarities with *R* v *Mason* [1988] 1 WLR 139 where a confession was made after the accused (and his solicitor) were deceived by the police in a similar way. In that case the Court of Appeal suggested that the confession should have been excluded under s. 78. There is no obvious reason why the same result should not follow here. (Quaere whether a deliberate deceit might amount to 'harsh, burdensome' etc. conduct so as to amount to oppression under s. 76(2)(a) or whether it is necessary that the suspect at least realises that he is being oppressed — perhaps the lie in combination with the unjustified refusal of access might amount to oppression?) Alternatively, the lie is something said or done which was likely to render a confession by Ambrose unreliable. Ambrose *may* have decided that if the police had already 'trumped up' evidence against him then there was not much point in maintaining his innocence.

Clearly there is plenty of scope for arguing that the confession he admits making is inadmissible. The argument should be dealt with on a voir dire — whether the case is in the magistrates' court or the Crown Court. The voir dire is not concerned with the truth or falsity of the confession but with the statutory tests under s. 76 or s. 78. However, as regards the statement Ambrose denies making, the issue is one of fact (i.e., for the jury) and should be fought out in front of them. See *Ajodha* v *The State* [1982] AC 204 and *R* v *Flemming* (1987) 86 Cr App R 32. However, there would seem to be nothing in principle wrong if Ambrose said that he didn't think the statement was made but if he was wrong (and it was made) it was rendered inadmissible either by s. 76 or s. 78. Moreover it is apparently not necessary for the accused to reveal his case in respect of the confession on the *voir dire* — see *R* v *Keenan* [1989] 3 All ER 598.

Chapter 11: Opinion Evidence and Judgments as Evidence of the Facts on Which They are Based

QUESTION 1

[D]

QUESTION 2

[C]

QUESTION 3

Yes, PCEA 1984, s. 74(1) and (2).

QUESTION 4

By virtue of CEA 1968, s. 11, the conviction is admissible. Notice should be given under RSC Ord. 18, r. 7A.

QUESTION 5

As to the procedure, pre-trial notification by D to P of intention to object so that (i) there is no reference to the disputed evidence in the P opening speech and (ii) *a voir dire* is requested at the appropriate time. As to the question of admissibility/discretionary exclusion, *see R* v *O'Connor* (1986) 85 Cr App R 298, *R* v *Curry* [1988] Crim LR 527, CA, *R* v *Lunnon* [1988] Crim LR 456, CA etc.

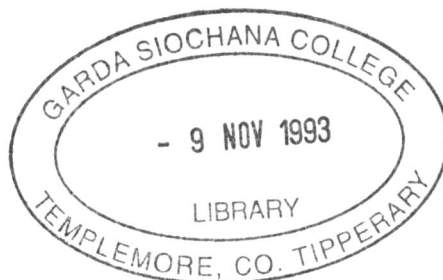

Appendix 2
Part I: Excerpts from Code C: Detention, Treatment and Questioning of Persons by Police Officers
Part II: Practice Direction on Code E (Tape Recording of Interviews)

Part I: Excerpts from Code C

1 General

1.1 All persons in custody must be dealt with expeditiously, and released as soon as the need for detention has ceased to apply.

1.2 This code of practice must be readily available at all police stations for consultation by police officers, detained persons and members of the public.

1.3 The notes for guidance included are not provisions of this code, but are guidance to police officers and others about its application and interpretation. Provisions in the annexes to this code are provisions of this code.

1.4 If an officer has any suspicion, or is told in good faith, that a person of any age may be mentally disordered or mentally handicapped, or mentally incapable of understanding the significance of questions put to him or his replies, then that person shall be treated as a mentally disordered or mentally handicapped person for the purposes of this code. [See *Note 1G*]

1.5 If anyone appears to be under the age of 17 then he shall be treated as a juvenile for the purposes of this code in the absence of clear evidence to show that he is older.

1.6 If a person appears to be blind or seriously visually handicapped, deaf, unable to read, unable to speak or has difficulty orally because of a speech impediment, he should be treated as such for the purposes of this code in the absence of clear evidence to the contrary.

1.7 In this code 'the appropriate adult' means:

(a) in the case of a juvenile:

(i) his parent or guardian (or, if he is in care, the care authority or voluntary organisation);
(ii) a social worker; or

195

(iii)   failing either of the above, another responsible adult aged 18 or over who is not a police officer or employed by the police.

(b)   in the case of a person who is mentally disordered or mentally handicapped:

(i)   a relative, guardian or other person responsible for his care or custody;
(ii)   someone who has experience of dealing with mentally disordered or mentally handicapped persons but is not a police officer or employed by the police (such as an approved social worker as defined by the Mental Health Act 1983 or a specialist social worker); or
(iii)   failing either of the above, some other responsible adult aged 18 or over who is not a police officer or employed by the police.

[See *Note 1E*]

1.8   Whenever this code requires a person to be given certain information he does not have to be given it if he is incapable at the time of understanding what is said to him or is violent or likely to become violent or is in urgent need of medical attention, but he must be given it as soon as practicable.

1.9   Any reference to a custody officer in this code includes an officer who is performing the functions of a custody officer.

1.10   This code applies to persons who are in custody at police stations whether or not they have been arrested for an offence and to those who have been removed to a police station as a place of safety under sections 135 and 136 of the Mental Health Act 1983. Section 15, however, applies solely to persons in police detention.

1.11   Persons in police detention include persons taken to a police station after being arrested under section 14 of the Prevention of Terrorism (Temporary Provisions) Act 1989 or under paragraph 6 of Schedule 5 to that Act by an examining officer who is a constable.

Notes for Guidance

1A   Although certain sections of this code (e.g., section 9 — treatment of detained persons) apply specifically to persons in custody at police stations, those there voluntarily to assist with an investigation should be treated with no less consideration (e.g., offered refreshments at appropriate times) and enjoy an absolute right to obtain legal advice or communicate with anyone outside the police station.

1B   This code does not affect the principle that all citizens have a duty to help police officers to prevent crime and discover offenders. This is a civic rather than a legal duty; but when a police officer is trying to discover whether, or by whom, an offence has been committed he is entitled to question any person from whom he thinks useful information can be obtained, subject to the restrictions imposed by this code. A person's declaration that he is unwilling to reply does not alter this entitlement.

1C   The parent or guardian of a juvenile should be the appropriate adult unless he is suspected of involvement in the offence, is the victim, is a witness, is involved in the investigation or has received admissions. In such circumstances it will be desirable for the appropriate adult to be some other person. If the parent of a juvenile is estranged from the juvenile, he should not be asked to act as the appropriate adult if the juvenile expressly and specifically objects to his presence.

1D   If a child in care admits an offence to a social worker, another social worker should be the appropriate adult in the interest of fairness.

1E   In the case of persons who are mentally disordered or mentally handicapped, it may in certain circumstances be more satisfactory for all concerned if the appropriate adult is someone who has experience or training in their care rather than a relative lacking such qualifications. But if the person himself prefers a relative to a better qualified stranger his wishes should if practicable be respected.

1F   A solicitor who is present at the station in a professional capacity may not act as the appropriate adult.

1G   The generic term 'mental disorder' is used throughout this code. 'Mental disorder' is defined by the Mental Health Act 1983 as 'mental illness, arrested or incomplete development of mind, psychopathic disorder and any other disorder or disability of mind.' It should be noted that 'mental disorder' is different to 'mental handicap' although the two forms of disorder are dealt with similarly throughout this code.

2   Custody Records

2.1   A separate custody record must be opened as soon as practicable for each person who is brought to a police station under arrest or is arrested at the police station having attended there voluntarily. All information which has to be recorded under this code must be recorded as soon as practicable, in the custody record unless otherwise specified.

2.2   In the case of any action requiring the authority of an officer of a specified rank, his name and rank must be noted in the custody record. The recording of names does not apply to officers dealing with persons detained under the Prevention of Terrorism (Temporary Provisions) Act 1989. Instead the record shall state the warrant number and duty station of such officers.

2.3   The custody officer is responsible for the accuracy and completeness of the custody record and for ensuring that the record or a copy of the record accompanies a detained person if he is transferred to another police station. The record shall show the time of and reason for transfer and the time a person is released from detention.

2.4   When a person leaves police detention or is taken before a court he or his legal representative or his appropriate adult shall be supplied on request with a copy of the custody record as soon as practicable. This entitlement lasts for 12 months after his release.

2.5   The person who has been detained, the appropriate adult, or legal representative who gives reasonable notice of a request to inspect the original custody record after the person has left police detention should be allowed to do so. A note of any such inspection should be made in the custody record.

2.6   All entries in custody records must be timed and signed by the maker. In the case of a record entered on a computer this should be timed and contain the operator's identification. Warrant numbers should be used rather than names in the case of detention under the Prevention of Terrorism (Temporary Provisions) Act 1989.

2.7   The fact and time of any refusal by a person to sign a custody record when asked to do so in accordance with the provisions of this code must itself be recorded.

3   Initial Action

(a)   Detained persons: normal procedure

3.1   When a person is brought to a police station under arrest or is arrested at the police station having attended there voluntarily the custody officer must inform him clearly of the following rights and of the fact that they are continuing rights which may be exercised at any stage during the period in custody.

(i)   the right to have someone informed of his arrest in accordance with section 5 below;
(ii)   the right to consult privately with a solicitor in accordance with section 6 below, and the fact that independent legal advice is available free of charge; and
(iii)   the right to consult this and the other codes of practice.

[See *Note 3E*]

3.2   The custody officer must give the person a written notice setting out the above three rights, the right to a copy of the custody record in accordance with paragraph 2.4 above and the caution in the terms prescribed in section 10 below. The notice must also explain the arrangements for obtaining legal advice. The custody officer must also give the person an additional written notice briefly setting out his entitlements while in custody. [See *Notes 3A and 3B*] The custody officer shall ask the person to sign the custody record to acknowledge receipt of these notices and any refusal to sign must be recorded on the custody record.

3.3   A citizen of an independent Commonwealth country or a national of a foreign country (including the Republic of Ireland) must be informed as soon as practicable of his rights of communication with his High Commission, Embassy or Consulate. [See *Section 7*]

3.4   If the custody officer authorises a person's detention he must inform him of the grounds as soon as practicable and in any case before that person is then questioned about any offence.

3.5   The person shall be asked to sign on the custody record to signify whether or not he wants legal advice at this point. The custody officer is responsible for ensuring that the person signs the custody record in the correct place to give effect to his decision. Where legal advice is requested (and unless Annex B applies) the custody officer must act without delay to secure the provision of such advice to the person concerned.

(b)   **Detained persons: special groups**

3.6   If the person appears to be *deaf* or there is doubt about his *hearing* or speaking ability or ability to understand English, and the custody officer cannot establish effective communication, the custody officer must as soon as practicable call an interpreter and ask him to provide the information required above. [See *Section 13*]

3.7   If the person is a juvenile, the custody officer must, if it is practicable, ascertain the identity of a person responsible for his welfare. That person may be his parent or guardian (or, if he is in care, the care authority or voluntary organisation) or any other person who has, for the time being, assumed responsibility for his welfare. That person must be informed as soon as practicable that the juvenile has been arrested, why he has been arrested and where he is detained. This right is in addition to the juvenile's right in section 5 of the code not to be held incommunicado. [See *Note 3C*]

3.8   In the case of a juvenile who is known to be subject to a supervision order, reasonable steps must also be taken to notify the person supervising him.

3.9   If the person is a juvenile, is mentally handicapped or is suffering from a mental disorder, then the custody officer must, as soon as practicable, inform the appropriate adult (who in the case of a juvenile may or may not be a person responsible for his welfare, in accordance with paragraph 3.7 above) of the grounds for his detention and his whereabouts, and ask the adult to come to the police station to see the person.

3.10   It is imperative that a mentally disordered or mentally handicapped person who has been detained under section 136 of the Mental Health Act 1983 should be assessed as soon as possible. If that assessment is to take place at the police station, an approved social worker and a registered medical practitioner should be called to the police station as soon as possible in order to interview and examine the person. Once the person has been interviewed and examined and suitable arangements have been made for his treatment or care, he can no longer be detained under section 136. The person should not be released until he has been seen by both the approved social worker and the registered medical practitioner.

3.11   If the appropriate adult is already at the police station when information is given to the person as required in paragraphs 3.1 to 3.4 above then the information must be given to the detained person in his presence. If the appropriate adult is not at the police station when the information is given then the information must be given to the detained person again in the presence of the appropriate adult once that person arrives.

3.12   The person should be advised by the custody officer that the appropriate adult (where applicable) is there to assist and advise him and that he can consult privately with the appropriate adult at any time.

3.13   If, having been informed of the right to legal advice under paragraph 3.11 above, the appropriate adult considers that legal advice should be taken, then the provisions of section 6 of this code apply. [See *Note 3G*]

3.14   If the person is blind or seriously visually handicapped or is unable to read, the custody officer should ensure that his solicitor, relative, the appropriate adult or some other person likely to take an interest in him (and not involved in the investigation) is available to help in checking any documentation. Where this code requires written consent or signification, then the person who is assisting may be asked to sign instead if the detained person so wishes. [See *Note 3F*]

(c)   **Persons attending a police station voluntarily**

3.15   Any person attending a police station voluntarily for the purpose of assisting with an investigation may leave at will unless placed under arrest. If it is decided that he should not be allowed to do so then he must be informed at once that he is under arrest and brought before the custody officer, who is responsible for ensuring that he is notified of his rights in the same way as other detained persons. If he is not placed under arrest but is cautioned in accordance with secton 10 below, the officer who gives the caution must at the same time inform him that he is not under arrest, that he is not obliged to remain at the police station but that if he remains at the police station he may obtain free legal advice if he wishes.

3.16   If a person who is attending the police station voluntarily (in accordance with paragraph 3.15) asks about his entitlement to legal advice, he should be given a copy of the notice explaining the arrangements for obtaining legal advice. [See *paragraph 3.2*]

(d)   **Documentation**

3.17   The grounds for a person's detention shall be recorded, in his presence if practicable.

3.18   Action taken under paragraphs 3.6 to 3.14 shall be recorded.

Notes for Guidance

3A   The notice of entitlements is intended to provide detained persons with brief details of their entitlements over and above the statutory rights which are set out in the notice of rights. The notice of entitlements should list the entitlements contained in this code, including visits and contact with outside parties (including special provisions for Commonwealth citizens and foreign nationals), reasonable standards of physical comfort, adequate food and drink, access to toilets and washing facilities, clothing, medical attention, and exercise where practicable. It should also mention the provisions relating to the conduct of interviews, the circumstances in which an appropriate adult should be available to assist the detained person and his statutory rights to make representation whenever the period of his detention is reviewed.

3B   In addition to the notices in English, translations into Welsh, the main ethnic minority languages and the principal EC languages should be available whenever they are likely to be helpful.

3C   if the juvenile is in the care of a local authority or voluntary organisation but is living with his parents or other adults responsible for his welfare then, although there is no legal obligation on the police to inform them, they as well as the authority or organisation should normally be contacted unless suspected of involvement in the offence concerned. Even if a juvenile in care is not living with his parents, consideration should be given to informing them as well.

3D   Most local authority Social Services Departments can supply a list of interpreters who have the necessary skills and experience to interpret for the deaf at police interviews. The local Community Relations Council may be able to provide similar information in cases where the person concerned does not understand English. [See Section 13]

3E   The right to consult the codes of practice under paragraph 3.1 above does not entitle the person concerned to delay unreasonably any necessary investigative or administrative action while he does so. Procedures requiring the provision of breath, blood or urine specimens under the terms of the Road Traffic Act 1988 need not be delayed.

3F   Blind or seriously visually handicapped persons may be unwilling to sign police documents. The alternative of their representative signing on their behalf seeks to protect the interests of both police and suspects.

3G   The purpose of paragraph 3.13 is to protect the rights of a juvenile, mentally disordered or mentally handicapped person who may not understand the significance of what is being said to him. If such a person wishes to exercise the right to legal advice the appropriate action should be taken straightaway and not delayed until the appropriate adult arrives.

6   Right to Legal Advice

(a)   Action

6.1   Subject to paragraph 6.2, any person may consult and communicate privately, whether in person, in writing or on the telephone with a solicitor. [See *Note 6B*]

6.2   The exercise of the above right may be delayed only in accordance with Annex B to this code. Whenever legal advice is requested (and unless Annex B applies) the custody officer must act without delay to secure the provision of such advice to the person concerned.

6.3   A poster advertising the right to have legal advice must be prominently displayed in the charging area of every police station. [See *Note 6H*]

6.4   No attempt should be made to dissuade the suspect from obtaining legal advice.

6.5   Reminders of the right to free legal advice must be given in accordance with paragraphs 11.2, 15.3 and paragraphs 2.15(ii) and 5.2 or code of practice D.

6.6   A person who wants legal advice may not be interviewed or continue to be interviewed until he has received it unless:

   (a)   Annex B applies; or
   (b)   an officer of the rank of superintendent or above has reasonable grounds for believing that:

      (i)   delay will involve an immediate risk of harm to persons or serious loss of, or damage to, property; or
      (ii)   where a solicitor, including a duty solicitor, has been contacted and has agreed to attend, awaiting his arrival would cause unreasonable delay to the process of investigation; or

   (c)   The solicitor nominated by the person, or selected by him from a list:

      (i)   cannot be contacted; or
      (ii)   has previously indicated that he does not wish to be contacted; or
      (iii)   having been contacted, has declined to attend;

and the person has been advised of the Duty Solicitor Scheme (where one is in operation) but has declined to ask for the duty solicitor, or the duty solicitor is unavailable. (In these circumstances the interview may be started or continued without further delay provided that an officer of the rank of Inspector or above has given agreement for the interview to proceed in those circumstances — see *Note 6B*)

(d)   The person who wanted legal advice changes his mind. In these circumstances the interview may be started or continued without further delay provided that the person has given his agreement in writing or on tape to being interviewed without receiving legal advice and that an officer of the rank of Inspector or above has given agreement for the interview to proceed in those circumstances.

6.7   Where 6.6(b)(i) applies, once sufficient information to avert the risk has been obtained, questioning must cease until the person has received legal advice or 6.6(a), (b)(ii), (c) or (d) apply.

6.8   Where a person has been permitted to consult a solicitor and the solicitor is available (i.e. present at the station or on his way to the station or easily contactable by telephone) at the time the interview begins or is in progress, he must be allowed to have his solicitor present while he is interviewed.

6.9   The solicitor may only be required to leave the interview if his conduct is such that the investigating officer is unable properly to put questions to the suspect. ([See *Notes 6D* and *6E*]

6.10   If the investigating officer considers that a solicitor is acting in such a way, he will stop the interview and consult an officer not below the rank of superintendent, if one is readily available, and otherwise an officer not below the rank of inspector who is not connected with the investigation. After speaking to the solicitor, the officer who has been consulted will decide whether or not the interview should continue in the presence of that solicitor. If he decides that it should not, the suspect will be given the opportunity to consult another solicitor before the interview continues and that solicitor will be given an opportunity to be present at the interview.

6.11   The removal of a solicitor from an interview is a serious step and, if it occurs, the officer of superintendent rank or above who took the decision will consider whether the incident should be reported to the Law Society. If the decision to remove the solicitor has been taken by an officer below the rank of superintendent, the facts must be reported to an officer of superintendent rank or above who will similarly consider whether a report to the Law Society would be appropriate. Where the solicitor concerned is a duty solicitor, the report should be both to the Law Society and to the Legal Aid Board.

6.12   In this code 'solicitor' means a solicitor qualified to practice in accordance with the Solicitors Act 1974. If a solicitor wishes to send a clerk or legal executive to provide advice on his behalf, then the clerk or legal executive shall be admitted to the police station for this purpose unless an officer of the rank of inspector or above considers that such a visit will hinder the investigation of crime and directs otherwise. Once admitted to the police station, the provisions of paragraphs 6.6 to 6.10 apply.

6.13   In exercising his discretion under paragraph 6.12, the officer should take into account in particular whether the identity and status of the clerk or legal executive has been satisfactorily established; whether he is of suitable character to provide legal advice (a person with a criminal record is unlikely to be suitable unless the conviction was for a minor offence and is not of recent date); and any other matters in any written letter of authorisation provided by the solicitor on whose behalf the clerk or legal executive is attending the police station. [See *Note 6F*]

6.14   If the inspector refuses access to a clerk or legal executive or a decision is taken that such a person should not be permitted to remain at an interview, he must forthwith notify a solicitor on whose behalf the clerk or legal executive was to have acted or was acting, and give him an opportunity of making alternative arrangements. The detained person must also be informed and the custody record noted.

6.15   If a solicitor arrives at the station to see a particular person, that person must (unless Annex B applies) be informed of the solicitor's arrival and asked whether he would like to see him. This applies even if the person concerned has already declined legal advice. The solicitor's attendance and the detained person's decision must be noted in the custody record.

(b)   **Documentation**

6.16   Any request for legal advice and the action taken on it shall be recorded.

6.17   If a person has asked for legal advice and an interview is begun in the absence of a solicitor or his representative (or the solicitor or his representative has been required to leave an interview), a record shall be made in the interview record.

Notes for Guidance

6A   In considering whether paragraph 6.6(b) applies, the officer should where practicable ask the solicitor for an estimate of the time that he is likely to take in coming to the station, and relate this information to the time for which detention is permitted, the time of day (i.e., whether the period of rest required by pararaph 12.2 is imminent) and the requirements of other investigations in progress. If the solicitor says that he is on his way to the station or that he will set off immediately, it will not normally be appropriate to begin an interview before he arrives. If it appears that it will be necessary to begin an interview before the solicitor's arrival he should be given an indication of how long police would be able to wait before paragraph 6.6(b) applies so that he has an opportunity to make arrangemens for legal advice to be provided by someone else.

6B   A person who asks for legal advice should be given an opportunity to consult a specific solicitor (for example, his own solicitor or one known to him) or the duty solicitor where a Duty Solicitor Scheme is in operation. If advice is not available by these means, or he does not wish to consult the duty solicitor, the person should be given an opportunity to choose a solicitor from a list of those willing to provide legal advice. If this solicitor is unavailable, he may choose up to two alternatives. If these attempts to secure legal advice are unsuccessful, the custody officer has discretion to allow further attempts until a solicitor has been contacted and agrees to provide legal advice.

6C   Procedures undertaken under section 7 of the Road Traffic Act 1988 do not constitute interviewing for the purposes of this code.

6D   In considering whether paragraph 6.9 applies, a solicitor is not guilty of misconduct if he seeks to challenge an improper question to his client or the manner in which it is put or if he advises his client not to reply to particular questions or if he wishes to give his client further legal advice. It is the duty of a solicitor to look after the interests of his client and to advise him without obstructing the interview. He should not be required to leave an interview unless his interference with its conduct clearly goes beyond this. Examples of misconduct may include answering questions on the client's behalf, or providing written replies for the client to quote.

6E   In a case where an officer takes the decision to exclude a solicitor, he must be in a position to satisfy the court that the decision was properly made. In order to do this he may need to witness what is happening himself.

6F   If an officer of at least the rank of inspector considers that a particular solicitor or firm of solicitors is persistently sending as clerks or legal executives persons who are unsuited to provide legal advice, he should inform an officer of at least the rank of superintendent, who may wish to take the matter up with the Law Society.

6G   Subject to the constraints of Annex B, a solicitor may advise more than one client in an investigation if he wishes. Any question of a conflict of interest is for the solicitor under his professional code of conduct. If, however, waiting for a solicitor to give advice to one client may lead to unreasonable delay to the interview with another, the provisions of paragraph 6.6(b) may apply.

6H   In addition to the poster in English, a poster or posters containing translations into Welsh, the main ethnic minority languages and the principal EC languages should be displayed wherever they are likely to be helpful and it is practicable to do so.

8   Conditions of Detention

(a)   Action

8.1   So far as is practicable, not more than one person shall be detained in each cell.

8.2   Cells in use must be adequately heated, cleaned and ventilated. They must be adequately lit, subject to such dimming as is compatible with safety and security to allow persons detained overnight to sleep. No additional restraints should be used within a locked cell unless absolutely necessary, and then only suitable handcuffs.

8.3   Blankets, matresses, pillows and other bedding supplied should be of a reasonable standard and in a clean and sanitary condition. [See *Note 8B*]

8.4   Access to toilet and washing facilities must be provided.

8.5   If it is necessary to remove a person's clothes for the purposes of investigation, for hygiene or health reasons or for cleaning, replacement clothing of a reasonable standard of comfort and cleanliness shall be provided. A person may not be interviewed unless adequate clothing has been offered to him.

8.6   At least two light meals and one main meal shall be offered in any period of 24 hours. Drinks should be provided at mealtimes and upon reasonable request between mealtimes. Whenever necessary, advice shall be sought from the police surgeon on medical or dietary matters. As far as practicable, meals provided shall offer a varied diet and meet any special dietary needs or religious beliefs that the person may have; he may also have meals supplied by his family or friends at his or their own expense. [See *Note 8B*]

8.7   Brief outdoor exercise shall be offered daily if practicable.

8.8   A juvenile shall not be placed in a police cell unless no other secure accommodation is availale and the custody officer considers that it is not practicable to supervise him if he is not placed in a cell. He may not be placed in a cell with a detained adult.

8.9   Reasonable force may be used if necessary for the following purposes:

(i)   to secure compliance with reasonable instructions, including instructions give in pursuance of the provisions of a code of practice; or
(ii)   to prevent escape, injury, damage to property or the destruction of evidence.

8.10   Persons detained should be visited every hour, and those who are drunk, every half hour. [See *Note 8A*]

(b)   Documentation

8.11   A record must be kept of replacement clothing and meals offered.

8.12   If a juvenile is placed in a cell, the reason must be recorded.

Notes for Guidance

8A   Whenever possible juveniles and other persons at risk should be visited more regularly.

8B   The provisions in paragraphs 8.3 and 8.6 respectively regarding bedding and a varied diet are of particular importance in the case of a person detained under the Prevention of Terrorism (Temporary Provisions) Act 1989. This is because such a person may well remain in police custody for some time.

9   Treatment of Detained Persons

(a)   General

9.1   If a complaint is made by or on behalf of a detained person about his treatment since his arrest, or it comes to the notice of any officer that he may have been treated improperly, a report must be made as soon as practicable to an officer of the rank of inspector or above who is not connected with the investigation. If the matter concerns a possible assault or the possibility of the unnecessary or unreasonable use of force then the police surgeon must also be called as soon as practicable.

(b)   Medical treatment

9.2   The custody officer must immediately call the police surgeon (or, in urgent cases, send the person to hospital or call the nearest available medical practitioner) if a person brought to a police station or already detained there:

(a)   appears to be suffering from physical illness or a mental disorder; or
(b)   is injured; or
(c)   does not show signs of sensibility and awareness; or
(d)   fails to respond normally to questions or conversation (other than through drunkenness alone);
or
(e)   otherwise appears to need medical attention.

This applies even if the person makes no request for medical attention and whether or not he has recently had medical treatment elsewhere (unless brought to the police station direct from hospital). It is not intended that the contents of this paragraph should delay the transfer of a person to a place of safety under section 136 of the Mental Health Act 1983 where that is applicable. Where an assessment under that Act is to take place at the police station, the custody officer has discretion not to call the police surgeon so long as he believes that the assessment by a registered medical practitioner can be undertaken without undue delay. [See *Note 9A*]

9.3   If it appears to the custody officer, or he is told, that a person brought to the police staton under arrest may be suffering from an infectious disease of any significance he must take steps to isolate the person and his property until he has obtained medical directions as to where the person shoud be taken, whether fumigation should take place and what precautions should be taken by officers who have been or will be in contact with him.

9.4   If a detained person requests a medical examination the police surgeon must be called as soon as practicable. He may in addition be examined by a medical practitioner of his own choice at his own expense.

9.5   If a person is required to take or apply any medication in compliance with medical directions, the custody officer is responsible for its safekeeping and for ensuring that he is given the opportunity to take or apply it at the appropriate time. No police officer may administer controlled drugs subject to the Misuse of Drugs Act 1971 for this purpose. A person may administer such drugs to himself only under the personal supervision of the police surgeon.

9.6   If a detained person has in his possession or claims to need medication relating to a heart condition, diabetes, epilepsy or a condition of comparable potential seriousness then, even though paragraph 9.2 may not apply, the advice of the police surgeon must be obtained.

(c)   Documentation

9.7   A record must be made of any arrangements made for an examination by a police surgeon under paragraph 9.1 above and of any complaint reported under that paragraph together with any relevant remarks by the custody officer.

9.8   A record must be kept of any request for a medical examination under paragraph 9.4, of the arrangements for any examinations made, and of any medical directions to the police.

9.9   Subject to the requirements of section 4 above the custody record shall include not only a record of all medication that a detained person has in his possession on arrival at the police station but also a note of any such medication he claims he needs but does not have with him.

Notes for Guidance

9A   The need to call a police surgeon need not apply to minor ailments or injuries which do not need attention. However, all such ailments or injuries must be recorded in the custody record and any doubt must be resolved in favour of calling the police surgeon.

9B   It is important to remember that a person who appears to be drunk or behaving abnormally may be suffering from illness or the effects of drugs or may have sustained injury (particularly head injury) which is not apparent, and that someone needing or addicted to certain drugs may experience harmful effects within a short time of being deprived of their supply. Police should therefore always call the police surgeon when in any doubt, and act with all due speed.

9C   If a medical practitioner does not record his clinical findings in the custody rcord, the record must show where they are recorded.

10   Cautions

(a)   When a caution must be given

10.1   A person whom there are grounds to suspect of an offence must be cautioned before any questions about it (or further questions if it is his answers to previous questions that provide grounds for suspicion) are put to him for the purpose of obtaining evidence which may be given to a court in a prosecution. He therefore need not be cautioned if questions are put for other purposes, for example, to establish his identity or his ownership of any vehicle or the need to search him in the exercise of powers of stop and search.

10.2   Whenever a person who is not under arrest is initially cautioned before or during an interview he must at the same time be told that he is not under arrest and is not obliged to remain with the officer (see paragraph 3.15).

10.3   A person must be cautioned upon arrest for an offence unless:

(a)   it is impracticable to do so by reason of his condition or behaviour at the time; or
(b)   he has already been cautioned immediately prior to arrest in accordance with paragraph 10.1 above.

(b)   Action: general

10.4   The caution shall be in the following terms:

You do not have to say anything unless you wish to do so, but what you say may be given in evidence.

Minor deviations do not constitute a breach of this requirement provided that the sense of the caution is preserved. [See *Notes 10C* and *10D*]

10.5   When there is a break in questioning under caution the interviewing officer must ensure that the person being questioned is aware that he remains under caution. If there is any doubt the caution should be given again in full when the interview resumes. [See *Note 10A*]

(c)   Juveniles, the mentally disordered and the mentally handicapped

10.6   If a juvenile or a person who is mentally disorderd or mentally handicapped is cautioned in the absence of the appropriate adult, the caution must be repeated in the adult's presence.

(d)   Documentation

10.7   A record shall be made when a caution is given under this section, either in the officer's pocket book or in the interview record as appropriate.

Notes for Guidance

10A   In considering whether or not to caution again after a break, the officer should bear in mind that he may have to satisfy a court that the person understood that he was still under caution when the interview resumed.

10B   It is not necessary to give or repeat a caution when informing a person who is not under arrest that he may be prosecuted for an offence.

10C   If it appears that a person does not understand what the caution means, the officer who has given it should go on to explain it in his own words.

10D   In case anyone who is given a caution is unclear about its significance, the officer concerned should explain that the caution is given in pursuance of the general principle of English law that a person need not answer any questions or provide any information which might tend to incriminate him, and that no adverse inferences from this silence may be drawn at any trial that takes place. The person should not, however, be left with a false impression that non-cooperation will have no effect on his immediate treatment as, for example, his refusal to provide his name and address when charged with an offence may render him liable to detention.

11   Interviews: General

(a)   Action

11.1   Following a decision to arrest a suspect he must not be interviewed about the relevant offence except at a police station (or other authorised place of detention) unless the consequent delay would be likely:

   (a)   to lead to interference with or harm to evidence connected with an offence or interference with or physical harm to other persons; or
   (b)   to lead to the alerting of other persons suspected of having committed an offence but not yet arrested for it; or
   (c)   to hinder the recovery of property obtained in consequence of the commission of an offence.

Interviewing in any of these circumstances should cease once the relevant risk has ben averted or the necessary questions have been put in order to attempt to avert that risk. For the definition of an interview see *Note 11A*.

11.2   Immediately prior to the commencement or re-commencement of any interview at a police station or other authorised place of detention, the interviewing officer should remind the suspect of his entitlement to free legal advice. It is the responsibility of the interviewing officer to ensure that all such reminders are noted in the record of interview.

11.3   No police officer may try to obtain answers to questions or to elicit a statement by the use of oppression or shall indicate, except in answer to a direct question, what action will be taken on the part of the police if the person being interviewed answers questions, makes a statement or refuses to do either. If the person asks the officer directly what action will be taken in the event of his answering questions, making a statement or refusing to do either, then the officer may inform the person what action the police propose to take in that event provided that that action is itself proper and warranted.

11.4   As soon as a police officer who is making enquiries of any person about an offence believes that a prosecution should be brought against him and that there is sufficient evidence for it to succeed, he should ask the person if he has anything further to say. If the person indicates that he has nothing more to say the officer shall without delay cease to question him about that offence. This should not, however, be taken to prevent officers in revenue cases or acting under the confiscation provisions of the Criminal Justice Act 1988 or the Drug Trafficking Offences Act 1986 from inviting suspects to complete a formal question and answer record after the interview is concluded.

(b)   **Interview records**

11.5   (a)   An accurate record must be made of each interview with a person suspected of an offence, whether or not the interview takes place at a police station.
   (b)   The record must state the place of the interview, the time it begins and ends, the time the record is made (if different), any breaks in the interview and the names of all those present; and must be made on the forms provided for this purpose or in the officer's pocket-book or in accordance with the code of practice for the tape-recording of police interviews with suspects.
   (c)   The record must be made during the course of the interview, unless in the investigating officer's view this would not be practicable or would interfere with the conduct of the interview, and must constitute either a verbatim record of what has been said or, failing this, an account of the interview which adequately and accurately summarises it.

11.6   The requirement to record the names of all those present at an interview does not apply to police officers interviewing persons detained under the Prevention of Terrorism (Temporary Provisions) Act 1989. Instead the record shall state the warrant number and duty station of such officers.

11.7   If an interview record is not made during the course of the interview it must be made as soon as practicable after its completion.

11.8   Written interview records must be timed and signed by the maker.

11.9   If an interview record is not completed in the course of the interview the reason must be recorded in the officer's pocket book.

11.10   Unless it is impracticable the person interviewed shall be given the opportunity to read the interview record and to sign it as correct or to indicate the respects in which he considers it inaccurate. If the interview is tape-recorded the arrangements set out in the relevant code of practice apply. If the person concerned cannot read or refuses to read the record or to sign it, the senior police officer present shall read it over to him and ask him whether he would like to sign it as correct (or make his mark) or to indicate the respects in which he considers it inaccurate. The police officer shall then certify on the interview record itself what has occurred.

11.11   If the appropriate adult or the person's solicitor is present during the interview, he should also be given an opportunity to read and sign the interview record (or any written statement taken down by a police officer).

11.12   Any refusal by a person to sign an interview record when asked to do so in accordance with the provisions of the code must itself be recorded.

11.13   A written record should also be made of any comments made by a suspected person, including unsolicited comments, which are outside the context of an interview but which might be relevant to the offence. Any such record must be timed and signed by the maker. Where practicable the person shall be given the opportunity to read that record and to sign it as correct or to indicate the respects in which he considers it inaccurate. Any refusal to sign should be recorded.

(c)   Juveniles, the mentally disordered and the mentally handicapped

11.14   A juvenile or a person who is mentally disordered or mentally handicapped, whether suspected or not, must not be interviewed or asked to provide or sign a written statement in the absence of the appropriate adult unless Annex C applies.

11.15   Juveniles may only be interviewed at their places of education in exceptional circumstances and then only where the principal or his nominee agrees. Every effort should be made to notify both the parent(s) or other person responsible for the juvenile's welfare and the appropriate adult (if this is a different person) that the police want to interview the juvenile and reasonable time should be allowed to enable the appropriate adult to be present at the interview. Where awaiting the appropriate adult would cause unreasonable delay and unless the interviewee is suspected of an offence against the educational estalishment, the principal or his nominee can act as the appropriate adult for the purposes of the interview.

11.16   Where the appropriate adult is present at an interview, he should be informed that he is not expected to act simply as an observer; and also that the purposes of his presence are, first, to advise the person being questioned and to observe whether or not the interview is being conducted properly and fairly, and secondly, to facilitate communication with the person being interviewed.

Notes for Guidance

11A   An interview is the questioning of a person regarding his involvement or suspected involvement in a criminal offence or offences. Questioning a person only to obtain information or his explanation of the facts or in the ordinary course of the officer's duties does not constitute an interview for the purpose of this code. Neither does questioning which is confined to the proper and effective conduct of a search.

11B   It is important to bear in mind that, although juveniles or persons who are mentally disordered or mentally handicapped are often capable of providing reliable evidence, they may, without knowing or wishing to do so, be particularly prone in certain circumstances to provide information which is unreliable, misleading or self-incriminating. Special care should therefore always be exercised in questioning such a person, and the appropriate adult should be involved, if there is any doubt about a person's age, mental state or capacity. Because of the risk of unreliable evidence it is also important to obtain corroboration of any facts admitted whenever possible.

11C   A juvenile should not be arrested at his place of education unless this is unavoidable. In this case the principal or his nominee must be informed.

12   Interviews in Police Stations

(a)   Action

12.1   If a police officer wishes to interview, or conduct enquiries which require the presence of, a detained person the custody officer is responsible for deciding whether to deliver him into his custody.

12.2   In any period of 24 hours a detained person must be allowed a continuous period of at least 8 hours for rest, free from questioning, travel or any interruption arising out of the investigation concerned. This period should normally be at night. The period of rest may not be interrupted or delayed unless there are reasonable grounds for believing that it would:

    (i)   involve a risk of harm to persons or serious loss of, or damage to, property;
    (ii)   delay unnecessarily the person's release from custody; or
    (iii) otherwise prejudice the outcome of the investigation.

If a person is arrested at a police station after going there voluntarily, the period of 24 hours runs from the time of his arrest and not the time of arrival at the police station.

12.3   A detained person may not be supplied with intoxicating liquor except on medical directions. No person who is unfit through drink or drugs to the extent that he is unable to appreciate the significance of questions put to him and his answers may be questioned about an alleged offence in that condition except in accordance with Annex C. [See *Note 12B*]

12.4   As far as practicable interviews shall take place in interview rooms which must be adequately heated, lit and ventilated.

12.5   Persons being questioned or making statements shall not be required to stand.

12.6   Before the commencement of an interview each interviewing officer shall identify himself and any other officers present by name and rank to the person being interviewed, except in the case of persons detained under the Prevention of Terrorism (Temporary Provisions) Act 1989 when each officer shall identify himself by his warrant number and rank rather than his name.

12.7   Breaks from interviewing shall be made at recognised meal times. Short breaks for refreshment shall also be provided at intervals of approximately two hours, subject to the interviewing officer's discretion to delay a break if there are reasonable grounds for believing that it would:

    (i)   involve a risk of harm to persons or serious loss of, or damage to, property;
    (ii)   delay unnecessarily the person's release from custody; or
    (iii) otherwise prejudice the outcome of the investigation.

12.8   If in the course of the interview a complaint is made by the person being questioned or on his behalf concerning the provisions of this code then the interviewing officer shall:

    (i)   record it in the interview record; and
    (ii)   inform the custody officer, who is then responsible for dealing with it in accordance with section 9 of this code.

(b)   **Documentation**

12.9   A record must be made of the times at which a detained person is not in the custody of the custody officer, and why; and of the reason for any refusal to deliver him out of that custody.

12.10   A record must be made of any intoxicating liquor supplied to a detained person, in accordance with paragraph 12.3 above.

12.11   Any decision to delay a break in an interview must be recorded, with grounds, in the interview record.

12.12   All written statements made at police stations under caution shall be written on the forms provided for the purpose.

12.13   All written statements made under caution shall be taken in accordance with Annex D to this code.

Notes for Guidance

12A   If the interview has been contemporaneously recorded and the record signed by the person interviewed in accordance with paragraph 11.10 above, or has been tape recorded, it is normally unnecessary to ask for a written statement. Statements under caution should normally be taken in these circumstances only at the person's express wish. An officer may, however, ask him whether or not he wants to make such a statement.

12B   The police surgeon can give advice about whether or not a person is fit to be interviewed in accordance with paragraph 12.3 above.

16   Charging of Detained Persons

(a)   Action

16.1   When an officer considers that there is sufficient evidence to prosecute a detained person, and that there is sufficient evidence for a prosecution to succeed, and that the person has said all that he wishes to say about the offence, he should without delay (and subject to the following qualification) bring him before the custody officer who shall then be responsible for considering whether or not he should be charged. When a person is detained in respect of more than one offence it is permissible to delay bringing him before the custody officer until the above conditions are satisfied in respect of all the offences (but see paragraph 11.4). Any resulting action should be taken in the presence of the appropriate adult if the person is a juvenile or mentally disordered or mentally handicapped.

16.2   When a detained person is charged with or informed that he may be prosecuted for an offence he shall be cautioned in the terms of paragraph 10.4 above.

16.3   At the time a person is charged he shall be given a written notice showing particulars of the offence with which he is charged and including the name of the officer in the case (in terrorist cases, the officer's warrant number instead), his police station and the reference number for the case. So far as possible the particulars of the charge shall be stated in simple terms, but they shall also show the precise offence in law with which he is charged. The notice shall begin with the following words:

You are charged with the offence(s) shown below. You do not have to say anything unless you wish to do so, but what you say may be given in evidence.

If the person is a juvenile or is mentally disordered or mentally handicapped the notice shall be given to the appropriate adult.

16.4   If at any time after a person has been charged with or informed he may be prosecuted for an offence a police officer wishes to bring to the notice of that person any written statement made by another person or the content of an interview with another person, he shall hand to that person a true copy of any such written statement or bring to his attention the content of the interview record, but shall say or do nothing to invite any reply or comment save to caution him in the terms of paragraph 10.4 above. If the person cannot read then the officer may read it to him. If the person is a juvenile or mentally disordered or mentally handicapped the copy shall also be given to, or the interview record brought to the attention of, the appropriate adult.

16.5   Questions relating to an offence may not be put to a person after he has been charged with that offence, or informed that he may be prosecuted for it, unless they are necessary for the purpose of preventing or minimising harm or loss to some other person or to the public or for clearing up an ambiguity in a previous answer or statement, or where it is in the interests of justice that the person should have put to him and have an opportunity to comment on information concerning the offence which has come to light since he was charged or informed that he might be prosecuted for it, unless they are necessary for the purpose of preventing or minimising harm or loss to some other person or to the public or for clearing up an ambiguity in a previous answer or statement, or where it is in the interests of justice that the person should have put to him and have an opportunity to comment on information concerning the offence which has come to light since he was charged or informed that he might be prosecuted. Before any such questions are put he shall be cautioned in the terms of paragraph 10.4 above. [See *Note 16A*]

16.6 Where a juvenile is charged with an offence and the custody officer authorises his continuing detention he must try to make arrangements for the juvenile to be taken into the care of a local authority to be detained pending appearance in court unless he certifies that it is impracticable to do so in accordance with section 38(6) of the Police and Criminal Evidence Act 1984. [See *Note 16B*]

(a)   Documentation

16.7 A record shall be made of anything a detained person says when charged.

16.8 Any questions put after charge and answers given relating to the offence shall be contemporaneously recorded in full on the forms provided and the record signed by that person or, if he refuses, by the interviewing officer and any third parties present. If the questions are tape-recorded the arrangements set out in the relevant code of practice apply.

16.9 If it is not practicable to make arrangements for the transfer of a juvenile into local authority care in accordance with paragraph 16.6 above the custody officer must record the reasons and make out a certificate to be produced before the court together with the juvenile.

Notes for Guidance

16A   The service of the Notice of Intended Prosecution under sections 1 and 2 of the Road Traffic Offenders Act 1988 does not amount to informing a person that he may be prosecuted for an offence and so does not preclude further questioning in relation to that offence.

16B   Neither a juvenile's behaviour nor the nature of the offence with which he is charged provides grounds for the custody officer to retain him in police custody rather than seek to arrange for his transfer to the care of the local authority.

Annex B: Delay in Notifying Arrest or Allowing Access to Legal Advice

A.   Persons detained under the Police and Criminal Evidence Act 1984

(a)   Action

1. The rights set out in sections 5 or 6 of the code or both may be delayed if the person is in police detention in connection wit a serious arrestable offence, has not yet been charged with an offence and an officer of the rank of superintendent or above has reasonable grounds for believing that the exercise of either right:

(i)   will lead to interference with or harm to evidence connected with a serious arrestable offence or interference with or physical injury to other persons; or
(ii)   will lead to the alerting of other persons suspected of having committed such an offence but not yet arrested for it; or

(iii)   will hinder the recovery of property obtained as a result of such an offence.

[See *Note B3*]

2.   These rights may also be delayed where the serious arrestable offence is either:

(i)   a drug trafficking offence and the officer has reasonable grounds for believing that the detained person has benefited from drug trafficking, and that the recovery of the value of that person's proceeds of drug trafficking will be hindered by the exercise of either right or;

(ii)   an offence to which Part VI of the Criminal Justice Act 1988 (covering confiscation orders) applies and the officer has reasonable grounds for believing that the detained person has benefited from the offence, and that the recovery of the value of the property obtained by that person from or in connection with the offence or if the pecuniary advantage derived by him from or in connection with it will be hindered by the exercise of either right.

3.   Access to a solicitor may not be delayed on the grounds that he might advise the person not to answer any questions or that the solicitor was initially asked to attend the police station by someone else, provided that the person himself then wishes to see the solicitor. In the latter case the detained person must be told that the solicitor has come to the police station at another person's request, and must be asked to sign the custody record to signify whether or not he wishes to see the solicitor.

4.   These rights may be delayed only for as long as is necessary and, subject to paragraph 9 below, in no case beyond 36 hours after the relevant time as defined in section 41 of the Police and Criminal Evidence Act 1984. If the above grounds cease to apply within this time, the person must as soon as practicable be asked if he wishes to exercise either right, the custody record must be noted accordingly, and action must be taken in accordance with the relevant section of the code.

5.   A detained person must be permitted to consult a solicitor for a reasonable time before any court hearing.

(b)   **Documentation**

6.   The grounds for action under this Annex shall be recorded and the person informed of them as soon as practicable.

7.   Any reply given by a person under paragraphs 4 or 9 must be recorded and the person asked to endorse the record in relation to whether he wishes to receive legal advice at this point.

B.   Persons detained under the Prevention of Terrorism (Temporary Provisions) Act 1989

(a)   **Action**

8.   The rights set out in sections 5 or 6 of this code or both may be delayed if paragraph 1 above applies or if an officer of the rank of superintendent or above has reasonable grounds for believing that the exercise of either right:

(a)   will lead to interference with the gathering of information about the commission, preparation or instigation of acts of terrorism; or

(b)   by alerting any person, will make it more difficult to prevent an act of terrorism or to secure the apprehension, prosecution or conviction of any person in connection with the commission, preparation or instigation of an act of terrorism.

9.   These rights may be delayed only for as long as is necessary and in no case beyond 48 hours from the time of arrest. If the above grounds cease to apply within this time, the person must as soon as practicable be asked if he wishes to exercise either right, the custody record must be noted accordingly, and action must be taken in accordance with the relevant section of this code.

10.   Paragraphs 3 and 5 above apply.

(b)   **Documentation**

11.   Paragraphs 6 and 7 above apply.

Notes for Guidance

B1   Even if Annex B applies in the case of a juvenile, or a person who is mentally disordered or mentally handicapped, action to inform the appropriate adult (and the person responsible for a juvenile's welfare, if that is a different person) must nevertheless be taken in accordance with paragraph 3.7 and 3.9 of this code.

B2   In the case of Commonwealth citizens and foreign nationals see Note 7A.

B3   Police detention is defined in section 118(2) of the Police and Criminal Evidence Act 1984.

B4   The effect of paragraph 1 above is that the officer may authorise delaying access to a specific solicitor only if he has reasonable grounds to believe that that specific solicitor will, inadvertently or otherwise, pass on a message from the detained person or act in some other way which will lead to any of the three results in paragraph 1 coming about. In these circumstances the officer should offer the detained person access to a solicitor (who is not the specific solicitor referred to above) on the Duty Solicitor Scheme.

B5   The fact that the grounds for delaying notification of arrest under paragraph 1 above may be satisfied does not automatically mean that the grounds for delaying access to legal advice will also be satisfied.

Annex C: Urgent Interviews

1.   If, and only if, an officer of the rank of superintendent or above considers that delay will involve an immediate risk of harm to persons or serious loss of or serious damage to property:

     (a)   a person heavily under the influence of drink or drugs may be interviewed in that state; or

     (b)   an arrested juvenile or a person who is mentally disordered or mentally handicapped may be interviewed in the absence of the appropriate adult; or

     (c)   a person who has difficulty in understanding English or who has a hearing disability may be interviewed in the absence of an interpreter.

2.   Questioning in these circumstances may not continue once sufficient information to avert the immediate risk has been obtained.

3.   A record shall be made of the grounds for any decision to interview a person under paragraph 1 above.

Note for Guidance

C1   The special groups referred to in Annex C are all particularly vulnerable. The provisions of the annex, which override safeguards designed to protect them and to minimise the risk of interviews producing unreliable evidence, should be applied only in exceptional cases of need.

Annex D: Written Statements under Caution (see paragraph 12.13)

(a)   **Written by a person under caution**

1.   A person shall always be invited to write down himself what he wants to say.

2.   Where the person wishes to write it himself, he shall be asked to write out and sign before writing what he wants to say, the following:

I make this statement of my own free will. I understand that I need not say anything unless I wish to do so and that what I say may be given in evidence.

3.   Any person writing his own statement shall be allowed to do so without any prompting except that a police officer may indicate to him which matters are material or question any ambiguity in the statement.

(b)   Written by a police officer

4.   If a person says that he would like someone to write it for him, a police officer shall write the statement, but, before starting, he must ask him to sign, or make his mark, to the following:

I,............................., wish to make a statement. I want someone to write down what I say, I understand that I need not say anything unless I wish to do so and that what I say may be given in evidence.

5.   Where a police officer writes the statement, he must take down the exact words spoken by the person making it and he must not edit or paraphrase it. Any questions that are necessary (e.g., to make it more intelligible) and the answers given must be recorded contemporaneously on the statement form.

6.   When the writing of a statement by a police officer is finished the person making it shall be asked to read it and to make any corrections, alterations or additions he wishes. When he has finished reading it he shall be asked to write and sign or make his mark on the following certificate at the end of the statement:

I have read the above statement, and I have been able to correct, alter or add anything I wish. This statement is true. I have made it of my own free will.

7.   If the person making the statement cannot read, or refuses to read it, or to write the above mentioned certificate at the end of it or to sign it, the senior police officer present shall read it over to him and ask him whether he would like to correct, alter or add anything and to put his signature or make his mark at the end. The police officer shall then certify on the statement itself what has occurred.

Annex E: Summary of Provisions Relating to Mentally Disordered and Mentally Handicapped Persons

1.   If an officer has any suspicion or is told in good faith that a person of any age, whether or not in custody, may be suffering from mental disorder or mentally handicapped, or cannot understand the significance of questions put to him or his replies, then he shall be treated as a mentally disordered or mentally handicapped person. [See *paragraph 1.4*]

2.   In the case of a person who is mentally disordered or mentally handicapped, 'the appropriate adult' means:

(a)   a relative, guardian or some other person responsible for his care or custody;
(b)   someone who has experience of dealing with mentally disordered or mentally handicapped persons but is not a police officer or employed by the police; or
(c)   failing either of the above, some other responsible adult aged 18 or over who is not a police officer or employed by the police.

[See *paragraph 1.7(b)*]

3.   If the custody officer authorises the detention of a person who is mentally handicapped or is suffering from a mental disorder he must as soon as practicable inform the appropriate adult of the grounds for the person's detention and his whereabouts, and ask the adult to come to the police station to see the person. If the appropriate adult is already at the police station when information is given as required in paragraphs 3.1 to 3.4 the information must be given to the detained person in his presence. If the appropriate adult is not at the police station when the information is given then the information must be given to the detained person again in the presence of the appropriate adult once that person arrives. [See *paragraphs 3.9 and 3.11*]

4.   If the appropriate adult, having been informed of the right to legal advice, considers that legal advice should be taken, the provisions of section 6 of the code apply as if the mentally disordered or mentally handicapped person had requested access to legal advice. [See *paragraph 3.13*]

5.   If a person brought to a police station appears to be suffering from mental disorder or is incoherent other than through drunkenness alone, or if a detained person subsequently appears to be mentally disordered, the custody officer must immediately call the police surgeon or, in urgent cases, send the person to hospital or call the nearest available medical practitioner. It is not intended that these provisions should delay the transfer of a person to a place of safety under section 136 of the Mental Health Act 1983 where that is applicable. Where an assessment under that Act is to take place at the police station, the custody officer has discretion not to call the police surgeon so long as he believes that the assessment by a registered medical practitioner can be undertaken without undue delay. [See *paragraph 9.2*]

6.   It is imperative that a mentally disordered or mentally handicapped person who has been detained under section 136 of the Mental Health Act 1983 should be assessed as soon as possible. If that assessment is to take place at the police station, an approved social worker and a registered medical practitioner should be called to the police station as soon as possible in order to interview and examine the person. Once the person has been interviewed and examined and suitable arrangements have been made for his treatment or care, he can no longer be detained under section 136. The person should not be released until he has been seen by both the approved social worker and the registered medical practitioner. [See *paragraph 3.10*]

7.   If a mentally disordered or mentally handicapped person is cautioned in the absence of the appropriate adult, the caution must be repeated in the adult's presence. [See *paragraph 10.6*]

8.   A mentally disordered or mentally handicapped person must not be interviewed or asked to provide or sign a written statement in the absence of the appropriate adult unless an officer of the rank of superintendent or above considers that delay will involve an immediate risk of harm to persons or serious loss of or serious damage to property. Questioning in these circumstances may not continue in the absence of the appropriate adult once sufficient information to avert the risk has been obtained. A record shall be made of the grounds for any decision to begin an interview in these circumstances. [See *paragraph 11.14* and *Annex C*]

9.   Where the appropriate adult is present at an interview, he should be informed that he is not expected to act simply as an observer; and also that the purposes of his presence are, first, to advise the person being interviewed and to observe whether or not the interview is being conducted properly and fairly, and secondly, to facilitate communication with the person being interviewed. [See *paragraph 11.16*]

10.   If the detention of a mentally disordered or mentally handicapped person is reviewed by a review officer or a superintendent, the appropriate adult must, if available at the time be given opportunity to make representations to the officer about the need for continuing detention. [See *paragraphs 15.1 and 15.2*]

11.   If the custody officer charges a mentally disordered or mentally handicapped person with an offence or take such other action as is appropriate when there is sufficient evidence for a prosecution

this must be done in the presence of the appropriate adult. The written notice embodying any charge must be given to the appropriate adult. [See *paragraphs 16.1 to 16.3*]

12. An intimate search of a mentally disordered or mentally handicapped person may take place only in the presence of the appropriate adult of the same sex, unless the person specifically requests the presence of a particular adult of the opposite sex. [See *Annex A, paragraph 4*]

Notes for Guidance

E1 In the case of persons who are mentally disordered or mentally handicaped, it may in certain circumstances be more satisfactory for all concerned if the appropriate adult is someone who has experience or training in their care rather than a relative lacking such qualifications. But if the person himself prefers a relative to a better qualified stranger his wishes should if practicable be respected. [See note 1E]

E2 The purpose of the provision at paragraph 3.13 is to protect the rights of a mentally disordered or mentally handicapped person who does not understand the significance of what is being said to him. It is not intended that, if such a person wishes to exercise the right to legal advice, no action should be taken until the appropriate adult arrives. [See Note 3G]

E3 It is important to bear in mind that although persons who are mentally disordered or mentally handicapped are often capable of providing reliable evidence, they may, without knowing or wishing to do so, be particularly prone in certain circumstances to provide information which is unreliable, misleading or self-incriminating. Special care should therefore always be exercised in questioning such a person, and the appropriate adult involved, if there is any doubt about a person's mental state or capacity. Because of the risk of unreliable evidence, it is important to obtain corroboration of any facts admitted whenever possible. [See Note 11B]

E4 Because of the risks referred to in Note E3, which the presence of the appropriate adult is intended to minimise, officers of superintendent rank or above should exercise their discretion to authorise the commencement of an interview in the adult's absence only in exceptional cases, where it is necessary to avert an immediate risk of serious harm. [See Annex C, sub-paragraph 1(b) and Note C1]

Part II: Excerpts from Code E: Tape Recording of Interviews

For the full text of Code E, see *Archbold*, 44th edition and Blackstone's 1992 edition.

Code E has been brought into effect by the Police and Criminal Evidence Act 1984 (Tape Recording of Interviews Order 1991 (SI 1991 Nos, 2686 and 2687) in the following police areas:

Avon and Somerset	Greater Manchester
Bedfordshire	Gwent
Cambridgeshire	Hampshire
Cheshire	Hertfordshire
City of London	Humberside
Cleveland	Kent
Cumbria	Lancashire
Derbyshire	Leicestershire
Devon and Cornwall	Lincolnshire
Dorset	Merseyside
Durham	Metropolitan Police District
Dyfed-Powys	Norfolk
Essex	Northamptonshire
Gloucestershire	Northumbria

North Wales	Surrey
North Yorkshire	Sussex
Nottinghamshire	Warwickshire
South Wales	West Mercia
South Yorkshire	West Midlands
Staffordshire	West Yorkshire
Suffolk	Wiltshire

Practice Direction

TAPE RECORDING OF POLICE INTERVIEWS: PREPARATION FOR PROCEEDINGS IN THE CROWN COURT

1. Paragraph 5.4 and note 5(b) of the Code of Practice on Tape Recording issued in accordance with section 60 of the Police and Criminal Evidence Act 1984, envisage that a case in the Crown Court in which a tape recording of a police interview with a suspect has been made will normally be conducted using a Record of Interview if such a Record has been agreed by the defence.

2. Sufficient notice must be given to allow consideration of any amendment to the Record of Interview or the preparation of any transcript of a tape recorded interview or any editing of a tape for the purpose of playing it back in Court. To that end, the following practice should be followed:

(a) Where the defence is unable to agree a Record of Interview or transcript (where one is already available) the prosecution should be notified no more than 21 days from the date of committal or date of transfer with a view to securing agreement to amend. The notice should specify the part to which objection is taken or the part omitted which the defence consider should be included. A copy of the notice should be supplied to the Court within the period specified above.

(b) If agreement is not reached and it is proposed that the tape or part of it be played in Court, notice should be given to the prosecution by the defence no more than 14 days after the expiry of the period in 2(a) above in order that counsel for the parties may agree those parts of the tape that should not be adduced and that arrangements may be made, by editing or in some other way, to exclude that material. A copy of the notice should be supplied to the Court within the period specified above.

(c) Notice of any agreement reached under 2(a) or (b) above should be supplied to the Court by the prosecution as soon as is practicable.

(d) Alternatively, if, in any event, prosecuting counsel proposes to play the tape or part of it, the prosecution should, within 28 days of the date of committal or date of transfer notify the defence and the Court and the defence should notify the prosecution and the Court within 14 days of receiving the notice if they object to the production of the tape on the basis that a part of it should be excluded. If the objections raised by the defence are accepted, the prosecution should prepare an edited tape or make other arrangements to exclude the material part and should notify the Court of the arrangements made.

(e) Whenever editing or amendment of a Record of Interview or of a tape or of a transcript takes place, the general principles set out in paragraphs 4–186, 4–187 and 4–188 of the 43rd edition of *Archbold Criminal Pleadings, Evidence and Practice* should be followed. [See now *Archbold*, 44th Edition, at paragraphs 4–295 to 4–300.]

3. If there is a failure to agree between counsel under paragraph 2 above, or there is a challenge to the integrity of the master tape, notice and particulars should be given to the Court and to the prosecution by the defence as soon as is practicable. The Court may then, at its discretion, order a Pre-trial Review or give such other directions as may be appropriate.

4. If a tape is to be adduced during proceedings before the Crown Court, it should be produced and proved by the interviewing officer, or any other officer who was present at the interview at which the recording was made. The prosecution should ensure that such an officer will be available for this purpose.

5. Where such an officer is unable to act as the tape machine operator, it is for the prosecution to make some other arrangement.

6.   In order to avoid the necessity for the Court to listen to lengthy or irrelevant material before the relevant part of a tape recording is reached, counsel shall indicate to the tape machine operator those parts of a recording which it may be necessary to play. Such an indication should, so far as possible, be expressed in terms of the time track or other identifying process used by the interviewing police force and should be given in time for the operator to have located those parts by the appropriate point in the trial.

7.   Once a trial has begun, if, by reason of faulty preparation or for some other cause, the procedures above have not been properly complied with, and an application is made to amend the Record of Interview or transcript or to edit the tape, as the case may be, thereby making necessary an adjournment for the work to be carried out, the Court may make at its discretion an appropriate award of costs.

8.   Where a case is listed for hearing on a date which falls within the time limits set out above, it is the responsibility of the parties to ensure that all the necessary steps are taken to comply with this Practice Direction within such shorter period as is available.

9.   In paragraphs 2(a) and 2(d) above, 'date of transfer' is the date on which notice of transfer is given in accordance with the provisions of section 4(1)(c) of the Criminal Justice Act 1987.

10.   This Practice Direction should be read in conjunction with the Code of Practice on Tape Recording referred to above and with the Home Office Circular 76/1988 issued on 17 August, 1988.

This Practice Direction is to take effect from 6 June, 1989.

26 May, 1989   *Lane CJ*

Appendix 3
Excerpts from Code D: Identification of Persons by Police Officers

2   Identification by Witnesses

(a)   Cases where the suspect is known

2.1   In a case which involves disputed identification evidence, and where the identity of the suspect is known to the police, the methods of identification by witnesses which may be used are:

     (i)   a parade;
     (ii)   a group identification;
     (iii)   a video film;
     (iv)   a confrontation.

2.2   The arrangements for, and conduct of, these types of identification shall be the responsibility of an officer in uniform not below the rank of inspector who is not involved with the investigation ('the identification officer'). No officer involved with the investigation of the case against the suspect may take any part in these procedures.

Identification parade

2.3   In a case which involves disputed identification evidence a parade must be held if the suspect asks for one and it is practicable to hold one. A parade may also be held if the officer in charge of the investigation considers that it would be useful, and the suspect consents.

2.4   A parade need not be held if the identification officer considers that, whether by reason of the unusual appearance of the suspect or for some other reason, it would not be practicable to assemble sufficient people who resembled him to make a parade fair.

2.5   Any parade must be carried out in accordance with Annex A.

Group identification

2.6   If a suspect refuses or, having agreed, fails to attend an identification parade or the holding of a parade is impracticable, arrangements must if practicable be made to allow the witness an opportunity of seeing him in a group of people.

2.7   A group identification may also be arranged if the officer in charge of the investigation considers, whether because of fear on the part of the witness or for some other reason, that it is, in the circumstances, more satisfactory than a parade.

2.8   The suspect should be asked for his consent to a group identification and advised in accordance with paragraphs 2.15 and 2.16. However, where consent is refused the identification officer has the discretion to proceed with a group identification if it is practicable to do so.

2.9   A group identification should, if practicable, be held in a place other than a police station (for example, in an underground station or a shopping centre). It may be held in a police station if the identification officer considers, whether for security reasons or on other grounds, that it would not be practicable to hold it elsewhere. In either case the group identification should, as far as possible, follow the principles and procedures for a parade as set out in Annex A.

Video film identification

2.10   The identification officer may show a witness a video film of a suspect if the investigating officer considers, whether because of the refusal of the suspect to take part in an identification parade or group identification or other reasons, that this would in the circumstances be the most satisfactory course of action.

2.11   The suspect should be asked for his consent to a video identification and advised in accordance with paragraphs 2.15 and 2.16. However, where such consent is refused the identification officer has the discretion to proceed with a video identification if it is practicable to do so.

2.12   A video identification must be carried out in accordance with Annex B.

Confrontation

2.13   If neither a parade, a group identification nor a video identification procedure is arranged, the suspect may be confronted by the witness. Such a confrontation does not require the suspect's consent, but may not take place unless none of the other procedures are practicable.

2.14   A confrontation must be carried out in accordance with Annex C.

Notice to suspect

2.15   Before a parade takes place or a group identification or video identification is arranged, the identification officer shall explain to the suspect:

(i)   the purposes of the parade or group identification or video identification;
(ii)   the fact that he is entitled to free legal advice;
(iii)   the procedures for holding it (including his right to have a solicitor or friend present);
(iv)   where appropriate the special arrangements for juveniles;
(v)   where appropriate the special arrangements for mentally disordered and mentally handicapped persons;
(vi)   the fact that he does not have to take part in a parade, or co-operate in a group identification, or with the making of a video film and, if it is proposed to hold a group identification or video identification, his entitlement to a parade if this can practicably be arranged;
(vii)   the fact that, if he does not consent to take part in a parade or co-operate in a group identification or with the making of a video film, his refusal may be given in evidence in any subsequent trial and police may proceed covertly without his consent or make other arrangements to test whether a witness identifies him;
(viii)   whether the witness had been shown photographs, photofit, identikit or similar pictures by the police during the investigation before the identity of the suspect became known. [See *Note 2B*]

2.16   This information must also be contained in a written notice which must be handed to the suspect. The identification officer shall give the suspect a reasonable opportunity to read the notice after which he shall be asked to sign a second copy of the notice to indicate whether or not he is willing to take part in the parade or group identification or co-operate with the making of a video film. The signed copy shall be retained by the identification officer.

(b)   **Cases where the identity of the suspect is not known**

2.17   A police officer may take a witness to a particular neighbourhood or place to see whether he can identify the person whom he said he saw on the relevant occasion. Care should be taken however not to direct the witness's attention to any individual.

2.18   A witness must not be shown photographs or photofit, identikit or similar pictures if the identity of the suspect is known to the police and he is available to stand on an identification parade. If the identity of the suspect is not known, the showing of such pictures to a witness must be done in accordance with Annex D. [See *paragraph 2.15(viii)*]

(c)   **Documentation**

2.19   The identification officer shall make a record of the parade, group identification or video identification on the forms provided.

2.20   If the identification officer considers that it is not practicable to hold a parade, he shall tell the suspect why and record the reason.

2.21   A record shall be made of a person's refusal to co-operate in a parade, group identification or video identification.

Notes for Guidance

2A   Except for the provisions of Annex D para 1, a police officer who is a witness for the purposes of this part of the code is subject to the same principles and procedures as a civilian witness.

2B   Where a witness attending an identification parade has previously been shown photographs or photofit; identikit or similar pictures, it is the responsibility of the officer in charge of the investigation to make the identification officer aware that this is the case.

3   Identification by Fingerprints

(a)   **Action**

3.1   A person's fingerprints may be taken only with his consent or if paragraph 3.2 applies. If he is at a police station consent must be in writing. In either case the person must be informed of the reason before they are taken and that they will be destroyed as soon as practicable if paragraph 3.4 applies. He must be told that he may witness their destruction if he asks to do so within five days of being cleared or informed that he will not be prosecuted.

3.2   Powers to take fingerprints without consent from any person over the age of ten years are provided by section 61 of the Police and Criminal Evidence Act 1984. Reasonable force may be used if necessary.

3.3   Section 27 of the Police and Criminal Evidence Act 1984 describes the circumstances in which a constable may require a person convicted of a recordable offence to attend at a police station in order that fingerprints may be taken. [See *Note 3A*]

3.4   The fingerprints of a person and all copies of them taken in that case must be destroyed as soon as practicable if:

(a)   he is prosecuted for the offence concerned and cleared; or
(b)   he is not prosecuted (unless he admits the offence and is cautioned for it).

An opportunity of witnessing the destruction must be given to him if he wishes and if, in accordance with paragraph 3.1, he applies within five days of being cleared or informed that he will not be prosecuted.

3.5   When fingerprints are destroyed, access to relevant computer data shall be made impossible as soon as it is practicable to do so.

3.6   References to fingerprints include palm prints.

(b)   Documentation

3.7   A record must be made as soon as possible of the reason for taking a person's fingerprints without consent and of their destruction. If force is used a record shall be made of the circumstances and those present.

Note for Guidance

3A   References to recordable offences in this code relate to those offences for which convictions are recorded in national police records. (See section 27(4) of the Police and Criminal Evidence Act 1984.)

4   Identification by Photographs

(a)   Action

4.1   The photograph of a person who has been arrested may be taken at a police staton only with his written consent or if paragraph 4.2 applies. In either case he must be informed of the reason for taking it and that the photograph will be destroyed if paragraph 4.4 applies. He must be told that he may witness the destruction of the photograph or be provided with a certificate confirming its destruction if he applies within five days of being cleared or informed that he will not be prosecuted.

4.2   The photograph of a person who has been arrested may be taken without consent if:

(i)   he is arrested at the same time as other persons, or at a time when it is likely that other persons will be arrested, and a photograph is necessary to establish who was arrested, at what time and at what place; or
(ii)   he has been charged with, or reported for a recordable offence and has not yet been released or brought before a court [see *Note 3A*]; or
(iii)   he is convicted of such an offence and his photograph is not already on record as a result of (i) or (ii). There is no power of arrest to take a photograph in pursuance of this provision which applies only where the person is in custody as a result of the exercise of another power (e.g., arrest for fingerprinting under section 27 of the Police and Criminal Evidence Act 1984).

4.3   Force may not be used to take a photograph.

4.4   Where a person's photograph has been taken in accordance with this section, the photograph, negatives and all copies taken in that particular case must be destroyed if:

(a)   he is prosecuted for the offence and cleared; or
(b)   he is not prosecuted (unless he admits the offence and is cautioned for it).

An opportunity of witnessing the destruction or a certificate confirming the destruction must be given to him if he so requests, povided that, in accordance with paragraph 4.1, he applies within five days of being cleared or informed that he will not be prosecuted. [See *Note 4B*]

(b) **Documentation**

4.5   A record must be made as soon as possible of the reason for taking a person's photograph under this section without consent and of the destruction of any photographs.

Notes for Guidance

4A   All references to photographs include computer images.

4B   This paragraph is not intended to require the destruction of copies of a police gazette in cases where, for example, a remand prisoner has escaped from custody, or a person in custody is suspected of having committed offences in other force areas, and a photograph of the person concerned is circulated in a police gazette for information.

5   Identification by Body Samples, Swabs and Impressions

(a) **Action**

5.1   Dental impressions and intimate samples may be taken from a person in police detention only:

(i)   if an officer of the rank of superintendent or above considers that the offence concerned is a serious arrestable offence; and
(ii)   if that officer has reasonable grounds to believe that such an impression or sample will tend to confirm or disprove the suspect's involvement in it; and
(iii)   with the suspect's written consent.

5.2   Before a person is asked to provide an intimate sample he must be warned that a refusal may be treated, in any proceedings against him, as corroborating relevant prosecution evidence. [See *Note 5A*] He must also be reminded of his entitlement to have free legal advice and the reminder must be noted in the custody record.

5.3   Except for samples of urine or saliva, intimate samples may be taken only by a registered medical or dental practitioner as appropriate.

5.4   A non-intimate sample, as defined in paragraph 5.11, may be taken from a detained suspect only with his written consent or if paragraph 5.5 applies. Even if he consents, an officer of the rank of inspector or above must have reasonable grounds for believing that such a sample will tend to confirm or disprove the suspect's involvement in a particular offence.

5.5   A non-intimate sample may be taken without consent if an officer of the rank of superintendent or above has resonable grounds for suspecting that the offence in connection with which the suspect is detained is a serious arrestable offence and for believing that the sample will tend to confirm or disprove his involvement in it.

5.6   Where paragraph 5.5 applies, reasonable force may be used if necessary to take non-intimate samples.

5.7   The suspect must be informed, before the intimate or non-intimate sample or dental impression is taken, of the grounds on which the relevant authority has been given, including the nature of the suspected offence, and that the sample will be destroyed if paragraph 5.8 applies.

5.8   Where a sample or impression has been taken in accordance with this section, it and all copies of it taken in the particular case must be destroyed as soon as practicable if:

(a)   the suspect is prosecuted for the offence concerned and cleared; or
(b)   he is not prosecuted (unless he admits the offence and is cautioned for it).

(b)   **Documentation**

5.9   A record must be made as soon as practicable of the reasons for taking a sample or impression and of its destruction. If force is used a record shall be made of the circumstances and those present. If written consent is given to the taking of a sample or impression, the fact must be rcorded in writing.

5.10   A record must be made of the giving of a warning required by paragraph 5.2 above.

(c)   **General**

5.11   The following terms are defined in section 65 of the Police and Criminal Evidence Act 1984 as follows:

(a)   'intimate sample' means a sample of blood, semen or any other tissue fluid, urine, saliva or pubic hair, or a swab taken from a person's body orifice;
(b)   'non-intimate sample' means:

(i)   a sample of hair other than pubic hair;
(ii)   a sample taken from a nail or from under a nail;
(iii)   a swab taken from any part of a person's body other than a body orifice;
(iv)   a footprint or similar impression of any part of a person's body other than a part of his hand.

5.12   Where clothing needs to be removed in circumstances likely to cause embarrassment to the person, no person of the opposite sex who is not a medical practitioner or nurse shall be present, (unless in the case of a juvenile, that juvenile specifically requests the presence of a particular adult of the opposite sex who is readily available) nor shall anyone whose presence is unnecessary. However, in the case of a juvenile this is subject to the overriding proviso that such a removal of clothing may take place in the absence of the appropriate adult only if the juvenile signifies in the presence of the appropriate adult that he prefers the search to be done in his absence and the appropriate adult agrees.

Note for Guidance

5A   In warning a person who refuses to provide an intimate sample or swab in accordance with paragraph 5.2, the following form of words may be helpful:

You do not have to [provide this sample] [allow this swab to be taken], but I must warn you that if you do not do so, a court may treat such a refusal as supporting any relevant evidence against you.

Annex A: Identification Parades

(a)   **General**

1.   A suspect must be given a reasonable opportunity to have a solicitor or friend present, and the identification officer shall ask him to indicate on a second copy of the notice whether or not he so wishes.

2.   A parade may take place either in a normal room or in one equipped with a screen permitting witnesses to see members of the parade without being seen. The procedures for the composition and conduct of the parade are the same in both cases, subject to paragraph 7 below (except that a parade involving a screen may take place only when the suspect's solicitor, friend or appropriate adult is present or the parade is recorded on video).

(b)   **Parades involving prison inmates**

3.   If an inmate is required for identification, and there are no security problems about his leaving the establishment, he may be asked to participate in a parade or video identification. (A group identification, however, may not be arranged other than in the establishment or inside a police station.)

4.   A parade may be held in a Prison Department establishment, but shall be conducted as far as practicable under normal parade rules. Members of the public shall make up the parade unless there are serious security or control objections to their admission to the establishment. In such cases, or if a group or video identification is arranged within the establishment, other inmates may participate. If an inmate is the suspect, he should not be required to wear prison uniform for the parade unless the other persons taking part are other inmates in uniform or are members of the public who are prepared to wear prison uniform for the occasion.

(c)   **Conduct of the parade**

5.   Immediately before the parade, the identification officer must remind the suspect of the procedures governing its conduct and caution him in the terms of paragraph 10.4 of the code of practice for the detention, treatment and questioning of persons by police officers.

6.   All unauthorised persons must be excluded from the place where the parade is held.

7.   Once the parade has been formed, everything afterwards in respect of it shall take place in the presence and hearing of the suspect and of any interpreter, solicitor, friend or appropriate adult who is present (unless the parade involves a screen, in which case everything said to or by any witness at the place where the parade is held must be said in the hearing and presence of the suspect's solicitor, friend or appropriate adult or be recorded on video).

8.   The parade shall consist of at least eight persons (in addition to the suspect) who so far as possible resemble the suspect in age, height, general appearance and position in life. One suspect only shall be included in a parade unless there are two suspects of roughly similar appearance in which case they may be paraded together with at last twelve other persons. In no circumstances shall more than two suspects be included in one parade and where there are separate parades they shall be made up of different persons.

9.   Where all members of a similar group are possible suspects, separate parades shall be held for each member of the group unless there are two suspects of similar appearance when they may appear on the same parade with at least twelve other members of the group who are not suspects. Where police officers in uniform form an identification parade, any numerals or other identifying badges shall be concealed.

10.   When the suspect is brought to the place where the parade is to be held, he shall be asked by the identification officer whether he has any objection to the arrangements for the parade or to any of the other participants in it. The suspect may obtain advice from his solicitor or friend, if present, before the parade proceeds. Where practicable, steps shall be taken to remove the grounds for objection. Where it is not practicable to do so, the officer shall explain to the suspect why his objections cannot be met.

11.   The suspect may select his own position in the line. Where there is more than one witness, the identification officer must tell the suspect, after each witness has left the room, that he can if he wishes change position in the line. Each position in the line must be clearly numbered, whether by means of a numeral laid on the floor in front of each parade member or by other means.

12.   The identification officer is responsible for ensuring that, before they attend the parade, witnesses are not able to:

(i)   communicate with each other about the case or overhear a witness who has already seen the parade;
(ii)   see any member of the parade;
(iii)   on that occasion see or be reminded of any photograph or description of the suspect or be given any other indication of his identity; or
(iv)   see the suspect either before or after the parade.

13.   The officer conducting a witness to a parade must not discuss with him the composition of the parade, and in particular he must not disclose whether a previous witness has made any identification.

14.   Witnesses shall be brought in one at a time. Immediately before the witness inspects the parade, the identification officer shall tell him that the person he saw may or may not be on the parade and if he cannot make a positive identification he should say so. The officer shall then ask him to walk along the parade at least twice, taking as much care and time as he wishes. When he has done so the officer shall ask him whether the person he saw in person on an earlier relevant occasion is on the parade.

15.   The witness should make an identifiation by indicating the number of the person concerned.

16.   If the witness makes an identification after the parade has ended the suspect and, if present, his solicitor, interpreter or friend shall be informed. Where this occurs, consideration should be given to allowing the witness a second opportunity to identify the suspect.

17.   If a witness wishes to hear any parade member speak, adopt any specified posture or see him move, the identification officer shall first ask whether he can identify any persons on the parade on the basis of appearance only. When the request is to hear members of the parade speak, the witness shall be reminded that the participants in the parade have been chosen on the basis of physical appearance only. Members of the parade may then be asked to comply with the witness's request to hear them speak, to see them move or to adopt any specified posture.

18.   When the last witness has left, the identification officer shall ask the suspect whether he wishes to make any comments on the conduct of the parade.

(d)   **Documentation**

19.   If a parade is held without a solicitor or a friend of the suspect being present, a colour photograph or a video film of the parade shall be taken. A copy of the photograph or video film shall be supplied on request to the suspect or his solicitor within a reasonable time.

20.   Where a photograph or video film is taken in accordance with paragraph 19, it shall be destroyed or wiped clean at the conclusion of the proceedings unless the person concerned is convicted or admits the offence and is cautioned for it.

21.   If the identification officer asks any person to leave a parade because he is interfering with its conduct the circumstances shall be recorded.

22.   A record must be made of all those present at a parade or group identification whose names are known to the police.

23.   If prison inmates make up a parade the circumstances must be recorded.

24.   A record of the conduct of any parade must be made on the forms provided.

Annex B: Video Identification

(a)   **General**

1.   Where a video parade is to be arranged the following procedures must be followed.

2.   Arranging, supervising and directing the making and showing of a video film to be used in a video identification must be the responsibility of an identification officer or identification officers who have no direct involvement with the relevant case.

3.   The film must include the suspect and at least eight other people who so far as possible resemble the suspect in age, height, general appearance and position in life. Only one suspect shall appear on any film unless there are two suspects of roughly similar appearance in which case they may be shown together with at least twelve other persons.

4.   The suspect and other persons shall as far as possible be filmed in the same positions or carrying out the same activity and under identical conditions.

5.   Provision must be made for each person filmed to be identified by number.

6.   If police officers are filmed, any numerals or other identifying badges must be concealed. If a prison inmate is filmed either as a suspect or not, then either all or none of the persons filmed should be in prison uniforms.

7.   The suspect and his solicitor, friend, or appropriate adult must be given a reasonable opportunity to see the complete film before it is shown to witnesses. If he has a reasonable objection to the video film or any of its participants, steps should, if practicable be taken to remove the grounds for objection. If this is not practicable the identification officer shall explain to the suspect and/or his representative why his objections cannot be met and record both the objection and the reason on the forms provided.

8.   The suspect's solicitor, or where one is not instructed the suspect himself, where practicable should be given reasonable notification of the time and place that it is intended to conduct the video identification in order that a representative may attend on behalf of the suspect. The suspect himself may not be present when the film is shown to the witness(es). In the absence of a person representing the suspect the viewing itself shall be recorded on video. No unauthorised persons may be present.

(b)   **Conducting the video identification**

9.   The identification officer is responsible for ensuring that, before they see the film, witnesses are not able to communicate with each other about the case or overhear a witness who has seen the film. He must not discuss with the witness the composition of the film and must not disclose whether a previous witness has made any identification.

10.   Only one witness may see the film at a time. Immediately before the video identification takes place the identification officer shall tell the witness that the person he saw may or may not be on the video film. The witness should be advised that at any point he may ask to see a particular part of the tape again or to have a particular picture frozen for him to study. Furthermore, it should be pointed out that there is no limit on how many times he can view the whole tape or any part of it. However, he should be asked to refrain from making a positive identification or saying that he cannot make a positive identification until he has seen the entire film at least twice.

11.   Once the witness has seen the whole film at least twice and has indicated that he does not want to view it or any part of it again, the identification officer shall ask the witness to say whether the

individual he saw in person on an earlier occasion has been shown on the film and, if so, to identify him by number. The identification officer will then show the film of the person identified again to confirm the identification with the witness.

12.   The identification officer must take care not to direct the witness's attention to any one individual on the video film, or give any other indication of the suspect's identity. Where a witness has previously made an identification by photographs, or a photofit, identikit or similar picture has been made, the witness must not be reminded of such a photograph or picture once a suspect is available for identification by other means in accordance with this code. Neither must he be reminded of any description of the suspect.

(c)   **Tape security and destruction**

13.   It shall be the responsibility of the identification officer to ensure that all relevant tapes are kept securely and their movements accounted for. In particular, no officer involved in the investigation against the suspect shall be permitted to view the video film prior to it being shown to any witness.

14.   Where a video film has been made in accordance with this section all copies of it must be destroyed if the suspect:

(a)   is prosecuted for the offence and cleared; or
(b)   is not prosecuted (unless he admits the offence and is cautioned for it).

An opportunity of witnessing the destruction must be given to him if he so requests within five days of being cleared or informed that he will not be prosecuted.

(d)   **Documentation**

15.   A record must be made of all those participating in or seeing the video whose names are known to the police.

16.   A record of the conduct of the video identification must be made on the forms provided.

Annex C: Confrontation by a Witness

1.   The identification officer is responsible for the conduct of any confrontation of a suspect by a witness.

2.   Before the confrontation takes place, the identification officer must tell the witness that the person he saw may or may not be the person he is to confront and that if he cannot make a positive identification he should say so.

3.   The suspect shall be confronted independently by each witness, who shall be asked 'Is this the person?' Confrontation must take place in the presence of the suspect's solicitor, interpreter or friend, unless this would cause unreasonable delay.

4.   The confrontation should normally take place in the police station, either in a normal room or in one equipped with a screen permitting a witness to see the suspect without being seen. In both cases the procedures are the same except that a room equipped with a screen may be used only when the suspect's solicitor, friend or appropriate adult is present or the confrontation is recorded on video.

Annex D: Showing of Photographs

(a)   **Action**

1.   An officer of the rank of sergeant or above shall be responsible for supervising and directing the showing of photographs. The actual showing may be done by a constable or a civilian police employee.

2.   Only one witness shall be shown photographs at any one time. He shall be given as much privacy as practicable and shall not be allowed to communicate with any other witness in the case.

3.   The witness shall be shown not less than twelve photographs at a time. These photographs shall either be in an album or loose photographs mounted in a frame or a sequence of not fewer than twelve photographs on optical disc, and shall, as far as possible, all be of a similar type.

4.   When the witness is shown the photographs, he shall be told that the photograph of the person he saw may or may not be amongst them. He shall not be prompted or guided in any way but shall be left to make any selection without help.

5.   If a witness makes a positive identification from photographs, then, unless the person identified is otherwise eliminated from enquiries, other witnesses shall not be shown photographs. But both they and the witness who has made the identification shall be asked to attend an identification parade or group or video identification if practicable unless there is no dispute about the identification of the suspect.

6.   Where the use of a photofit, identikit or similar picture has led to there being a suspect availa'le who can be asked to appear on a parade, or participate in a group or video identification, the picture shall not be shown to other potential witnesses.

7.   Where a witness attending an identification parade has previously been shown photographs or photofit, identikit or similar pictures (and it is the responsibility of the officer in charge of the investigation to make the identification officer aware that this is the case) then the suspect and his solicitor must be informed of this fact before the identity parade takes place.

8.   None of the photographs (or optical discs) used shall be destroyed, whether or not an identification is made, since they may be required for production in court. The photographs should be numbered and a separate photograph taken of the frame or part of the album from which the witness made an identification as an aid to reconstituting it.

(b)   **Documentation**

9.   Whether or not an identification is made, a record shall be kept of the showing of photographs and of any comment made by the witness.

LEGAL RESEARCH SKILLS

14 Introduction

14.1 The Barrister as Legal Expert

If you think that the highest function of the barrister is in court-room advocacy, think again. Barristers are 'learned' counsel. This is no formal compliment (like, e.g. 'Right Honourable Member'). They have earned their traditional title, and not by their in-court resourcefulness but by being the specialists of the legal profession, lawyers whom other lawyers consult.

The ability to provide counsel's opinion, based on researches into the darker areas and novel aspects of the law, is the first requisite of the barrister — first also because it comes long before advocacy, or even drafting of pleadings, in the particular case. There is of course a close connection between all of these functions; the opinion given is one which the barrister knows he or she must be prepared to make stand up in court. It must therefore be well-founded on thorough research, to which the argumentative skills of the advocate can then be applied. It is in their ability to find the law and their facility to adapt and apply it in their client's cause that the most able barristers can be recognised.

If you ask any barrister how he or she learned to research in law, the chances are that they will say by trial and error, jumping in at the deep end, or various other vague expressions. Many will say that they have never actually 'learned' to do it at all. Until now, the professional law schools have never attempted to teach the technique of systematic legal research. As for the universities, they expect their law students to absorb large amounts of legal doctrine and to apply it; but almost all of this is presented to them by textbooks and lectures, and the further reading these indicate. Not often are students set to find out for themselves. Even if they are, the academic law libraries do not have the materials a practitioner needs to use.

The result is that young barristers and solicitors arrive at their first job without any real training in one of its most essential functions. They are then expected to 'pick it up' as best they can. Some never do, and perhaps never need to if they find a niche for themselves in areas of practice where research plays little part. If such limited practice is possible at the Bar, it consigns one to the least interesting and stimulating work. At all events, every aspiring barrister should as a matter of self-respect and professional pride want to acquire skill in research and to merit that title of 'learned'.

14.2 From Theory to Practice

There is of course a traditional answer from the profession to this criticism of lack of training. Seasoned practitioners may say that this, like most other vocational skills, can only be learned by doing it in practice. (But then they once said this about English law itself!) Whether this is true or not, you can't even begin to research in law without some preliminary acquaintance with the sources of legal knowledge and the technique of tapping them. What follows seeks to guide you in that direction, providing sufficient information to start you off in acquiring the necessary skill for yourself.

14.3 Legal Research and the Pupil Barrister

From the day you start in chambers, you will be faced with questions, points of law, procedure, tactics, etc., which are quite new to you. This does not mean that the cases and papers you will see are likely to be bristling with complex legal problems. On the contrary, to a seasoned practitioner, there may be very little 'law' involved, everything turning on the facts as the court eventually finds them. But when everything is new and unfamiliar you must have the facility to know how to find out. To start with you need to know what people are talking about. At a more advanced level, when you are given papers to prepare an opinion, you must know how and where to get at the law.

Some answers will come readily from your pupil master, from sharing experience with other pupils, or from picking the brains of other barristers. That is part of the comradeship of the Bar. But if they say, 'It'll be in *MacGillivray*', it does not extend to taking you by the hand and showing you what that is. You are assumed to know how legal knowledge is organised on the library shelf: statute and case law, reference works, the main practitioners' textbooks, the cumulations and indexes: and how they all cite, classify, fit together and cross-refer. These are things you can and must equip yourself with before you even set foot in chambers. So if you did not learn it all at university, you must do so now. (If you did, or think you did, quaere!)

14.4 Order of Treatment

14.4.1 THE LIBRARY

The first part of this guide, **Chapter 15**, is concerned with the basic materials of English and European Community Law which you can expect to find in a practitioners' law library. This is part of the essential knowledge of the legal scene that you must now start to acquire. Without it you cannot even begin to research. It is important to get a general understanding of the way in which legal knowledge is organised, visually and spatially, in general and in your particular library. Most chambers' libraries have the basic sources only. For deeper research you will need to go to one of the Inns' libraries or further afield. But don't wait until a problem forces you to wander hopefully round the shelves. Get to know the library, its arrangement and contents, find the books described and browse through them to see the features indicated.

14.4.2 PROBLEM-SOLVING

The second part of this guide, **Chapters 16 to 20**, is about using the library. We have to go on and learn how to make it work for us in problem-solving. Problems in law vary greatly in type. The sequence adopted here is to start with problems in areas of law with which you must be familiar from your studies so far; going on to research in unknown territory; then the technique of 'following-through' to make sure your answer is completely up to date, which entails knowing how to access very recent law generally; and ending with the way in which computer-assistance can (and cannot) help.

14.4.3 THE DIAGRAMS

These have been added at the end to show in graphic form a suggested sequence for researching. If these are to be useful, it can only be after you have read and understood the relevant sections of the text, to which they refer back.

14.4.4 REPETITION

In this treatment of the resources for and methods of legal research, you will find that some things may seem to be repeated. This is where materials previously described as static apparatus on the library shelf are then deployed in problem-solving. This repetition has the advantage of reminding you of your earlier exploration of the shelves; or else sending you back to do it. Anyway, familiarity and skill only come with repetition.

15 Getting to Know the Library

15.1 Introduction

The first thing you must do is familiarise yourself with the law library. Find out what it has and where it has it. Find out which library you can go to research in when yours hasn't got what you need, and then have a look at that library too. By the time pupillage begins, the would-be barrister should be familiar with the basic tools of practical legal research and how they all fit together. So please read carefully what follows, and then use it as a guide-book to the shelves, finding and exploring each of the materials described.

15.1.1 EXERCISES

Merely looking at the shelves, and perhaps flicking through a few pages, will not do much for you. Do the simple exercises at the end of each section so as to get some basic dexterity with each of the sources in turn. You should then be able to tackle the problems which are set in the research technique section.

15.2 The Essential Parts of a Law Library

An English law library has at least five different sorts of materials: statutes, reports, journals, textbooks, and general reference works. Of these, statutes and law reports are sometimes called primary sources because their content, legislation and precedent, is The Law; whereas the other secondary sources, though they may sometimes be highly regarded, are only their writers' opinion of what the law is. It may have sufficed in tutorial to rely on a statement in the textbook but it will rarely do so in court.

15.2.1 THE NEW TECHNOLOGY

We must get used to thinking of the books on the shelves as 'hard-copy', by contrast with (a) micro-reproduction (in the years to come more and more of the big sets of law serials will be reduced to microfiche or CD-ROM) and (b) computerised sources (many chambers and solicitors' offices have LEXIS and some also have access to other databases). For these you will need to have a special course of instruction. There are some suggestions at the end of this chapter on the approach to using LEXIS, but otherwise these notes deal mainly with what is on the shelf. In any event you must master the lawyer's traditional tools first.

15.3 Legislation

15.3.1 PRIMARY LEGISLATION

Legislation may be primary or secondary. In the UK, primary legislation takes the form of statutes (or 'enactments') which are Acts of Parliament or Measures of the Church Assembly. Acts are either

Public General Acts, Local Acts, or Private and Personal Acts. Of all of these the only ones of importance for everyday practice are Public General Acts, which make up what is sometimes called our 'statute book'. Local and Personal Acts may be found in the Inns' libraries. Since 1992, Local Acts for each year are included in *Current Law Statutes*.

15.3.2   SECONDARY LEGISLATION

Secondary legislation, referred to as 'subordinate' or 'delegated', consists of law which has the full force of statute but which has been laid down not in Parliament but by lesser bodies authorised by Parliament. Thus local authorities and public utilities are often given power to make by-laws. (For how to find these, see Local Government Act 1972, s. 236 as amended.) But for present purposes we need consider only the regulations made by government departments and published in the form of Statutory Instruments (formerly called Statutory Rules & Orders).

15.4   Acts of Parliament

These appear in law libraries in three main forms:

1.   Queen' Printer's copies: these are the officially-issued Acts in the form in which they were passed by Parliament. For citation and use in court, these are the only versions the judges wish to refer to.

Each new Act on getting the royal assent is published by Her Majesty's Stationery Office (HMSO), whose head is also the Queen's Printer of Acts of Parliament. On the library shelf these Acts will be found in bound volumes with either 'Public General Acts and Measures' or 'Law Reports Statutes' on their spine. Inside, both these series are identical, Queen's Printer's copies. They have recently been enlarged into A4 page size.

2.   Annotated statutes: *Current Law Statutes* are arranged in annual volumes. Very recent Acts arrive in loose-leaf parts during the year. The annotations, written by specialist editors, give much helpful information, e.g. the legal and Parliamentary background; references following each section to cases, regulations, or other statutes affecting that section; and often a general running commentary. For research purposes annotated statutes are much more useful than the bare official versions.

3.   Classified annotated statutes: *Halsbury's Statutes* (not to be confused with *Halsbury's Laws of England*) are not only annotated but arranged in alphabetical order of subject-headings. This set thus organises in its many volumes the entire statute law of this country, of whatever date, which is still to any extent in force. The fourth edition (grey with red labels) is now almost complete. The whole set is kept up to date to the beginning of the present year by an annual cumulative supplement. This follows the same sequence of volumes and subject-headings as the main set. For still more recent developments there is a loose-leaf Noter-Up volume. A Current Statutes Service laid out in several loose-leaf volumes gives the text of Acts too recent to get into the appropriate bound volume. There is a separate index volume which lists both alphabetically and chronologically every Act extant with its reference in the main set; or in the Current Statutes, indicated by a letter S.

Annotations take time to prepare. It may be a while before the edited *Current Law* or *Halsbury* version of an Act arrives. (Meantime they may issue a temporary unannotated version on coloured paper.) During that delay you will have only the HMSO version to consult, and will have to do your own interpreting unaided; though usually there will have been running commentary on the Bill during its passage, which can be found in the practitioners' journals. See for these **15.12**.

15.4.1   CITATION OF STATUTES

Every modern Act of Parliament has a short title and year (e.g. Theft Act 1968), and a unique 'chapter' number (e.g. 1968 c. 60). Before 1963, chapter numbers were based on the regnal year or years during which the Parliament sat. So, for example, 15 & 16 Geo. 5 c. 20 is an old friend of yours. Personal Acts have their chapter number in italic e.g. *c. 11*. Local Acts have it as a Roman numeral (Port of London Act 1968 is 1968 c. xxxii).

15.4.2 LOOKING UP STATUTES

(a) *You know the short title?* In the annual bound volume or volumes of HMSO versions (see **15.4(1) above**) you will find an alphabetical index of the year's Acts giving the chapter number of each. The Acts are bound in chapter number order. Or you can do the same with the *Current Law Statutes* annual volumes. Always look for the index to these in the last volume for the year, where that year had more than one volume.

(b) *You show the short title but aren't sure of the year?* (e.g. when was the Data Protection Act?) The alphabetical index volume to *Halsbury's Statutes* will give it. Alternatively, *Current Law Legislation Citator* has at the beginning an alphabetical list of statutes which have been in any way active in the years covered by the two *Citator* volumes.

(c) *You don't know the short title, but do know the year and chapter number?* This is a bit unlikely, but may sometimes happen with older statutes. You can find it as in (a) above if it is a calendar year. If it is a regnal year and you have the HMSO bound volumes, you should be able to find any Act this century by looking at the spines, which give the regnal year as well as the calendar year. For older Acts, check the chronological index in *Halsbury's Statutes* index volume, or in the official two-volume *Chronological Table* (see **15.4.3**).

15.4.3 IS THE ACT IN FORCE?

Once you have found your Act, the next most important thing to find out is whether it is in force. This is really two questions:

(a) *Is it yet in force?* Many Acts have a delayed beginning and await activation. Having found your Act, the first thing to do is to see if it is in force, and the first place to look for that is in the commencement section. Go to the end of the Act and find the last two or three sections (of the Act itself, ignoring any schedules — pronounced 'shedule' — which are often appended at the end of Acts). These last sections give the short title, the extent (geographical) of operation, and the date of commencement. This may be the date of enactment (which you can find on the first page of the Act in a square bracket immediately after the long title), or a stated date after that, or it may be left to the government department concerned (nominally 'the Secretary of State', or 'Her Majesty in Council'), to bring it into operation, and in such stages, areas, etc., as it sees fit. If the last, this is done by Commencement Order made in a Statutory Instrument (see **15.5**).

If it is not clear from the Act itself whether it (or the particular bit that you need) is in force, the simplest way to find out is to refer to *Is It In Force?* This annual volume, part of the *Halsbury's Statutes* set, covers every Act of the last 25 years, and is up-to-date to the beginning of the present year. Acts are listed alphabetically within their year. If this says 'not yet in force', don't rest content. It may have been activated since. Have a look at the loose-leaf Noter-Up volume. You will find an *Is It In Force?* section in the binder. Alternatively (or, better, look here too), *Current Law* latest monthly part has all the commencement dates fixed for Acts so far this year. You are now up-to-date to sometime last month. The *New Law Journal* Practitioner section gives each week's commencement orders. To be right up to the minute, HMSO publish a *Daily List* which many libraries take.

(b) *Is it still in force?* There is nothing more embarrassing than finding you have based yourself on an Act which has, unknown to you, been repealed or substantially amended. There is no way of telling this from the Act itself. *Halsbury's Statutes* plus its annual cumulative supplement plus the Noter-Up should give you the present status of the Act. Equally good is *Current Law Legislation Citator* which gives every Act's subsequent life-history, down to the end of last year. For happenings since, check the last monthly part of *Current Law*, which has a Statute Citator section giving all the current year's happenings to any statutes.

The most comprehensive source for all statutes' subsequent statutory history is the two-volume *Chronological Table of the Statutes* published by HMSO. This is very helpful with older statutes, but is not issued sufficiently often to help with more recent happenings. The same is true of their *Statutes in Force*, a loose-leaf series which some libraries take. They aim to provide under subject groupings every extant Act and to continually update and amend the texts.

15.4.4   OLDER ACTS

Old Acts which are still in force will be found in *Halsbury's Statutes*. You will not often have to research old repealed Acts. If you do, and are unsure about the reference, check in the *Chronological Table of the Statutes*. You should then be able to locate the text in one of two official collections:

(a)   *The Statutes Revised:* or if not there,
(b)   *The Statues of the Realm*, huge volumes covering 1235 to 1713, produced by the Record Commission in the nineteenth century.

Neither set is easy to find, though theirs are the required versions of Acts for citation in court: see Interpretation Act 1978, s. 19. You are as likely to find one of the unofficial collections called *Statutes at Large*. These are reasonably accurate, and in size and coverage more useful as well as more widely available.

15.4.5   OTHER SOURCES OF STATUTES

Other collections of statutes may be found in the library, mainly where Acts relevant to a particular subject or jurisdiction are provided in works written for that area of practice, e.g. *Stone's Justices Manual, Paterson's Licensing Acts*, and the many encyclopedic textbooks (Housing Law, Medical Law, etc.).

Exercise 1 — Statutes

1.   What are the short titles of the following statutes?

(a)   21 Geo. 3 c. 49.
(b)   1971 c. 30
(c)   59 & 60 Vict. c. 14.

2.   Are the following in force?

(a)   Broadcasting Act 1990, s. 24.
(b)   Suppression of Religious Houses Act 1539.
(c)   National Health Service and Community Care Act 1990, s. 35.
(d)   Criminal Justice Act 1988, s. 29.

3.   What is the punishment prescribed by Piracy Act 1837, s. 2?

4.   What conduct is made illegal by the Chartered Associations Act?

5.   Which marriages are made void by the Royal Marriages Act?

6.   What is the heading to Part VIII of the Law of Property Act?

15.5   Delegated Legislation: the Statutory Instruments

15.5.1   PUBLICATION

The SIs are a vast series. Currently there are said to be about 12,000 in force, with a constant flow from Whitehall of new ones and revocations and amendments. The official texts are published as

Queen's Printer's copies by HMSO. Often these are just one sheet of paper. If your library takes these they will have to be carefully filed in sequence somewhere. In more durable form, the SIs will be found in one of three places in the library:

(a)   Annual Volumes: As with the statutes, HMSO publishes annual volumes of SIs in sequence. They fill several large blue volumes each year, for which few libraries have the shelf space; and especially now that they, like the HMSO statutes, have swelled to A4 format.

(b)   *Halsbury's Statutory Instruments:* This set of volumes, arranged alphabetically by subject-matter, lists all the SIs in force. But it prints the full texts of only a few, selecting the ones which the editors believe to be those most needed by lawyers and which (unlike, e.g. the Rules of the Supreme Court) are not likely to be found elsewhere in the library. The key to the set by subject-matter is the limp-bound Consolidated Index, revised annually, and supplemented during the current year by the index at the back of Service Volume 1. The key to the set by SI reference number is at the front of the same Service Volume, where you will find a numerical list indexing every SI in force up to last year. This list is then updated in the Monthly Survey, also in the same binder. Use the Key part of the Monthly Survey to check if your SI or subject-area is affected by recent developments. The key by short titles of SIs is the alphabetical list in the Consolidated Index.

Note that this *Halsbury* set, like the other multi-volume encyclopedic sets, is in a continous state of revision and replacement. The current set has grey volumes, but some of the outgoing black volumes may still be required. The various indexes indicate this by the use of italic or roman type respectively.

(c)   Textbooks: As with statutes, the main practitioners' works, especially the loose-leaf encyclopedic textbooks, should set out the SIs relevant to the scope of the book.

(d)   Older SIs and SR & Os: If still in force, they should at least be mentioned in *Halsbury's SIs*. For the text of an older instrument some of the big law libraries have the HMSO annual volumes going back for years. (The SR & Os which preceded the SIs are in red volumes.) In addition, you may find the set of *Statutory Rules & Orders and Statutory Instruments Revised*. This is a reorganisation under subject-headings of all the instruments in force at the end of 1948. There are indexes in the last volume; and the *Table of Government Orders* in a separate volume shows the impact of subsequent instruments.

15.5.2   CITATION OF STATUTORY INSTRUMENTS

Every SI is given a unique number in its year, shown as 1990/1234, or more fully as SI 1990 No. 1234. (The earlier series, before 1948, are still cited as, e.g. SR & O 1923 No. 752.) SIs also have short titles, e.g. Prison Rules 1964 (1964/388); Misuse of Drugs Regulations 1973 (1973/797).

Exercise 2 — Statutory Instruments

1.   The Access to Personal Files Act by s. 3 empowers the Secretary of State to make regulations enabling individuals to see files about them held by various bodies, and to make corrections and erasures, etc. Have any such regulations been made so far? If so, find the actual text of any.

2.   In a work on property law you find a reference, Rule 301 of SR & O 1925 No. 1093. What is this? Is it in the library? Have there been any recent cases on it?

3.   What is the date of the earliest piece of subordinate legislation that is still in force?

4.   Find the statutory provision that allows the Inland Revenue to charge interest on unpaid income tax. What is the rate of interest they currently charge? When was this fixed and how?

15.6   Law Reports

Every law library will have series of reports which are general, covering all courts and subjects; and some which are specialised, covering a limited jurisdiction or area of law. There are now many specialised series, some of which are published as part of a practitioners' periodical.

15.6.1   REFERENCES

The first problem you may encounter is decrypting the various initials used in citation. You will be familiar with WLR, All ER, Cr App R, and such commonly occurring references. For any initials which you aren't sure of, check in one of the following:

Current Law Case Citator.

Halsbury's Laws of England, Vol. 1.

The Digest, Annual Supplement.

Legal Journals Index.

Index to Legal Citations & Abbreviations.

Sweet & Maxwell's Guide to Law Reports and Statutes.

15.6.2   BRACKETS, SQUARE AND ROUND

Where the year is given in square brackets thus; [1990] 1 WLR 270, it is part of the reference. You therefore need page 270 of the particular volume of those reports with that date on the spine; if there were two or more volumes for that year, the reference will indicate the volume number. Most of our standard series of reports use this 'square-bracket' method. Where a date is supplied in round brackets, it is just given to you as useful but non-essential information; because in such series the publishers give each volume its own volume number in sequence in the set. For example, (1985) 80 Cr App R 117 tells you it was a case in 1985, but you wouldn't need to know the year to find Volume 80.

15.6.3   *THE LAW REPORTS*

Our major, semi-official series of reports, produced by the legal profession in the guise of the Incorporated Council of Law Reporting, are called simply *The Law Reports*. They started in 1865. There are now just four series:

1.   *Appeal Cases* cited as AC, has reports of the House of Lords and Judicial Commitee of the Privy Council.

2.   *Chancery* cited as Ch. contains reports of cases on all matters heard in the Chancery Division and in the Court of Appeal therefrom.

3.   *Queen's Bench* (formerly *King's*) cited as QB or KB, contains reports of cases in that Division, including its ordinary, commercial, maritime, appellate and review jurisdictions, and in the CA (Civil Division) therefrom; and also decisions of the CA (Criminal Division).

4.   *Family* cited as Fam, containing reports of the Family Division in its ordinary and appellate jurisdiction, and in the CA on appeal therefrom. (Until 1971 this Division was called the Probate, Divorce and Admiralty Division and its reports were cited in a P series.)

15.6.4   THE AUTHORITY OF *THE LAW REPORTS*

These are our senior series. They are checked by the judges concerned prior to publication. In addition to the usual headnotes, facts and judgments, they usually give a summary of counsel's arguments, which is helpful in ascertaining what points the court must have had in mind in coming to its decision. For all these reasons, these are the preferred series for citation in court. See *Practice Note* [1991] 1 All ER 352. Their corresponding disadvantage is that they are slow to arrive in the library, even in their unbound parts. To fill this gap lawyers go to one of the weekly series.

15.6.5   THE WEEKLY SERIES

(a)   The Incorporated Council since 1953 have put out a junior series to fill the gap: the *Weekly Law Reports*. These arrive in paper parts within a month or so of a case being decided. They are grouped into three volumes each year: Volumes 2 and 3 contain cases intended to appear in *The Law Reports*. Volume 1 has cases which are not intended to get that full treatment. Each paper part may contain cases destined for Volume 1 as well as for Volume 2 or 3. Look carefully at the cover to see the exact content.

(b)   Since 1936 Butterworths have provided us with the *All England Law Reports* (All ER), which in most respects are comparable with the WLR. There are three or four volumes a year, but these are merely consecutive.

15.6.6   INDEXES TO THESE REPORTS

The Law Reports publishes during the course of each year a cumulative index in a pink booklet. This includes not only *The Law Reports* cases and WLR but also the All ER and many other current series: see its front cover for the list. These indexes are conflated with those for past years, becoming the (limp) red indexes; and each ten years of these are made into a bound red index volume. (The usefulness of these indexes for research on statutes and SIs is explained in **Chapter 18**.)

15.6.7   MORE RECENT REPORTS

Almost every day in the broadsheet newspapers (*Times, Independent, Guardian, Financial Times*, formerly *Daily Telegraph*, recently *The Scotsman*, and *Lloyd's List*), there are citable law reports. In many law libraries the librarians extract and file these. Some of the more important may be reprinted after two or three weeks in one or more of the practitioners' weeklies (*New Law Journal, Solicitors' Journal, Law Society's Gazette*). These cases, if important, eventually get edited into full-strength law reports. But until they do, the newspaper or weekly is the only source. Many, moreover, never get reported further and these newspaper reports remain the sole source. There is now a comprehensive means of accessing them: *Daily Law Reports Index*.

15.6.8   *DAILY LAW REPORTS INDEX*

DLRI started in 1986. It appears in red coloured limp-bound parts, cumulated quarterly and ending as an annual bound volume. Every case that has been in any of the five dailies is included, and is accessible in four alternative ways: (1) by the parties' names; (2) by subject-matter, for which several different key-words may be extracted from a case; (3) by any statute, SI, RSC, etc., involved in the case. Every newspaper report of the case will be cited. But before trying to find the newspaper report indicated, turn to (4) cases digest, containing a useful summary of the facts and decision.

DLRI is up to date to about the last fortnight. It is thus the most up to date permanent serial reference work in the law library. Surprisingly few lawyers (as distinct from librarians) seem to use it. You should familiarise yourself with it at the first opportunity and get to know how the cumulations are organised.

15.6.9   OLDER REPORTS

(a)   Continuous series: There were various continuous series which started in the nineteenth century and ended in the middle of the twentieth: the *Law Journal Reports, Law Times Reports* and *Times Law Reports*. One such series survives: *Justice of the Peace Reports*.

(b)   Named reporters: For much of our legal past, law reporting was left to private individuals, lawyers or judges, who made their own collections of cases and which eventually got printed and published. They are recognisable by their names, e.g. Coke's Reports, Vesey Senior, Meeson & Welsby, etc., or their corresponding initials. Some libraries may have some of these in the original volumes. However they have been more conveniently collectd into 176 volumes as the *English Reports*, which can be accessed in the following ways:

(i)   If you have the case-name: the last two volumes of the set are an index of case-names. This gives both the original reporter's volume and page, and the volume and page in the ER set.
(ii)   If you have the reference but not the case-name (e.g. 1 Cl & F 527), there is a chart which comes with the ER set that lists all the reporters by name and initials, and tells you which courts they reported and in which volumes of the ER they appear. Look at the spine of the volume(s) cited and see which includes your reporter's volume reference.
(iii)   Citing the *English Reports*: Strictly, we don't. The ER is just a rationalised reprint. We still cling to the original reporter's name, volume and page when citing his reports as if we were using the old leather tomes. For this purpose you will find the original pagination preserved in the midst of ER pages by numbers in square brackets in the text.

(c)   The All England Reprint (All ER Rep): this somewhat misleadingly-named series selects older cases reported in the LT and LJ reports and from the named reporters ((a) and (b) above) which still have practical importance. It is therefore a useful alternative source, especially in smaller modern libraries which may lack the older series.

(d)   The oldest reports: the anonymous law reports known as the Year Books run from the late 1200s into the sevententh century. 1535 was the last year to be printed. These are very rarely needed in modern litigation.

15.7   To Find a Specific Case Report

If you have absorbed the above information you should with a little practice be able to find any case to which you have the reference. Where you have a case by name only, or the reference seems to be wrong, you need a comprehensive case index. This is provided by the citator volumes of the *Current Law* service.

15.7.1   CURRENT LAW CASE CITATOR

This lists the names of every case — *of whatever date* — which has had any 'life' (decided, distinguished, followed, not followed, etc.) in the period since 1947. It is arranged alphabetically by case name in two volumes, 1947–76 and 1977–88. A third volume has been started from 1989. Each year a cumulating red booklet will appear and will eventually make a third bound volume. Every report of the case is given, as well as any articles or case-notes on it and where it is digested in *Current Law Year Book*. In other words, you have the subsequent case-history of every case that has had any. The latest monthly part of *Current Law* continues the case citator into the present year, giving new cases in capitals and citations of older cases in small type.

15.8   To Find Case Law in General

If you know that you need to find cases on a topic or line of authority, the sensible place to look may be the practitioners' textbook, where they should all be at least in the footnotes. If however you want to know of cases since a definite date, try *Current Law Year Book* and the current year's parts, or *Halsbury's Laws* Annual Abridgment volumes; and the annual and recent parts of *Daily Law Reports Index*. All of these have good subject-matter or key-words indexes. However, the widest trawl through case law of any date is achieved by searching *The Digest*.

15.8.1 *THE DIGEST*

This is a multi-volume encyclopaedia of case law, organised under subject-headings. It was formerly called the *English & Empire Digest* and that name reveals one of its virtues: it digests virtually all the reported cases of the common law world outside USA. It now also includes cases of European Community and Human Rights law. It is slightly complicated to use, because of its copious indexes, tables of contents, replacement and continuation volumes, and its system of numbering cases. It is kept up to date by supplements; but it can be misleading in that it never seems to jettison cases which have been, for example, overruled in effect by statute, or whole areas of law which are defunct, such as copyhold. Nevertheless it is a most valuable source once you have learned how to use it, and provided you are sure that it is instances of precedent that you need. It is particularly useful in extending the library both historically and geographically: if you have a reference to an old case, or one from outside England, a glance at *The Digest* via its cases index may save you a lot of unnecessary outside research.

Exercise 3 — Cases

1. What are BCLC, BWCC, WWR, Co Rep, WN, NILR, Com Cas, EG, STC? Which of them does your library have?

2. How many reports are there of *Street* v *Mountford* in the House of Lords?

3. Find the most recent cases in the library on:—

   (a) market overt;
   (b) *donatio mortis causa*;
   (c) seizure of an aeroplane because its owners had failed to pay airport charges;
   (d) whether it is contributory negligence if a motorcyclist injured in a collision didn't have the chinstrap of his crash helmet done up.

4. What types of goods were involved in *Hurry* v *Mangles* (1808)?

5. Find a case reported in 1989 that says that for canon law purposes there is no difference between a corpse in a grave and cremated ashes.

6. Using *The Digest*, find:

   (a) a case from Australia on whether the ringing of church bells on a Sunday morning could be a nuisance;
   (b) a case involving Switzerland which says that a corporation has no right to freedom of conscience or religion.

15.9   Sources for Words and Phrases

A very high percentage of legal problems boil down in the end to the meaning of words. It then becomes essential to discover what meaning, if any, has been given to specific words and phrases by the law in the past. A law library must have several sources from which these meanings can be ascertained.

15.9.1 DICTIONARIES OF WORDS AND PHRASES

These very useful compilations seek to expound every word or phrase to which any judicial, legislative or other recognised legal meaning has been attached. In doing so, they give detailed references, examples of usage and other helpful information. The two works are *Stroud's Judicial Dictionary* and *Words & Phrases Legally Defined*. Both are multi-volume sets with periodic supplements keeping them up to date. Although covering much the same ground, their manner of treatment can be quite different and it is always wise to consult both works. Incidentally, should you ever need to use the American equivalent to these compilations, it is called *Words and Phrases*. The set contains about ninety large volumes, plus supplements!

15.9.2 *HALSBURY'S LAWS*, VOLUME 56 AND ANNUAL ABRIDGMENT

Following the general index to this encyclopaedia there is in Vol. 56 an index of words and phrases occurring anywhere in it. This sometimes throws up a phrase missed by the dictionaries. This is carried on for each year by the Annual Abridgment volumes which have a separate section of the year's words and phrases listed near to the beginning.

15.9.3 THE PINK AND RED INDEXES

The indexes to *The Law Reports* have a section of words and phrases under the letter 'W' in the subject-matter index. The *All England Reports* annual and cumulated indexes have a similar list.

15.9.4 *CURRENT LAW*

Each year book has a section of words and phrases as interpreted by the courts that year. The monthly parts have a cumulative list under 'W' in the subject-headings, so by looking at the latest monthly you will find a list of all the present year's words.

15.9.5 *DAILY LAW REPORTS INDEX:* INDEXES BY KEY-WORDS

Although not strictly the same as words and phrases, you can get useful further leads here to recent cases and those not reported elsewhere. Moreover the editors of law reports and *Current Law* don't single out as many cases on words as they might, so a further source is welcome.

15.9.6 LEXIS

The computer is at its most useful in searching for usage of words and phrases, if not necessarily for their interpretation. But unless your word or phrase is very unusual, just offering it to the Cases file will give you far too many instances to check. You should give it W/5 of constr! or defin! or mean! or interpret!

15.9.7 ORDINARY DICTIONARIES

Don't forget that it is quite proper and sometimes necessary to have one or two of the standard dictionaries' definitions available. A good law library should have at least the two-volume Shorter Oxford.

15.10 Foreign Legal Vocabulary

You can expect to have to translate from time to time legal terms from and to other European languages. There are professional legal translators who specialise in this work for big transactions, court documents, etc. But where it is just a term or concept in, say, a letter to or from a lawyer on the continent, it may suffice to refer to a foreign law dictionary. These may be two-way or they may be polyglot, giving legal equivalent terms across several languages. Most law libraries now have such dictionaries, covering at least the major European languages. Check to see which yours has. Also, if your library has the *Official Journal* of the European Community, check if it has the Eurovoc Thesaurus, volume 3 of which gives corresponding terms in the Community's languages. That brings us at last to EC documents in general.

Exercise 4 — Words and Phrases

1. Find the most recent judicial explanations of:—

    (a) 'curtilage';
    (b) 'reasonable time';
    (c) 'land covered with water';
    (d) 'likely'.

2. Has it been held defamatory to describe a lawyer as 'a dunce'?

3. An Act requires a notice to be displayed outside premises. Is it sufficient to stick it to the inside of the window of the building so that it is visible outside but remains inside?

4. A recent will left a large legacy 'to X, if he returns to England'. X has returned from Australia, where he lives, and is claiming the legacy. He says that he intends to go back as soon as he has it. The executors say this isn't what the testator meant. Are they right?

5. What do *'purger une hypotheque'* and *'Ubertragung einer schuld'* mean in foreign legal documents?

15.11   European Community Legal Documents

The legal literature of the EC is vast and every-increasing. A few official and university libraries have been designated European Documentation Centres and as such receive automatically all official publications of the various organs of the Community. The larger firms of solicitors and some chambers hold a selection of EC legal materials. The selection tends to be rather arbitrary and to vary greatly. See what your library has. You may find it has unofficial publications put out by commercial publishers: these can be more helpful than the EC's own sources. But find out where your nearest Documentation Centre is. It will be listed in what is a very useful source for EC law finders: *Directory of EC Information Sources*. If you can, see how the Documentation Centre is organised and what the legal documents consist of.

The EC produces various types of law. These correspond in type with UK domestic law: legislation, both primary and secondary, and case law. They are also comparable in the way they are either judicially noted or proved. [See European Communities Act 1972, s. 3.)

15.11.1   EC LEGISLATION

15.11.1.1   Primary
This consists of the treaties which established the three communities (EEC, ECSC, Euratom), plus amending treaties and the Single European Act. There is an official edition of these, a small pale lavender book with thumb-holes, published in 1987. But in most libraries they may be found in Sweet & Maxwell's *European Community Treaties* (1980), the same publisher's *Encyclopedia of European Community Law*, B volumes, or *Halsbury's Statutes*, Vol. 50. Some libraries may have Smit & Herzog's *Law of the European Economic Community* (New York: Matthew Bender).

15.11.1.2 Secondary: regulations, directives or decisions
(For the difference betwen these, see Art. 189 of the EEC Treaty.) These are cited by their year, community and running number, e.g. Reg (EEC) 123/88; Dir 85/123/Euratom; Dec 89/123/ECSC.

15.11.2 FINDING SECONDARY LEGISLATION

All EC secondary legislation, including draft legislation, and also recommendations and opinions, are published in the *Official Journal* (OJ) which is the main organ and official gazette of the EC. In theory, with a reference to a particular instrument, it can be found in the OJ via the index (alphabetical order, by subject) or methodological table (numerical order, for each type of instrument). In practice this may be difficult. Not many libraries have the entire OJ. (There are about 32 volumes a year!) The indexing is slow and only monthly and annual, not cumulated.

Various commercial publishers produce collections of EC secondary legislation. In this country there is Sweet & Maxwell's loose-leaf multi-volume *Encyclopedia of European Community Law*, C volumes; and CCH's *Common Market Reporter*, despite its name, gives legislation arranged under subject matter.

15.11.2.1 Is it in force?
EC secondary legislation is constantly amended and supplemented. As with UK legislation you must check to see the present state of any particular instrument. The EC publishes a *Directory of Community Legislation in Force* about twice a year. Volume 1 contains an Analytical Register, classifying by subject-matter. Volume 2 has a chronological index, if you know the number; and a broad subject-category alphabetical index, which is useful for getting into the subject-matter headings used by Volume 1.

A more up-to-date and easier to use service for updating is provided by Butterworths' *European Communities Legislation: Current Status* in 3 volumes, supplemented by a telephone service for subscribers.

15.11.2.2 Subject-headings
Searching for EC legislation by subject-matter can be difficult because the legal vocabulary of the European Community is more varied and at times more obscure than our own. Some help can be got from the Eurovoc volumes which come as an annex to the OJ. These are a thesaurus: alphabetical, subject-oriented and multi-lingual, to aid in word- and concept-searching. Once you have an acceptable subject-heading, the index to *Current Statutes* should lead you to the applicable legislation.

15.11.2.3 Implementation of directives
Directives from Brussels tell member governments to legislate but leave them to do it in their national way. It may be easy enough to find the directive but often difficult to find if it has been put into law by the UK, let alone by other member states; and if so, how. Butterworths *EC Legislation Implementator*, a soft-cover twice-yearly volume sets out most of the EC's directives since the UK's accession (continued by fortnightly blue sheets) giving for each the instrument of implementation, if any, by the UK.

15.11.2.4 Draft legislation
Generally speaking, the Commission proposes new directives and the Council eventually approves them, but the progress can be tortuous. The Commission's proposals first appear in their numbered COM series. These should be noted in the various current news sources, and are carried by the House of Commons *Weekly Information Bulletin*, which some law libraries take especially for these EC pages. The proposals may go to the European Parliament and also to the Economic and Social Committee, in which case their discussion of them will appear in due course in the OJ's C Series. As noted earlier, however, the OJ index requires you to know the month or year. When finally adopted, the directive will appear in the OJ's L Series.

15.11.3   EC LAW REPORTS

Decisions of the European Court at Luxembourg (abreviated CJEC or ECJ) and the more recently formed Court of First Instance (CFI) are reported in an official series, the *European Court Reports* (ECR). But these are very slow to appear and are not well-indexed. A few libraries get transcripts of judgments straight from Luxembourg. These are the quickest of all their reports — but you may have to translate them from French! A compromise, slightly less up-to-date, is the Court's *Proceedings* series, which come weekly in duplicated sheets, about three months after the decisions. These summarise case facts and extract the vitals of the judgments.

More useful for most purposes are the *Common Market Law Reports* (CMLR), and they also include relevant decisions of the courts of member states. The CCH *Common Market Reporter*, mentioned earlier, gives selected recent cases and these are then re-published in a bound companion series, *European Community Cases* cited as CEC.

15.11.4   DIGESTS OF CASE LAW

The EC is in the process of producing a loose-leaf *Digest of Case Law* which seeks to summarise the effect of decisions. The *Gazetteer of European Law: Case Search* series, in two volumes continued monthly, attempts to provide up to date summaries, with a cumulative index. Our own *Digest* (**15.8.1**) has a European volume, Volume 21. It cannot be as comprehensive as the specialised sources but may have enough of a particular case you have been referred to to spare you a trip to a more specialised library. Even with its supplement, however, do not take it as the last word.

15.11.4.1 Finding EC Cases
Butterworths *EC Case Citator*, is based on the ECR and CMLR, but also gives OJ references to assist in finding cases not in those series. It indexes every EC Case by every means of reference: name, nick-name, subject-matter, docket number, etc. Butterworths continue it with a fortnightly Case Citator Service, pink sheets listing all the most recent cases by number, name and subject-area.

15.11.5   PERIODICAL LITERATURE

A large number of official periodicals emanate from various organs of the EC. The most important general one is the monthly *Bulletin of the European Communities*. Various publishers produce their own journals: *Common Market Law Review, European Law Review, Journal of Common Market Studies,* etc. All significant articles on EC law relevant to the UK are indexed in *Current Law* (**18.4.1**) and *Legal Journals Index* (**18.4.3**).

15.11.6   GENERAL SURVEYS OF EC LAW

There are now many textbooks by individual authors explaining EC law and legal structure to beginners, as well as monographs on particular aspects, e.g., competition. Every library differs in its holdings of these, but all will have *Halsbury's Laws*, Volumes 51 and 52 and Supplement, which attempt to give a wide-ranging survey of all aspects of EC law, as part of their encyclopedic treatment of English law.

15.11.7   REGULAR NEWS BULLETINS

Such is the ferment of EC law-making, proposals and commentaries that several publishers offer monthly, weekly, or even daily news-sheets of current legal intelligence. The following are just a few examples.

(a)   *EC Brief.* Butterworths began publishing in 1989 their *EC Brief*, a weekly newsletter reporting legal happenings of every sort, supported by a telephone service. This is recast into an annual volume summarising all EC (and related UK) legal happenings, proposals, publications, etc., over the year.

(b) *European Access*. Published six times a year by Chadwyck-Healey, gives very detailed references and some useful descriptions of current EC activities, literature and comment.

(c) *Current Law*. The monthly editions have for some years had a 'European Communities' subject-heading. A new specialised *European Current Law* covers every country in Europe cumulating monthly and with a year book. If your library does not take it, it would be well to remember that the ordinary *Current Law* will now contain rather less European matter than formerly. Conversely, *Current Law* will continue to list major articles on European law because the new publication does not list any periodical articles.

15.11.8   COMPUTER DATABASES

There is now a bewildering array of on-line databases which have EC materials. Since you are most likely to be using LEXIS, you should note how it also accesses EC materials. LEXIS has its European Communities library, EURCOM. This has CASES and COMDEC files. CASES has all the ECR and CMLR reports since these series began, as well as other series such as *European Commercial Cases* and *European Human Rights Reports*. COMDEC has all the decisions of the Commission on competition matters, mainly under Articles 85 and 86. In addition LEXIS now has an Intlaw library which includes an ECLAW file containing much of the OJ L and C Series. Details of these libraries are in the literature supplied to subscribers by LEXIS.

The EC has its own official database, Celex, covering virtually the whole of the EC's massive legislative, judicial and preparatory output, and almost all in full text. Parts of it are accessible through LEXIS or Profile or on CD-ROM (video disc), with regular updates.

Spearhead is another much-favoured database. It summarises legislation related to the single market, at every stage of its life-cycle from the merely projected to the fully implemented. One of its special virtues is that because it is produced by the DTI, it gives the names of responsible officials to contact at government level.

Exercise 5 — European Community Law

1.   Find out what the following are about and whether they are still in force:—1677/88/EEC; 87/153/EEC.

2.   Find the regulation fixing the minimum price to be paid to producers of Williams pears.

3.   The CJEC two or three years ago ruled that the Commission, having mistakenly awarded too large an amount of aid to an applicant, could not after two years withdraw the award and make a fresh one for a lesser amount. Who was the Advocate-General in the case?

4.   Which is the EC Directive which gave rise to the Consumer Protection Act 1987? Who signed it?

5.   Find the EC Directive which enables lawyers and other professionals to be qualified to practise in any other EC country. What are the two 'compensatory mechanisms', one or other of which the host country may require?

15.12   Legal Journals

Practitioners' libraries may have some periodicals you will recognise from your academic studies but the emphasis will be on practitioners' specialised periodicals. The weeklies (NLJ, SJ, LSG) keep up a running commentary on all current and pending legal happenings, professional news and opinion. A browse through one of these every week must now become a habit for you in order to be well-informed. In every specialised area of legal practice there are now legal or professional periodicals which you will want to scan if those areas are of concern to you. It is however virtually impossible to keep up with the vast range of periodical literature now offered to lawyers. The usefulness of *Current Law* and *Current Law Year Book* in listing periodical articles was mentioned earlier. However, we now have some more efficient ways of accessing this literature.

15.12.1 *LEGAL JOURNALS INDEX*

This started in 1986. It lists every article in a very wide range of periodicals (some of them only quasi-legal) by title, subject-matter, and author's name; and where it is a case-note or statute-note, by the case or statute name. It comes out in monthly parts and is cumulated quarterly and annually. It is a most valuable new tool for research into recent developments, and can be the first port of call before venturing into the unknown as well as the final checkpoint, when you think you have the answer from primary sources.

15.12.2 JOURNALS ON LEXIS

In addition to its files of cases and statutes, LEXIS has a UKJNL library which gives access to every article printed in the NLJ and LSG since 1986. Since almost every legal and professional happening is written about in these periodicals, and at around the time it occurs, this is a most valuable source of contemporary comment on the legal scene. It is especially useful where a change in the law is in contemplation or mere speculation, and the possible impact on existing law is discussed. Keying in a suitable expression from existing law should then reveal what commentators think is going to happen to it, a very useful sort of updating.

Exercise 6 — Journals

1. Find an article in 1988 about pupillage in chambers being more like unpaid labour than education.

2. Find the most recent article you can on:— (a) Romalpa clauses; (b) Dogs Act 1871.

3. How many articles has Alec Samuels published so far this year?

[See also **Chapter 22** which lists the most common books used in practice.]

16   Starting to Research

Having now surveyed the apparatus of the law, we have to bring it to bear in solving specific problems. This and the following chapters aim to show how this is done. The order adopted here is to start with searching in more familiar areas of law; then going on to research in unknown territory; then to updating and to accessing very recent law; some further thoughts on construing words and phrases; and a few remarks on computer-assisted research. Exercises are set for each section. At the end are some diagrams presenting a suggested sequence in graphical form.

Although reference back to **Chapter 15** may be necessary, some of its content has been repeated from a problem-solving standpoint as a reminder.

There are a few preliminary observations which need to be kept in mind throughout:

   (a)   *The Right Way:*   there is no one invariable or correct way to research in law. There are almost always two or more parallel routes to the same destination. With experience and instinct practising barristers know where and how to look up the law (or whose brains to pick). Many a pupil must have had the experience of sweating for two or three days to produce an opinion on some seemingly esoteric point. Their master scans it with a faint smile and then dictates a full (and very different) opinion off the cuff. But this need not discourage you. In legal research everyone makes mistakes, misclassifies, follows false trails to dead ends. The important thing is to learn from mistakes and to develop an approach which avoids them. For the beginner there *is* one right way: be very methodical and thorough.

   (b)   *Subject-Headings:*   the most usual point of entry into the law books is by way of the subject-matter of the problem, which you have first to recognise and classify. An initial difficulty here is that legal labelling tends to vary from one period to another and from one law publisher to another. For example, if you have a matrimonial dispute to advise on, do you look under 'husband and wife', or 'divorce', or 'family law' or 'domestic relations'? Similarly with what used to be called 'master and servant' and is now called 'employment law' (or is it 'labour law', 'industrial law', 'trade union law', 'equal opportunities', 'discrimination', or whatever?) One discovers with experience, trial and error, which category is used by which publisher.

   (c)   *The End-Product:*   the pupil barrister's ultimate purpose is to produce an opinion which is a well-constructed statement of thoroughly-researched law applied to the essential facts. The proper approach to opinion-writing, described elsewhere in the Manual, has to affect the way you research. Counsel's opinions are not broad and discursive overviews of an area of law such as might have won you high marks in university or polytechnic law school. They have to be clear, concise, realistic, reliable, client-oriented applications of the law to the facts as stated. If you bear this in mind it will help to keep your feet on the ground and to ensure that your research does not pull you in all directions. Be resourceful but not perfectionist.

   (d)   *Finding Nothing:*   the problems set in the exercises which follow all have more or less 'correct' and ascertainable solutions in the law. That this should be so is necessary, or at any rate desirable, for learning purposes. However, to some extent this may give a false picture of law in practice, where sometimes there is no clear-cut answer, and sometimes no discoverable law at all. Finding nothing, no case on the point, no legislation, nothing written about it, is not necessarily

251

failure. Always provided you have done your researches thoroughly, it is success. If there is really no authority, you are free to construct what arguments or analogies you can. But of course your instinct should tell you when and where there is likely to be some relevant law on the point and should prompt you to search more widely or thoroughly before accepting a nil finding. Anyway, in the accompanying exercises there will always be something to find. In one situation, finding 'nothing' is quite normal, and usually good news: in the process of following-through. See further below.

(e) *Further Reading:* There are several books dealing with aspects of legal research. These include:

(i) Dane J. & Thomas P.A., *How to Use a Law Library*, 3rd ed. (London,: Sweet & Maxwell 1987)

(ii) Farrar J.H. & Dugdale A.M., *Introduction to Legal Method*, 3rd ed. (London: Sweet & Maxwell 1990).

(iii) *Legal Research in England and Wales,* 2nd ed. (Hebden Bridge: Legal Information Resources 1990).

(iv) Logan R.G. (ed.), *Information Sources in Law*, (London: Butterworths 1986).

(v) Tunkel V., *Legal Research: Law Finding and Problem Solving* (London: Blackstone Press 1992).

But no amount of book-learning will give you the skill necessary for effective research in law. So read and absorb these pages, do the exercises and learn from your successes and failures.

16.1 Finding Law You Already Know Something of

Although in pupillage you will be thrust into areas of law totally strange and new to you, there will be occasions when the ground seems slightly familiar, where you recognise the legal context (contract, tort, crime, procedure, etc.) even though you do not know the actual answer.

Exercise 7
Consider how you would go about looking up the law on these:

(a) What is the maximum fee on counsel's brief allowable on scale 2 and scale 3 in the county court?

(b) What is the maximum fine for an offence under the Tattooing of Minors Act?

(c) While on holiday in France, John, an Englishman, found some valuable jewellery in the hotel. He kept it and brought it back to England. The jewels (in his possession) have now been identified as stolen and on these facts he has now been charged in London with handling stolen goods, How would you advise him?

(d) Peter, who has just failed the Bar Finals, says the multiple-choice exams he had to sit were unfair in setting too high a pass mark and are anyway not a suitable test of legal aptitude. Has he any legal remedy?

Analysis
However blank you may feel about any of these, you do actually know enough to at least set off in the right direction. A moment's reflection should suggest that the answer to (a) will be somewhere in the Green Book. For (b) you will have first to find the Act: either by knowing or discovering its date, or by reference to a comprehensive work on criminal law. These will not necessarily give you the answer, but will point you in the right direction. You must have realised that for (c) you will have to go first to the relevant sections of the principal statute, and that you will then have to see if there has been any case law to interpret them. By contrast, the remedy in (d) (if there is one) must presumably lie in the field of administrative law, essentially a case-law area without much statutory material.

16.2   Use of Textbooks

Where you recognise the area of law involved and have some acquaintance with it, it makes sense to go straight to the known appropriate source: the Act or case itself, if you know it; or, better, the general secondary source, the textbook. Until now textbooks for you have meant students' textbooks. These may still be a useful starting-point, but do remember that you need to switch to the corresponding practitioners' works, with their detailed indexes, comprehensive coverage, multiplicity of decisions cited, updating supplements and general in-court citability. Academic books have the advantage when it comes to speculation about uncertainties in the law, answering difficult questions as yet unresolved in litigation, perhaps drawing inspiration from other jurisdictions. For this purpose some of the major academic works in, for example, criminal law and evidence, are cited from time to time in court. But it will usually suffice to get leads from these rather than to cite the writers' opinions verbatim.

You need to familiarise yourself with what is the practitioners' text in each area of law you are likely to have to research.

Exercise 8
Identify and find the main practitioners' books in the following fields:—

contract, conveyancing, company law, civil procedure, landlord and tenant, evidence, custody of children, defamation, licensing, town planning, damages, jurisdiction of magistrates, insurance, motor vehicles, industrial tribunal cases, professional ethics of barristers.

Which, if any, of these do not have supplements?

If you were correct in your guess at the subject area of your problem, you should by intelligent use of the appropriate textbook index (or table of contents), plus the supplement, have obtained one or more useful references. Find these in the law reports, statutes or wherever and see if they are what you want.

Can't find them? If your difficulty is in decoding the reference itself, you may need to refer to one of the legal citation manuals. You have been reminded in **Chapter 15** how we cite and find statutes (short title, regnal/calendar year etc.) and the more common series of law reports (round and square brackets etc.). More cryptic initials are explained in any of:

Current Law Case Citator.

Halsbury's Laws of England, vol. 1.

The Digest. Supplement Volume.

Legal Journals Index.

D. Raistrick, *Index to Legal Citations and Abbreviations.*

Various law dictionaries.

Exercise 9
What do the following commonly used legal abbreviations stand for?

LGR, CLY, OFT, FSR, SI, SFO, CPS, H & N, RPC, CCR.

16.3 The Right Case or Act?

In law reports a quick scan of the lines of catchwords which are provided between the case name and the headnote may help to eliminate unwanted cases. Statutes don't have catchwords but the annotated series (*Current Law Statutes Annotated* and *Halsbury's Statutes*) offer introductory notes, explanations of sections and cross-references which may be helpful for the same purpose. Annotated statutes are much more useful for the researcher than the official Queen's Printer's versions. Remember, however, that it is the official version that you will need for citation in court.

16.4 Following Through

Never be satisfied with what you have found until you have checked that it is still extant, unoverruled, unrepealed etc. A glance at a supplement taking only a few seconds may transform what the body of the book says.

Exercise 10

1.   Mary was left property by the will of her husband, Tom, who died in June. Tom's will, made in November 1982 when Tom and Mary were engaged, stated that Tom was looking forward to marrying Mary. He did marry her in March 1983. Mary wants advice on her rights under the will. She has been told by Tom's family that her marriage to Tom revoked it.

2.   Percy, a company director, wants to borrow £20,000 from the bank. He has offered his company as guarantor. The bank manager has agreed, 'if it's allowed'. Can the company guarantee the loan?

3.   Daphne employed a firm of heating contractors to replace the central heating system in her house. She warned them of the special need to take care of art treasures in the house. One of the workmen using a blowlamp set fire to a priceless tapestry. The fire was soon put out and little damage was done but Daphne suffered nervous shock. The contractors' insurers have agreed to pay for the damage but not for the nervous shock, since Daphne was admittedly not in fear for her own safety but only for her property. Can she nevertheless claim against the contractors for nervous shock?

16.5 Other Members of the Bar as a Resource

Other barristers can be a very useful research resource in many cases. It is a strong tradition of the Bar that one barrister will help another, and it is natural to talk informally to other members of chambers when you have a problem. This point is fairly obvious and will only be dealt with briefly here. Of course, consulting others should not replace doing proper research yourself, but it can be a valuable addition in many circumstances.

Amongst the circumstances in which one might wish to consult another member of the Bar are the following:

(a)   Where an aspect of a case involves an area of law one is not entirely familiar with, one might consult a person who regularly practises in the area. (If the whole brief is in an area with which one is not familiar, one should consider returning it to the solicitor).

(b)   Where you wish to check you are up to date on a particular point.

(c)   Where you are aware that another barrister has recently acted in a similar case to the one you are presented with.

(d)   Where you have a legal or factual hypothesis about your case and you wish to try it on someone.

Ethical considerations must be kept clearly in mind if you do wish to discuss a case. The case is the client's and the client has a right to privacy. Names should not be used and personal details should not be revealed. If it is valuable to discuss points in a case with another practitioner only relevant facts without names should be given, and points may usefully be discussed in an impersonal or hypothetical way, for example, 'I'm appearing for a man who . . .' or 'If a person does not know that . . .'

17 Cold-starting

You can be set a legal problem that has no obvious starting point. The area of law may be just about recognisable, or not even that. This rarely happens to an experienced lawyer. If it does, he or she will apply some thoughtful analysis to the facts, consider the source or origin of the problem, probe the client for background knowledge, do some brain-picking etc. until some pointers emerge sufficient to indicate the right approach.

17.1 Unfocused Problems

Sometimes one is starting cold not so much because the area is unrecognisable as because the problem is unfocused i.e., you are asked to advise generally in a situation where no actual problem has yet arisen, in order to forestall any problem. If a client comes with a summons in his hand you know broadly what the issue is and will seek out the facts and then the law. If, however, he says 'I am thinking of doing so-and-so. Is that all right?', you may have to pose problems to yourself in thinking of all forseeable snags which might arise.

17.2 Keywords

Obviously any problems set for you here as an exercise have to be hypothetical, so you cannot do any of these things except the first: analysis. This involves a careful examination of the facts, attempting to identify the area of law involved and/or to establish what keywords the facts provide. Keywords are any terms which are legally significant and therefore index-worthy (or LEXIS-worthy, but see later for that). The broadest general index in the law library is in the index volumes to *Halsbury's Laws of England*. It descends to factual subjects, not just legal categories. When you have no idea where to begin, begin here. *Halsbury's Laws of England* is a legal encyclopaedia and provided you use it properly (index, volume, supplement, current service) and see where it tells you to go, it is one of your best friends in the library.

Example
A Bar students' magazine wants to run a competition. Readers are asked to guess the number of Bar exam candidates this year who pass in all subjects. Entry is free. Only one entry is allowed per reader, who must be a Bar Finals student. If no one gets exactly the right figure, the prize (new edition of the White Book) will go to the closest guess. Some officious lecturer at the Bar School says he thinks the magazine ought to get legal advice in case there are any restrictions or regulations applicable. You are asked to check.

Analysis
Can there be any legal objection to this? What area of law would it be? It doesn't look like wagering or betting. No money is involved. It's not a lottery with tickets. Indeed, some skill is involved. Freedom of the press? Competition law? Prize law? (Surely they are something quite different?) But maybe 'competition' or 'prize' could be worth trying as keywords.

Assuming that you have succeeded in finding the answer, it is worth noting that the above problem could have been formulated without using the actual words 'prize' or 'competition'. The point is that you must not expect that the keyword which unlocks the law will always be explicit and obvious. You may have to find synonyms or paraphrases before the particular index you are using will respond. A good index will usually give cross-references (drunkenness — see intoxication; drug — see narcotic, pharmaceutical, prescription). But not all indexers are so helpful. You will often have to use your imagination, stretch your vocabulary, and translate from plain lay terms to legal concepts to arrive at the vital keyword.

Exercise 11 — Simple Keyword Problems
1. When is the close season for snipe?
2. Must London taxis have meters?
3. In what circumstances may a Coroner hold an inquest on a Sunday?
4. If an auctioneer gives away free gifts during the course of an auction, what legal effect may this have on the auction?
5. If the police tow away a car abandoned in the street, can they sell it?
6. At what time(s) of day may a loudspeaker be used in the street for purposes of advertising or selling?
7. North Sea gas is odourless but when it comes into our houses it smells. In legal terms, why?
8. May a schoolmaster in an independent school cane a pupil?
9. How old must one be to get a licence to operate a CB radio?
10. Are the winnings of a successful gambler or the earnings of a prostitute subject to income tax?

17.3   Concealed Keywords

The keyword approach will not work if, for example, the statutory source we need uses a precise and narrow word which we tend to widen or paraphrase in ordinary usage.

Example
Henry, a landlord, granted tenancies of rooms in a newly converted house on weekly terms. To avoid giving security of tenure under the Rent Act he installed a free coffee-machine in the basement kitchen so that his tenants can help themselves in the mornings. Henry would like you to confirm that his tenants are thus not protected.

Analysis
The landlord's thinking is that if he is providing more for his tenants than merely lodging, they are, like paying guests, outside the Act. This is an inevitable distinction which the Acts have always recognised. So a trawl through one of the standard textbooks should eventually reveal how far the law allows it to be pushed. Alternatively, we could try 'food' or 'drink' as keywords. But the books don't respond to these (and they are too general for LEXIS). The real keyword is 'board', but no one not knowing it would be likely to guess it. That, however, is the Act's word, and all the cases are based on it, including a House of Lords case in 1988 which you will need to find.

17.4   Red Herrings

There may be a plethora of keywords in a problem. Some careful analysis is called for to identify the narrow issues and focus on them to the exclusion of all else.

Exercise 12 — Less Obvious Keywords
1. Charles's house was badly damaged in a severe gale last night. The upper part is in danger of falling. Charles's surveyor says it must be pulled down and made safe without delay. Workmen are standing by to do the necessary. But the house is a listed building and no authorisation has been obtained. Can Charles go ahead?

2.   Peter, Paul and Mary want to go carol singing for charity on Christmas Day. They intend to stand together, each with a collecting box, outside Euston Station. They have also trained their dog to carry a collecting box. Any advice?

3.   Oscar, a chiropractor, has been told by thé Customs and Excise that he has to add VAT to his charges to patients. Oscar says that he has always understood that there is an EC Directive which exempted the medical and related professions from having to charge VAT. He asks you to advise with a view to appealing to the VAT Tribunal.

4.   The City Council is divided equally between Conservative and Labour members. The mayor, who presides, is a Labour member. Whenever the Council votes on what is a politically loaded matter, the result is a tie. So the mayor, who has already voted with the Labour side, then purports to vote for that side again, tipping the balance. The Conservatives wish to challenge his right to do this. Will they succeed?

5.   You are consulted by a firm of investment consultants who have recently bought an estate agents' business. They want to make changes in the way it is run. Until now the estate agents have issued occasional printed lists of properties (residential and commercial) for sale and to let. The new owners want to issue these as a regular monthly circular, in a glossy brochure, making a small charge to their clients just to cover expenses. Can they go ahead?

18 Following Through

Just as you should not be discouraged if at first you do not succeed, so conversely you should not be satisfied when you find what seems to be the right case, section, regulations or whatever. Because until you have checked its current status you cannot be sure you have found the last word on the matter. You must get into the habit of searching cumulatively, right up to date.

18.1 Statutes

The first question to ask of a statute is: is it operative? That is really two questions: is it yet in force? and is it still in force?

Is it yet in force? Do not assume this. Look first at the commencement section. Nowadays this is always at the end of the Act proper, before any schedules. (Or almost always: see, however, Local Government Act 1985). Does the commencement section indicate that the bit you want has a delayed start, waiting for the Secretary of State to activate it? If so, check *Is It in Force?* or the *Current Law Legislation Citator*. If according to these it is not yet activated, check the citator part of the *Current Law* service file, and then the latest monthly part of *Current Law* for the table of this year's commencement dates. Commencement orders even more recent than that are given in the legal weeklies.

Is it still in force? You will look pretty silly if you base your opinion on a statute or section since repealed. *Current Law Legislation Citator* and the latest monthly part index will tell you of any repeals or amendments and the later Act which made them. Remember that the citator gives you every statute — of whatever date — to which anything has happened since 1947. Alternatively, if you are using *Halsbury's Statutes*, you must check its supplement and current service, updating your information to the beginning of the current year and month respectively. Notice that these give not only subsequent statutory happenings, but also SIs with regulations and orders which flesh out the sections; and, most helpfully, cases on the section.

This exercise in cumulative checking is essential. It is made easy for you by the sets (all three *Halsbury's, The Digest, Current Law*) which have cumulative supplements. We are often too lazy or rushed to follow through properly. Yet it takes only an additional minute, or not even that when, as one hopes, there are no subsequent entries to affect the information got from the main set. (Remember what was said earlier about finding 'nothing'.)

18.2 Subsequent Happenings

There are four main ways in which the law as we know or discover it can be affected by later happenings:

(a) statutes affecting earlier statutes;
(b) cases interpreting earlier statutes;

(c) cases affecting earlier case law;

(d) statutes affecting earlier case law.

Of these, the methods of checking for (a) and (b) have been considered already. (c) is easily ascertained by the use of the *Current Law Case Citator* volumes. These give every case — of whatever date — of which anything like a report exists, which has had any happenings (decided, distinguished, overruled, etc.) since 1947. Again, it is necessary to continue your follow-through to the latest monthly part of *Current Law* with its cumulative case citator for the current year.

It is (d) which is the most difficult to find out; at least where a well-known case or body of case law has been affected by recent legislation. The statute may not yet have reached the textbook's supplement. The authors may not even see it as relevant, if its impact is an incidental side-effect. One cannot expect law reports on the library shelf to be annotated to take account of later legislation. One might have thought that the *Current Law Case Citator* or *The Digest* could have indicated when a case they cite has been completely overturned by Parliament. But they do not.

Example

Any effective example depends on recentness, and will therefore quickly lose its point because of updating by the standard books and sources. The following problem illustrates the general point:

A company had a warehouse built for it in 1980. The company moved in in October 1980. Faults in the structure began to appear for the first time in 1986. A structural engineer has reported to the company that the cause is corrosion in the steelwork used in the frame of the building; and this is because the steel used was below the quality specified in the original contract. The engineer thinks that the corrosion could have started to occur within a year of the completion of the building. The cost of reinstatement is very high. The company wants your advice on whether it can proceed against the original structural engineer responsible for supervising the building.

Analysis

Assuming there was negligence on someone's part, the action is barred after six years from the accrual of the cause of action (Limitation Act 1980, s. 2). *Pirelli General Cable Works Ltd* v *Oscar Faber & Partners* [1983] 2 AC 1 says that time runs from occurence of the damage, irrespective of whether discoverable. Therefore action in tort is barred. But the Latent Damage Act 1986 was passed to alter the effect of the *Pirelli* case. It gives a further three years from when the damage should have been discovered, provided that the action was not statute-barred before the 1986 Act. The Act, by s. 5, is to commence two months from royal assent, which was on 18 July 1986. So if the damage first occurred after 18 September 1980, the cause of action was still extant at the passing of the 1986 Act, and therefore if the six-year period expired before the damage was discoverable, there are a further three years from the date of reasonable discoverability in which to sue.

In 1986 a Bar student faced with this type of problem might have gone straight to the *Pirelli* case, which he or she knew from the tort course at university, and not realised that Parliament has meanwhile intervened. The normal case-law sources would not have revealed that the House of Lords had been overruled. As this was done by way of amendment to the 1980 Act, the impact of the 1986 Act should have shown up if the student had checked *Current Law Legislation Citator* or *Halsbury's Statutes* for subsequent happenings to the 1980 Act. But if it had been a pure common law precedent that is affected by statute, there was until recently no easy way of discovering this impact pending the textbooks and supplements taking it on board. It may now be revealed by the use of *Legal Journals Index* and, more reliably, by the ALLJNL file of LEXIS.

18.3 Statutory Instruments and their Subsequent Happenings

Statutory instruments are something of a law unto themselves, with their great bulk and constant flow, their manner of creation, amendment and revocation, their separate literature, their low profile (for the general public, at least), and the complications of accessing them. Section 15.5 has outlined the various ways they are found and updated in the library. They are all now contained on the STATIS file of LEXIS. So with a little practice you should be able to find them by their number, by their parent Act or by their subject-matter, on the shelf or the screen.

18.3.1   RESEARCHING IN THE STATUTORY INSTRUMENTS

18.3.1.1   Why might you be looking for a SI?

(a)   You have an Act which is to commence on an appointed day, and want to see whether there has been a commencement order and, if so, what it says:— if that is all you want, don't bother to look for the SI (if any) unless you have some very special reason for wanting its exact words. Instead:—

(i)   Check *Is It In Force?* and continue as explained in **15.4.3** above.
(ii)   Alternatively there is a list of commencement and appointed day orders in the first loose-leaf volume of *Halsbury's SIs* updated to the present month by the Monthly Survey section in the same binder.
(iii)   In either case, follow through for the most recent orders by checking the *New Law Journal* weekly lists.

(b)   You have a section of an Act which says 'regulation may be made under this section. . .' or words to that effect, and you want to know if there has been any, you can find out in various ways:—

(i)   the annotations to that section in *Halsbury's Statutes*, with Cumulative Supplement and noter-up;
(ii)   *Current Law Legislation Citator* and latest monthly index under subject-matter;
(iii)   the Table of Statutes in *Halsbury's SIs* indexes all enabling Acts with their implementations;
(iv)   the *Index to Government Orders* and its monthly supplement, published by HMSO;
followed in all cases by a scan of the last few issues of the *New Law Journal* which lists all newly published SIs. To be right up-to-date, HMSO publishes a daily list.

(c)   You have been referred to a SI by its number:—

(i)   *Halsbury's SIs* has a chronological list in the first loose-leaf volume, which will tell you in which main volume the SI is located. If your SI is more recent than the latest listed, check the Monthly Survey.
(ii)   Alternatively, if you have the blue HMSO annual volumes, you will find the years and numbers in each stated on the spine.

(d)   You have the name of a SI but not its number (e.g. the Road Vehicle Construction & Use Regulations of uncertain date). There isn't a comprehensive name index of all SI short titles. Since 1984, *Current Law Year Book* and *Current Law* monthly have listed all of the year's SIs alphabetically. *Halsbury's Laws* Annual Abridgment volumes have a similar list. You could try the likely years here first. If that does not work (perhaps because you have the SI name incorrectly),

(i)   try to classify the subject-matter and then find it in the Title Key in the first loose-leaf volume of *Halsbury's SIs*; or if that doesn't work
(ii)   search the Consolidated Index by trying suitable key-words.

(e)   You think your problem is in a typical SI area of law, but don't know any more than that (e.g. are there any restrictions on the movement of radioactive substances?) This isn't a very likely point of entry and you should do more preparatory research before plunging in. You could try the Consolidated Index of *Halsbury's SIs* or the current *Index to Government Orders*, the official two-volume index by subject-matter. However a more methodical approach would be to go to the appropriate practitioners' textbook; or to *Halsbury's Laws of England* index and follow through.

(f)   You have the SI but don't know if it has been considered in any cases:—

(i)   At the back of the pink annual index to the *Law Reports* is a list of SIs etc. considered. Depending on the date of your SI, check also the cumulated red indexes for previous years. Note that these indexes relate not only to the *Law Reports* themselves but many other series. Nevertheless bear in mind that SIs are very often on minute areas of technical law, too specialised to be reported in any of these series. If yours is such, you should check if there is a multi-volume loose-leaf specialised textbook on the subject-area, or an appropriate specialised series of reports which have a running index.

(ii)   The indexes to the *All England Law Reports* have a similar index to SIs referred to, but covering only cases reported in their series. The remarks above apply with added force.

(iii)   *Daily Law Reports Index* (see below) has a Legislation Index which includes SIs by name which have had cases based on them.

(iv)   The CASES file of LEXIS can be searched by the SI number, name or key words.

(v)   The UKJNL file of LEXIS can be searched to find not only discussion of such case law, if any, but any other professional discussion of the particular SI which you think there might have been recently.

(g)   Your SI is ambiguous? Could its purpose have been explained during Parliamentary scrutiny? Very few SIs are debated. If yours was, it will appear in one of the SI Standing Committee volumes (see **19.3**).

(h)   What are you looking for, although a SI in origin, is better known in another form. The best examples are the various courts' rules. These are in the HMSO SIs as issued but are more conveniently to be found in the 'White' or 'Green' Books, *Stone's* or *Archbold*, etc., or their supplements.

Finally, before leaving the SIs, remember that with such an active and prolific series, whatever answer you may have found must be checked to ensure it is up to date. All the sources mentioned above have supplements, current services, etc. You should also be aware of *Current Law Legislation Citator*, which has an index of 'Statutory Instruments Affected' 1947–1989. Follow through in the subject-index to the last monthly part of *Current Law* for recent or pending happenings.

Exercise 13 — Statutory Instruments

1.   What is the daily maximum fine for breach of the Insolvency Act 1986, s. 109(2)? Has the Secretary of State increased it snce the Act was passed?

2.   How much tomato must there be in tomato ketchup? What other fruit or vegetable, if any, may it contain?

3.   When you have contact lenses fitted, to what after-sales service are you legally entitled?

4.   After an evening out, Reg drove his girlfriend Gloria home. They parked outside her house talking in the car. As it was a cold night, Reg kept the engine running, revving it from time to time. Pc Killjoy was pushing his bike along the pavement, approaching the parked car from the rear. As he drew level with the car, Gloria opened the front passenger door to get out. The door struck the Pc's bike but he managed to take evasive action and no damage was done. Pc Killjoy told Gloria that she would be prosecuted for not looking before opening the door. He also told Reg that he would be reported with a view to prosecution for keeping his engine running. Reg and Gloria say they have never heard of such offences and ask you to advise them.

5.   Uplift, while travelling by hovercraft across the Channel, was injured in an accident caused by the negligent navigation of the craft; and some of his luggage was damaged. What is the maximum Uplift can claim for his injuries and loss?

18.4   Very Recent Happenings

More than any other professional, the practising lawyer has to be right up to date, aware of this morning's law reports, this afternoon's debate in Parliament. When it comes to research, the need to find very recent law arises in two main ways: one may have a vague recollection that there was something about this not long ago; or, more methodically, one should be following through to update what one has found.

In big law firms the librarians each day prepare and circulate to members all manner of current legal news. These circulars may be filed and even indexed. Barristers' chambers offer no such service to their members, other than by subscribing to the legal weeklies. How, then, do we find cases which are too recent for the WLR and All ER (which usually appear two months or more after their deciding), new legislation or newly activated legislation?

18.4.1 *CURRENT LAW*: MONTHLY PARTS

These appear about the middle of the month following. *Current Law* tries to capture every occurrence in the law; legislation, cases, articles, books, committee reports etc., under subject headings. Make yourself thoroughly familiar with its contents, layout and classification scheme. Note specially that its index is cumulative: you only need to look at the latest month's index to cover the whole year to then.

Note also that at the end of year the contents of the monthly parts are reorganised into an annual volume: *Current Law Year Book 1992* has all the law fully indexed for that year. So if you know that it is a 1992 case, statutory instrument or whatever that you need, you may as well start here. Or where, for example, your textbook goes up to end 1991 or early 1992, the [1992] CLY subject heading, plus the latest monthly index, will cover all developments since.

18.4.2 *HALSBURY'S LAWS OF ENGLAND*: CURRENT SERVICE

This keeps the main encyclopaedia up to date to the current month if read together with the supplement volumes. It is not as easy to use as *Current Law* but covers similar ground. It also has annual volumes, the Annual Abridgment, which contain much the same as CLY.

18.4.3 *LEGAL JOURNALS INDEX*

This is a monthly index to articles appearing in a wide range of law periodicals. It indexes by title, author, subject-matter, case names, statute names and even statutory instruments where these have names. You will realise that a comprehensive source for recent comment on all manner of law must be an invaluable indirect source for the law itself; and not only of recent happenings but even of things which have not happened yet, such as the impact of pending changes. The pity is that no one thought of compiling this before 1986 when LJI began.

18.4.4 *DAILY LAW REPORTS INDEX*

Another new and most valuable index, up to date to the last fortnight. It summarises cases not yet reported, even on LEXIS, (and perhaps never to be reported), which have appeared in any of the dailies which carry law reports (*The Times, The Independent, The Daily Telegraph, Financial Times, The Guardian* and *Lloyd's List*). Whenever you think you can recall a recent case that might be relevant, this is where to check. Again, like its stable-mate the *Legal Journals Index*, it is well indexed and accessible.

18.4.5 LEXIS

The LEXIS service is discussed in **Chapter 20**. It constantly adds new material, up to date to about six weeks of the present. It is therefore roughly comparable with *Current Law* in that respect.

Exercise 14
Find the following:

(a)   The largest award so far this year for personal injuries.
(b)   A ruling in 1989 about barristers who accept two briefs for trials starting the same day.
(c)   Any recent decision on Clergy (Ordination) Measure 1990, s. 1.

Find the most recent article on:

(d)   Women at the Bar.

(e)   *Smith* v *Mutasa* (1989).

(f)   An unreported case about development in the Green Belt.

19   Researching Words and Phrases

Sometimes a legal problem comes down to the precise meaning to be given to a word or words. The uncertain words may be in an Act or regulations; or they may occur in a contract, insurance policy, lease etc, between the parties. Or, conversely, you may be at the drafting stage and trying to find an expression which will have the legal effect you want without any risk of unwanted side-effects. What follows deals mainly with the first type of situation: the expression is already there, imposed on you by the document, and you need to know how strictly or flexibly the law allows it to be interpreted. Where you are drafting and have a free hand, the research process is ultimately the same: checking against future problems instead of present ones.

You already know something of the interpretation of statutes and documents, the various approaches (literal, mischief etc.) and subrules (*eiusdem generis* etc.). Those may be needed if at the end of all your researches and interpretative efforts, you are left with ambiguity. However, the initial question is whether the law has already defined the term used, giving it an authoritative interpretation. How is this discoverable?

19.1   Stages of Inquiry

There are four stages of inquiry here. It is really only stage (c) which concerns us for present purposes but to be methodical we need to glance at all stages.

(a)   Does the Act or document provide its own definitions? Look for these. If the expression is defined, that should end doubt. But it may not be, e.g. where it is an inclusionary definition, or where it is expressly subject to exception 'where the context otherwise requires'. Even a definition section may sometimes need interpreting.

(b)   Does the Interpretation Act 1978 help? It lays down some very basic clarifications (e.g. masculine includes feminine, singular interchangeable with plural, England includes Wales, etc.). It only applies to statutes, however.

(c)   Has any other statute or case provided a definition? (See below).

(d)   Would dictionaries help? They are quite often produced in court to assist in establishing the accepted meaning of words, on the assumption that Parliament (or the parties) had that in mind. An interesting recent example is *R* v *Fulling* [1987] QB 426 which shows this can be done even where there is a definition in the statute, provided the definition is not exhaustive.

19.2   Definitions of the Term in Other Contexts

The task for the legal researcher: to find whether the law has defined the word already. Research is necessary to find out if the word or expression has been given any authoritative construction elsewhere in the law. This could be a definition in another statute, or in a case. But before commencing the search, consider whether what you may find will be relevant:

(a) Other statutory definitions. To make what should be an obvious preliminary point, one cannot mechanically import a definition of the same word from one statute to another. A definition of, say, 'child' in an Act dealing with succession is unlikely to be thought applicable to the construction of the same word in a statute on, say, employment conditions or education. On the other hand Acts on the same subject (tax, theft, road traffic etc.) have to be read together, including their definitions, so that, e.g. 'income', 'deception' and 'motor vehicle' have a consistent meaning throughout. Between these two obvious extremes lie Acts which to varying extents may be arguably *in pari materia*, i.e. on legally comparable or equivalent subject-matter. If so, their definitions may be worth borrowing for the purposes of your argument. The index to *Halsbury's Statutes* may be a helpful place to start looking.

(b) Precedents of interpretation. More commonly the situation is that you are faced with an undefined word in an Act and you want to know if it has been previously defined judicially, either in the same context or more generally.

Example

A new Act of Parliament allows compensation for disturbance in certain circumstances. The disturbance must be shown to be of 'significant proportion or degree'. The Act does not define this expression. You are consulted by a (slightly) disturbed client. How would you advise him?

Analysis

The problem is the word 'significant'. The dictionaries do not help; it can mean substantial, appreciable, more than negligible, or just showing signs. Has it perhaps been defined in any other statute and been construed by a court? Where do we look?

Reference works for words and phrases: some of these were mentioned in **15.9.1**. Most libraries have *Stroud's Judicial Dictionary* and *Words and Phrases Legally Defined*. These are multi-volume works. They not only give the words and their established judicial meanings, but full references to the cases and statutes involved. They are kept up to date by supplements. But for more recent information the indexes to the *Law Reports*, the WLR and All ER all have a section of 'words and phrases'. Then, following through, we go to the latest *Current Law* monthly part and under 'W' in the subject headings is a list of all the words and phrases construed this year so far, with references.

So if you now return to your quest for 'significant' you should find a case about a sex shop. See what it says and use your judgment whether, notwithstanding that it is far from being *in pari materia*, it could be applied to your case.

While on the subject and in that part of the library, take the opportunity to look at the other, general, law dictionaries. You will probably find *Jowitt's Dictionary of English Law, Wharton's Law Lexicon*, and the *Oxford Companion to Law*. They cover a wider field, including all manner of legal terms, maxims, concepts and institutions, with references. It is no shame to not know the meaning of some technical expression or piece of lawyers' Latin on the first occasion it confronts you. You have less excuse on subsequent occasions.

19.3   Unresolved Ambiguity

If after a methodical search no help is found, which is not unlikely with a recent statute, the Lords decision in *Pepper* v *Hart* [1993] 1 All ER 42 requires a look at the Parliamentary proceedings. The following procedure must be observed in sequence:

(a) The meaning of the words must be ambiguous or obscure or absurd; and this must be patent *before* any recourse to Parliamentary material —

(i)   *Ambiguous:* fairly capable of more than one meaning.
(ii) *Obscure:* not capable of any clear meaning.

(iii)   *Absurd:* the clear meaning makes the statute nugatory, or self-contradictory; or would subvert fundamental legal principle (e.g., confiscation without compensation, profiting from crime, retrospective effect, impact beyond UK jurisdiction, etc.).

(b)   Identify and find the reports of relevant debates on the Bill in both Houses, and in the Standing Committee. Look for the references to these in *Current Law Statutes* after the long title. Hansard volumes (red for Lords and green for Commons) and loose parts are available in the Inns', Westminster and Guildhall libraries. Standing Committee volumes (mud-yellow) are held only by the last two libraries.

(c)   Find in these reports the statement, if any, by the Minister or other promoter (only that person) as to what the words in question were intended to mean. Follow through to make sure this meaning was not altered in any way during the rest of the legislative process.

(d)   Consider whether you need to look at the clause in context. If so, find the Bill when it was at that stage. The Inns' libraries have copies of all Bills as published.

(e)   If a clear Ministerial statement is found, this is conclusive. If not, you are free to argue for your interpretation in the usual way, based on the principle of interpretation. These are in the standard works on statutes, of which *Bennion* is the most up-to-date.

In **Chapter 21** there is a diagram setting out a suggested sequence in which to approach problems on the meanings of words, especially in construing statutes.

Exercise 15

1.   The police called at the office of Snoop, a private detective, and found there a bugging device for listening in to telephone conversations. Snoop was charged under a statute which makes it an offence to use such apparatus without a licence. His counsel made a submission that, since there was no evidence of his actually using the device he could not be found guilty of the offence. The magistrates rejected this saying that he must have had the device for use. Snoop was convicted. Advise him if he should appeal.

2.   Peter insured his factory against damage from 'flood, bursting or overflowing of water tanks, apparatus or pipes'. While moving some office furniture, his employees dropped a heavy metal cabinet on to a water pipe which fractured, flooding the office and causing extensive damage to the firm's records. Peter's insurers say this loss is not within the insured perils. Advise him.

3.   Slinger moved into a house recently. He found in the loft an old tin bath, some rolls of carpet and broken chairs. He asked the local authority to take these away. They have refused to do so, saying tht their duty under the Public Health Act is to remove house refuse, which this is not. Are they right?

20 LEXIS

This is not an attempt to teach you how to use LEXIS. You have to attend a training session or two, study thoroughly the LEXIS user's guide and gain experience using a terminal. The notes and examples which follow assume that you have had that initial introduction and offer some guidance on when LEXIS is likely to help, either initially or after a hard-copy start. (If you had a course but now feel you have forgotten what you learned — a common experience — the best brief reminder is in J. Dane and P.A. Thomas, *How to Use a Law Library*. For full information you need the LEXIS user's guide. You are entitled to a copy if you have a LEXIS number.)

20.1 Contents

Make yourself familiar with the ENGGEN library, its scope and limitations. Note especially what it has that ordinary libraries have not, e.g. the Court of Appeal (Civil) transcipts of unreported cases since 1980; and, vice versa, cases reported in the *Criminal Law Review* before 1980.

Remember that LEXIS contains no law. It only contains words. To make it work effectively for you, think only in terms of words. All LEXIS can do is to compare the words or combinations you choose to give it with those it has got, giving you any that correspond. It is therefore totally literal and you have to think the same way.

The words of the law come in two distinct styles: judges' and legislators'. These may be quite different from each other, even on the same subject-matter. Keep this in mind when trying out words on the CASES and STATIS files.

20.2 Search Strategy

You should always have what LEXIS calls a search strategy worked out in advance. Consider which keywords with which connectors would seem most promising and try to devise and have in reserve a second level to refine your search should this be necessary.

20.3 UKJNL library

This most important addition to the database gives access to the contents of the *New Law Journal* and *Law Society's Gazette* since 1986. Among that material are numerous articles describing changes in the law, actual, foreseen or speculative. One especial updating advantage of this was mentioned earlier: anything significant affecting existing cases or statutes will almost certainly have been spotted and commented on by somebody. Say, for example, the rule in *Hedley Byrne & Co. Ltd* v *Heller & Partners Ltd* was cut down or extended in a particular direction by a new case. You could of course find this by conventional searching. But if a statute, law reform report, government white paper, EC

Directive, or whatever have any impact, actual or anticipated, on the principle laid down in *Hedley Byrne*, the sure way of detecting this would be by calling up UKJNL library, selecting the ALLJNL file, calling up the case name and seeing if it has had any flicker of life in the recent past. To take the example given in **18.2**, calling up just 'Pirelli' might have been enough in 1986 to reveal an article or two mentioning the case by way of explanatory background to the Latent Damage Bill, as it then was.

20.4   Recent Material

The time-lag for LEXIS updating can be as much as six or eight weeks for full texts of cases, two or three weeks for statutes and statutory instruments. For the most recent information, *Daily Law Reports Index* is quicker. So is *Legal Journals Index* which includes statute notes.

20.5   LEXIS and Hard-Copy Research Compared

LEXIS does best, easily beating hard-copy research, where an unusual significant word, whether legal usage or otherwise, is involved. Where, on the other hand, a problem concerns everyday legal concepts and verbiage it will need two or three levels of refinement and, even then, you may still have to scroll through many cases before finding one relevant. In the latter instance, hard-copy research may well prove quicker than LEXIS, because the practised human eye is far from superseded as a rapid scanner of columns and footnotes. The two exercise problems at the end of this chapter exemplify this point.

Exercise 16
Almost any of the exercises so far in the Legal Research Skills part of this file can be done for useful practice on LEXIS. There may, however, be the same initial difficulty as noted in the example given in **17.3** where no keyword is apparent. In that case LEXIS will offer nothing relevant in exchange for 'coffee' or 'coffee AND machine'. 'Landlord OR tenant! w/20 meal!' might have been better. But a reference to the books first, for an overview of the law, would have revealed 'board'. This is of course a word used in many contexts in the law. So you will need an apt association and connector to get to the case in point.

(a)   Your opinion is sought by Green, who has a garden centre situated in an outer London suburb. He intends to fly a large helium balloon above the garden centre as an advertisement. He would like to fly it as high as possible. He wants it there for the whole summer season. He intends to tie it to the roof of a caravan which he has on the site. Can he go ahead?

(b)   Your opinion is sought by Brown. He is a tenant under a lease which has a covenant 'not to assign or underlet any part of the premises without the written consent of the landlord'. Brown intends to sublet the entire premises to one sublessee. Brown says that he does not need any consent for this, since he is not underletting a 'part' but the whole. Is he right?

21 Legal Research Technique

21.1 Diagrams

The diagrams which follow are meant to offer suggested sequences for tackling basic research. They are necessarily very generalised and introductory, and after a few exercises you should have found your way around sufficiently to be able to dispense with them.

The diagrams are not self-sufficient. They presuppose that you have read the relevant sections of the text of the preceding chapters, and, in particular, that you have looked at all the source-materials there described.

The stages in these diagrams should give you some guidance not only on how to carry out research, but how to make notes to present the research in written form. Notes could usefully follow a sequence like that set out in these diagrams, a separate paragraph being used to cover the results of each stage in following the diagram.

SUGGESTED TECHNIQUE

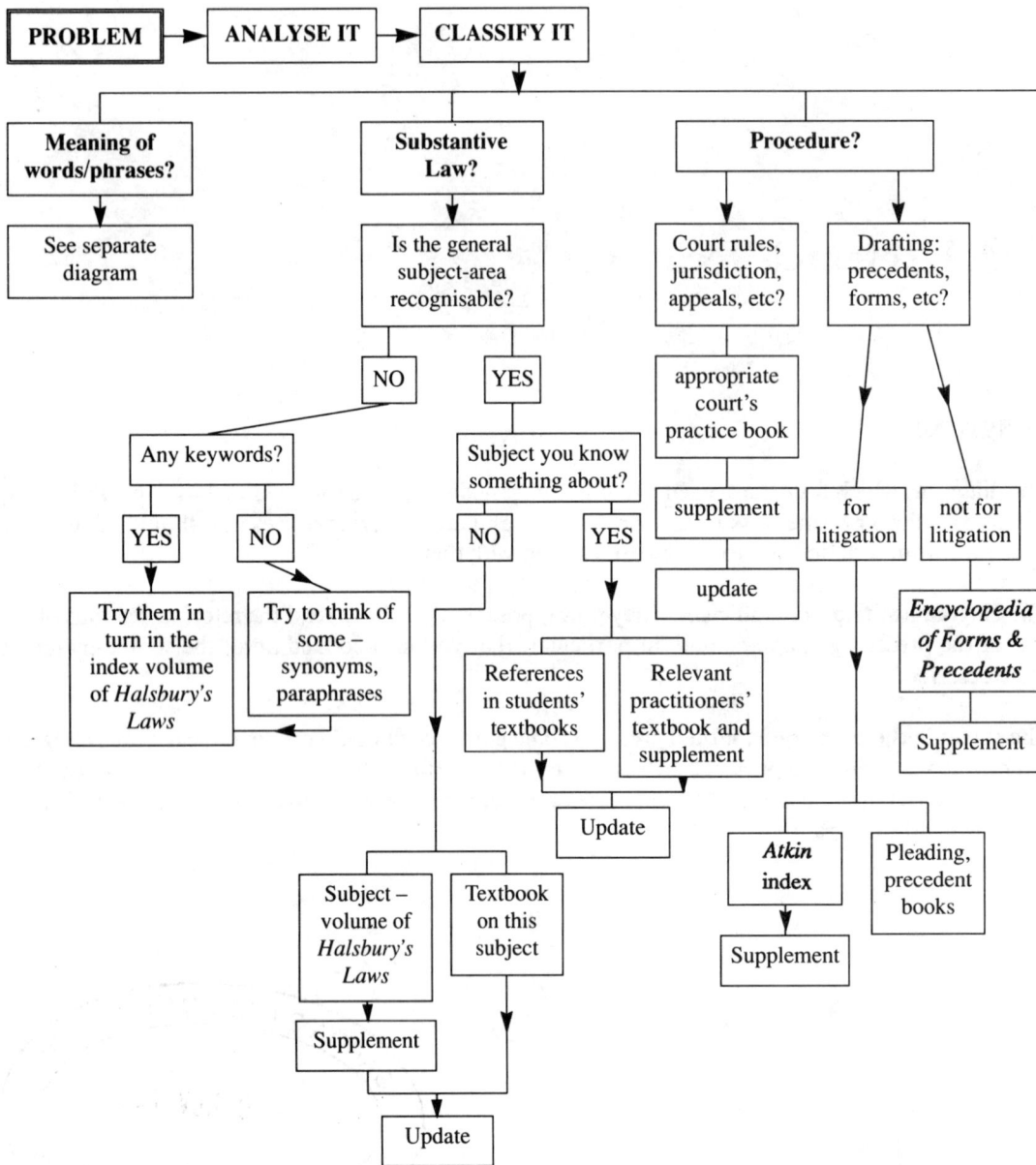

PROBLEM → ANALYSE IT → CLASSIFY IT

Meaning of words/phrases?
→ See separate diagram

Substantive Law?
→ Is the general subject-area recognisable?
- NO → Any keywords?
  - YES → Try them in turn in the index volume of *Halsbury's Laws*
  - NO → Try to think of some – synonyms, paraphrases
- YES → Subject you know something about?
  - NO → References in students' textbooks → Subject – volume of *Halsbury's Laws* → Supplement → Update
  - YES → Relevant practitioners' textbook and supplement → Update; Textbook on this subject → Update

Procedure?
- Court rules, jurisdiction, appeals, etc? → appropriate court's practice book → supplement → update
- Drafting: precedents, forms, etc?
  - for litigation → *Atkin index* → Supplement; Pleading, precedent books
  - not for litigation → *Encyclopedia of Forms & Precedents* → Supplement

NOTES

1. This diagram is only a rudimentary outline, indicating some of the main directions that might usefully be pursued in legal problem-solving. In so far as you find that it states the obvious, you must already have some skill or instinct for basic legal research.

2. Where, having followed one particular line, the result suggests that your original classification was incorrect, go back and recommence at the appropriate heading.

3. 'Supplement' means that you must refer efficiently to all the supplement(s) and services supplied with the source indicated.

4. 'Update' means go through the appropriate updating procedures, some of which are indicated under the 'Law Known' heading.

5. LEXIS-searching may be useful at many points, either initially or once a certain amount of information has been obtained. LEXIS has been left out of the diagram, however, to avoid overloading it.

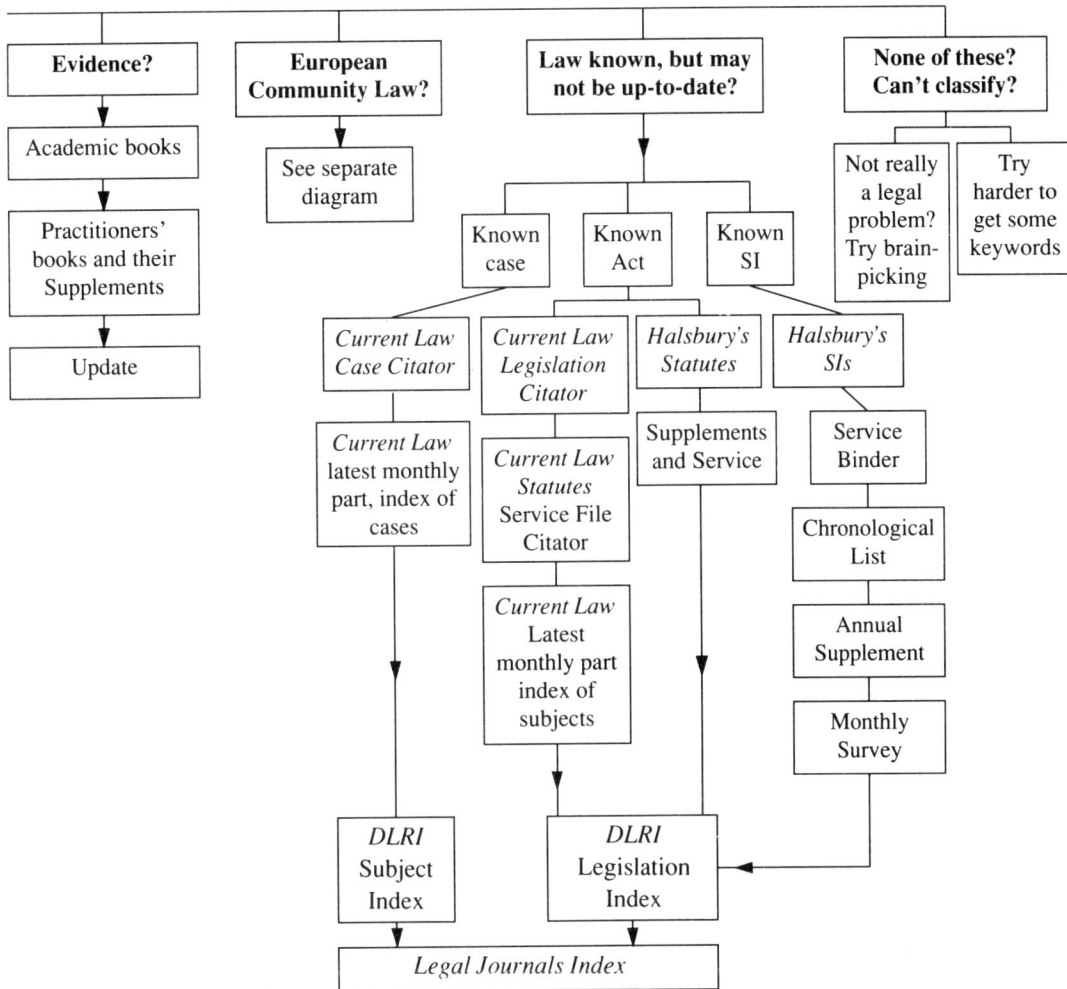

WORDS AND PHRASES IN STATUTES, ETC.

There follows a suggested sequence for construing their meaning. It may also be used for construing documents, by analogy; and when drafting your own. The sequence may not need to be followed through every stage if a definition or interpretation is revealed early, e.g. in the annotations to a statute. Similarly, if a meaning before or after a specific date is sought, *CLYB* or *Halsbury's* Annual Abridgment may be a useful approach.

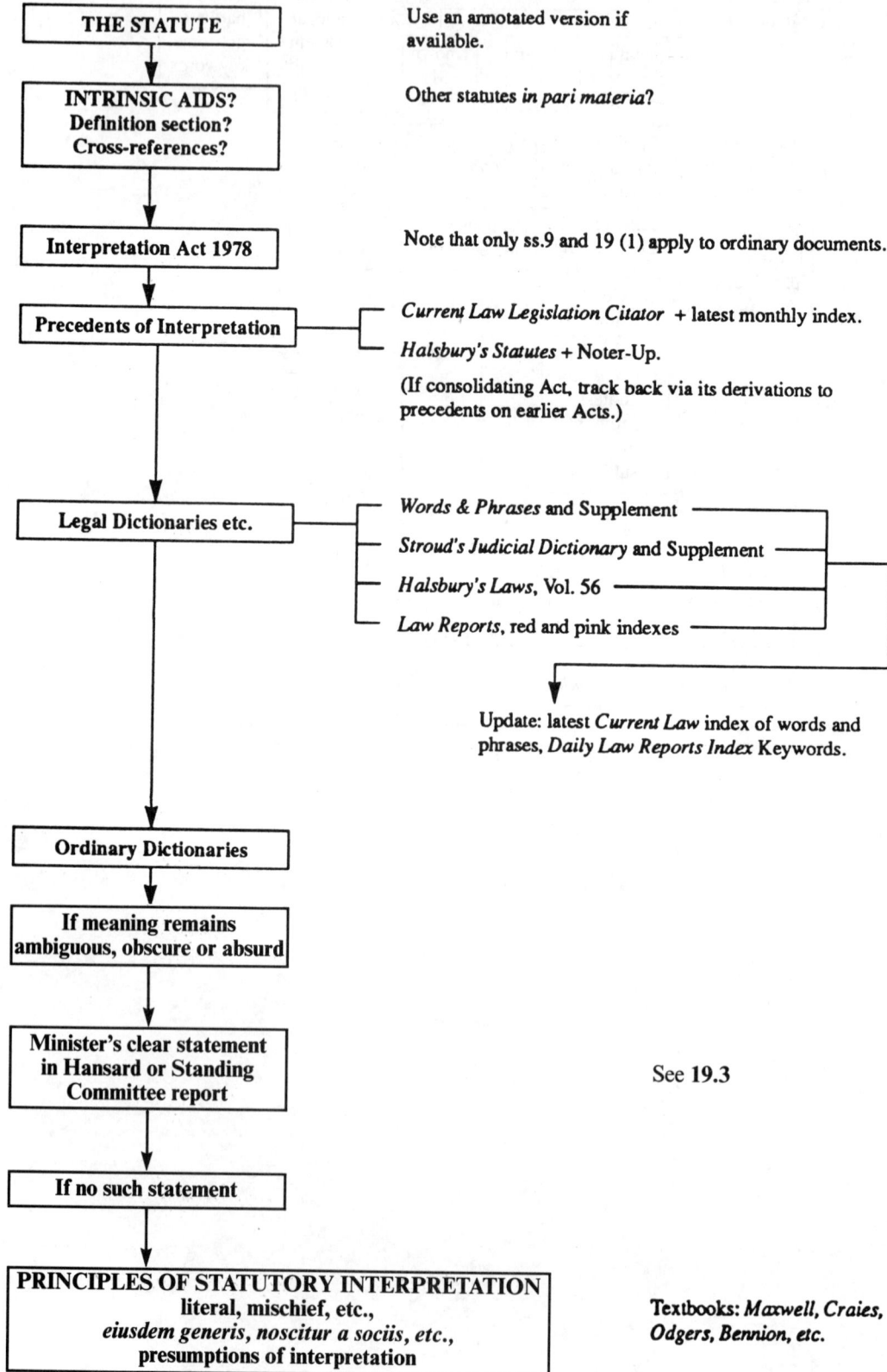

THE STATUTE	Use an annotated version if available.
INTRINSIC AIDS? Definition section? Cross-references?	Other statutes *in pari materia*?
Interpretation Act 1978	Note that only ss.9 and 19 (1) apply to ordinary documents.
Precedents of Interpretation	*Current Law Legislation Citator* + latest monthly index. *Halsbury's Statutes* + Noter-Up. (If consolidating Act, track back via its derivations to precedents on earlier Acts.)
Legal Dictionaries etc.	*Words & Phrases* and Supplement *Stroud's Judicial Dictionary* and Supplement *Halsbury's Laws*, Vol. 56 *Law Reports*, red and pink indexes
	Update: latest *Current Law* index of words and phrases, *Daily Law Reports Index* Keywords.
Ordinary Dictionaries	
If meaning remains ambiguous, obscure or absurd	
Minister's clear statement in Hansard or Standing Committee report	See **19.3**
If no such statement	
PRINCIPLES OF STATUTORY INTERPRETATION literal, mischief, etc., *eiusdem generis, noscitur a sociis, etc.,* presumptions of interpretation	Textbooks: *Maxwell, Craies, Odgers, Bennion, etc.*

Researching European Community Law

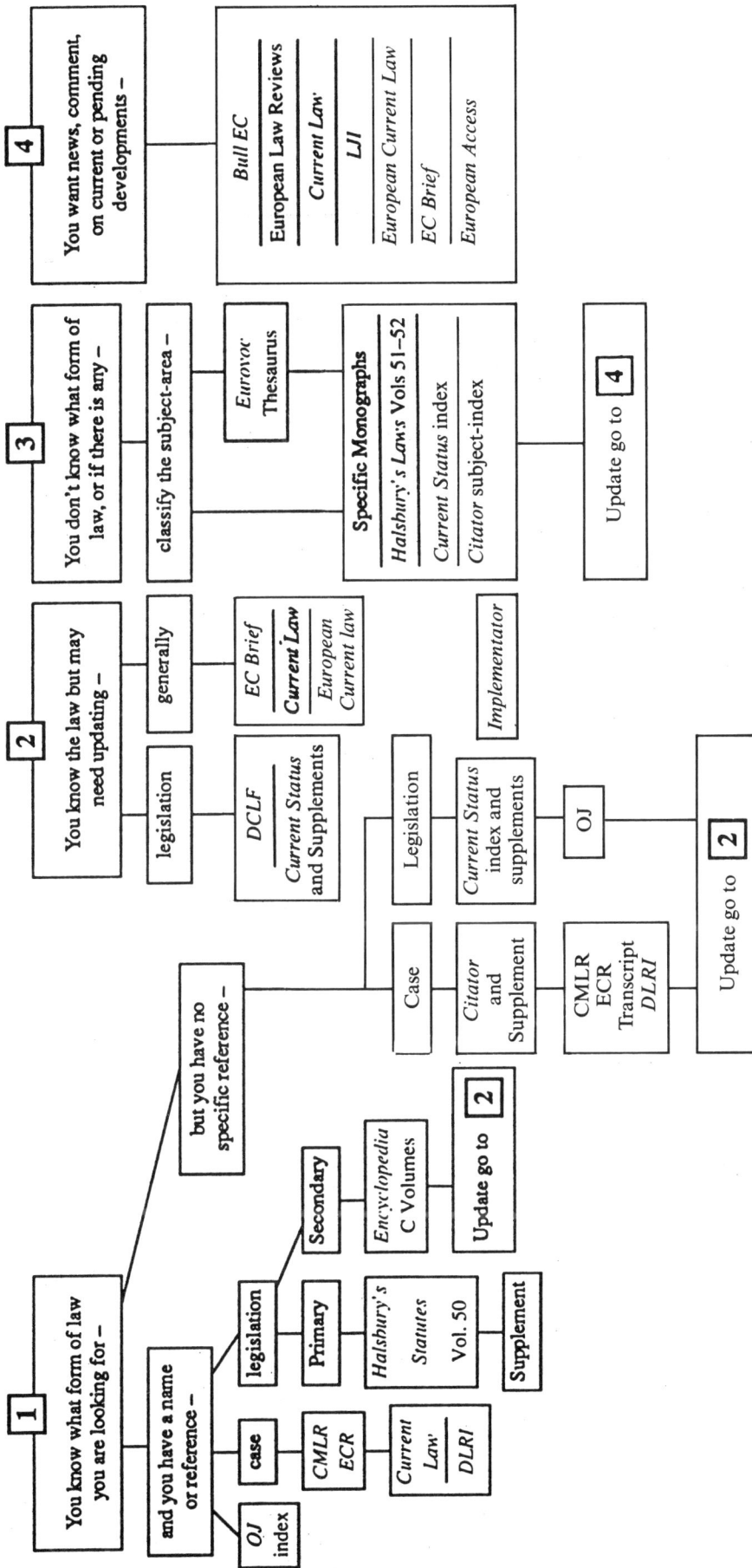

1

You know what form of law you are looking for –

and you have a name or reference –

OJ index

case
— *CMLR*
— *ECR*
— *Current Law*
— *DLRI*

legislation

Primary
— *Halsbury's Statutes*
— Vol. 50
— Supplement

Secondary
— *Encyclopedia* C Volumes

Update go to **2**

but you have no specific reference –

Case
— *Citator* and Supplement
— *CMLR*
— *ECR*
— Transcript
— *DLRI*

Legislation
— *Current Status* index and supplements
— *OJ*

Update go to **2**

2

You know the law but may need updating –

legislation
— *DCLF*
— *Current Status* and Supplements

generally
— EC Brief
— *Current Law*
— *European Current law*

Implementator

3

You don't know what form of law, or if there is any –

classify the subject-area –
— *Eurovoc Thesaurus*

Specific Monographs
— *Halsbury's Laws* Vols 51–52
— *Current Status* index
— *Citator* subject-index

Update go to **4**

4

You want news, comment, on current or pending developments –

Bull EC

European Law Reviews
— *Current Law*
— *LJI*
— *European Current Law*
— *EC Brief*
— *European Access*

KEY

Bull. EC	Bulletin of the European Communities (official publication).
Citator	Butterworths EC Case Citator
CMLR	Common Market Law Reports.
Current Law	the English monthly (Sweet & Maxwell).
Current Status	European Communities Legislation: Current Status (Butterworths).
DCLF	Directory of Community Legislation in Force (official publication).
DLRI	Daily Law Reports Index.
EC Brief	European Community Brief (Butterworths).
ECR	European Court Reports (official publication).
Encyclopedia	Encyclopedia of European Community Law (Sweet & Maxwell).
European Access	bi-monthly (Chadwyck-Healey)
European Current Law	English monthly (Sweet & Maxwell)
Eurovoc	**Eurovoc Thesaurus** (official publication).
Implementator	Butterworths EC Legislative Implementator
LJI	**Legal Journals Index.**
OJ	Official Journal of the European Communities.

275

22 Books for the Practitioner

22.1 Introduction

We are all familiar with such legal textbooks as Smith and Hogan on *Criminal Law* and *Cheshire, Fifoot and Furmston's Law of Contract*. It therefore comes as a shock to learn that, while such books are excellent for students and may still assist a practitioner on occasions, they are not often used in practice. The likely effect of this is a bookshelf of out-of-date legal textbooks and a large bill to replace them with practitioners' works!

That being said, most chambers have an extensive chambers library, with all having at least a basic selection of law reports, statutes, precedents and practitioners' books. It is therefore unlikely that you will need to purchase more than one or two books in your first year of pupillage or practice.

The following is a guide to some of the most common books used in practice. They have a more detailed coverage than a general encyclopaedia like *Halsbury's Laws*. You will see them time and again in the court room or under the arm of counsel on his or her way to court; you will hear many of them being cited as authority in court. The list, however, is not exhaustive: there are many excellent, practical books on the market which are not included here. Indeed, it is difficult to find a legal subject which has not been covered extensively by at least one author. The purpose of this list is to provide a basic guide to the main practitioners' books so that you become familiar with using them for your practical work on the course and during pupillage. Some specialist law reports are included where appropriate. Other books can be located via the subject index in a law library.

It is vital that you use the latest editions of these or any books. Those which are not re-edited annually are normally updated by supplements. The law changes so rapidly that it is foolhardy to rely on out-of-date material. If the textbook is in loose-leaf format it will be regularly updated. The front page of each section should tell you how up-to-date it is. Recent developments may be set out in a service volume rather than in the main text. Bound texts may have soft-cover supplements which deal with recent developments. The following list is up-to-date as at May 1992.

22.2 A Guide to Practitioners' Books

22.2.1 ADMINISTRATIVE LAW

De Smith/Evans: *Judicial Review of Administrative Action*, 4th ed. (Sweet & Maxwell, 1980).

Wade: *Administrative Law*, 6th ed. (Oxford University Press, 1988).

22.2.2 AGENCY

Bowstead/Reynolds: *Law of Agency*, 15th ed. (Sweet & Maxwell, 1985) updated.

22.2.3 ARBITRATION

Mustill/Boyd: *Commercial Arbitration*, 2nd ed. (Butterworths, 1989).

22.2.4 BANKING

Byles: *Bills of Exchange*, 27th ed. (Sweet & Maxwell, 1992).

Paget/Megrah/Ryder: *Law of Banking*, 10th ed. (Butterworths, 1989).

Encyclopaedia of Banking Law (Butterworths) updating service.

22.2.5 BANKRUPTCY AND INSOLVENCY

Muir Hunter: *Personal Insolvency* (Sweet & Maxwell, 1987), updated.

22.2.6 BUILDING

Keating: *Building Contracts*, 5th ed. (Sweet & Maxwell, 1991), updated.

Emden *et al: Construction Law* (Butterworths), updated.

See also: *Building Law Reports*.

22.2.7 CHARITIES

Tudor/Maurice/Parker: *Tudor on Charities*, 7th ed. (Sweet & Maxwell, 1984), updated.

22.2.8 COMPANY LAW

Butterworths: Company Law Service (updated).

Gore-Browne: *Companies,* 44th ed. (Jordans, 1986), updated.

Palmer/Schmitthoff: *Palmer's Company Law*, (Sweet & Maxwell), updated.

22.2.9 CONFLICT OF LAWS

Dicey/Morris: *Conflict of Laws*, 11th ed. (Sweet & Maxwell, 1987), updated.

Cheshire/North: *Private International Law*, 12th ed. (Butterworths, 1992).

22.2.10 CONTRACT LAW

Chitty/Guest: *On Contracts*, 26th ed. (Sweet & Maxwell, 1989), updated.

Goff/Jones: *Law of Restitution*, 3rd ed. (Sweet & Maxwell, 1986).

22.2.11 CONVEYANCING LAW

See also *Real Property*.

Emmet/Farrand: *Emmet on Title*, (Longman), updated.

Fisher/Lightwood: *Law of Mortgage*, 10th ed. (Butterworths, 1988).

Ruoff/Roper: *Law and Practice of Registered Conveyancing*, (Sweet & Maxwell, 1991), updated.

Preston/Newsome: *Restrictive Covenants Affecting Freehold Land*, 8th ed. (Sweet & Maxwell, 1991).

Encylopaedia of Compulsory Purchase, (Sweet & Maxwell), updating service.

22.2.12   CRIMINAL LAW

Archbold: *Criminal Pleading, Evidence and Practice*, (Sweet & Maxwell, annual), plus supplement.

Blackstone's Criminal Practice, (Blackstone Press) annual.

Wilkinson/Wallis: *Road Traffic Offences*, 15th ed. (Longman Group Ltd, 1991), updated.

See also: *Criminal Appeal Reports, Criminal Appeal Reports (Sentencing), Criminal Law Review*.

22.2.13   DAMAGES

Kemp/Kemp: *Quantum of Damages*, (Sweet & Maxwell), updating service.

Butterworths Personal Injury Litigation Service, (Butterworths), updating service.

McGregor: *Damages*, 15th ed. (Butterworths, 1988) updated.

22.2.14   EMPLOYMENT LAW

Harvey: *Industrial Relations and Employment Law*, (Butterworths), updating service.

Redgrave/Fife/Machin: *Health and Safety* (Butterworths, 1990).

Encyclopaedia of Health and Safety at Work, (Sweet & Maxwell), updating service.

Encyclopaedia of Labour Relations Law, (Sweet & Maxwell), updating service.

See also: *Industrial Relations Law Reports, Industrial Cases Reports*.

22.2.15   EQUITY AND TRUSTS

Underhill/Hayton: *Law of Trusts and Trustees*, 14th ed. (Butterworths, 1987), updating service.

Snell: *The Principles of Equity*, 29th ed. (Sweet & Maxwell, 1991)

22.2.16   EUROPEAN COMMUNITY LAW

Vaughan: *Law of the European Communities*, (Butterworths, 1986), updating service.

Bellamy/Child: *Common Market Law of Competition*, 3rd ed. (Sweet & Maxwell, 1987), plus supplement.

Green: *Commercial Agreements and Competition Law*, (Kluwer, 1986).

Encyclopaedia of EEC Law, (Sweet & Maxwell), updating service.

22.2.17   EVIDENCE

Phipson et al: *On Evidence*, 14th ed. (Sweet & Maxwell, 1990), updated.

Cross: *Evidence*, 7th ed. (Butterworths, 1990).

22.2.18   FAMILY LAW

Rayden/Jackson: *Divorce and Family Matters*, 16th ed. (Butterworths, 1991), updated.

Jackson/Davies: *Matrimonial Finance and Taxation*, 5th ed. (Butterworths, 1992).

Brown: *On Divorce*, 2nd ed. (Shaw & Sons, 1986), updated.

Clarke Hall/Morrison: *Law Relating to Children*, (Butterworths), updated.

Bird/Turner: *Forms and Precedents in Matrimonial Causes*, 3rd ed. (Sweet & Maxwell, 1992), updated.

Clark/Parker: *Practical Matrimonial Precedents* (Longman), updating service.

Butterworth's Family Law Service, updating service.

See also: *Family Law Reports*.

22.2.19   HOUSING LAW

Encyclopaedia of Housing Law and Practice, (Sweet & Maxwell), updating service.

Arden/Partington: *Housing Law*, 2nd ed. (Sweet & Maxwell, 1992), updated.

See also: *Housing Law Reports*.

22.2.20   IMMIGRATION

Butterworths Immigration Law Service, updating service.

Macdonald: *Immigration Law and Practice* 3rd ed. (Butterworths, 1991).

22.2.21   INSURANCE LAW

MacGillivray/et al: *Insurance Law*, 8th ed. (Sweet & Maxwell, 1988).

Hardy Ivamy: *General Principles of Insurance Law*, 5th ed. (Butterworths, 1986).

See also: *Insurance Law Reports*.

22.2.22   INTELLECTUAL PROPERTY

Kerly: *Law of Trade Marks and Trade Names*, 12th ed. (Sweet & Maxwell, 1986).

Copinger/Skone James: *Copyright*, 13th ed. (Sweet & Maxwell, 1991).

Terrell: *On the Law of Patents*, 14th ed. (Sweet & Maxwell, 1991).

Cornish: *Intellectual Property: Patents Etc.,* 2nd ed. (Sweet & Maxwell, 1989).

22.2.23   LANDLORD AND TENANT

Hill/Redman/Barnes: *Landlord and Tenant*, (Butterworths), updated.

Woodfall/Wellings: *Landlord and Tenant Law*, (Sweet & Maxwell), updating service.

22.2.24   LEGAL AID

Legal Aid Handbook (Sweet & Maxwell), annual.

22.2.25   LIBEL

Gatley/Lewis: *Libel and Slander*, 8th ed. (Sweet & Maxwell, 1981), updated.

Carter-Ruck: *Libel and Slander*, 4th ed. (Butterworths, 1992).

Duncan/Neill/Rampton: *Defamation*, 3rd ed. (Butterworths, 1992).

22.2.26   LICENSING

Paterson: *Licensing Acts*, (Butterworths), annual.

22.2.27   LOCAL GOVERNMENT

Encyclopaedia of Local Government Law, (Sweet & Maxwell), updating service.

22.2.28   PARTNERSHIP LAW

Lindley/Scammell: *Law of Partnership*, 16th ed. (Sweet & Maxwell, 1990).

22.2.29   PLANNING LAW

Encyclopaedia of Planning Law and Practice, (Sweet & Maxwell), updating service.

Butterworths Planning Law Service, updating service.

See also: *Planning Law Reports*.

22.2.30   PRACTICE AND PROCEDURE

Stone's Justices' Manual, (Butterworths) annual.

Archbold: *Criminal Pleading, Evidence and Practice* (Sweet & Maxwell) annual, with supplements

Anthony/Berryman: *Magistrates' Court Guide* (Butterworths), annual.

Blackstone's Criminal Practice (Blackstone Press), annual.

County Court Practice ('Green Book'), annual.

Supreme Court Practice ('White Book') (Sweet & Maxwell, 1991), updated.

Bullen/Leake/Jacob: *Precedents of Pleadings*, 13th ed. (Sweet & Maxwell, 1990) updated.

Chitty/Jacob: *Queen's Bench Forms*, 21st ed. (Sweet & Maxwell, 1986), updated.

Butterworth's County Court Precedents, updating service.

22.2.31   RATING

Ryde: *Rating & Community Charge* (Butterworths), updated.

Encyclopaedia of Rating and Local Taxation, (Sweet & Maxwell), updated.

22.2.32   REAL PROPERTY

See also **Conveyancing**.

Gale: *The Law of Easements*, 15th ed. (Sweet & Maxwell, 1986).

Megarry/Wade: *Law of Real Property*, 5th ed. (Sweet & Maxwell, 1984).

See also: *Estates Gazette Law Reports; Property, Planning and Compensation Reports.*

22.2.33   ROAD TRAFFIC LAW

Wilkinson/Wallis: *Road Traffic Offences*, 15th Ed. (Longman Group, 1991), updated.

Bingham/Taylor: *Motor Claims Cases*, 9th ed. (Butterworths, 1986), supplement.

22.2.34   SALE OF GOODS AND CONSUMER LAW

Benjamin/Guest: *Sale of Goods*, 3rd ed. (Sweet & Maxwell, 1987), updated.

Butterworths Law of Food and Drugs, updating service.

Encyclopaedia of Consumer Credit Law (Sweet & Maxwell), updating service.

Encyclopedia of Consumer Law (Sweet & Maxwell), updating service.

Goode: *Consumer Credit Law*, (Butterworths, 1989).

22.2.35   SENTENCING

Thomas: *Current Sentencing Practice* (Sweet & Maxwell), updating service.

22.2.36   SHIPPING

Carver/Colinvaux: *Carriage by Sea*, 13th ed. (Sweet & Maxwell, 1982).

Scrutton: *On Charterparties*, 19th ed. (Sweet & Maxwell, 1984).

Colinvaux/et al.: *Forms and Precedents* (Sweet & Maxwell, 1973).

Sassoon: *CIF and FOB Contracts*, 3rd ed. (Sweet & Maxwell, 1984).

See also generally: *British Shipping Law* series.

22.2.37   SOCIAL SECURITY AND WELFARE LAW

Ogus/Barendt: *Law of Social Security*, 3rd ed. (Butterworths, 1989), updated.

*Encyclopaedia of Social Services Law (*Sweet & Maxwell), updating service.

Social Security and State Benefits (Tolley), annual.

22.2.38   TAXATION

Whiteman/et al.: *On Income Tax*, 3rd ed. (Sweet & Maxwell, 1988), updated.

Whiteman/et al.: *On Capital Gains Tax*, 4th ed. (Sweet & Maxwell, 1988), updated.

Bramwell/et al.: *Taxation of Companies*, 5th ed. (Sweet & Maxwell, 1991), updated.

Butterworths Orange Tax Handbook, annual.

Butterworths Yellow Tax Handbook, annual.

British Tax Encyclopaedia (Sweet & Maxwell), updating service.

Simons Taxes (Butterworths), updating service.

22.2.39   TORTS

Charlesworth/Percy: *On Negligence*, 8th ed. (Sweet & Maxwell, 1990), updated.

Clerk/Lindsell: *On Torts*, 16th ed. (Sweet & Maxwell, 1989), updated.

22.2.40   WILLS AND PROBATE, SUCCESSION

Theobald/Clark: *The Law of Wills*, 14th ed. (Sweet & Maxwell, 1982), updated.

Williams: *Wills*, 3rd ed. (Butterworths, 1987), updated.

Tristram/Coote: *Probate Practice*, 27th ed. (Sweet & Maxwell, 1989), updated.

Sherrin/Bonehill: *Law and Practice of Intestate Succession* (Sweet & Maxwell, 1987), updated.

23   Assessing Legal Research

The assessment of legal research focuses on each stage of the research process:

(a) *Identifying the issues*

Having digested the facts of the problem, your next step should be to identify the issues which need to be researched. In some cases, your instructing solicitors will already have done this and your instructions will contain a series of questions. Even then, ask yourself if there are any other questions which the solicitor should have asked but has not done so. In other cases, you will have to identify the questions yourself.

(b) *Finding the appropriate primary sources*

In most cases, there will be more than one starting point to solving a problem. Indeed, it will often be that another user of the library has got the book you wish to consult and so you will have to think of an alternative. Remember that the main subject-matter index in your library will help you. There is also the list of practitioner books in **Chapter 22** of this Manual. It is best to use a practitioner's text, if one is available (and remember, if it is not in loose-leaf format you will need to check if there is a supplement). If you cannot identify an appropriate practitioners' text, or the one you want is not available, the best starting point is likely to be *Halsbury's Laws of England*.

Once you have identified the correct book you will have to use the index and/or contents pages to locate the appropriate part of the book. This involves identifying an appropriate keyword. If the first keyword you think of yields nothing, try another.

It is rarely sufficient (although very tempting!) to rely on what textbooks (including footnotes) say about primary sources. On matters which are central to the problem, you should always consult the primary sources (cases, statutes, etc.).

In any event, you will have to check that the law you have found is up-to-date. At the very least you must check the latest cumulative supplement to the work you are using. Ideally you should also use something like *Current Law*.

(c) *Interpreting the law*

In some cases, the law will be so clear that only one interpretation is possible. However, this is not always so. The language of a particular statutory provision may be ambiguous — is there a definition section, or relevant case law? In an area governed by case law, it may be that you will have to deduce a principle from a line of cases; or it may be that a case, or series of cases, sets out a narrow principle which can be used to establish a wider principle.

Textbooks and/or the commentary in *Halsbury's Laws* often show how various authorities relate to each other, point out any inconsistencies, and suggest ways in which the cases may be reconciled.

(d) *Applying the law to the facts of the case*

A barrister does not carry out legal research in the abstract. The purpose is to give the best advice to your client or to ensure that the strongest case is put before the court on your client's behalf. You must therefore apply the law in a realistic and practical way. Your advice must not be an essay on the law. It must be specific to the case upon which your advice is sought.

It may be necessary to consider whether the facts of the present case are distinguishable from the facts of the authorities you have found. If there are conflicting authorities, it may be necessary to decide which is more likely to be followed.

You must attempt to answer all the questions or issues raised in your instructions. It may or may not be possible to give a definite answer. If you are unable to give a categorical answer, you must attempt to assess the likely result and the degree of probability that the court will come to the conclusion you suggest. Each answer arrived at must be a 'satisfactory' one, in that it must have at least a reasonable prospect of being upheld by the court.

23.1 Tasks

In a legal research assessment you are required to produce two documents: notes to pupil-master and memorandum to assessor.

23.1.1 NOTES TO PUPIL-MASTER

This task does not require you to produce a full opinion, but rather the notes which would form the basis for your opinion. The notes must be clear, concise and accurate. The following guidelines may help you:

(a)   You may write in note form (rather than writing complete sentences which conform with the rules of grammar) if you wish to do so, but do remember that the result must be intelligible to another reader (i.e. your assessor or pupil master).

(b)   Your answers must be satisfactory, in the sense of being sustainable given the present state of the law which applies to the questions you are answering.

(c)   Your answers must be supported by relevant authority (usually, statutory or case law):

(i)   Only cite relevant authority, as the citation of irrelevant sources adds to the length of your notes and tends to create confusion. Something is relevant if it actually makes a difference to your answer.

(ii)   Show how the authority you cite is relevant. This will involve relating that authority to the facts of the case upon which you are advising. When you are citing precedent, you will normally find it easier to show its relevance by referring to a particular dictum rather than simply referring to the case as a whole. If you do not set out your legal reasoning, your pupil master cannot check the soundness of your reasoning.

(iii)   Correct citations must be given for all the authorities you cite. For example, 'the Ecclesiastical Judges and Legal Officers (Fees) Order 1991 (S.I. 1991 No. 1756)'; or *R v Roberts* [1993] 1 All ER 583, at p. 590 per Lord Taylor CJ'. If you do not give the correct citation for the authority which supports your conclusion, your pupil master will not be able to find that authority quickly.

(iv)   Verbatim quotation of statutes and judgments should be kept to a minimum. If the passage upon which you wish to rely is very short, or the precise words are crucial, then you will have to write it out in full. Otherwise, you should simply distil the essentials, which will involve paraphrasing the material rather than copying it out.

(v)   You should always cite 'primary' sources (i.e. statutes, case law etc.) in preference to 'secondary' sources (textbooks, articles etc.). However, if there is no authority, or there are conflicting authorities, then it may be appropriate to cite academic opinion. In that case, you should wherever possible refer to a source which could be cited in court (that is a textbook written for practitioners rather than students, or an article in a publication which is aimed, at least in part, at practitioners).

(d)   Finally, some guidance on the incorporation of background detail in your notes. If you are unfamiliar with an area of law, it may well be that you will have to do a certain amount of background reading before you can put the questions which you have to answer into context. However, your notes should contain only reasoned answers to the questions which are posed (expressly or by implication) in your instructions. Otherwise you will find that you are writing a legal essay, not the notes which form the starting point for an opinion.

23.1.2   MEMORANDUM TO ASSESSOR

This is not something that a pupil would be asked to do. Its purpose is to enable the assessor to follow, and give feedback on, the research techniques you have used. No set form is prescribed, but you must set out clearly what books and indexes you consulted, what keywords you used and what primary sources (cases, statutes etc.) you found together with the steps which led you to your answer. Where your instructions require you to answer more than one question, you should set out the route to each answer separately in your Memorandum to Assessor. This note should be relatively short and in any event should not exceed two sides of A4 paper.

23.2   *Re Arthur Zachary* — A Sample Exercise in Legal Research

There is no single 'right' way of conducting legal research. In this section we consider one way of approaching a particular PTX problem, *Re Arthur Zachary*. It is not the only approach that is possible. These papers were used as a formal assessment in legal research in 1991/92. It is a fairly typical exercise, though inevitably others will be more straightforward, others more complex.

Re Arthur Zachary
Artistic Corporation

INSTRUCTIONS TO COUNSEL
TO ADVISE ON VARIOUS
TRADE MARK AND RELATED MATTERS

Scruton Atkins & Co.
94 Coronation Road
London W2

Re Arthur Zachary Artistic Corporation

Instructions to Counsel

Counsel will please find herewith:

(i) letter to client from Van Manet Paints;
(ii) letter to client from Cross Finger & Dolittle Solicitors

We act on behalf of Arthur Zachary, who trades as the Arthur Zachary Artistic Corporation. This is not a limited company. Mr Zachary recently has encountered a number of problems relating to how he conducts his business on which counsel is asked to advise.

He owns a shop in Kensington High Street which sells amongst other things artists' materials. There are two leading manufacturers in the field of artists' paints, Van Manet and El Hals. Each of these names is a registered trade mark in part A of the register. Each has written a letter to Mr Zachary complaining of alleged acts of infringement. The allegations of fact made in each letter are correct. Would counsel advise in each case whether or not he considers there has been an act of infringement. Would counsel please note there is no question of challenging either mark.

Mr Zachary's customers come largely from the areas of Kensington, Chelsea and Fulham, which are covered by a local weekly newspaper, *The Westerner*. Mr Zachary has reached an arrangement with the company which distributes this newspaper under which every fourth issue contains an insert advertising his services. He did not make an approach to the newspaper itself about doing this. He has now received a letter from the newspaper's solicitors demanding that he desist. Is he under any obligation to stop? Would adding words to his insert pointing out that they were not placed as a result of agreement with the newspaper make a difference?

A slightly corrupted acronym of Mr Zachary's trade name is ANZAC. He has recently purchased some letterheads on which this is imprinted. He has been in correspondence with the government of New South Wales' London office with whom he has been doing some business. He received an extremely frosty reply to that letter telling him it is a criminal offence to use the word ANZAC like that. This sounds extraordinary — can it be right? If so, what are the possible penalties? Unfortunately, he has mislaid the relevant letter in which reference was made to the specific provision. We did not feel it would be wise to contact the NSW office to obtain another copy of this letter.

Mr Zachary's business activities also include the manufacture of paint brushes. This is done at a small factory in Kensington. The brushes are sold by the name 'Kennsingtons'. Over the past five years these have acquired a reputation for quality amongst the artists who use them. Mr Zachary would like to know if it would be possible for him to register 'Kennsingtons' as a trade mark.

The Van Manet Paint Co. Ltd,
9 Syon Park Industrial Estate,
Twickenham, Middlesex.

A. Zachary
69 Kensington High Street,
London W8

Dear Sir,

Re Van Manet Paints

It has recently come to our attention that you are advertising paints manufactured in Korea as 'As good as Van Manet's but half the price'.

This is a flagrant breach of our trade mark in the word Van Manet.

We must ask you to desist forthwith failing which we will have no choice but to instruct our solicitors to obtain an injunction and damages against you.

Yours faithfully,

Camille Pissarro
Manager

Cross Finger & Dolittle
Solicitors
The Old Manse
Frierton
Nr Northampton

Our Ref: MF/SA/ECl

The Proprietor
Zachary's
69 Kensington High Street
London W8

Dear Sirs,

Re: El Hals Paints

We act on behalf of Brown Products plc who are the owners of the trade mark El Hals Paints.

We have been informed by our clients that you have recently taken to placing piles of our client's paints next to those of Karishika, which are produced in the Far East. Their paints come in similar size packets to our clients' and you are able to arrange displays of similar appearance for each product. However, you prominently show the price of each product on your display to the detriment of clients' product which is considerably more expensive.

This in fact constitutes infringement of our clients' trade mark.

We trust that you will cease this practice in which case our clients would not wish to take any action against you.

Yours faithfully,

Cross Finger and Dolittle

23.3 *Re Arthur Zachary* — The Research Process

23.3.1 GETTING STARTED

Appropriate textbooks are Kerly: *Law of Trade Marks and Trade Names* and Cornish: *Intellectual Property — Patents Etc*. The latter is sometimes used as a student text, but in fact has sufficient standing to be cited in court.

So that the rest of this chapter has the greatest general value, we are going to assume that neither of these books is available and that we are going to use *Halsbury's Laws of England*.

Quite a lot of the material in the following section also appears in the suggested notes to pupil-master or the notes to assessor. This is to show how the raw material of the results of the research can be turned into useful notes for your pupil-master or assessor.

23.3.2 THE ISSUES

In *Zachary* there are seven issues:

(a) Has the 'Van Manet' trade mark been infringed?
(b) Has the 'El Hals' trade mark been infringed?
(c) Can Mr Zachary be stopped from placing advertising inserts in the *Westerner*?
(d) Would the answer to (c) differ if the inserts carried a disclaimer?
(e) Is the use of the word 'ANZAC' an offence?
(f) If so, what is the penalty?
(g) Can the word 'Kennsingtons' be registered as a trade mark?

(a) Has the 'Van Manet' trade mark been infringed?
The first key word is 'trade marks'. Use of the general index takes you to volume 48. We move on to index of volume 48, remembering that where a single volume deals with more than one subject, there is a separate index for each subject. The index gives us 'infringement — trade mark, of — acts constituting' and takes us to paras 85–92.

Paragraph 85 sets out what constitutes an infringement and the footnotes refer to the Trade Marks Act 1938, s. 4 and to the definition section of that Act, s. 68.

Reading on, para. 87 is headed 'Importing a reference and other infringing uses'. It deals with what has been held to amount to importing a reference. Case law, together with some further commentary, is cited in the footnote. It is clear that the leading case is *Bismag Ltd* v *Amblins (Chemists) Ltd* [1940] Ch 667. This case was doubted by the House of Lords in *Aristoc Ltd* v *Ryste Ltd* [1945] AC 68. However, *Bismag* has been followed at first instance in cases such as *British Northrop Ltd* v *Texteam Blackburn Ltd* [1974] RPC 57.

Consulting the sources
Halsbury's Statutes (being updated, so subsequent statutory amendments are shown) normally provide the best source of general Acts of Parliament. Like *Halsbury's Laws*, *Halsbury's Statutes* are divided according to subject-matter. Coincidentally, the volume dealing with trade marks is volume 48. Acts within each area are set out chronologically.

Section 4(1) of the 1938 Act is far from easy to understand. Some help will be gained from the commentary in *Halsbury's Laws* and *Halsbury's Statutes*.

Find the case of *Bismag* (*supra*). It deals in detail with the wording and effect of s. 4. Note that Mackinnon LJ dissented, so don't waste time reading his judgment.

Find the case of *Aristoc* (*supra*). The headnote shows that the case is about what is capable of being registered as a trade mark and so is not relevant to the present issue. It is quite a long case (40 pages) and is not worth reading in full. Skim through the speeches, looking for the name of the *Bismag* case. At pp. 93–4, Viscount Maugham says that the decision could be criticised. At p. 97, Lord Macmillan prefers the dissenting judgment of Mackinnon LJ.

Find the case of *British Northrop* (*supra*). It deals with a number of issues. Only the trade marks point is relevant to the present problem. The headnote sets out the order in which the points in issue in that case are dealt with. Towards the end, we see that the trade marks point is dealt with. Turning to pp. 76–9, we see that Megarry J applies *Bismag* without questioning its validity.

Applying the law to the facts
By applying the law to the facts of the problem we should be able to produce an answer to the issue posed. In this case, the facts of our problem are indistinguishable from the facts of *Bismag* and that case is almost certain to be followed at first instance. Although the decision was criticised in *Aristoc*, it can only be overruled by the House of Lords. Given the small scale of Mr Zachary's business, it is unlikely that he will want to go that far, and so the best advice is that he should regard his advertisement as an infringement.

(b) Has the 'El Hals' trade mark been infringed?
The research process is essentially the same as for issue (a). The facts, however, do not fall within the actual decision in *Bismag*. The Master of the Rolls in that case (p. 684) did refer to a situation very similar to the present facts but, given the criticism of *Bismag* in *Aristoc*, this is unlikely to be held to be an infringement.

(c) Can Mr Zachary be stopped from placing advertisement inserts in The Westerner?
The cause of action here is 'passing off'. Looking up 'passing off — misrepresentation — manner in which effected' in *Halsbury's Laws*, volume 48 index gives para. 150. This is of general help, but more importantly, when the corresponding section (48.150) of the cumulative supplement is consulted, a recent decision is referred to, which should be consulted. Alternatively, looking up 'passing off' in the subject-matter index of the Law Reports, or the All England Law Reports, produces *Associated Newspapers* v *Insert Media* [1991] 3 All ER 535, CA. At first glance, the facts of that case appear very similar to the facts of the present case. However, on closer examination, it is clear that the plaintiffs succeeded on a number of issues only because of the particular evidence they were able to adduce on the issue of whether a substantial body of the public at large perceived or assumed that the inserts were made by the plaintiffs or with their authority. The case deals specifically with national newspapers. A well-known national newspaper and a local newspaper may well be treated differently, making the present case distinguishable from *Associated Newspapers*, with the result that the injunction may well not be granted.

(d) Would the answer to (c) differ if the inserts carried a disclaimer?
It was held in *Associated Newspapers* that a disclaimer would make no difference to the outcome as it would not necessarily correct the perception that the plaintiffs were responsible for the inserts. However, if no injunction is granted under issue (c), this is irrelevant.

(e) Is the use of the word 'ANZAC' an offence?
Looking up 'ANZAC' in the index to *Halsbury's Laws* produces two references. The first, volume 7(1), relates to use by a company. That is irrelevant as Mr Zachary is a sole trader. It also refers to volume 48, para. 352. This sets out the offence, using the word 'ANZAC' in connection with a business.

(f) If so, what is the penalty?
The entry referred to under issue (e) also states that the penalty is a fine on level 3. The Criminal Justice Act 1982 is cited in a footnote, but looking in a criminal procedure text or the front cover of *Stone's Justices' Manual* gives the present definition of level 3.

(g) Can the word 'Kennsingtons' be registered as a trade mark?
The contents section at the front of *Halsbury's Laws*, volume 48, gives 'registered trade marks — requirements for registration'. That takes us to para. 25, which gives a summary of the requirements and contains cross-references to the paragraphs dealing with each of the requirements. Paragraph 25 indicates that the main issue is whether the word 'Kennsingtons' is 'distinctive' for the purposes of registration in Part A, or, alternatively, is 'capable of distinguishing' for the purposes of registration in Part B. Footnotes indicate further paragraphs which should be consulted, though a quick skim through this part of volume 48, using the sub-headings in bold type, is equally productive.

The question of distinctiveness (Part A) is considered in paras 33 to 53. Paragraph 33 refers to the relevant statutory provision, the Trade Marks Act 1938, s. 9. This should be consulted in *Halsbury's Statutes*.

It is clear from these materials that some marks are regarded as being distinctive without the need to adduce evidence, whereas others must be proved to be distinctive. Marks of the first type are listed in s. 9(1)(a)-(d). Paragraphs (a) and (b) are obviously irrelevant as they deal with company, individual and firm names and signatures.

Paragraph (c) deals with invented words. This is considered in para. 36 of *Halsbury's Laws*. This states the test as being whether the word is a substantially new word when first used by the applicant. 'Kensington' (correctly spelt) is the name of a long-standing London district. The text to note 17 says that misspelling is not sufficient to constitute invention and cites *Electrix Ltd* v *Electrolux Ltd* [1960] AC 722. Turning to that report, it states that 'electrics' was regarded as inherently unregistrable and a misspelt version, 'electrix', was also unregistrable.

Paragraph (d) deals with words having no direct reference to the quality or character of the goods. Clearly, this is the case here. However, paragraph (d) is subject to exceptions relating to geographical names. *Halsbury's Laws,* para. 42, is headed 'geographical names' and the text to note 3, citing *Re Boots Pure Drug Co. Ltd* [1938] Ch 54, states that a name only ceases to be a geographical name if it is of no commercial value and is unknown in the UK. Clearly that is not the case here.

Next, we have to consider registration under Part A on proof of distinctiveness under the Trade Marks Act 1938, s. 9(1)(e). Further definition of what is meant by 'distinctive' is given by s. 9(2) and (3). Commentary is provided by *Halsbury's Laws*, para. 44ff. Paragraph 45 says that geographical names cannot be used unless they clearly have no reference either to the character or the origin of the goods, and note 2 contains a cross-reference to para. 42 (geographical names). Note 3, on evidence of distinctiveness, cites two House of Lords cases: *Yorkshire Copper Works Ltd* v *Registrar of Trade Marks* [1954] 1 All ER 570 and *York Trailer Holdings Ltd* v *Registrar of Trade Marks* [1982] 1 All ER 257. Consulting the latter (as the more recent decision) we find that Lord Wilberforce reviews earlier case law (including the earlier House of Lords decision). The result is that some words, like 'York', are inherently incapable of being 'distinctive', even if the applicant's goods achieve what is known as '100 per cent factual distinctiveness.' Lord Wilberforce explains why, at p. 261.

This reasoning must surely apply to 'Kensington'. Further, we have seen that misspelling (the added 'n' and 's') makes no difference.

Lastly, we have to consider registration in Part B. Text on this can be found in *Halsbury's Laws*, volume 48, para. 54, via the contents section at the beginning of that volume. This refers to the Trade Marks Act 1938, s. 10 and to *York Trailer Holdings* (*supra*) which holds that some geographical names are incapable in law of distinguishing goods for the purpose of s. 10. A well-known and distinct name such as 'Kensington' must surely fall within this category. Again, the misspelling is irrelevant.

Checking the present year's cumulative supplement to *Halsbury's Laws* produces two cases which appear at first sight to be relevant: under para. 34 (meaning of 'distinctive') *Coca Cola Trade Marks* [1985] FSR 315 and under para. 37 (examples of invented words) *Exxate Trade Mark* [1986] RPC 567. Closer examination of these authorities reveals that they add nothing. Therefore, the advice to Mr Zachary is that his mark is clearly not registrable as a trade mark.

23.4 *Re Arthur Zackary* — Suggested Format for Notes to Pupil-Master and Notes to Assessor

Your answer to *Re Arthur Zachary* might look something like this.

23.4.1 NOTES TO PUPIL-MASTER

(a) *Has the 'Van Manet' trade mark been infringed?*
In *Bismag Ltd* v *Amblins (Chemists) Ltd* [1940] Ch 667 the defendants used the plaintiff's trade mark 'Bisurated' in an advertisement which compared the plaintiff's product with the defendant's product and purported to show that the latter was better value for money. Sir Wilfred Greene MR (at p. 681), applying Trade Marks Act 1938, s. 4, held that D was using P's trade mark as a method of describing the merits of D's goods and that this constituted an infringement of P's trade mark.

This was doubted in the House of Lords case, *Aristoc Ltd* v *Ryste Ltd* [1945] AC 68 (Viscount Maugham at pp. 93–4 and Lord Macmillan at p. 97) but *Bismag* was not overruled. It is therefore good law and would be followed at first instance, as it was, for example, in *British Northrop Ltd* v *Texteam Blackburn Ltd* [1974] RPC 57 (Megarry J at pp. 76–9).

Mr Zachary's use of the trade mark 'Van Manet' in comparison with his own product is therefore an infringement of that trade mark.

(b) *Has the 'El Hals' trade mark been infringed?*
In *Bismag Ltd* v *Amblins (Chemists) Ltd* (*supra*), the Master of the Rolls (at p. 684) answered the suggestion that a consequence of his decision was that displaying one's own goods and branded goods in the same shop or catalogue could constitute an infringement of the trade mark of the branded goods. His Lordship said that each case must be decided on its own facts, clearly implying that common sense would not allow such a conclusion.

To regard such a situation as an infringement would be to extend the decision in *Bismag* beyond its ratio decidendi. Given the criticism of *Bismag* (see above), this is unlikely to be done.

Proximate display of a set of goods against branded goods — without more — would therefore not amount to an infringement.

(c) *Can Mr Zachary be stopped from placing advertising inserts in* The Westerner?

In *Associated Newspapers* v *Insert Media* [1991] 3 All ER 535 (CA), the plaintiff publishers sought an injunction to prevent the defendant from placing advertising inserts in their newspapers and magazines. Held — an injunction would only be granted if a substantial body of the public at large would perceive or assume that the inserts were made with the plaintiff's authority. There was evidence before the court that the effectiveness of an insert depended on the newspaper into which it was placed. The court inferred from this fact that there would therefore be a misrepresentation to the public that the inserts formed part of the newspaper and that the publishers therefore accepted responsibility for the inserts. There was a risk to the reputation of the publishers in that if there was inaccuracy or dishonesty in the advertising in the inserts the publishers would be blamed by the public even though, in fact, they had no control over the inserts. An injunction was granted to prevent this misrepresentation from taking place.

That case concerned national newspapers (including the *Daily Mail*). The fact that the newspaper had a national circulation was an important part of the reasoning of the court (ibid. pp. 540–1, per Browne-Wilkinson V-C). It is therefore unlikely that the same result would obtain in the case of a local newspaper such as *The Westerner*. The injunction would probably be refused.

(d) *Would an injunction still be granted even if the inserts carried a disclaimer?*
At p. 542 of the *Associated Newspapers* case (*supra*) the Vice-Chancellor said that a disclaimer would be ineffective, as it was unlikely to come to the attention of the reader and may well confuse him further if it does come to his attention. A disclaimer therefore makes no difference.

(e) *Is the use of the word 'ANZAC' an offence?*
Yes. ANZAC (Restriction on Trade Use of Word) Act 1916, s. 1(1): it is an offence to use the word ANZAC in connection with a trade.

(f) *If so, what is the penalty?*
Section 1(2), ibid., a fine on level 3: £1,000 (Criminal Justice Act 1991, s. 17), 10 units (CJA 1991, s. 18).

(g) *Can the word 'Kennsingtons' be registered as a trade mark?*
Registration can be under Part A or Part B of the Trade Marks Act 1938.

Part A: The trade mark must be 'distinctive': s. 9.
Part B: The trade mark must be 'capable of distinguishing: s. 10.

Part A
Section 9 can be satisfied in various ways, including:

(i) s. 9(1)(c) — invented words,i.e., the word is a substantially new one when first used by the applicant. The word 'Kensington' (properly spelt) is not a new word. Misspelling is not enough to create a new word when it is phonetically the same as another word: *Electrix Ltd* v *Electrolux Ltd* [1960] AC 772: 'electrix' is a misspelling of 'electrics'. The latter is not a new word, so neither is the former. Both therefore unregistrable. Same applies to 'Kensington' and 'Kennsingtons'.

(ii) s. 9(1)(d) — words having no direct reference to character or quality of goods, excluding geographical names. *Boots Pure Drug Co. Ltd* [1938] Ch 54 — a name only ceases to be a geographical name if it is of no commercial value and unknown in the UK. Kensington suggests quality (high-class London district) and is known in the UK. Therefore, Kensington unregistrable, and so is the misspelt version 'Kennsingtons'.

(iii) s. 9(1)(e) — words proved by evidence to be distinctive. In *York Trailer Holdings Ltd* v *Registrar of Trade Marks* [1982] 1 All ER 257 (HL) Lord Wilberforce said that 'York' is inherently incapable of being distinctive even if the trade mark has been used to denote the trader's goods and those of no one else ('100% factual distinctiveness'). This is because (p. 261) traders cannot obtain a monopoly in the use of such words to the detriment of other people who might, in the future, desire to use them in connection with other goods. The same must apply to 'Kensington' and to the misspelt 'Kennsingtons'.

Part B
York Trailer Holdings Ltd v *Registrar of Trade Marks* (*supra*) also considers s. 10 — geographical names incapable of distinguishing goods for purpose of s. 10. Must apply to 'Kensington' and 'Kennsingtons'.

Therefore 'Kennsingtons' not registrable at all.

23.4.2   NOTES TO ASSESSOR

Issue (a)
Halsbury's Laws general index — 'trade marks' — vol. 48.
Trade Marks index to vol. 48: 'infringement — trade mark, of acts constituting: paras 85–92.
Para. 85: ss. 4 and 68, Trade Marks Act 1938 (Act in vol. 48 *Halsbury's Statutes*):
Para. 87: importing a reference — cites *Bismag, Aristoc, British Northrop* (all read).

Issue (b)
Reading *Bismag* gives answer.

Issue (c)
Halsbury's Laws, vol. 48 trade marks index — passing off — misrepresentation — manner in which effected: para. 150.
Cumulative supplement under para. 48.150 gives *Associated Newspapers*.

Issue (d)
Reading *Associated Newspapers* gives the answer.

Issue (e)
Halsbury's Laws general index — 'ANZAC': vol. 7(1) — irrelevant: companies; vol. 48 para. 352 gives ANZAC (etc.) Act 1916, s. 1(1).

Issue (f)
Halsbury vol. 48 para. 352, s. 1(2) ANZAC Act — level 3.
Blackstone's *Criminal Practice* index — fines — magistrates courts — standard scale of maximum fines: E13.4, E13.5.

Issue (g)
Halsbury's Laws vol. 48 contents section gives 'registered trade marks — requirements for registration' para. 25. Also Part A, para. 25 and Part B, para. 53.
Skim reading gives:
para. 33: s. 9, Trade Marks Act 1938.
para. 36: invented words, s. 9(1)(c), note 17 gives *Electrix* (read headnote).
para. 42: geographical names, s. 9(1)(d), note 3 gives *Boots Pure Drug Co.* (read headnote).
para. 44: proof of distinctiveness, s. 9(1)(e), note 2 refers to para. 42 so same law applies, note 3 refers to *York Trailer* (read, as most recent HL case).
para. 54: part B registration, gives s. 10 and *York Trailer* again.

23.5   Summary

Legal research involves:

  (a)   Analysing the issues raised by the case so that you can identify which questions of law have to be answered.
  (b)   Identifying and locating sources of information such as textbooks, *Halsbury's Laws*, etc.
  (c)   Correct identification of keywords to enable efficient and effective use of indexes.

(d)   Identifying and locating relevant sources and materials, such as reported cases, statutes, statutory instruments.

(e)   Distinguishing between relevant and irrelevant sources and materials.

(f)   Summarising or paraphrasing relevant materials: a succinct summary, not mindless copying out.

(g)   Cross-referencing between materials to ensure answer complete.

(h)   Checking that the law you have found is current (e.g. that the statute is in force, that the case has not been overruled).

(i)   Coming to a satisfactory answer to each of the questions you have to answer; satisfactory meaning (in this context) an answer which could be argued with a reasonable prospect of success.

(j)   Adopting a practical (rather than academic) approach to the law, in that your research will always focus on the facts of the case you are dealing with.

23.6   Criteria by which Performance will be Assessed

In assessing the quality of your performance in carrying out a legal research exercise, any of the following basic criteria may be developed or modified, but you will always be informed of the precise criteria for each exercise. You can use these criteria for self-assessment, or to give feedback to a fellow student.

In order to be graded as competent or above you must show your ability to:

(a)   Identify the legal issues raised by your instructions correctly and completely.

(b)   Identify relevant sources and materials so that you can disregard those which are irrelevant.

(c)   Extract the key points from, and correctly cite, those sources and materials.

(d)   Apply the law to the facts of the case so as to produce satisfactory answers to the questions posed (explicitly or implicitly) in your instructions.

(e)   Give brief reasons for the answers you have arrived at, showing how those answers have been reached.

(f)   Produce clear and concise notes which encapsulate the results of your research.

(g)   Produce clear and concise notes which show the research process you followed.

FACT MANAGEMENT:
PREPARATION TO PROOF

24 The Course

24.1 Outline of the Fact Management Course

24.1.1 AIM

The course aims to develop skills which will assist the barrister in thinking about facts, assessing their importance and organising them to construct a logical argument in order to achieve the client's objectives and to prove the case.

Fact management is fundamental to every aspect of the work of a barrister and underlies all the other skills of negotiating, opinion writing, drafting and advocacy, and conference skills, which all depend on the effective comprehension, identification and use of relevant information. This skill will be needed from the first moment of preparation when the brief is received to the last stage of the trial.

Fact management is perceived not as a 'one-off activity' but as a continuing process whereby the issues are continuously reviewed and reassessed at different stages as the case progresses. For instance, an issue may have to be rethought after a conference with a client or a strategy reconsidered after a statement is made by a witness at trial. However, once the fundamental skills of fact management are acquired by the student, they can be reapplied with ease in different situations and at different stages of a case.

24.1.2 OBJECTIVES

The course is designed to develop the fundamental skills of Fact Management and at the end of the course the student should be able to:

(a) understand data presented in a variety of ways;
(b) identify gaps, ambiguities and contradictions in information;
(c) identify the objectives of the client both in terms of practical outcomes and legal remedies;
(d) place the information in context;
(e) identify the factual issues;
(f) identify the legal issues raised by the facts;
(g) select possible solutions to the client's problem;
(h) recognise the interaction between law and fact;
(i) assess the strengths and weaknesses of a case;
(j) organise information in a variety of ways:

    (i) to aid understanding;
    (ii) to prove propositions of law;
    (iii) to assist at trial;

(k) distinguish between relevant and irrelevant facts;

(l) distinguish between fact and inference;

(m) construct an argument from the facts to support the client's case:

    (i) by developing a theory of the case;

    (ii) by selecting a theme or themes to fit that theory;

(n) evaluate the issues in response to new information and in the light of tactical considerations.

24.2 Design of the Course

The course is planned to develop and practise each component of the skill through lectures, tutorials and private study before linking the skill with others as part of the practical exercises which will combine fact management with legal research, negotiating, opinion writing, drafting, advocacy and conference skills.

Whilst opportunities will be provided in lectures and tutorials to practise individual aspects of the skill, it must be realised that it is impossible to treat one aspect as divorced from the others. Each part of the skill is interrelated. The brief is seen as the focal point of this skill and the same brief will be used as the basis of many of the teaching exercises to illustrate different aspects of the skill.

In every exercise you do from the moment you start to read your instructions, you should be making use of fact management skills. Decide what notes need to be made, what charts, tables and diagrams will be helpful to you, what means of organising the information is best suited to the nature of the case, and do whatever is necessary. This is a natural part of the preparation of every case, and it should become second nature. You should use fact management skills in every case, whether it involves advocacy, conference skills, negotiation, opinion writing, drafting or legal research, and however simple or difficult the case is.

Fact management skills, as you develop through the rest of the course, pupillage and practice, will become more and more intuitive and will be used more and more subconsciously. Many senior barristers, whose skill in preparing cases and organising information is exemplary, would claim to be quite unaware of fact management as a skill in itself at all. This is a stage you may reach one day; but with the conscious and structured training you have had in fact management, it is to be hoped that your ability to use these skills will grow sooner, faster and in the end further than that of lawyers who have not had such training.

The course on fact management attempts to identify some of the ways in which your skills in managing facts can be improved by consciously thinking about what you are doing. **Chapters 25 to 30** present possible methods of developing your abilities in the crucial fact management skills so that you can effectively:

(a) identify what you are trying to do;

(b) collect the facts;

(c) identify the issues of law and fact;

(d) identify whether the case can be proved;

(e) present the case effectively and persuasively.

24.3 Assessment of Fact Management Skills

24.3.1 BASIS FOR ASSESSMENT

During the course your ability to demonstrate fact management skills will be tested. You may be set a variety of tasks, such as preparing for a negotiation or a conference, making notes for use at trial, or you may be asked to answer specific questions such as how you will prove your case, or challenge the evidence.

The degree of success you achieve in any assessment will depend on the extent to which, in answering the questions or in performing the tasks required, you fulfil the specified criteria for that assessment selected from the list of criteria as appropriate.

24.3.2   ASSESSMENT CRITERIA

In assessing the quality of your performance in carrying out any fact management task, any of the following basic criteria may be used. For any particular exercise these general criteria may be developed or modified, but you will always be informed of the precise criteria for assessment. You can use these criteria for self-assessment, or as the basis for giving feedback to a fellow student.

In order to be graded as competent or above you must show your ability to:

    (a)   Identify your objectives.
    (b)   Identify your client's objectives.
    (c)   Collect and order facts.
    (d)   Identify the legal relevance of facts.
    (e)   Identify the factual issues.
    (f)   Identify the legal issues.
    (g)   Show the strengths and weaknesses of your case.
    (h)   Show the strengths and weaknesses of the opponent's case.
    (i)   Choose the best explanation in support of the client's case.
    (j)   Identify alternative courses of action.
    (k)   Identify any further information required.
    (l)   Present material clearly and concisely.
    (m) Use facts to support an argument.

25   Introduction to Fact Management Skills

At the heart of a barrister's work are facts: an incident has occurred, a person injured, property damaged, loss sustained. From the first moment of receiving the brief until the last stage of the trial it is the facts of a case that the barrister is working from. They are the basis of any evidence given, any speeches made, and any questions asked. It is the barrister's ability to manage the facts, to understand their implications and to use them as the basis of argument, which will be crucial to the success of a case. The majority of cases involve disputes of fact, not, despite one's academic training, disputes about questions of law, as was recognised by the Ormrod Committee on Legal Education in its report in 1971 when it considered the skills needed by practising lawyers:

> The raw material of every practising lawyer is facts, and a great deal of his time will be spent, whether he is a judge or a barrister or a solicitor, in finding the facts. The law cannot be properly applied until they are ascertained. If the facts are wrong, the advice of the most learned lawyer will be, at best, worthless — and may be dangerous. Facts, therefore, are of crucial importance to the practising lawyer at all levels, and his ability to handle facts is among his most essential skills. The handling of facts has many aspects. The practitioner must first obtain the client's instructions and the surrounding facts, and then investigate and scrutinise them for accuracy. Analysis of all the available data, to separate the relevant from the irrelevant and to perceive the relation between one set of facts and another and so to check reliability or expose errors, is an essential process in every case. In every case, also, he must synthesise his facts in order to present them lucidly and cogently, whether as an advocate, or as a pleader, or as a draftsman, or negotiator, or even as a letter writer. All stages of these processes will of course be controlled and informed by his knowledge of the relevant law, without which the exercise would be futile.

The ability of barristers to carry out the task of managing facts has in the past been developed by experience and little attempt has been made to formulate the individual processes involved. The teaching of fact management as a skill, however, necessitates a closer analysis of what the barrister actually does and requires that the intellectual processes are made explicit.

In most cases you will be sent a set of papers by your instructing solicitors, which will contain their instructions as to what they want you to do with the papers. The instructions will make clear, for example, what advice is required and/or whether you are to draft the pleadings in the case. Before you can adequately perform any of these tasks you will need to manage the facts, which in practice consists of four operations:

(a)   a determination of the legal and practical ambit of the client's problem, complaint or question;
(b)   collecting the facts;
(c)   analysing the facts;
(d)   presenting the facts.

25.1 The Legal and Practical Ambit

This is a 'range finding' exercise which must be completed whenever a question or problem is set for the barrister by the client. Inevitably, because usually a legal resolution of the problem is sought, the 'best fit' legal patterns must be selected before any more detailed work on the facts can take place. These patterns must be selected from both causes of action (that is legal analyses of the problem) and remedies (that is, the legal methods of achieving the client's practical objectives). The client's practical objectives are 'facts' and are the first facts to be established. The first exercise is setting up general maps of the likely factual terrain to be covered. It is very important to avoid formulating theories, explanations or analyses at this stage in such a way as to colour the next exercise. It is for this reason that Sir Arthur Conan Doyle makes Sherlock Holmes warn Dr Watson against formulating an explanation before collecting and examining all the facts of the case.

25.2 Collecting the Facts

You will start with the facts which have been collected by your solicitor and which are presented to you in the papers. It is important that the barrister fully understands the mechanisms of fact collection and investigation so as to be able to make constructive suggestions for further investigation by the solicitor and to recognise defects and gaps in the work that has already been done. In effect, the activity of collecting facts is usually divided between the barrister and the solicitor.

The barrister is directly involved in the collecton and investigation of facts when:

    (a) examining documentary evidence, in large cases he may assist in discovery;

    (b) examining exhibits;

    (c) carrying out site views;

    (d) interviewing the client; and

    (e) examining and cross-examining witnesses.

The barrister is indirectly involved in the collection and investigation of facts when:

    (a) drafting requests for further and better particulars;

    (b) drafting interrogatories;

    (c) advising on discovery; and

    (d) advising the solicitor on the investigation of the case.

There are two essential elements to the conduct of this exercise: the completeness of the task and recognition of the context and interrelationship of the facts. Just as an archaeologist is as much, if not more, concerned with the physical relationship of a particular article to other articles and the subsoil, so is someone collecting and investigating facts concerned with the contexts and interrelationships of those facts. The significance of a particular piece of information very often will depend on its place in a larger pattern. The significance of a particular fact can frequently be affected by the absence of other facts, for example, a document missing from the bundle.

25.3 Analysing the Facts

In analysing the facts, start by taking an overview of all the facts so as to see whether there are any patterns which can be used to establish the relevance of particular pieces of information to the client's problem and to achieving the desired solution. One way of doing this is to read through all the papers very quickly.

Next try to order the facts in a number of different ways by:

    (a) constructing patterns;

    (b)   listing chronologies, dramatis personae and flow charts of events;
    (c)   tabulating (for example, family trees, company structures, conveyancing histories);
    (d)   preparing maps, pictures and diagrams to establish the physical relationship of pieces of information.

Next, check whether you will be able to prove the existence of particular facts. This includes determining what facts prove other facts and what facts are dependent on others.

Next answer the five essential questions of who, why, where, when and what for.

You will then be in a position to analyse the client's problem and the possible methods of achieving a practical solution to it in the light of the known facts. You will be in a position to interpret the facts which you have collected and analysed in order to assess the degree of relevance of each, their relevance to particular stages in the legal analysis and determine the inferences which can be drawn from those facts.

25.4   Presenting the Facts

In presenting the facts the key words are clarity, appropriateness of method, relevance and accuracy. There are a number of different methods of presenting facts, each of which requires either more or less action on the part of the presenter. Some facts can be presented to the tribunal by direct observation, for example, exhibits, site views, the appearance or demeanor of witnesses and original or copy documents. Others can be presented by visual methods, for example, tables, schedules, lists, maps, photographs, drawings, plans, etc. Others can be presented by audio methods, for example, narrative, recordings and the testimony of witnesses.

25.5   The Skills Needed in Fact Management

The barrister needs the ability to:

    (a)   be aware of and acquire facility in the use of different ordering techniques;
    (b)   become used to travelling up and down the scale of detail by the use of summary, precis and expansion;
    (c)   focus on single facts and then put them into a wider context;
    (d)   interpret facts, recognise 'best fit' patterns and see significant gaps in the pattern;
    (e)   evaluate by grading facts according to their relevance to particular parts of the analysis of the problem and finding the solution;
    (f)   gather facts through reading, understanding visual information and qustioning;
    (g)   narrate facts in writing and orally using visual information;
    (h)   select facts which assist the chosen 'logic' that is most useful for the purpose.

Always remember that your job is to tell a story with a purpose and that purpose will govern the level of detail which is required; for example, compare a general opinion at an early stage with preparation for trial.

26 Understanding your Instructions

26.1 Introduction

Once you have obtained the facts (or as many as you can) you need to clarify what you are being asked to do about them. Facts only have meaning in context; they can be and are interpreted differently depending on the standpoint of their interpreter.

You will need to ask and to answer a number of questions before any detailed analysis can be undertaken:

Who is your client?
Which stage of the legal process has the case reached?
What are you trying to do?
Why are you being instructed?
What is your client hoping to achieve?
What needs and interests does your client hope to satisfy?

Your view of the facts will depend on whether you are acting for the plaintiff or for the defendant, the prosecution or the defence. Your point of view will be different depending on whether your client is an employer or an employee, a consumer or a manufacturer.

26.2 The Stage of the Proceedings

You will need to ascertain which stage of the legal process the case has reached. Your approach and your task will be different if you are being asked to advise on a preliminary matter from that which is necessary if the case is being prepared for trial.

For example, a barrister might be briefed to write an advice on evidence. This is the particular task that has been set but it can occur at different stages of the legal process. It will often be asked for when litigation has started and the solicitor is preparing for trial. This may be before discovery of documents occurs (see **Civil Litigation Manual** on 'Discovery') or afterwards, or both. It may be before litigation has started — perhaps the lay client wants to know if a claim can be made and, if so, who should be sued. This will usually involve advising on the available evidence.

It is necessary to determine the particular stage that has been reached in the process since this determination will play a crucial part in answering the third question, 'What am I trying to do?' There is little chance of successfully defining your objectives until you know where you are already.

26.3 Your Role

As a junior barrister, you will often find that you are briefed to appear on an interlocutory hearing in a 'heavy' case. You may spend hours reading through bundles of papers, to prepare in case the Master asks you a difficult question. This is laudable — one should always seek to be as knowledgeable about a case as possible. But, if you don't work out first where in the litigation process you (and this court hearing) are, you will be reading the papers with the wrong purpose. You will be a legally qualified sponge, soaking up information in order to master the history of this case. You ought to be a barrister preparing for courtroom advocacy, dissecting the papers in order to appreciate the arguments that can be used at the hearing, either for or against you.

You will often find that these arguments have already been worked out — the senior barrister with overall responsibility for the case will have a strategy prepared for this hearing. If you decide that the brief is yours to do with as you will, the hearing may not achieve its real purpose (either long-term or short-term); you may highlight the wrong area, or give away points unnecessarily because you don't see their significance. In short, you have not determined correctly what your role was. In order to determine this properly, you may need to:

(a) read the papers in the brief;
(b) speak to the solicitor handling the case;
(c) speak to the barrister with overall responsibility for the case (if there is one).

26.4   Your Objectives

When a barrister gets a brief, he or she has a very simple, superficial objective — to win the case (or succeed at a particular hearing). It should not be forgotten that there is a lay client involved, too; who usually wants you to win the case but may have other additional aims. 'What am I trying to do?' is best answered by the barrister after establishing what the client is trying to do.

Remember also to identify all your objectives. The most obvious aim is not necessarily the only one or even the most important one. There may be latent aims as well as manifest ones. When a barrister in court asks his own witness 'What is your name and address?', the manifest purpose is to put on record who the witness is and where she lives. The latent purpose is usually to settle the witness down in the witness-box by asking easy, non-contentious questions. There may be other latent purposes, for example to show the court that the witness comes from a poor part of town (if this is part of your story or theme).

The last point to make is that barristers usually have audiences, most frequently magistrates, judges, juries. When clarifying your own objectives, remember to consider your audience. Who are they? At what stage of what process are they? What are they trying to do? Consider the senior barrister, prosecuting for the Crown in the *Lady Chatterley* libel trial, who asked the jury 'Is this a book you would allow your wife or servant to read?' — in 1963! Had he given any consideration to the nature of his audience?

When you have thought about all of these matters, you will stand a much better chance of achieving your aims, whatever they may be.

26.5   Your Client's Objectives

By the time the case is referred to you, the client's objectives may already be settled. These objectives may be the original ones of the client, or may be those which the client has adopted having had the advice of the professional client. You need to recognise the client's objectives but may only be able to assess these when you see the client in conference. Otherwise you will be acting on your professional client's view of the lay client's objectives or perhaps on the objectives of the professional client. This will have an impact on the way the problem-solving process is managed. You may well have to start the whole process again once you have had the opportunity to discuss with the lay client what his or her objectives are. Remember as well that it is easy to allow your own objectives to influence your understanding of the problem and of the client's objectives. For example, you may be very keen to negotiate a settlement in order to avoid having to appear in court and your client may want a public investigation of the case (may want his or her day in court) and be completely opposed to any idea of a settlement whatever the financial cost. Your task is to identify your client's values and objectives, to know the extent to which your own objectives may affect the resolution of the problem and to know the client's real intentions.

Remember that the client may have legal and non-legal objectives, and these may or may not be articulated. You should try to obtain as full a picture of the situation as possible. In a dispute about contact with children on a Sunday, an analysis of your client's objectives might look something like this:

	Articulated	Unarticulated
Legal	Wants the court to order contact – Sundays	Wants to exercise parental rights
Non-legal	Wants the children to attend church on Sundays	Wants to show the childcarer that he still has power over the children's upbringing

(See R. Mager, *Goal Analysis*, 2nd edn, D.S. Lake Publications, 1984, pp. 39–63.)

27 Understanding the Problem and Collecting and Analysing the Facts

27.1 Introduction

When you receive the papers in a case you will read them; they will contain a variety of information. The first apparently simple task is one of comprehension. Specialist terminology may be used in a report and you will need to know what the words mean. You may need to consult a glossary and an example is contained in the Appendix to this Manual.

You will certainly need to be able to understand information presented in numerical form. Not only will you need to be able to analyse a bank statement or a set of accounts but you may also need to make sense of graphs or statistics. Indeed you may have to develop your own numerical skills in order to check any figures you have been given and to make your own accurate calculations where necessary. (See further **Chapter 32, Dealing with Figures**).

It is impossible to list the various ways in which facts are presented but some facility in comprehending a variety of forms of information is essential and opportunities will be provided to help you develop this.

Once you have read and understood the contents of your brief you can begin to clarify in your mind exactly what is said to have occurred. You must develop a critical and questioning approach to any information you receive, as the information you do not have may be as important as the facts that are available. You will need to identify any gaps in the information you have and any inconsistencies in the facts before you.

It may be that your written instructions are minimal. In that event you will have to find out what happened in conference. Here again you will need to sift carefuly the information you receive to make sure that you understand exactly what happened, checking what you are told for different interpretations of the facts. Again, what you are not told may be as important as what is related to you. The conference is one of your opportunities to clarify any misunderstandings or areas of doubt and to obtain any further information you require.

It is important to remember that fact-finding is an on-going process and new facts may become available at different stages of a case, for instance on discovery of documents or as a result of the examination of a witness at trial. As each new fact emerges, your view of the case will need to be reconsidered and your original conclusions reassessed and possibly modified. You may never obtain all the facts.

27.2 Understanding the Problem

It must always be remembered that it is the client's problems which need to be identified and solved. It is the client who needs to be advised as to the way the problem may be overcome. More than one solution may be possible and the client must be made aware of the implications involved for him in choosing a particular course of action. It is for the client to choose which solution is preferable and the choice may well be made not on whether a legally convincing case can be established but on whether the client's true needs and interests can be met. It is therefore vital to ensure that you have identified clearly what the problem is.

Attempting to identify the problem specifically may be helpful, for example:

Who did or failed to do what to whom, when, where and with what result?
When does the problem occur?
In what situations does the problem occur?
Under what circumstances does the problem occur?
Under what conditions is the problem most severe/least severe?
When does the decision have to be made or the problem solved?
What are the costs of finding the solution?
What interferes with a solution?
Are the costs warranted?

By posing these questions, you will not only be gaining an understanding of the problem but will also be focusing your mind on the task of collecting the facts.

27.3   Collecting the Facts

The barrister must know and understand the problem which he or she is asked to solve. You have to collect, analyse and understand all the facts so that you are in a position to understand the problem. The cause of the problem must also be identified. For example, if the problem which is presented for you to solve is that your client wants contact with his children on a Sunday rather than a Saturday, you should investigate first why this issue has arisen between the parties. You will want to know:

Whether Saturday contact had been agreed or was the subject of a court order?
Whether the agreement or order has worked well, properly or with difficulties?
What the nature of any difficulties has been?
Whether changing the day is considered by the client and/or child carer to make arrangements easier or more difficult?
How the children have responded?
Whether the children wish to maintain contact?
Why your client wants to see the children on Sundays?
Whether the children want to have contact on Sunday rather than Saturday?
Why he believes his proposal has been refused?
Whether there are any other difficulties between the parties which may be masked by this dispute?

Only with all this information at your finger-tips will you be able to fully understand the problem and begin to consider ways of solving it which will meet the client's objectives.

27.3.1   TECHNIQUES OF FACT COLLECTION

There are many techniques which you can use to help you to collect the facts and so increase your understanding of the problem. The purpose of all of them is the same, to ensure that every aspect of the problem is explored thoroughly and from every angle.

27.3.1.1   Sorting
Sorting will help you to categorise, for example:

When does the problem occur — date, time, etc.

Where does the problem occur — home, work, etc.?

With whom does the problem occur — friend, relative, employer, supplier, women, men, ethnic minority group, etc.?

Why does the problem occur — drunkenness, anger, lack of funds, lack of supplies, etc.?

Does the problem have a pattern to it — the problem arises whenever the bank rate goes up, when contact is refused, whenever maintenance is unpaid, etc.?

Does anything seem to trigger the problem — smell, noise, rain, etc.?

27.3.1.2 Making checklists

The following checklist is provided to give you an example of what you need to identify when you prepare your cases. You will find that when you have a little experience you will develop your own style and order of working but what is important is that you have a system which provides you with an efficient means of having at your fingertips all the information you need at whatever stage in preparation you have reached.

Of course, there may be times when you receive the papers in a case at the last minute and will not have time to prepare copious checklists. However, once you have got into the habit of this way of preparation, your mind will automatically take you through the checklists, thereby ensuring that even in the last minute case you are properly prepared and able to do the very best for your client.

Civil action: collecting the facts of your lay client's case

Who is your client?

Where does your client live?

When did the event which is the basis of the action/defence take place?

How does your client say that it happened?

What does your client say happened?

What, if anything, did your client say or do at the time of the occurrence of the event?

Who heard what your client said, or saw what your client did?

What, if any, statement did your client make or what action did your client take at the time of the occurrence of the event?

To whom was the statement made?

Who has a copy of this statement?

When was the statement made?

Who witnessed the action taken?

Who can give evidence about the action taken?

Who witnessed the event (names and addresses)?

What did each witness see or hear?

Witness A:

What can this witness prove?

Witness B:

What can this witness prove? etc.

What exhibits are there?

Where are they?

Who has them?

What can each exhibit prove?

What has your client suffered as a result of the event? (e.g. personal injury, pain and suffering, nervous shock, inconvenience, distress, etc.)

If your client has suffered personal injury, what is the nature of that injury?

What is the medical prognosis?

Will your client make a full recovery?

If not, to what extent will your client recover?

What expert witness(es) have given/should give their opinion on your client's medical condition?

What type of loss has your client suffered? e.g. lost income? lost profit? property lost or damaged? pain and suffering? etc.

If income has been lost:

What is/was your client's gross income?

What is/was your client's net income?

What payments were/are being received from the State?

What steps, if any, could/should have been taken to minimise that loss?

If steps could/should have been taken, why should they have been?

If profit has been lost:

What profit should have been made?

How is that profit calculated?

Why was it lost?

What steps could/should have been taken to minimise that loss?

If steps could/should have been taken, why should they have been?

If property has been lost or damaged:

What was its value before the event?

What was its value after the event?

What is its value now?

Can it be repaired?

If it can be repaired what is the cost of repairing it?

What steps could/should have been taken to minimise the loss?

If steps could/should have been taken, why should they have been?

Does your client have insurance? If so, with whom?

Does the policy cover this loss?

Has a claim been made?

When was it made?

Does the other party have insurance?

Does that insurance contract cover this loss assuming that liability can be proved?

Has a claim been made?

27.4 Analysing the Facts

All barristers have their own particular methods of analysing the facts. There are, however, a number of basic tasks which are commonly undertaken and which you may find helpful in preparing your papers, regardless of whether you are instructed to advise, negotiate, draft a pleading or appear as an advocate.

27.4.1 CONSTRUCT A CHRONOLOGY

Listing the events in the order in which they occurred clarifies what has happened, assists understanding, and can be invaluable as the basis of an opening speech. Increasingly a chronology is handed up to the judge at the start of both civil and criminal trials to assist the court in understanding the case and to provide a structure for the presentation of the case.

27.4.2 DRAW A PLAN OF THE *LOCUS IN QUO*

The *'locus in quo'* simply means the place where the events with which you are concerned occurred. Strictly speaking, the plan of the *locus in quo* should not contain any matters which are in dispute or it should be clearly marked in such a way as to identify controversial matters. The reason for this is that if you draw a plan showing one version of events, or a plan which makes assumptions about facts which are yet to be proved, the plan becomes fixed in your mind as the way things actually happened. This makes it much more difficult for you to keep an open mind and consider other possible explanations. A plan may be particularly useful in a client conference, where there is doubt about the credibility of a witness's evidence.

Take a bank robbery, for example. You are told that a witness was on the opposite side of the road, but you do not know precisely where. If you guess a position and put it on your plan, you will subconsciously assume that the witness was indeed standing there. So mark it in a way that shows there is doubt, or even wait until you have more information. It may be important — what was the witness' line of view? In what direction was the witness walking?

It may sometimes be helpful to draw a series of plans. The first is entirely uncontroversial. The additional plan or plans may then show various alternative explanations of what occurred.

27.4.3 IDENTIFY THE AGREED FACTS

The agreed facts are those facts which are conceded and do not therefore have to be proved. In criminal cases they may sometimes be set out in a 'formal admission' (see **Evidence**). More often, counsel simply tells the court, 'It is not in dispute that . . .' In civil cases you can see from the pleadings what is agreed between the parties. Put simply, if a fact is 'admitted', that fact is not in issue and no evidence has to be adduced to prove it.

Noting down what facts are agreed between the parties helps you to narrow down the issues of the case. It may help you in negotiating to be able to start from some common ground. It may shorten the length of the trial.

27.4.4 IDENTIFY THE FACTUAL ISSUES

This means facts which are in dispute between the parties and which will therefore have to be proved by evidence. In a civil case, facts may be 'not admitted' or may be 'denied'. If a fact is 'not admitted', the party seeking to prove the fact has to adduce evidence; by making 'no admissions', the other party is saying 'I will not adduce evidence to contradict this fact but I reserve the right to cross-examine your witnesses to test their evidence on this point'. If a fact is 'denied', the party relying on that fact has to adduce evidence to prove it and the other party will probably adduce evidence to contradict it.

An issue may well have to be broken down into separate issues. In the bank robbery example, it may be that the identity of the robber is in issue. One element of the identification evidence concerns the colour of his hair. One witness says that he had fair hair, another that he had brown hair. The colour of the hair is therefore a factual issue.

It may help you to divide the case into fairly broad factual issues and then look at the facts which are in dispute within each of those broader issues.

27.4.5 IDENTIFY THE GAPS OR AMBIGUITIES

This simply means matters which require clarification. It is sometimes said that you can only conduct a case well if you know so much about it that it is as if you had been there when the events were happening.

Try to picture the story and then see what pieces are missing or unclear. Returning to the bank robbery, in **27.4.2**, the fact of a witness on the road opposite was mentioned. Before you can complete that part of the picture, you need to know where the witness was standing, the direction he or she was facing, whether there was anything to obstruct a clear view etc.

Consider also how you will obtain such further information. It may be that your client can give you the answer, in which case you may need a conference with your client. It may be that the case concerned expert evidence, in which case you will need a conference with your expert witness. In Civil proceedings it may be necessary to serve interrogatories on your opponent (see **Civil Litigation Manual, Chapter 18**). It may be, however, that the information can only come from a witness whom you cannot see in conference. In such a case you may need to ask your instructing solicitors to take a further proof of evidence from an existing witness or even to seek further witnesses.

It may even be that you will have to wait until cross-examining a witness called by your opponent at trial.

27.4.6 IDENTIFY THE LEGAL ISSUES

This is simply a list of the questions of law which will have to be answered.

List all potential causes of action/offences.
List all potential defences.
List all potential legal outcomes.
List all procedural and evidential questions.

27.4.7   IDENTIFY THE AREAS FOR LEGAL RESEARCH

For more detail on this see **Legal Research Skills**.

Briefly, the notes which would be of use in dealing with the legal issues of a case are:

(a)   Sources, so that you can refer back to them later. Note down relevant page or paragraph numbers of textbooks, and set out full citations of relevant case law.

(b)   A summary of the relevant law.

(c)   Your view of the answer to the question which has to be answered, showing how the law which you have found leads to the answer for which you will be contending.

27.4.8   IDENTIFY THE STRENGTHS AND WEAKNESSES OF YOUR CASE

You have already listed the facts which are not in dispute. To what extent do they assist or weaken your case? You have considered the factual issues. How much evidence is there on each issue which is favourable to you, and how much is there against you?

Your analysis may of course change when the gaps and ambiguities which you have identified are resolved.

There are two important questions which you must think about:

(a)   Once you have identified weaknesses, how can those weaknesses be remedied?

(b)   What evidence which supports your case do you want to bring out in examination-in-chief of your witnesses and/or cross-examination of your opponent's witnesses?

You also need to consider the legal strengths and weaknesses of your case. You will need to note authorities which support your case, as well as authorities which go against you and how you propose to distinguish those authorities.

27.4.9   IDENTIFY THE STRENGTHS AND WEAKNESSES OF YOUR OPPONENT'S CASE

This is really the same process as in **27.4.8** above, except that you are now looking at the case from your opponent's point of view.

The major question you have to ask yourself is, how can you exploit the weaknesses of your opponent's case? Anticipating the points your opponent is likely to make will enable you to decide in advance how you will deal with these points, reducing the risk of being taken by surprise.

27.4.10   FORMULATE A 'THEORY OF THE CASE'

This is dealt with more fully in **Chapter 30, Presenting the Case**. Essentially, it means trying to decide what you think actually happened. It really underpins most of your analysis. However, it is particularly important when preparing for trial for two reasons:

(a)   *Cross-examining witness.* You can cross-examine on inconsistencies between what the witness is saying now and

(i)   other things that witness has said;

(ii)   things said by other witnesses;

(iii)   common sense.

It is to the latter that your theory of the case is most important. At the same time as the robber emerged from the bank, there was an accident in the road outside. A witness identifies your client as the robber. Is it not likely that the witness' attention was distracted by the accident, thus weakening the evidence?

(b)   *Formulating a closing speech*. Imagine you are now making your closing speech. What is the best version of events that you can put before the court on your client's behalf?

This helps in preparing the case because it causes you to ask questions like these. What are the weak points which you will have to deal with? What can be done to show the court that your version of events is the correct one?

28   Choosing the Solution

28.1   Introduction

When the client's problem and your own objectives are understood, you can begin to consider the legal issues raised by the facts and how these issues will affect the client. It is likely that you will, while collecting the facts and considering your instructions, already have begun to match the facts to your own preconceived patterns of legal thought. But it is important to be wary of putting too firm a label on the facts too soon, as it will restrict your thoughts about the case and narrow down too quickly the possible ways of achieving the client's objectives and so providing a solution to the client's problems.

Instead it is suggested that you try to keep an open mind and, starting with the facts, consider each element separately and identify how it might have a legal implication. Rather than attempt to fit the facts to the law, try to fit the law to the facts.

The best legal argument has no point in a court if it is not soundly based on the facts. Equally, the facts of the case need the best legal argument to achieve the best result. Although consideration of a case should start with consideration of the facts, as the case progresses, the role of law and fact is equally important, and the two are closely inter-related. More than that, they are interactive; one moves with the other as more legal or factual input is provided for a case.

It is vital, therefore, to select relevant law with a sound knowledge of the facts, and then also to consider the facts in the light of the law to ensure coherence. However, although law and fact become interrelated, never be deceived into thinking the law has become more important — dealing with facts will always be as important as dealing with law.

When you have considered how the facts might be legally relevant you can attempt to group the areas of relevance together as identifiable legal issues, such as defences or causes of action.

You will need to be constantly reviewing the facts, and now that you have some criteria by which to judge, reassessing the facts for relevance to the legal issues. Some issues may need to be researched by you if they are in an area of law you are unfamiliar with and this further research may necessitate a new review of the facts.

As you proceed with the legal analysis some potential methods of achieving your client's objectives will become apparent. Some will prove unworkable, and new issues may open up, but you should finally be able to put forward some possible arguments which may help to solve your client's problem.

When you have identified a working hypothesis — an identified legal proposition on which to base your case — you will need to review the facts to see if you can prove it.

28.2   Stages in Identifying the Appropriate Legal Solution

Having started with facts, you need a basis for using the facts to identify an appropriate legal solution. The following steps might be followed once the available facts have been collected and analysed. It is important to try to identify all possible routes to a solution rather than settling for the first that occurs. Every possibility should be found and tested before a selection is made.

The process of identifying all the legal possibilities for a case may not be difficult for the barrister who has been in practice for many years, but it may be for the student. In starting to learn this process, never be happy with your list of possibilities if there could be more, and never be happy with a particularly clever answer — it may have weaknesses, or there may still be another even more inventive!

It can be difficult to identify a range of legal solutions at first; the tendency is to use familiar pigeon-holes, from the basic 'Contents' pages of legal textbooks: 'Contract', 'misrepresentation', 'mistake', and the like. This can have uses, but its limitations must be realised. The legal solution is not necessarily going to come from a simple textbook label.

28.2.1   IDENTIFY ALL POTENTIAL LEGALLY RELEVANT ELEMENTS

Do not attempt immediately to attach an overall legal categorisation, but try to find and list every possible legally relevant fact in the case. Make no initial judgments, just write them all down. The following general categories may have legal relevance:

(a)   people, e.g. minor, spouse, professional, owner;
(b)   places, e.g. occupier's liability, Factories Acts, waterways;
(c)   objects/items, e.g. animals, cars, guns;
(d)   documents, e.g. wills, contracts;
(e)   acts, e.g. negligence;
(f)   omissions, e.g. failure to act;
(g)   words, e.g. misrepresentation, fraud;
(h)   dates, e.g. limitation.

Don't list only those elements that you know appear in legal textbooks, or only those elements of which you have some legal knowledge. Just find all those elements of the case that may possibly have any legal ramifications. A source for ideas of the wide variety of things that may have legal implications is the index of *Halsbury's Laws*.

In making the list of possible legally relevant elements, do not limit yourself to words that appear in the facts. Include everything that underlies or surrounds the facts that you have. If the case includes a jam jar, you may well be aware that there is no Jam Jars Act, but you may still need to write down 'jam jar'; there are laws relating to the manufacture of jam jars, filling jam jars either in a factory or at home (if the contents are for sale to the public), labelling jam jars (including EEC regulations), not dealing with jam jars negligently to cause injury to another, etc. The more comprehensive your list of basic legal elements, the more pieces you have for putting together a case.

28.2.2   IDENTIFY LEGAL ISSUES FROM THE LEGALLY RELEVANT ELEMENTS

Once you have identified every possible element of the case that may have legal implications, you then proceed to rationalise all those elements into legal issues. Only once you have identified all the possible legal elements should you start to judge which of the elements are actually most important, and how the separate elements can be grouped together in legal issues.

You need to organise and group together the legally relevant elements you have identified. In doing this, you should show full appreciation of context and standpoint.

As a suggestion for putting legally relevant elements together to find legal issues, the following headings might be used:

(a)   parties;
(b)   causes(s) of action;

(c) defence(s);
(d) relief sought.

Put all your elements under appropriate general headings. Do not judge too quickly which element goes under which heading. If there are alternatives, list them as such. This may sound pedantic to the confident lawyer who is rushing to get on with things, but there are many cases where taking that bit longer to prepare thoroughly will give you that insight into the case which makes all the difference to how well you do it, by giving you a fresh perspective.

If there are some potentially relevant legal elements that do not fit into one of the headings of legal issues, do not necessarily ignore them. Keep them in a general category at the end. It may still be valuable to glance at them later to see if they reveal a gap in the case you are evolving.

28.2.3   DEVELOP A FULL FRAMEWORK OF LEGAL ISSUES

Once you have identified all the legal issues, they need to be put together in a comprehensive framework. To do this:

(a) List the legal issues under the headings suggested in **28.2.2**.
(b) Put the legally relevant elements in under the issue to which they relate.
(c) Emphasise which legal issues are most important.
(d) Ensure that all the legal issues and legally relevant elements are included in the framework.

This framework should then provide a basic outline of the case, even if it does still include options and question marks. All the legally relevant facts should now be grouped in a legally relevant way.

The framework should be expanded to include all procedural and evidential points that can be identified and which might help to achieve the client's objectives. Note in the framework those areas where you have identified weaknesses and problems, and those areas where further factual information is required.

28.2.4   DEVELOP POTENTIAL LEGAL SOLUTIONS FROM THE FRAMEWORK

The framework of legal issues should provide the basis for identifying potential legal solutions. However, it will not as such necessarily provide the legal solution, as a case is won not on the law alone but on proof. Therefore the legal framework must be reviewed in the light of the facts, and particularly in the light of which facts are agreed and which are in issue, and how good the proof is. Review your framework in the light of all the facts to see which bits of it are strong and which weak. Putting together the strengths should suggest a good legal solution. In developing the legal solution, every effort should be made to achieve all the client's objectives, including extra-legal objectives.

This review may produce a clear legal solution which simply needs to be followed through. If it leaves any options or areas of doubt, as it often will, further research must be done on the potential legal solutions to see which it is best to pursue, and the client may need to be consulted.

28.2.5   DRAW UP A RESEARCH PLAN TO INVESTIGATE POTENTIAL LEGAL SOLUTIONS

From the legal framework reviewed in the light of the facts already available, you need to construct a plan for legal and factual research. From the framework it should be possible to decide not only what areas require research but also their relative importance and priority. Do keep the lists for legal and factual research clear and distinct.

Although you need to deal with basic facts before trying to identify a legal solution, more research will be needed once you have a potential legal solution. It would be very expensive and therefore unrealistic to have all the factual information before starting work on the case. To start with you need enough factual information to start the process, then further research should be done to investigate your provisional legal solution. In finding the factual support, remember that every fact will need to be proved, so in developing your legal solution list each fact you need to prove with the item of evidence that proves it or a note that evidence is still required. Such lists should include an assessment of the reliability of the evidence and possible inferences where clear evidence is not available.

Carrying out legal research is dealt with in a separate part of this Manual. When the legal and factual research is done, it should be possible to see clearly all the relative strengths and weaknesses of different parts of the framework, to clear up doubts, and to take decisions where there are options.

Only after research can you finally identify the appropriate legal solution. Even when you have done that, do make one final check that all the facts available and the legal elements that you identified do support that solution.

Exercise
Your client is the mother of a nine year old child. She took the child on a picnic in the countryside. They ate their picnic at the side of a cultivated field near a stream. After eating their picnic your client fell asleep and was woken by her child crying out as he had fallen into the stream and cut his arm quite badly. It appears that the child had tripped on some rusty wire at the edge of the stream, but it is not clear how he cut himself. The client is worried that the water in the stream did not seem to be very clean. She took the child to hospital but had to wait some time to get attention for him. The child was not well for several weeks after the incident.

(a)   List the factual issues that you would wish to pursue before trying to identify the possible legal solutions.

(b)   Make a key list of as many potentially legally relevant elements as you can that might be involved in finding a legal solution.

28.3   Methods of Choosing the Appropriate Legal Solution

Putting together a framework of issues and doing the appropriate research may give you an answer in a straightforward case. But often it will not; the law may not be clear, all the facts may not be available, or there may be alternatives. Professional skill and judgment must come into play in filling gaps and making choices.

28.3.1   THE 'BEST FIT' PATTERN

If the framework does not provide a single obvious answer, it should get you some distance down the road. It should at least define where there are legal and factual certainties and where there are legal options, and in such a case, what the options are. One way to proceed is simply to find that solution which best fits the framework — that which makes best use of the legal and factual strengths of the case while placing least reliance on its weaknesses. Although you should not immediately label a case 'misrepresentation' without reviewing all the options as outlined above, it may be that at the end of the day 'misrepresentation' is the 'best fit'.

In deciding what legal solution fits best, do not forget those elements which do not fit well. They may still have some use in reviewing the case at a later stage, or in looking for options for a settlement. The 'best fit' approach must not be seen as suggesting that superficial analysis or sloppy thought will do so long as it gives a roughly right answer. It should only ever be the result of wide-ranging and deep consideration.

28.3.2   THE POTENTIAL PENULTIMATE PROBANDUM

This slightly grandiose phrase summarises an alternative approach to identifying an appropriate legal solution, which has some points of overlap with finding the 'best fit' but is a separate and slightly more complex process. The 'potential penultimate probandum' (or probanda, plural) is the central proposition(s) that you must prove to win your case. The process is to identify precisely what the probandum or probanda are for a particular legal solution and then check carefully to see if they can actually be shown in the case in question.

To give a simple example, for a misrepresentation case you would need to show:

(a)   that representations were made;
(b)   what those representations were;
(c)   that they were relied on in making a contract;
(d)   that they were false; and
(e)   that the fact that they were false lead to loss.

This must be done with great care to work properly; if you just use general legal propositions your analysis of the case may be woolly or inaccurate. The skill is to state precisely what you have to prove to win and then check in detail that you can prove it. If you can prove all you need to, or have a good chance of doing so, you have a potential legal solution to the case. The statement of what needs to be proved should be comprehensive, and should, for example, include the relevant standard of proof. Whilst this process is largely objective, it will also involve making professional judgments on the chances of success — you will very rarely have a 100 per cent chance of proving every element of the case!

In all but a fairly simple case it may not be a question of just defining what ultimately needs to be proved to win the case. It may be necessary to delve deeper — what do you need to prove to support the elements you will need to prove to win the case? (Potential pre-penultimate probanda!) What would you need to demonstate to show that a contract was made in reliance on misrepresentations?

28.3.3   TENTATIVE THEORY OF THE CASE

The tentative theory of the case is different from the 'best fit' approach. The 'best fit' is based on an objective valuation of the framework of legal issues, whereas a theory of the case, whilst securely founded on that framework, uses guesswork to fill in gaps rather than simply identifying and relying on the main strengths of the framework. The theory of the case puts cement between the bricks of the framework, to fill in any factual and legal gaps and make the whole thing fit together. But as few gaps as possible should be filled; the more you fill in yourself, the weaker the case.

Finding a theory of the case is done by thinking why and how the events in the case are likely to have come about. It can be done by looking for themes, or by using analogies from other cases or from general knowledge of life. Intelligent use of theories can be a valuable way into a case, but the dangers of developing an imaginative theory that is not well founded on the facts, must not be underestimated. Putting forward a theory of the case is often a basis for persuasive advocacy, and this is dealt with in the **Advocacy, Negotiation and Conference Skills Manual**, but before you present the case in court it is a method of dealing with facts.

Any potential theory of the case must be carefully analysed. It should not simply be the best theory for the client, but should look objectively at how things are most likely to have happened. Remember that a theory of the case can easily be destroyed when extra evidence becomes available — do not be too confident on too little. It is useful to consider how the other side may view your theory!

Once you have identified a theory for the case it is not simply a matter of arguing it in court, but of finding evidence to support it. Any theory of the case must be analysed for legal and factual weaknesses, and it must be coherent and as capable of proof as possible, or you will not have a sound foundation for advocacy.

Exercise
A man and a woman who are in the living-room of the man's house, are heard arguing by a neighbour. Shortly afterwards two shots are heard. The man shouts for help, and the neighbour

rushes in to find the man nursing the woman, who has a severe head wound. A doctor is called and the woman is taken to hospital but she later dies.

You have evidence that a handgun was found in the man's pocket shortly after the incident by a policeman investigating what happened. The man admits that he has owned the gun for several years. You also have evidence that the man and woman had been living together for several years, but their relationship had not been happy recently.

You are acting for the defence of the man on a charge of murder.

    (a)   List the factual aspects of the case that will require investigation on behalf of the defence.

    (b)   Construct as many potential theories of the case as possible which may show the man's innocence.

28.4   Methods of Evolving a Theory

If you have substantial factual information and proof, you may be able to proceed with a 'best fit' legal solution, or one firmly based on an analysis of the elements you need to prove. If you do not, you will have to wholly or partly evolve a theory of the case to identify and pursue a legal solution. There are various approaches to evolving a theory.

28.4.1   LOGICAL THINKING

Logical thought is vital in seeking a legal solution for a case. Look for all plausible logical possibilities. However, do not assume that the first solution which occurs to you is right, simply because it is logical. An answer must be based on proof, not simply on logic. If your logical construction of how events came about posits that something happened or did not happen, see if there is any evidence to that effect, even if it is purely circumstantial. In constructing a logical approach to a case, be sure to base your analysis on proved or provable facts as far as possible. Beware of emotion, intention and knowledge elements, which are particularly difficult to prove. In thinking logically yourself, never assume that others have acted logically!

Use the great strength of logic, but beware the great weakness. The great strength is the need for any legal development of a case to be logical. The great drawback is the danger of assuming that just because a theory is logical it is actually true.

28.4.2   LATERAL THINKING

Although the development of cases should be logically based, there is a role for inventive thought in finding a legal solution. It is not simply a matter of thinking of how events are most likely to have happened, but of thinking of all the possible ways in which they could have happened. Once one has eliminated the impossible, all the other theories might be true!

The concept of lateral thinking, invented and propounded by Edward de Bono, is now widely known. Even those who have not read any of the books on the subjct may be aware of some of the classical lateral thinking problems. There are many elements in lateral thinking that are of potential value to the practical lawyer.

Lateral thinking may be useful for anyone who needs to find new ways of looking at problems and finding answers. To illustrate with a classic lateral thinking problem:

John states that when he went into the living room of his house he saw immediately that James was lying naked on the floor, and that he was dead. There was broken glass on the floor, and a small pool of water. The window was open.

What simple questions should you ask John to establish what has happened, to decide whether any crime has been committed, and if so, by whom?

Think about this before reading on. There are some clear lines of questioning that a lawyer would naturally pursue, to find out more about James, to find in what way he might have died, and why, and to evolve factual and legal theories.

The simplest answer is actually contained in the facts given with little or no further questioning, but with a little lateral thinking. It is natural to assume that James has been murdered, or has died of a heart attack. It is natural to concentrate attention on the fact that he is naked. But the simple answer, dismissing all assumptions, is that James is in fact a goldfish, and has died naturally after the cat has knocked his bowl over and run out through the window!

The student may feel on reflection that this particular example is of limited value, as the barrister would know that James was a fish. But beware such simple faith. The barrister is not initially offered the full facts of the case, and it is easy to assume something is true because it seems likely right up to the day of the trial.

Although lateral thinking has not yet been developed to have specific applications for lawyers. De Bono himself mentions lawyers amongst those groups who might benefit from a lateral thinking approach. He also suggests two contrasting examples which suggest the relevance of lateral thinking for lawyers, both coming from Shakespeare. In *The Merchant of Venice* the fact that Shylock has a contract for a pound of flesh appears to have no defence. But Portia finds one by the lateral thinking approach of using a different entry point — Shylock can have his pound of flesh, but he can have not a drop of blood! In contrast, Othello unfortunately fails to use lateral thinking and believes Desdemona to be unfaithful because he accepts limited facts of their face value rather than trying to look for alternative explanations. Lateral thinking shows the importance not only of organising information, but of reviewing it regularly, and of not being bound by existing impressions. Many detective stories are based on a sudden addition of information or a sudden change of viewpoint and many legal cases unravel in this way. In preparing a legal solution to a case one should be ready for this.

In developing insight and creativity to find potential solutions to problems, lateral thinking emphasises the following:

  (a)   the importance of reviewing one's viewpoint;
  (b)   the need not just to arrange but to rearrange information to solve a problem;
  (c)   the need to seek a full range of extra information;
  (d)   dividing the problem into its constituent elements;
  (e)   looking at what really underlies the problem;
  (f)   checking the limits and boundaries of the problem;
  (g)   looking for new inputs;
  (h)   using analogies;
  (i)   using a different entry point;
  (j)   random stimulation of possible answers;
  (k)   the possibility of redefining the problem;
  (l)   the importance of generating alternatives;
  (m)   suspending judgment in looking for a solution;
  (n)   asking for an independent viewpoint of the problem;
  (o)   never being happy with simply finding one cause or explanation that satisfies you personally.

Finally, a general idea from lateral thinking which may be of use in trying to identify a legal solution. Beware of being too swayed by the order in which information arrives — the sequence trap. The fact that a piece of information comes to you early in a case does not mean it is particularly important, and it should not prejudice your attitude to information that arrives later.

327

Identifying a legal solution is an important element of problem solving, and lateral thinking offers some ideas for this such as:

(a) moving away from labels and set patterns of thinking;
(b) not being afraid of being wrong in looking at options;
(c) learning to suspend judgment;
(d) escaping from dominant ideas, arrogance and ego; and
(e) an emphasis on not being limited by one's own experience, emotions or assumptions.

A particular concept advocated in problem solving is 'Po': the idea is that traditional logical thinking is bounded by 'Yes' and 'No', and that in looking at a problem these may limit possibilities. 'Po', however, can be used to suspend judgment, to encourage alternatives, to challenge established positions, and to make disconnected jumps when a dead-end is reached. The point being made is that in looking at a problem, rather than deciding 'Yes' or 'No' on a course of action or a possible solution, one can say 'Po' to interrupt, to challenge, to start again, to rearrange, to liberate or to provoke. This can be particlarly useful if you are working on a brief late at night, or thinking about it on the tube.

All the books on lateral thinking are relatively easy and amusing to read, but the four by Edward de Bono (see Further Reading section) may be particularly useful to the student who is not familiar with lateral thinking.

Exercise
1. There are three witnesses who saw a woman running away from the scene of the armed robbery shortly ater the robbery occurred. How many different factual reasons might there be for her conduct? How many different legal hypotheses can these factual possibilities lead to?
2. You are representing Cinderella's stepmother, who has been charged with ill-treating her stepdaughter. Tell the story from the point of view of the stepmother, offering possible lines of defence.
3. A man believes that he had developed a way of predicting how an individual's career may progress by looking at specific factors. He charges a fee for his service, which is popular with young people. He accepts that he is not infallible, and it is a term of paying for his service that if his prediction is wrong, he will return double the original fee. He makes a lot of money. He has just been arrested. What might he have been arrested for?

28.4.3 MIND MAPPING

An alternative technique to developing a theory of a case is mind mapping.

Man's mind does not work in a linear or list-like manner.

When you receive information, a complex process of sorting and selecting is taking place in the mind. Whole networks of words and ideas are being juggled and interlinked in order to communicate a certain meaning.

When you peruse a brief, it is not simply a process of observing a long list of words. Each word is received in the context of the words which surround it. Thus key concepts are interlinked and integrated.

The mind mapping process takes place in the mind automatically and the mind map is a physical representation of that process. When legal and factual elements of a case are being recalled, key concept overviews are given outlining the main characters, settings and events together with descriptive detail in the form of 'branches' from the central theme.

In addition to or as an alternative to lists of the various legal and factual elements of the case, you should start from the centre or main theme and branch out into those elements. The more important elements are placed nearer the centre of the map and less important ones nearer the edge. The links between the key concepts are immediately recognisable because of their proximity and connection on the 'branches'.

The result should be an organically drawn map which would enable you to recall and review the elements of the case much more effectively and rapidly. New information can also be added more easily and tidily. This should prove a great asset as new developments occur during the trial.

Having classified your thoughts in this way, you should obtain a better overview of the case and so ensure that no item is missed when developing a theory.

28.5   Methods of Supporting a Legal Solution

A potential legal solution will rarely be entirely founded on incontrovertible legal principles any more than on incontrovertible facts. Although the basic legal principles supporting the case may be clear, there will always be some areas where the law is not clear. If the case could be simply answered from a legal textbook the solicitor would have done it rather than send it to a barrister.

The barrister should not be worried by encountering areas where the law is not clear; arguing the law is part of the job and is an area where many professional reputations are made.

28.5.1   STATUTE LAW

Once you have established a statutory section as being relevant to the legal solution in a case, do not simply write it down. Consider its real role in your legal solution:

Does the section really apply to your case or not?
If it does, is its effect clear or is there any doubt?
Are there any relevant principles of statutory interpretation?
Are there cases interpreting the words of the statute?

A more complex process must be followed with subordinate legislation and statutory instruments:

Is the statutory instrument within the enabling legislation?
Does it apply?
Has it been interpreted?

28.5.2   CASES

Simply finding a case which appears to be relevant is only a starting-point in fitting it into a coherent legal solution. There are many questions to deal with concerning the pecedent value of the case. Consider the following:

Is the case in your favour or not?
If it is, you wish to defend its precedent value; if it is not, you wish to challenge it. A case is hardly ever directly on point; there is always some room to consider its value in contructing a legal case.

On what facts was the decision made?
What precisely was the decision and what was obiter?
Did all the judges agree?
What was the level of the court making the decision?
When was the case decided?
Has the case been reviewed subsequently?

There is rarely a single case on a particular point but a variety of cases or even a line of cases, so one has to review the whole line, not simply to make the line of cases coherent, as one does as an undergraduate, but to consider what line through the cases one can and should take for the present purpose.

If appropriate, note the procedural basis on which the decision was made. In some cases it is not open to the judges to review the facts, they may simply have jurisdiction to consider if the decision before them was properly reached.

28.5.3   TEXTBOOKS

While some of the leading textbooks can be quoted in court, a legal theory for a case should not be based primarily on textbook comment, but on original sources.

28.5.4   PROCEDURE AND EVIDENCE

Procedure and evidence should not be swept aside as peripheral — they are tools that can be central in achieving an objective if one investigates the range of possibilities that are available, learns how to use them, and always looks to see what can be useful in helping to achieve objectives in a particular case. Any potential legal solution can only be achieved with a proper use of procedure and evidence. Can you prove every fact on which your legal solution is based, if so how and when?

28.6   Reviewing the Potential Legal Solution

Always keep the potential legal solution that you favour under review. Do not let the case be bound by initial impressions. Totally re-evaluate it constantly in the light of factual and legal research. Any theory of the case will need to be regularly updated. Keep a note of alternatives you have identified earlier in case they need to be re-examined. It is a stength, not a weakness, to allow your perception to change. Be prepared to restructure the case and your ideas of it if you need to. Barristers do not easily admit they are wrong, but if you are you need to accept it immediately rather than continue on the wrong course.

Whatever legal solution you propose, check it for consistency with all the facts and legal research available. Make sure of its strength in the light of all of the facts, and be very wary if any fact appears to contradict it. Don't just do this once, keep doing it right through the case.

In addition, review your potential legal solution in the light of the available evidence. A legal theory firmly based on a fact you cannot prove has limited value. Draw up a chart of all the facts you have to prove to succeed with a particular theory, noting which you can already prove and which you still have to find proof for. Consider the possibilities and dangers of inference from the facts that can be proved.

Finally, try to assess the chance your proposed legal solution has of winning. The client will want to know this before clear instructions can be given as to how to proceed.

28.7   Getting the Client's Instructions

The criteria against which your client will make his or her decision should not be forgotten. Apart from your client's overall objectives, other criteria will also be relevant. For example, such matters as cost, time efficiency, the desire to avoid stress, the desire to attain a fair result, the impact on others, the desire to avoid risk, the desire to be exonerated and/or the desire to be understood may be the factors which determine which decision is taken. As an illustration, your client may well feel that her marriage has broken down and, in theory, want a divorce, but her decision to pursue an action for divorce may have more to do with the impact which a divorce might have on her children than on your advice that, on the facts, a divorce would be granted. In seeking to solve your client's problem you should recognise the existence of this sort of criterion and be able to assess its potential impact on your client. You will then be in a position to present the possible solution to your client in such a way that all the consequences of a particular course of action or inaction are made known so that an informed decision can be made.

The client will make his or her decision after being advised in conference by you or after having read your witten opinion and been further advised by the solicitor as to the best way forward. The feedback from your client in conference may require you to revise your proposed solution because you had not understood the problem fully from your client's point of view, or because you had failed to recognise what your client's objectives were or the constraints which might otherwise influence the result. If you have taken care to consider the problem fully this should rarely occur because, having been through the whole process you should have been able to recognise which of the optional solutions would be the most appropriate. However, you must be prepared on occasion for an iterative process and ensure that you have finally understood your client's wishes which initially may have been obscured by embarrassment, unwillingness to act decisively or other hidden personal motives.

28.8 Checklist for Identifying a Legal Solution

1. Identify all the client's objectives.
2. Collect and analyse all basic factual information about the problem.
3. List all potentially legally relevant elements.
4. From the elements, identify legal issues.
5. Put together a framework for the case from the legal issues.
6. In developing the framework look at:

   (a) the relative importance of issues;
   (b) the 'best fit' pattern;
   (c) the 'potential ultimate probandum';
   (d) a potential theory of the case.

7. Develop each legal issue in the framework to include:

   (a) all the substantive parts of each legal issue;
   (b) all the sub-issues related to each legal issue;
   (c) all procedural and other supporting points;
   (d) potential problems.

8. Using your framework to assess relevance, decide:

   (a) what facts must be proved for the client to succeed;
   (b) which available facts support your case;
   (c) which available facts cause difficulties for your case;
   (d) which facts can already be proved;
   (e) which facts still require proof;
   (f) which facts still need to be ascertained.

9. From the framework developed as suggested under (6) and (7), draw up a plan for factual research and for legal research.
10. Review statutory and case law material to support your case.
11. As research is completed, review your potential legal solution. In particular check that:

   (a) legal research does not undermine the central legal issues of your potential solution;
   (c) that you do have admissible evidence to prove all the elements of each of the central legal issues in your potential legal solution.

Be ready to change your mind if necessary!

29 Assessing the Strength of the Case

29.1 Introduction

The question which most clients ask their barristers is 'will I win my case'? The answer will depend on what can be proved. Before you can answer it, you will need to identify

(a) What must be proved and by whom.
(b) What evidence there is in support of each proposition which must be proved.
(c) Any conflicting or contradictory evidence.
(d) Whether the evidence is sufficient to satisfy the standard of proof required.

In a civil case, the issues for trial will have been narrowed down by the pleadings. It will be clear from an analysis of the pleadings which facts are in issue and which are admitted and therefore need not be proved. By identifying which side carries the burden of proof on each issue and by looking at the witness statements and any documentary evidence to see what evidence there is in relation to each issue, you can assess the likelihood of successfully establishing your client's case.

Without careful analysis of the strengths and weakness of your case you will be unable to give sound advice to your client on the likelihood of success at trial. This will also affect your ability to negotiate effectively, advise on whether to accept a payment into court, or on whether further evidence is necessary, or indeed plan the presentation of the case at the trial.

In a criminal case, it is the commission of the offence by the accused that must be proved by the Prosecution before there can be a conviction. Therefore, whether you are briefed for the Prosecution or the Defence, you will need to scrutinise the facts of the case and consider carefully whether inferences can be drawn from the facts from which it can be established beyond reasonable doubt that each and every element of the offence is made out against the accused. The strength of those inferences will then have to be weighed against others which may weaken the Prosecution case before any advice can be given as to the likely outcome of the trial.

29.2 Organising Information for Proof

The method you use to analyse the evidence will depend on the nature of the case you are dealing with, the stage of the proceedings it has reached, the particular objectives you have in mind, the time frame within which you are operating and not least the way in which your own mind works. Different people have different methods of doing this analysis.

One way of carrying out this analysis is to use a table such as that shown below and referred to in the **Opinion Writing and Drafting Manual** at **11.1.6.3**.

Another alternative method would be to use the mind mapping technique described at **28.4.3**.

Identifying Issues and Relating Evidence to Issues

Ref.	Issue	Para. of statement of claim	Para. of defence	Para. of reply	Burden of proof	Name of witness	Available oral evidence	Available documentary evidence	Notes/ comments e.g. procedure, evidence, gaps

It is, however, essential that the method you use is rigorous. It must enable you to identify exactly what inferences you are seeking to draw from the facts which are logically probative of the issues which must be proved. It should show, not simply whether the case can be proved, but how it can be proved. It should enable you not only to give sound advice on what further evidence is needed but help you, if necessary, to argue why a particular piece of information is relevant and thus admissible.

The Wigmorean method of analysing evidence which is explained below is a highly sophisticated and well-developed system which illustrates how thorough and detailed an analysis of evidence can and should be.

29.3 Wigmorean Analysis

The device which is here recommended is a chart based on a scheme originally proposed by Wigmore. (See J H Wigmore 'The Problem of Proof' (1913) 8 Ill L Rev 77; *The Science of Judicial Proof* (1937).) Wigmore's ideas have recently been taken up and elaborated by Terence Anderson and William Twining in *Analysis of Evidence* (Weidenfeld, 1991). Further reference may be made to William Twining, *Theories of Evidence: Bentham and Wigmore* (1985). *Rethinking Evidence: Exploratory Essays* (1990); N. Gold, K. Mackie & W. Twining, *Learning Lawyer's Skills* (1989), pp. 216–255.

The way in which the chart is developed will depend to some extent on the purpose for which it is being drawn up. This in turn depends on the standpoint of the person making it. (For the purpose of practising Wigmorean analysis a useful standpoint is that of a historian reviewing the evidence in some *cause célèbre* where there is a suggestion that a miscarriage of justice occurred.) So before you begin the chart, clarify your standpoint:

(a) Who are you?
(b) What are you doing?
(c) Why are you doing it?

29.4 Ultimate Probandum and Penultimate Probanda

Wigmore's analysis works from the top downwards. The starting-point in any case is, therefore, the ultimate probandum — something which must finally be proved. Examples are:

(a) Bessie Boot stole a bottle of whisky, the property of Super Stores plc.
(b) Charles Charnel murdered Daisy Dove.
(c) Ernest Fish raped Gertrude Heap.
(d) The defendant is in breach of a landlord's repairing covenant.
(e) The respondent committed adultery with Dolly Dainty.

In order to establish an ultimate probandum it will generally be necessary to prove a number of matters which lead directly to it. What these matters are will be determined in each case by reference to pleadings or substantive law. These matters are known as the penultimate probanda.

Thus, in the examples above:

(a) Ultimate probandum: Bessie Boot stole a bottle of whisky, the property of Super Stores plc. Penultimate probanda:

(i) BB appropriated a bottle of whisky.
(ii) The whisky belonged to Super Stores.
(iii) She did so dishonestly.
(iv) At the time, she intended to deprive Super Stores permanently of the whisky.

335

(b)   Ultimate probandum: Charles murdered Daisy Dove.
      Penultimate probanda:

   (i)   CC stabbed DD.
   (ii)   He did so intending to kill her.
   (iii)   The stabbing caused DD's death.

(c)   Ultimate probandum: Ernest Fish raped Gertrude Heap.
      Penultimate probanda:

   (i)   EF had sexual intercourse wth GH.
   (ii)   GH did not consent.

(d)   Ultimate probandum: Defendant is in breach of a landlord's repairing covenant.
      Penultimate probanda:

   (i)   Defendant is plaintiff's landlord by a lease dated 4 April 1988.
   (ii)   The lease contains a covenant obliging the landlord to repair the roof of the demised
premises upon notice being given by the tenant.
   (iii)   The roof of the demised premises fell into disrepair in January 1989.
   (iv)   Plaintiff gave notice of the disrepair in February 1989.
   (v)   Defendant has failed to repair the roof.

(e)   Ultimate probandum: Respondent committed adultery with Dolly Dainty.
      Penultimate probanda:

   (i)   Respondent is married to petitioner.
   (ii)   After the marriage the respondent had sexual intercourse with D.D.

The diagram below shows the way in which the ultimate probandum and penultimate probanda are
charted. The example is the first of those given above. (Note: here and in the subsequent illustrations
the standpoint is that of prosecuting counsel advising on the strength of the case against the accused.)

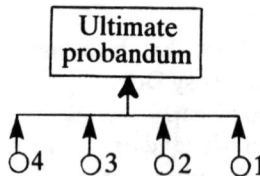

Key List:

1.   BB appropriated a bottle of whisky,
2.   The whisky belonged to Super Stores.
3.   BB appropriated the whisky dishonestly.
4.   At the time, she intended to deprive Super Stores of the whisky permanently.

The chart shows that the four penultimate probanda lead to the ultimate probandum. In other words,
the truth of the ultimate probandum can be inferred from the truth of the penultimate probanda. (The
symbol of the arrow signifies this.) Note that the working goes from right to left, as well as from top
to bottom. The key list explains the items in the chart and should itself, when read, give a coherent
account of the items charted.

29.5   Chains of Inference: Generalisations

In the example just given, the facts which formed the penultimate probanda were almost certainly not facts known directly by the person reviewing the evidence and trying to organise it in the form of a Wigmore chart. They were inferences which he drew from other information. The chart has to take this into account so as to give an accurate picture of the extent to which the evidence supports the ultimate probandum. Suppose the store detective has made a statement to the police and that part of it reads as follows:

> I saw the defendant take a bottle of whisky from the spirits display. She did not put it in the store's wire basket which she was carrying but instead she put it in an inside pocket in the mackintosh which she was wearing. She went to a check-out and paid for the goods in the wire basket but made no attempt to pay for the bottle of whisky. She then left the store. I followed her and stopped her in the street outside.

We shall concentrate on item 1 in the key list and show how this is established from the information given in this extract. The chart and key list will appear as follows:

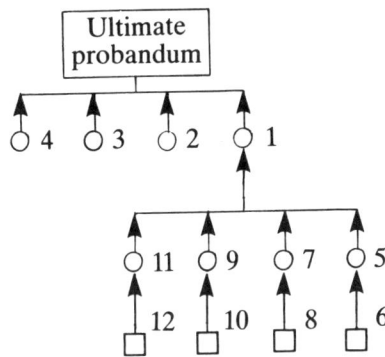

Key List:

1.   BB appropriated a bottle of whisky.
2.   The whisky belonged to Super Stores.
3.   BB appropriated the whisky dishonestly.
4.   At the time, she intended to deprive Super Stores of the whisky permanently.
5.   BB took the whisky from the display.
6.   Store detective's statement to this effect.
7.   BB put it in her mackintosh instead of the basket.
8.   Store detective's statement to this effect.
9.   BB failed to produce or pay for the whisky at check-out.
10.   Store detective's statement to this effect.
11.   BB left store with whisky.
12.   Store detective's statement to this effect.

Notice that the chart now shows that item 1 is to be inferred from the combination of items 5, 7, 9 and 11. But these are still not facts to which the maker of the chart has direct access. They are only inferences from, respectively, 6, 8, 10 and 12. These last *are* facts to which the chart-maker has direct access (on the assumption that he has the statement, or at least a copy of it, before him.) The special nature of these facts is shown by the different symbol representing them. Strictly speaking, there is another stage of thought which the chart might have shown. The move from the store detective's statement to the inference that what she stated was in fact the case involves a generalisation and could be charted thus:

337

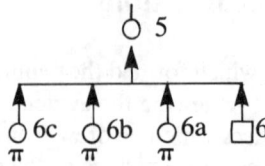

Key list:

5.   BB took the whisky from the display.
6.   Store detective's statement to this effect.
6a.   In the absence of a motive to lie or opportunity for erroneous observation, a person's account of what he has seen is likely to be true.
6b.   The store detective had no known motive to lie.
6c.   He had no known opportunity for erroneous observation.

The symbol π is used to designate a fact noticed as a matter of general knowledge or inference without evidence being introduced specifically on the point. Here 6a takes the form of a generalisation about the trustworthiness of a particular type of evidence, whilst 6b and 6c may be inferred from the absence of evidence to the contrary.

The objective of the chart is to clarify, and since clarity is likely to be obscured by density of items it may be thought unnecessary to chart all the generalisations on which inferences depend. But care should be taken because some generalisations which are necessary to support an inference are a good deal more questionable than might at first appear. See, for example, Profesor Twining's discussion of the relevance of the age of the accused in *R* v *Bywaters & Thompson* (**29.7** below). With or without explicit generalisations, the chart should always show the fact that a witness states something to be the case and the inference that that is indeed the case as two distinct items. One of the dangers of the Wigmoran exercise is that it can lead to the production of a rigid pattern of unnaturally solid 'facts', whereas reality is altogether more fragile and elusive. The point is well made in Peter Ackroyd's *Hawksmoor*. The detective in Ackroyd's novel had just been shown a number of witness statements, but:

> None of these apparent sightings interested Hawksmoor, since it was quite usual for members of the public to come forward with such accounts and to describe unreal figures who took on the adventitious shape already suggested by newspaper accounts. There were even occasions when a number of people would report sightings of the same person, as if a group of hallucinations might create their own object which then seemed to hover for a while in the street of London. And Hawksmoor knew that if he held a reconstruction of the crime by the church, yet more people would come forward with their own versions of time and event; the actual killing then became blurred and even inconsequential, a flat field against which others painted their own fantasies of murderer and victim. (**Chapter 8**).

29.6   Strengthening and Weakening Inferences

Suppose the evidence of the store detective's observation is not so clear-cut. There are difficulties because he admits in his statement that the store was crowded and so he did not have the defendant in view for the whole time at the spirits display. But an assistant manager who had been alerted was also observing the defendant and he confirms the detective's account that the bottle of whisky was taken. The appropriate section of the chart will look something like this:

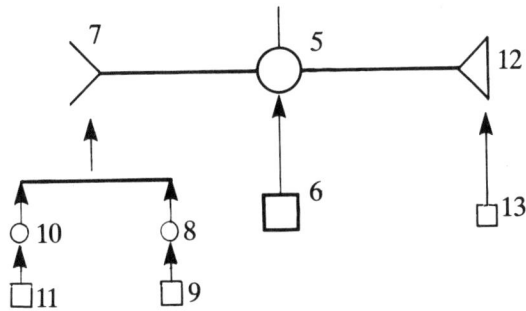

Key list:

5. BB took whisky from display.
6. Detective's statement to this effect.
7. Her observation may have been mistaken.
8. Store was crowded.
9. Detective's statement to this effect.
10. Detective could not have defendant in view all the time at the spirits display.
11. Detective's statement to this effect.
12. Assistant manager confirms 5.
13. His statement to this effect.

(The numbers of the items shown in earlier illustrations will have to be adjusted.)

The symbol > shows something which weakens the effect of another piece of charted information. It appears on the left of the symbol which represents the weakened information. The symbol ◁ shows something which strengthens the effect of another piece of charted information. It appears on the right of the symbol which represents the strengthened information.

The most basic features of Wigmore's system have been shown. It should now be possible to construct a chart and key list either for a whole case or for part of one.

The important points to remember are:

(a) Clarify standpoint.
(b) Work out ultimate probandum and penultimate probanda.
(c) Draw the chart from top to bottom and from right to left.
(d) Think carefully about any generalisations.
(e) Work on the basis that one item stands for one proposition and no more.

With the task completed you will have a better idea of how your information hangs together. The chart cannot, of course, tell you which propositions are likely to be accepted by the court but your own judgement will be greatly assisted in dealing with that problem by the construction of the chart. Wigmore observed that the use of this method came more readily to some than to others. Experience has shown, however, that initial difficulties disappear if the student persists in trying to make the method work. The best way to learn this technique is to use it.

29.7   Examples of Inference

The whole of this section is an extract from William Twining, *Theories of Evidence: Bentham and Wigmore* (1985) pp. 142–6, and is reproduced by permission of the publishers, Weidenfeld & Nicholson.

V is found dead from a stab wound in the back. W, a forensic scientist, testifies that a particular knife was the murder weapon. He also testifies that there was one clear set of fingerprints on the weapon with characteristics x, y, z etc. and that M's finger patterns conform precisely to the prints. In this simple example, particular scientific findings establish the cause of death, the identity of the murder weapon and the identity of a person who had handled the weapon. They all form part of a chain of reasoning which has strong, but not necessarily conclusive, probative force despite the length of the chain. It is possible that W is lying or mistaken, or that the prints were planted, or that M's fingerprints were there innocently or that V was killed by accident or in self-defence. In short, the argument is open to attack at a number of points. Nevertheless, most people would agree there is a strong prima facie case against M.

How do we arrive at this judgment? The standard answer lies in the fact that several, but not all, of the links in the chain are backed up by a body of well-founded *general* scientific knowledge. In ordinary discourse we tend to gloss over the background generalisations that support such inferences. For example, we tend to move directly from the fact that M's finger patterns coincided with the prints on the knife to the conclusion that it was almost certainly or very probably M who killed V. If called on to justify such inferences and our assessments of their strength we invoke generalisations of the kind 'A finger pattern x, y, z etc. can be borne by one person only' or, more cautiously, 'Where a person's finger patterns coincide with a set of clear fingerprints it is very probable indeed that the prints were that person's.' The generalisation thus forms the major premiss of a syllogism:

A finger pattern x, y, z can be borne by one person only
M bears that finger pattern
M is that person

In this instance the major premiss is based on a well-developed body of scientific knowledge; yet it is striking that even in this context forensic scientists are very reluctant to give precise numerical estimates of the chances of more than one person in a given population having the same fingerprints. It is only exceptionally that we are in a position to appeal to such scientific generalisations as a basis for making inferences from evidence. Typically we have to appeal to our own personal or vicarious experience, often referred to as 'common sense', 'general knowledge' or 'experience of the common course of events'. Some of the problems surrounding such generalisations can be illustrated by another example.

Edith Thompson was accused of inciting her lover, Frederick Bywaters, to murder her husband, Percy. Edith was twenty-eight years old at the time, Freddy was only twenty. Is this discrepancy in age relevant to the *probandum* of incitement? Many people would intuitively feel that it is; counsel for the prosecution in the case, the trial judge and many commentators have all assumed it to be relevant. Yet an argument which goes: 'X was older than Y, therefore she incited Y' seems highly dubious. Can the inference be justified analytically and, if so, how?

The standard answer to this kind of question is that the *factum probans* is linked to the factum probandum by an implicit generalisation. Common sense does suggest that there is *some* connection between age and influence in human relationships but this is too vague. What precisely is the generalisation? Let us consider just two possible candidates:

(i) All older women always dominate younger men in all circumstances.
(ii) There is a tendency for the older person in an intimate relationship to be the dominant partner.

The first proposition provides the major premiss for a syllogism proving that Edith dominated Freddy. The argument is valid, but the premiss is easily falsified. There is no scientific evidence to support such a broad generalisation and most people can produce counter-examples from their own experience to show that (i) is at the very least grossly over-generalised. Furthermore, it appears to be both prejudiced and prejudicial.

At first sight, (ii) seems to meet these objections. It is not framed in sexist terms and it is more likely to be true than (i). However, it is open to some further objections. First, it is very vague — it does not even differentiate between often, sometimes and occasionally, let alone quantify the estimate of frequency; secondly, how are we to know whether it is true or not? and thirdly, it is not universal. It therefore does not establish a *necessary* connection between the fact that Edith was older than Freddy and the allegation that she incited him to murder.

Thus (i), if it were true, would establish a very strong probative relation between the *factum probans* and the *factum probandum*; but it is not true. On the other hand, (ii) might be true, but its strength as a bridge between the *factum probans* and the *factum probandum* is both weak and indeterminate. To complicate matters (i) and (ii) are by no means the only possible generalisations that might provide a link between the relative ages of Edith and Freddy and the allegation of incitement. Indeed, taken in isolation from a whole mass of other general and particular background information it is not possible to make any confident judgment about the probative value, if any, of this particular fact.

. . .

Binder and Bergman state a commonly held view:

> A generalisation is, then, a premiss which rests on the general behaviour of people or objects. How does one formulate generalisations? Usually, one adopts conventional wisdom about how people and objects function in everyday life. All of us, through our own personal experiences, through hearing about the personal experiences of others, and through knowledge gained from books, movies, newspapers and television, have accumulated vast storehouses of commonly held notions about how people and objects generally behave in our society. From this storehouse one formulates a generalisation about typical behaviour. The generalisation, in turn, becomes the premiss which enables one to link specific evidence with an element one hopes to prove.

Sociologists of knowledge, sceptics and relativists of various kinds have done much to heighten our awareness of the difficulties and dangers of accepting 'common-sense' generalisations and the like as constituting 'objective knowledge'. In respect of any such generalisation one should not assume too readily that there is in fact a 'cognitive consensus' on the matter. The stock of knowledge in any society varies from group to group, from individual to individual and from time to time. Even when there is widespread consensus, what passes as 'conventional knowledge' may be untrue, speculative or otherwise defective; moreover 'common-sense generalisatons' tend not to be purely factual — they often contain a strong mixture of valuation and prejudice, as is illustrated by various kinds of social, national and racial stereotypes.

29.8   A Simplified Method

Your choice of a method of analysing the facts may depend upon a number of factors. You may have the time available to construct a Wigmorean chart, which can form the basis for the greatest degree of confidence in your conclusions. In the limited time available, in practice, a simpler method may be of more value. Your mind may be one which is assisted by the graphical presentation offered by a chart. It may, on the other hand, respond more effectively to text, and a system of lists may then be of more assistance. You should try different methods and determine which suits you best, although remember that none of these techniques is easy at first. Do not, therefore, judge a technique by the ease with which you make your first attempt. These are skills which take time to acquire, but are rewarding once achieved.

A simpler version of the Wigmorean method of analysing evidence is shown on pp. 344–346 in respect of *R* v *Peter Penny*. This example provides an analysis of the evidence in respect of the identification element only of a potential murder charge. It has certain advantages in visual clarity. Facts and inferences leading towards the conclusion are presented in rectangular boxes to distinguish them from those casting doubt on the conclusion (in round boxes). Fact is distinguished from inference by use of a thicker line, and generalisations distinguished from each by use of a dotted line. Everything is presented on one page. Visual presentation can help in clarifying individual inferences. The entire analysis also assists in identifying weaknesses in an argument on which an opponent may be expected to concentrate. The method can be carried out fairly quickly.

Having said this, there are disadvantages. Its very simplicity may tempt one into using the technique too quickly, with insufficient care. The validity of conclusions *must* be checked with care. Moreover, it does not attempt the thoroughness of Wigmorean analysis.

Exercise
1.   *R* v *Lang & Tait*
You are instructed on behalf of the Prosecution in these proceedings. Both Defendants have been committed for trial at Plymouth Crown Court on the charge of stealing a gold signet ring. Consider the prosecution statements below and construct a Wigmore chart to show the strength of the case, as the evidence now stands, against *Lang only*. Assume for the purposes of this exercise that *all* relevant evidence will be admitted at trial. In other words, ignore at this stage any exclusionary rules which might affect the admissibility of relevant evidence. (A suggested chart and key list appear below.)

Statement of Maggie Benson   I am a store detective employed by Jingles Ltd of Royal Parade, Plymouth. On 24th February, 1990 I was on duty in their jewellery department when I had occasion to observe a man and a woman whom I now know to be Gordon Lang and Lucy Tait. My attention was drawn to them when I noticed that they were carrying large plastic carrier bags which were not those used by Jingles Ltd. From my experience as a store detective I am able to say that people intending to steal from the store frequently carry such bags in order to conceal goods and avoid suspicion. When I first saw them they were standing by a display of wrist watches. They appeared to converse for a short time and they then moved towards a counter where rings were displayed. One of them said something to the assistant behind the counter and he began to produce rings for them to examine. I saw Lang pick up a ring and look at it carefully. Then he said something to the assistant and handed the ring to him. The assistant then examined the ring carefully and while his attention was distracted I saw Tait pick up another ring from the counter and put it in her coat pocket. By then the assistant had finished examining the ring which he had been holding and was saying something to Lang. He then began to put the rings away and Lang and Tait turned away from the counter. I followed them as they left the store, having previously alerted an assistant manager. Together we stopped them on the pavement outside the store. I told them what I had seen and asked them to come back with me to the manager's office. Lang said, 'Property is theft.' Tait said, 'You'll never make it stand up in Court. You were miles away from us. You couldn't have seen a thing.' In the manager's office I telephoned for the police and I then asked to Tait to empty her pockets. However, she refused to do anything or to answer any questions until the police arrived. After about 10 minutes PC Parker and WPC Abbot arrived. I told them what I had seen and WPC Abbot asked Tait to hand over her coat to be examined. This was done and a man's gold signet ring with a Jingles price tag on it was found in the left-hand pocket. PC Parker then arrested Lang and Tait. He cautioned them and they made no reply. They were then taken away.

Statement of PC Parker   On 24th February as a result of information received I went with WPC Abbot to Jingles Ltd in Royal Parade, Plymouth. In the manager's officer I saw a store detective, Miss Maggie Benson, and a man and woman whom I now know to be Gordon Lang and Lucy Tait. I said to them, 'Be quiet and listen while this lady tells me what she has seen.' Miss Benson then said that she had seen them at the counter in the jewellery department where rings were displayed. She said that while Lang had distracted the attention of the assistant, Tait had taken a ring and had put it in her pocket. WPC Abbot then examined Tait's coat and discovered a man's gold signet ring with a Jingles Ltd price tag on it. I then arrested Lang and Tait for theft of the signet ring. I cautioned them and they made no reply. They were taken to the police station where in due course they were searched and a letter in Tait's handwriting was found in Lang's wallet. I produce this letter as exhibit MP1. They were later both charged and cautioned and again they made no reply.

I have caused investigations to be made as to the Defendant' antecedents. Lang has three previous convictions for theft. All involved shoplifting. The last, in May 1989, was committed with a woman known as Joan Whitgift in a jeweller's shop in Swindon. While Lang distracted the attention of the shop assistant, Whitgift put a man's wristwatch in her pocket. Details of the other offences (both in 1987) are not known, save that they involved thefts from large department stores. Tait has two previous convictions for theft (shoplifting) in 1987 and 1988 respectively.

Exhibit MP1

Darlingest Gordon, lover of mine, thank you, oh thank you a thousand times for Friday — it was lovely — it's always lovely to go out with you. And then Saturday — yes I did feel happy — I didn't think a teeny bit about anything in this world, except being with you. Don't forget what we talked in the pub, I'll still risk and try if you will — try and help.

LUCY

R v. LANG & TAIT

R v LANG & TAIT

KEY-LIST

1. Tait stole the ring.

2. Lang was present when she did so.

3. He was distracting the assistant's attention.

4. He was doing this so that the assistant would not see Tait take the ring.

5. He was doing this dishonestly.

6. He was doing this by agreement with Tait.

7. Evidence of Maggie Benson to this effect.

8. Lang said 'Property is theft' when stopped.

9. Lang cared nothing for the store's property rights.

10. The remark may have been flippant.

11. A person caring nothing for the store's property rights would be more likely than one who did to steal from the store.

12. When taxed by Maggie Benson, Lang didn't deny involvement.

13. An innocent person would have made a denial.

14. There may have been an innocent reason for failure to deny.

15. Lang had used this system for obtaining men's jewellery in 1987.

16. Testimony of PC Parker to this effect.

17. A person of whom 15 is true is less likely to have distracted the assistant innocently than one who had not.

18. Exhibit MP1.

19. Lang and Tait had talked about risking and trying something.

20. That may have meant this offence.

21. It may not.

22. No evidence to show who was 'Lucy'.

23. No clear indication of what was discussed.

24. No evidence of when written.

25. It was a man's ring that was stolen.

26. A woman would want a man's ring to give to a man and not to keep for herself.

27. A man may have encouraged her to steal it for him.

28. She may have decided on her own to steal in order to give the ring to a man.

29. If a man did encourage her to steal, it was likely to have been Lang.

30. But there may have been other men in her life who would be likely to have encouraged her.

31. Lang had influence over her.

32. She loved Lang.

2. *R v Peter Penny*

The facts here are based on materials prepared by Professor Twining, which may be seen used in a different way in Anderson and Twining, 'Analysis of Evidence', in Gold, Mackie and Twining; *Learning Lawyers' Skills*, at p. 253. These materials are used with the permission of Professor Twining.

Report by PC Giles: dated 2 January 1992   In response to a call from a neighbour I visited 26 Acacia Court at 5 p.m. this afternoon. I spoke initially to John Thorp, the neighbour who called police. I found the front door ajar. On entering the flat I discovered a body in the living room. I called for assistance and made a thorough search of the flat. There was no one else present. While in the flat I ascertained that there was no rear entry.
PC David Giles, 8:30 p.m., 2/1/92.

Summary of Police report on the body discovered by PC Giles on 2/1/92   The body has been identified as that of David Star, of 26 Acacia Court, London SE11. Medical evidence suggests that he was strangled between 4 and 5 p.m., on 2/1/92.

John Thorp will say: I was in my lounge on the afternoon of 2nd January 1992, watching out of the window. From here I have a good view of the flats opposite. At around 4.30 p.m. I saw a tall dark-haired man with a moustache run from the flat opposite: 26 Acacia Court. He appeared to be in a great hurry and this made me suspicious, so I telephoned the police. A constable arrived at around 5 o'clock. I told him what I had seen and he entered the flat and found poor David Star dead. I had been watching from my window for most of the time between 4 and 5 p.m., and I am sure that no one entered or left the flat apart from the man I have described.

Paula Lyle will say: I am a neighbour of Peter Penny, who lives at 32 Tamarisk Court, London SE11. I was returning to my own flat on 2nd January 1992, when, at 4.05 p.m., I saw Peter Penny enter the flat at 26 Acacia Court. I know Peter and am confident that it was him I saw.

Alice Lion will say: I was at a New Year party to see 1992 in, where I saw two friends of mine, Peter Penny and David Star. They were engaged in a heated argument, but I do not know what it was about as I did not want to get involved.

Police report on Peter Penny: Mr Penny is 6ft 2in tall, has dark hair and a moustache, and walks with a pronounced limp. He lives at 32 Tamarisk Court SE11, a block of flats on the same estate as Acacia Court. He is known to have been an acquaintance of the deceased.

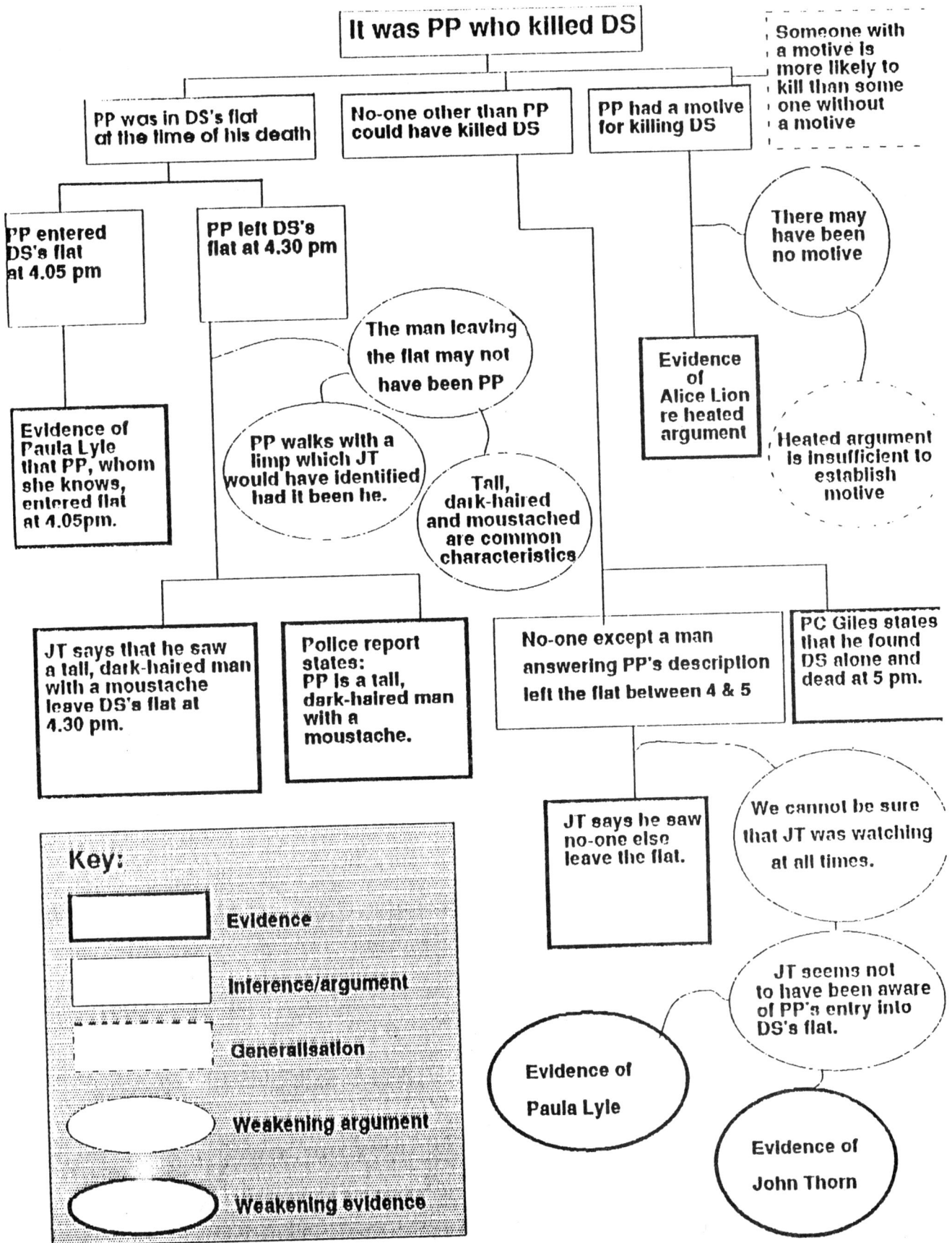

It was PP who killed DS

Someone with a motive is more likely to kill than someone without a motive

PP was in DS's flat at the time of his death

No-one other than PP could have killed DS

PP had a motive for killing DS

PP entered DS's flat at 4.05 pm

PP left DS's flat at 4.30 pm

There may have been no motive

The man leaving the flat may not have been PP

Evidence of Alice Lion re heated argument

Evidence of Paula Lyle that PP, whom she knows, entered flat at 4.05pm.

PP walks with a limp which JT would have identified had it been he.

Tall, dark-haired and moustached are common characteristics

Heated argument is insufficient to establish motive

JT says that he saw a tall, dark-haired man with a moustache leave DS's flat at 4.30 pm.

Police report states: PP is a tall, dark-haired man with a moustache.

No-one except a man answering PP's description left the flat between 4 & 5

PC Giles states that he found DS alone and dead at 5 pm.

JT says he saw no-one else leave the flat.

We cannot be sure that JT was watching at all times.

JT seems not to have been aware of PP's entry into DS's flat.

Key:

☐	Evidence
☐	Inference/argument
⌐ ¬	Generalisation
◯	Weakening argument
◯	Weakening evidence

Evidence of Paula Lyle

Evidence of John Thorn

347

30 Presenting the Case

30.1 Introduction

It should be clear by now that at a variety of stages in the course of litigation, the competent lawyer will exercise a number of fact management skills. In summary, the lawyer faced with a mass of raw data (whether volunteered or requested) will:

(a) attempt to comprehend it; and then
(b) attempt to organise it, on the basis of
(c) a careful selection of context (or standpoint) and
(d) an equally careful selection of an appropriate legal solution.

There are three further important skills that the lawyer must perform if the case is to proceed to trial:

(a) the development of a theory of the case
(b) the selection of a theme to fit that theory and
(c) the reorganisation of all the available data in ways that are suitable for its presentation in court.

The first and second of these skills are closely interrelated but it will be convenient to consider each in turn before turning to organisational devices for the purposes of the trial. First, then, what do we mean by 'theories' and 'themes'?

30.2 Theories and Themes

30.2.1 THEORIES

The formulation of the theory of a case is a relatively straightforward task because it is the natural conclusion to the steps in fact management that we have already taken. The result of taking these steps will be that the lawyer has:

(a) reached a decision as to the principles of law that are likely to be used at the trial;
(b) identified what has to be proved and/or disproved at the trial if the client represented is to succeed;
(c) eliminated all data which, by reason of the rules of evidence, will be (or in all probability will be) excluded at the trial;
(d) organised all of the remaining available data to see whether there is a theory of the case, i.e. to see whether he or she can explain why, in logic, the party represented is capable of succeeding if the case goes to trial.

349

In so far as the lawyer is able to give a number of different explanations as to why, in logic, the party represented is capable of succeeding at the trial, there is a choice. *The theory* of the case may be defined, then, as the best explanation of all the information to date which indicates that logically the party represented should succeed in the litigation.

Four matters should be stressed:

(a)   What is required is the best explanation, i.e. the lawyer must select from all the possible explanations of the information, the best one from the standpoint of the client being represented.

(b)   In practice, lawyers develop a theory of a case at a fairly early stage, typically before drafting pleadings — it should be remembered, however, that it is possible and desirable to develop provisional theories at an earlier stage, and that *the theory of a case may have to be altered or even replaced in its entirety* at some subsequent stage. This could happen prior to trial (in the light of one's opponents pleadings, further and better particulars, formal admissions, discovery etc.) or during the trial (in the light of the way in which the evidence emerges).

(c)   The theory must be *logical*, i.e. the explanation must indicate clearly that logic requires that the party you are representing should succeed.

(d)   Although the theory must be logical, *the ultimate form that it takes should be influenced by the choice made as to the theme of the case*, which as we shall see, goes beyond logic and may show that moral force is also on your side.

Developing a cohesive theory of a case may not be difficult, provided that the other skills in fact management have been mastered, but its importance, in relation to the trial of the action, should not be underestimated. Elkan Abramowitz (*Master Advocates' Handbook*, 1986) puts the matter this way:

Selecting a theory is simply one aspect of careful preparation and is the *sine qua non* of effective litigation. Without a coherent framework provided by a carefully considered strategy, the most exhaustive preparation, the most cogent argument, and the most sympathetic case will be unavailing. While a cohesive theory cannot take the place of thorough preparation and a favourable set of facts, it is the glue which holds together the other elements required for successful litigation.

30.2.2   THEMES

30.2.2.1   Definition

Selecting a theme (or themes) to fit the theory of a case is the next skill to master before the trial commences. The theme, for these purposes, may be defined as that part of the 'story' presented in court which the lawyer selects and presents because of its particularly persuasive effect in relation to the ultimate conclusion which the lawyer wants the tribunal of fact to draw. In an essay entitled 'Lawyers' Stories' (originally presented at the Seminar on Narrative in Culture, University of Warwick, in 1987) in *Rethinking Evidence, Exploratory Essays* (Blackwell, 1990), Professor William Twining defines theme in the following way:

Sometimes it is used to refer to the overall characterization of the situation or story or some element of it that appeals to a popular stereotype. For example: 'This is an example of a grasping landlord exploiting a helpless tenant'; or 'this is a case of property developers needlessly desecrating the countryside'. Another, more precise usage . . . refers to any element that is sufficiently important to deserve emphasis by repetition. An English barrister (Patrick Bennett QC) gives a vivid account of what he calls 'the mantra', as follows: 'In almost all cases there will be a key factor which has played a dominant role in the case from your point of view. It may be "stupidity", "fear", "greed", "jealousy", "selfishness". Pick your word, inject it into your opening. Put it on a separate piece of paper. Repetition will have a lasting effect. If you have hit the right note and have repeated it often enough, it will echo in the jury's mind when they retire. It will be the voice of the 13th juror. Try to hit the note as soon as possible in opening.'

Before considering some further examples, five matters should be stressed:

(a)   Although lawyers develop a theory of a case at a fairly early stage (see **30.2.1**), it is often impossible to develop a theme at the same time — in many cases, the correct theme will only present itself at the final stages of preparation for trial. '

(b)   The theme forms part of the 'story' which will usually be told in the opening and closing speeches but which will also underpin questioning in both examination-in-chief and cross-examination.

(c)   The 'story' should include any items of evidence by which it is supported and should exclude any items of evidence by which it is undermined.

(d)   Good themes are often very simple. An uncomplicated theme is easier to understand and for that reason often more appealing and credible to the tribunal of fact.

(e)   The theme goes beyond logic — it is often based on moral generalisations appropriate to the case and likely to influence the tribunal of fact in favour of the desired conclusion.

This final matter is of particular importance. Patrick Bennett QC puts it in this way (*Master Advocates' Handbook*, 1986):

> Having decided on a theory, you must pick a theme to fit that theory. You must have two goals in mind: first, why the other side is responsible for what happened and second, why your client is not. For example, big business at its intolerant and unimaginative worst; on the other hand, no one is perfect; there is a limit to the care and foresight which the ordinary man like your client cannot be expected to pass, etc.

The same issue is addressed in *The Trial Lawyer's Book: Preparing and Winning Cases* (1990), Lawyers Cooperative Publishing, NY, at pp. 87 and 92 (permission to reprint these excerpts has been granted by the copyright holder, Lawyers Cooperative Publishing, a division of Thomson Legal Publishing Inc.):

> To convince a jury, you must have a theme or storyline that, while consistent with the legal theory, appeals at a 'gut' level to the jurors' notion of equity and common sense. The theme, then, may be defined as the soul or moral justification of your case. It is rooted in human behaviour and sociocultural attitudes, and is sometimes more intuitive than analytical. . . . the 'story' appeals to the jury by providing . . . an equitable reason for deciding in favour of your client. Finding a theme in the facts and repeating it throughout the trial reinforces your version of the case because it appeals to the jurors' common sense, life experiences, and concern for fairness.

Because the theme should evolve from common human experience, the authors go on to suggest, as typical sources of the theme, well-known situations, personal experience or family history, classical and modern literature, the Bible, movies, plays and the television. *Norman Birkett* even made use of newspapers (see *Dennistoun* v *Dennistoun*, **30.2.2.2**).

The task for the practising lawyer, as we have said, is to develop a theory and then to select a theme which fits it. In other words, the theory and the theme must be consistent with each other. The experienced advocate is capable of making the theory and the theme so consistent that they are virtually indistinguishable. This is done because the better the theme fits in with the theory, the greater the plausibility or moral force of the theory and the greater the likelihood of persuading the tribunal of fact in favour of the desired conclusion. To cite again from *The Trial Lawyer's Book* (ibid. at p. 87):

> Together, your legal theory and its 'human' justification serve one primary goal: they supply the overall supporting rationale for your case. They are essential tools for any advocate. The theory provides the logical rigor necessary as a matter of law; the theme provides the common sense appeal that compels a decision-maker to interpret facts and decide disputed issues in a certain way.

30.2.2.2   Examples and exercises
The task of selecting a theme is not confined to cases in which novel points of law arise. It is doubtless true that in such cases theme is particularly important in persuading the tribunal that the common

law needs to be developed (or as the case may be, that a particular statutory provision needs to be construed) so as to provide a just legal solution to the facts as you present them. Theme, however, is also important in the many ordinary cases, at any level of practice, in which the law is reasonably settled and clear.

Take, for example, a relatively straightforward contested careless driving case in the magistrates' court: a pedestrian steps out on to a zebra crossing, causing the motorist to brake hard and skid; the only substantial dispute on the facts is whether the pedestrian looked to the right before stepping on to the crossing. In such a case, the defence theme may well be that there is a limit to the care and foresight to be expected of the ordinary competent motorist, especially when faced with a jay-walker. If, at the trial, it emerged that the pedestrian was late for an important engagement, another defence theme might be based on the adage 'more haste, less speed', and so on. In cases where the plaintiff is an individual and the defendant a bank, insurance company or other large corporation, the plaintiff's theme will often be a variation of the story of David and Goliath. In a professional negligence action against a solicitor for allegedly erroneous advice, the theme for the plaintiff may well be that since 'professionals' are paid for their expertise, they should be especially careful not to make mistakes, and should be responsible when they do. The defence theme, if appropriate on the facts, as when the advice given was on a complicated 'grey' area, might be that the standard of care to be expected of even professional advisers should not be pitched at an unrealistically high level. In many cases in which there is a direct conflict between the two stories told by the two parties to the litigation, the theme may be based on the motive which one of the parties has for not telling the truth, for example, fear, jealousy or greed.

The two exercises that follow are based on real cases taken from *Norman Birkett* by H. Montgomery Hyde. They are designed to illustrate the importance of *theme* (and not just theory) at the trial stage. The first example is not typical, because in effect the only issue in dispute was quantum. It is instructive, nonetheless, as an easy illustration of a 'moral generalisation'. Notice, in the second case:

    (a)   the choice of themes; and
    (b)   how the theme actually chosen was developed at each stage of the trial.

Notice also, in both cases, that the theme related to the motives of the litigants.

1. *Froggatt v Hoyland*   This action was for breach of promise of marriage. It came before Sankey J at Derbyshire Assizes in February 1923. The plaintiff sued a chemist's assistant. She alleged that they had known each other since 1907, that 1,400 love letters had passed between them and that the promise had been made in writing in 1914. The defendant said that in 1916 he confessed to his fiancée that he had committed adultery with a married woman over the previous four years and that his fiancée had struck him with her clenched fist and called him 'Dog', 'Pig' and 'Swine'. The engagement was then broken off. Five years later, by which time the defendant had married someone else, the plaintiff commenced her action. The defendant made a payment into court which the plaintiff declined to accept.

Assume that you are appearing for the defendant in this case. Think of a theme, based on a moral generalisation appropriate to the case, which is likely to influence the jury in your favour:

    (a)   on the question of liability and
    (b)   on the quantum of damages (so that even if they find against you on the question of liability, they do not award damages which exceed your payment into court).

Counsel for the defence, Norman Birkett, decided to call no evidence in the case but the theme he used in his cross-examination of the plaintiff and in his closing address brings to mind the generalisation to be found in the following lines of William Congreve in *The Mourning Bride*, III, viii:

> Heaven has no rage like love to hatred turned,
> Nor Hell a fury like a woman scorned.

Norman Birkett's first question in cross-examinaion of the plaintiff was to ask her why she had waited so long before beginning proceedings. She answered that she did not have the money. The questioning proceeded as follows:

Q. I suggest you brought this action out of spite?
A. No.
Q. Not at all?
A. No.
Q. You knew that the defendant was married when you issued the writ?
A. Yes.
Q. Did the fact that you learned that he married in 1920 influence you?
A. No, I did not know where he was.
Q. Did you think that it was a kind thing to bring the action and so pain an innocent wife as well as the husband, the defendant?

In his address to the jury, Birkett returned to the theme. He said that the real reason for the present action, after five years and five months, was to gain publicity and to do the defendant as much injury as possible.

The jury found for the plaintiff with damages of £25, which was exactly the sum which the defendant had been advised to pay into court. The plaintiff was ordered to pay the defendant's costs of the action since the date of payment in.

2. *Dennistoun* v *Dennistoun*   The plaintiff, Mrs Dennistoun, was the former wife of Lieutenant-Colonel Dennistoun, ex-Grenadier Guards, whom she had married in 1910 and whom she had divorced on the grounds of desertion and misconduct in 1921. The present, celebrated, action was brought by the plaintiff for maintenance. The salient facts of the case, which are far more complex than those of the case just considered, may be summarised as follows:

The plaintiff was an attractive woman of strong character. According to the defendant, he was unable to satisfy her physical demands and consequently she had indulged in a series of affairs with among others, a Hungarian nobleman, a Polish major, a Spanish bullfighter and a high-ranking English army officer. The officer was referred to in the plaintiff's opening speech as General X but during her examination-in-chief, the plaintiff revealed that it was Sir John Cowans (who had filled with distinction the post of Quartermaster-General of the British Army throughout the First World War). The plaintiff said that it was General Cowans to whom the defendant owed his promotion and appointment to a good staff job in the War Office.

The plaintiff alleged that the defendant was prepared to accept any sacrifice from his wife, even misconduct between her and General Cowans and other lovers from whom she received favours, including money; and that the defendant had accepted with gratitude the benefit of such money. The plaintiff put in evidence the following letter, written by the defendant to the plantiff, at a time when the plaintiff's affair with the General was developing:

My own girl,
I could not phone you as things are moving a bit, and I must get busy. Darling heart, take great care of yourself; you seem sometimes such a tiny, small brown mouse. Me feels just like a tiger in a cage behind great big iron bars. Oh, girlie darling, I hate you using the lovely body of yours as a gift.

You are all I have got in this world. It makes me despise myself and everything I do. I can't help it; there it is. Why should you be made a fool of, which is worst of all? Don't go further than you want — life is so short and I want you so dreadfully. Me wishes me were back in the little wee house. Good-night, precious. One big kiss.
Tiger.

The plaintiff alleged that the defendant encouraged his wife in her association with General Cowans. The defence denied this. Their version was that she could do anything with her weak and vacillating husband that she pleased; that he did his best to look after her and shield her as far as possible; but that he was so infatuated with her that a course which would seem to the ordinary man truly repugnant was to him a matter in which he could only acquiese.

At the time of the divorce, both parties were in debt and the defendant was unable to provide maintenance for the plaintiff. The plaintiff alleged that the defendant agreed to provide maintenance when he became solvent if she would refrain from petitioning for alimony. Shortly after the divorce she said that she sent the defendant sums of money, £20, then £100, then another £100. At about this time, the plaintiff was staying with friends, Lord and Lady Carnarvon. Lady Carnarvon was going to Paris and the plaintiff asked her to bring back some articles belonging to her which her husband, then living in France, would deliver to her. Lady Carnarvon met the defendant and a strong friendship, with no hint of impropriety, developed between them. Lady Carnarvon was a wealthy woman and the defendant was very poor — she gave him £20,000 and a furnished flat. Shortly afterwards, Lord Carnarvon died and Lady Carnarvon married the defendant and gave him a further £100,000.

While the defendant's financial affairs were improving, the plaintiff's deteriorated. Soon she was in severe financial straits and begged him for money. Eventually he gave her some £600. She made further financial appeals but his reply was that any further communication should be made through his solicitors.

It was at this stage that the plaintiff brought her action against the defendant. The claim was for the maintenance that he had allegedly agreed to provide when he became solvent and two further sums: (a) £472 which she said that she had lent him; and (b) £616 which she said had been borrowed at his request in 1913 and spent on paying his debts. On the day the writ was issued, the defendant closed his bank account by drawing a cheque payable to himself for £51,695. Although now nominally well off, the defendant's money in reality belonged to his new wife and she was totally opposed to a settlement of the case. The defendant denied the existence of the alleged agreement to provide maintenance but at a late stage pleaded, in the alternative that if the agreement was entered into, there was an implied term that the plaintiff should live a chaste life. (The defendant had available a variety of witnesses, hotel employees, to show that the plaintiff's life had been anything but chaste).

In his summing up to the jury, the judge, McCardie J, noting that the plaintiff did not contemplate bringing her action until after her former husband had married her friend Lady Carnarvon, implied that the mainspring of the action may have been the sentiment expressed in the lines of William Congreve to which reference has already been made. That, however, was not the theme advanced by counsel for the defence, who were Sir Edward Marshall Hall and Norman Birkett.

Imagine that you are appearing for the defence in this case. Think of another theme based on a moral generalisation appropriate to the case and likely to influence the tribunal of fact in your favour on the issue of liability.

The generalisation actually used as the basis for the theme was that one of the most potent weapons of the blackmailer is the threat of bringing court proceedings and the consequent threat of publicity. In other words, the plaintiff's claim was a 'try on' — she hoped that the threat of exposing the details of her married life to the public gaze would force the defendant and his new wife to acquiesce in an out of court settlement of her bogus claim. Her plan had back-fired, however, because the defendant and his new wife had bravely decided that, however embarrassing it might prove to be, they would not submit to blackmail but would go to court and tell the truth.

Consider the following extracts, which show how the theme was first advanced in the cross-examination of the plaintiff, then re-emphasised in the opening speech for the defence and finally driven home in the closing speech for the defence.

Sir Edward Marshall Hall's cross-examination of the plaintiff:

Q. Did you hear the specific charge that [your husband] forfeited the right, if he ever had it, to call himself a gentleman, and had lived on your immoral earnings?

A. I heard it said.

Q. Do you approve of it?

A. I think it is a very unfair question.

Q. Madam, fair or unfair, I propose to repeat it. Do you approve of that charge?

A. I was fond of my husband.

Q. How much do you think a woman who loved her husband would pay not to have this case in open court?

A. It is a great deal harder for me than my husband thinks. I am a woman alone and he is a man.

Q. A woman alone?

A. I am a woman alone.

Q. Is that true?

A. Absolutely and entirely.

Q. If the woman who has married your husband is a rich woman, a very rich woman, how much do you think that he would be prepared to pay to avoid a case like this being opened in open court?

A. I have never thought of it in that light at all.

Q. If you had married a man and loved him, if you can imagine it, how much would you have paid to prevent an attack on this man?

A. If the man cared for the woman he married, he would not want to expose the woman by himself. I asked him to provide for me, and only asked for a small sum — his pension. It did not seem a large sum of money. The rest of your question was not considered or thought about.

Q. Did you not think that Lady Carnarvon and your husband having married on December 19, 1923, there was some sort of reason why she would not sooner pay than have this case in court?

A. Such a thing never entered my head. I thought my husband would keep his promise.

The plaintiff, it may be thought, came out of these exchanges rather well. Nonetheless, when the defence opened their case, Norman Birkett returned to exactly the same theme.

Norman Birkett's opening speech for the defence:

Members of the jury, at last the moment has come when you will hear for the first time what my client has to say. . . There is only one phrase to describe what Colonel Dennistoun and Almina Lady Carnarvon have passed through during the past few days — unspeakable anguish. You may think this case might have been settled for a payment less than was expended to defend the case. Then there would have been no daily anguish of seeing column after column of this in the daily papers. Why did they fight? They took the view that if they gave way they would never be free from demands. Colonel Dennistoun and Lady Carnarvon said: 'This means the loss of everything dearest to me, but, though I am pilloried every day, I needs must fight, because I cannot do otherwise'.

At this stage, Birkett picked up a newspaper and read an extract from an article in which it stated that one of the most potent weapons of the blackmailer was to bring proceedings in court, with the consequent threat of publicity. He continued:

That puts into a concise form what the position really will be in this case, if it is found that there never was such an agreement as Mrs Dennistoun alleges. Th only reason this allegation was brought was because Almina Lady Carnarvon married Colonel Dennistoun and both are living in wealth. An action like this would form a weapon that no man could face; he would do anything and everything to avoid it. . .

Norman Birkett's closing speech for the defence:

She [pointing at Mrs Dennistoun] comes into court and, in order to extort money from the poor weak husband and from Lady Carnarvon, says that Colonel Dennistoun arranged for her to go with General Cowans. The use of misconduct from a choice and because she wanted to do it, as a means of getting money from Lady Carnarvon, is in the last grade of unforgivable sins!

355

Mrs Dennistoun says that she lived with General Cowans in order to gain military preferment for her husband. That conduct is just the opposite of love. If a woman wanted to do things for her husband, that is just the thing she would never do. . .

Never for one moment did Mrs Dennistoun dream that this case would be fought out to the end with such intensity. It was her inention that the action should be settled. . .

There was never a word of any legal claim until Colonel Dennistoun's marriage with Lady Carnarvon, until the countess's fortunes were linked with those of the man with whom she stands or falls and to whom she showed such wonderful devotion in the witness-box yesterday.

I have not shrunk from using the hideous term, 'blackmail', in connection with this action. Blackmail takes many forms, but this is about the most dreadful form that it can take. There are issues in this case of exceeding gravity. People in the position of Lady Carnarvon do not face the ordeal of publicity during nearly three weeks for nothing.

The jury's findings in the case were somewhat confusing: they found that the defendant had entered into a verbal agreement to 'assist to support' his wife, but not in the form alleged by the plaintiff; that the plaintiff had made certain payments on the defendant's behalf as loans; and assessed damages due to her under the agreement at £5,000. The judge, however, deprived the plaintiff of the £5,000 on the ground that the alleged verbal agreement was too vague to be enforceable by law, being a 'conjecture, unsupported by any evidence'. The plaintiff succeeded in recovering the loans totalling £472 (but not the sum of £616).

31 The Trial

31.1 Introduction

The trial tests not only the strengths of your case but also your skills as an advocate. Good advocacy depends on good preparation. Exactly what preparation is necessary will depend on the type of case. The **Advocacy, Negotiation and Conference Skills Manual** contains 'How to do it Guides' which include guidance as to the preparation needed for a variety of the more common types of applications you are likely to make in your first few years of practice.

Your preparation falls into two main categories ensuring the case is prepared and ensuring that you are prepared to present the case.

31.2 Ensuring the Case is Prepared

As you are the person presenting the case you should ensure that it is properly prepared which includes checking that those things on which you rely to prove your case are available and properly prepared for trial. This includes checking:

(a) *Documents.*

The solicitors should have prepared bundles of relevant documents (all those documents on which the parties will rely at trial). There should be:

(i)   a bundle of the originals of all relevant documents.
(ii) bundles of copies for the tribunal witnesses and counsel and solicitor for each parties.

You should ensure that you know where originals are not available and, if you intend to rely on copies, know on what basis you consider they are admissible.

In civil proceedings the rules on preparation of the bundle of documents must be followed (see **Civil Litigation Manual**).

In criminal proceedings each party has the responsibility to ensure that the originals and sufficient copies of documents on which it is intended to rely are available at the hearing.

(b) *Witnesses.*

The solicitors should have warned all the witnesses of the time, date and place of the hearing and issued summonses or subpoenas for the attendance of those who require it.

(c) *Witness statements/proofs of evidence.*

Check whether you have full unambiguous statements for all witnesses you intend to call. Where necessary have they been served on the other side?

(d) *Exhibits.*

The solicitor should have ensured that all relevant exhibits will be available at court but you should make sure that this has been done.

(e) *The law.*

You should have the reference for and copies of the cases, statutes or statutory instruments on which you intend to rely. It is your responsibility to ensure that there are sufficient copies of the case so as not to inconvenience the court or your opponent.

(f) *The pleadings/summons/indictment.*

Check they are in order, properly served etc.

The above is a list of the main items to check. For further details see the How to do it Guides in the **Advocacy Manual**.

31.3   Ensuring that You are Ready to Present the Case

By the time you go to court you should have a thorough knowledge, understanding and ready access to the relevant law (procedural and adjectival) and the facts and know how you intend to present the case and have readily accessible notes to assist you in your presentation. This means reorganising all the available data in ways that will facilitate its use and presentation in court. Thus, you should set out in some format notes on:

(a) relevant law;
(b) relevant facts;
(c) points to make in opening;
(d) points to make in closing (where appropriate);
(e) the order of witnesses to be called;
(f) examination and cross examination of each witness;
(g) the type of orders sought (where appropriate including those for costs).

In addition you should know how you intend to make notes during the hearing to ensure that you make as full notes as possible, that those notes are readily accessible during the trial and can be used to supplement the notes you have made in preparation.

Any method you use for setting out your prepared notes for trial should allow for the fact that you may alter your presentation as the case proceeds (e.g. leave sufficient space to add questions in cross examination or points in opening).

Everyone adopts their own method of organising this information to suit their own needs. Many barristers use blue notebooks for all their work done on preparing a case, from notes of conferences with clients, to preparations for trial (e.g. submissions to be made in opening).

31.4   The Trial Book

The 'trial book' and the 'chart system' as descriptive terms are borrowed from the United States. An excellent summary of the devices lawyers can and commonly do use in this context is to be found in Anderson and Twining's *Analysis of Evidence, Text Materials and Exercises Based upon Wigmore's Science of Judicial Thought*. The following section consists of extracts from Chapter 5, The Trial Lawyer's Standpoint.

A NOTE ON TRIAL BOOKS

The 'trial book' is simply a lawyer's device for organizing what he or she needs to try a particular lawsuit. Typically, it will include pleadings, checklists, copies of documents to be introduced and statements or depositions to be used, outlines for opening and closing speeches or anticipated 'scripts' for direct and cross-examination of witnesses, jury instructions, and memoranda of law addressing significant problems likely to arise during the particular trial.

The trial book serves three kinds of functions. First, preparation of the book is a systematic way to prepare for trial. The laywer is forced to analyse what he or she needs for each segment of the trial from voir dire through closing and verdict. The lawyer is also forced to organise the materials into a whole. Like the production book for a play, the trial book enables the participants to see the parts and the whole and to visualise concretely whether the whole makes sense. Second, during the trial, the trial book is a ready reference. The trial book has everything the lawyer needs in one place, organized to facilitate easy use. Finally, also during trial, the trial book serves as a checklist and an organised vehicle for keeping track of what has been and what needs to be done. Counsel (counsel's partner) can 'check off' that essential questions have been asked, that items of documentary evidence have been not only identified but also admitted into evidence. The lawyers can keep notes on particular witnesses and for reference in closing argument.

The following 'Outline for Trial Books' describes one format for trial.

For those who are interested, the following materials contain descriptions and other formats for trial books:

Gottlieb, *Systematic Litigation Planning* (BNA 1978)
Hagland, 'Trial Notebooks' from *Trial and Practice Skills* 140–43 (West 1978)
Sonsteng, et al. *The Trial Book* (West 1984)

Outline of Materials for Trial Books

I   *The Preliminary Memorandum*

A.   *The Introduction* (theory established, story and themes identified in a nutshell)
B.   *The Facts* (necessary to establish theory and themes with references to evidence and to the ultimate proposition to be proved)
C.   *The Law* (from which the ultimate probandum can be derived and which dictates the major strategic decisions)
D.   *Problems and Strategies Chosen*
E.   *Master Checklists* (for use during trial)

II   *The Trial Components*
A.   *Preliminary Matters* (if any)
B.   *Opening Statement:*

1.   An abstract (ordinarily the story that the evidence will show to establish the theory and theme illustrated by facts to be emphasised)

2.   An outline (from which counsel will speak)
C.   *Plaintiff's or Prosecution's Case*: The book should include, if you are counsel for

Pl. or Gov't		Def.	
1. For each witness:			
a.	Statement of objectives	a.	Statement of counter-objectives and checklist
b.	*Direct:*	b.	*Direct:*
(i)	Script for direct: question (Q) and anticipated (A) response (R)	(i)	A/direct lines of inquiry, danger areas, and proposed responses (strategic and legal)

<table>
<tr><td>

(ii) The outline (from which you will examine and which your partner will use as a checklist)

(iii) Exhibits to be identified or introduced

(iv) Notes for anticipated objections, responses, law, etc.

</td><td>

(ii) Notes for objections, A/R law, etc.

</td></tr>
</table>

<table>
<tr><td>

c. *Cross*

  (i) Cross-lines of inquiry, danger areas proposed responses (strategic and legal)

  (ii) Notes for objections, anticipated responses, law, etc.

</td><td>

c. *Cross*

  (i) Cross-lines of inquiry with script for central Q and A/R for each line

  (ii) Outline (for planned examination)

  (iii) Exhibits to be used or identified

  (iv) Notes for anticipated objections, responses, law, etc.

</td></tr>
</table>

2. Motions or anticipated motions at close of plaintiff's case, anticipated and planned responses, and supporting legal authority, and an outline for anticipated arguments.

D. *Defendant's Case*: The book should include, if you are counsel for

Pl. or Gov't	Def.
1. For each witness:	
a. Statement of counter objectives and checklist	a. Statement of objectives and checklist
b. *Direct:*	b. *Direct:*
(i) A/direct-lines, danger areas, proposed responses	(i) Script-Q and A/R
(ii) Notes	(ii) Outline
	(iii) Exhibits
	(iv) Notes
c. *Cross*	c. *Cross*
(i) Cross-lines of inquiry, script central Q and A/R	(i) A/Cross-lines, danger areas, proposed responses
(ii) Outline	(ii) Notes
(iii) Exhibits	
(iv) Notes	

2. Motions or anticipated motions at close of defendant's case, anticipated and planned responses, supporting legal authority, tentative speaking outlines.

E. *Plaintiff's Rebuttal* (If planned or anticipated, following same format as plaintiff' case)

F. *Close of Evidence*: Motions or anticipated motions, anticipated and planned responses, supporting legal authority, tentative speaking outlines.

G. *Closing Argument:*

1. An abstract (Theory and Theme: Facts integrated with law)
2. An outline (from which you hope you will be able to speak)

H. *Miscellaneous Requirements:*

1. The jury instructions central to the theory adopted.
2. The chart and keylist from which theory, theme and strategy were developed.

Reproduced with kind permission of the authors.

32   Dealing with Figures

32.1   Introduction

Dealing with figures is part of dealing with the facts of a case. This chapter introduces the role of figures in the work of the barrister, and the contexts in which work with figures may be required.

32.2   The Importance of Numeracy

Numeracy is vital to the barrister. Some people are quite confident in dealing with numbers, others are rather less confident, but in professional terms, no barrister can tell a client or solicitor, 'I never was much good at arithmetic' — the client wants to know what will be recovered in damages, and the solicitor can take briefs elsewhere. This chapter is designed to show you in what ways numeracy is important, and to help you develop your own skills.

Your immediate reaction to the proposition that you need to be numerate may well be 'Why?'. The law is about words, not figures — you see very few figures in legal textbooks — and also there will in any event be an accountant there if necessary. The student who has got a law degree or diploma without doing any addition or multiplication may well express the view that arithmetic was left behind happily at GCSE with no intention of ever returning to it.

Unfortunately for those who do not feel comfortable with figures, any suggestion that a barrister can get by without a facility with numbers is not true in practice. Although legal textbooks may have few figures in them, they do include substantial coverage of the legal principles for dealing with figures. A contract law textbook may not include figures, but most of the text ultimately relates to how much money you will get if you are successful in a claim for damages, so that when you have a contract case all the principles for the award of damages must be dealt with in terms of figures, not just words. Also, as outlined below, the barrister will most certainly not always have an accountant to help just because there are figures in the brief.

Thus although the immediate impression may be that a barrister can get by with limited numerical ability, a little thought should make it clear that this is not the case, and there are many contexts in which a lawyer will have to deal with figures every day. If you are not confident with numbers, now is the time to get to grips with the problem for the sake of your future clients and your career. If you are fairly confident with numbers, you can now start finding ways to develop your numeracy skills in a professional legal context.

In the simplest terms, as a barrister you must be able to tell the client what he or she might hope to get: you need to be able to deal with figures given to you: you need to be able to identify what further figures you need: and you need to be able to talk intelligently about figures to a solicitor or an accountant. Appreciating this is part of the vital move from the academic approach of university or college to the practical approach of the real barrister in practice.

32.3 The Relevance of Figures in the Life of a Barrister

32.3.1 TYPES OF PRACTICE

Numeracy is going to be important to a barrister in any area of practice from the solely civil to the wholly criminal, albeit in slightly different ways. To provide some examples:

(a) *Commercial practice.* The relevance of figures is obvious in dealing with companies or partnerships, especially as regards a detailed knowledge of accountancy and tax.

(b) *Chancery practice.* The relevance is clear in actions for breach of trust, or for the administration of an estate, including claims for provision from the estate. Again this will specifically require a thorough knowledge of relevant tax provisions and how to read a set of accounts.

(c) *General Common law practice.* This has many elements, but to give some basic examples:

(i) *Contract.* You ned to be able to deal with all figures relevant to a contract and to damages. Companies and partnerships will often be parties to the contract. Again a good knowledge of accounts and relevant taxation principles will often be required.

(ii) *Tort.* The importance of figures should be equally obvious here — damages assessment can be very complex in cases of severe injury or fatal accident. One should not be deflected from this by the possible complexity of the facts.

(iii) *Landlord and tenant.* Many financial issues arise in connections with leases and rent.

(iv) *Employment law.* Many questions relating to pay arise, and in some cases there will be a need to deal with statistics.

(v) *Family law practice.* Clearly the greatest relevance is to financial provision, both maintenance and capital payments. There is not simply the question of how much to pay, but also of how much is really available, how much a person needs to live on, the tax consequences and so on.

(vi) *Welfare law.* Clearly complex numerical issues can arise with regard to benefits, etc.

(vii) *Compensation.* There are various types of compensation, for example in discrimination cases, where numeracy is important.

(d) *Criminal practice.* The importance of numeracy here ranges from the complex fraud trial to the small-scale fiddling of the books. Complete understanding is essential for clear presentation to the judge and the jury. There are also other possibilities, from being able to deal with tracing the monetary proceeds from the sale of illegal drugs to simply finding out what fine a defendant may be able to afford.

32.3.2 WORKING WITH AN ACCOUNTANT

When dealing with a case that has a substantial financial factor it is possible that assistance will be available from an accountant. An accountant may actually be called in as an expert witness and you will see him or her in conference. If the client employs an accountant you may direct questions to the client's accountant through the client.

An accountant can be of great assistance, but having an accountant to help is not necessarily an answer, it is simply another element. You will still have to talk to the accountant, to know what to ask about, exactly what questions to ask, and you will have to be able to understand the answers.

However, in the vast majority of cases there will be no accountant to help, for the very simple reason that having an accountant costs money and the client either may not be able to afford this, or the financial issues may not be substantial or vital enough to justify the expense of an accountant. In a legally aided case the cost of an accountant may not be covered, although money issues may be especially important to the client in such a case even if the sums involved are small.

Whenever there is no accountant you will have to deal with all the figures and financial issues personally, finding the figures, analysing them and coming to conclusions that can be communicated to the client and be presented in court. You will personally have to deal with any relevant accounts and tax issues.

32.3.3 PROFESSIONAL ABILITY

A numerical ability is a matter of maintaining good professional standards. When you represent a client you have the duty to do the best you can, which includes not only winning the case if possible, but achieving the best result. You should get the highest figure that you properly can for a plaintiff. You must properly protect the position of a defendant.

This relates not just to the issue of damages, but to every arithmetical aspect of a case. If you think it is legally correct for a husband to pay £20,000 to his former wife you need to check with him whether he can afford to raise the sum without ruining his own financial position. If you advise your client that he or she can expect £40,000 in damages it is verging on the negligent not to advise that the money will be liable to 40% tax, if that is the case.

More personally, you need to impress each client, and each solicitor, with the range and quality of the advice that you give. A barrister can build up a reputation for good and thorough work just as quickly as a reputation for a Marshall Hall style of advocacy, and probably on a sounder basis.

32.3.4 PERSONAL RELEVANCE

There is also a personal relevance for the barrister in practice having a reasonable arithmetical ability and a knowledge of the principles of accounting and taxation. The point is simply that as a self-employed person each barrister will be responsible for drawing up a set of accounts each year and will be personally liable for paying their own tax.

Again the reaction of those starting to train for the Bar tends to be that this point is in fact not very important — you employ an accountant to do your accounts and you get a good accountant so that you pay as little tax as possible, so why does a barrister need to be personally concerned? Such a reaction again shows a lack of practical appreciation of how things really work. Even if you are going to have an accountant to draw up your annual accounts, you need to keep all the records on which those accounts are to be based. You need to know what is taxable and should be entered and what is not. It is also in your interests to know what is tax-deductible so that you know what to keep receipts for. Tax rules mean that there is sometimes a choice of doing things in a tax-effective or a non-tax effective way, and it is in your interests to know which is which. In addition to income tax, the barrister with sufficient income will be liable for value added tax, with the need to make quarterly returns.

32.4 Stages in an Action when You May Need to Deal with Figures

These notes provide a brief and simple outline of those stages in a case at which a barrister may need to deal with figures. This is intended to give you an awareness of when to look out for numeracy issues on this course: a numeracy issue will not always come clearly labelled — it is for you to appreciate it is there. As general fact management skills inter-relate closely with other skills, so does the need to manage figures.

32.4.1 IN A CONFERENCE

When planning for or carrying out a conference, dealing with relevant facts must of course include all the relevant figures. This is so not only where figures are an important element of the case, for example, when you are interviewing a client for whom you are seeking maintenance, but in any case where figures arise.

Any figures that the client provides should of course be noted. In addition you should identify the figures that will be required to pursue the case and ask the client about them. Often the client will not be able to provide the figures personally, in which case you will have to consider with the solicitor how the figure might be obtained.

32.4.2   IN PREPARING A CASE

Fact management principles cover figures as well as facts. In dealing with the facts of a case the barrister will need to identify:

(a)   in what areas of the case figures will be needed,
(b)   precisely what figures will be needed,
(c)   what figures are already known,
(d)   what figures need to be ascertained,
(e)   how each figure will be ascertained,
(f)   how each figure will be used,
(g)   how each figure can be proved.

32.4.3   IN WRITING AN OPINION

A good solicitor will send you most of the figures that you need, but a less good solicitor might not, and even a good solicitor is unlikely to send all the figures you need in the initial brief. At that stage the main issue is whether there is a case and the strength of the case. But figures will still need to be dealt with — the client will want to know not only whether he might win but also at least in general terms how much.

Thus in analysing a brief you must consider in what areas figures are relevant. In writing the opinion you should deal with figures as far as possible. All figures that are provided in the brief should be dealt with, and other areas where figures are relevant should be dealt with in principle if not in detail. You also need to decide on a suitable way to present the figures in the opinion, whether as part of the text or in a tabulated form.

In writing an initial opinion, it is easy to underestimate the numerical and arithmetical side of a case simply because detailed figures are not always provided. This feeling must be resisted — the barrister is not there simply to accept what is provided, it is for the barrister to decide what is important and to indicate what information is needed and how the case should progress. Areas where more detailed figures are required should be indicated in an opinion.

32.4.4   IN DRAFTING

When planning a draft you must consider to what extent figures should be set out in the draft. Just to give a few general examples, in a statement of claim, figures may need to be given for damages — figures for special damages should be listed in some detail, and the basis of the financial claims for general damages must at least be pleaded in outline. While damages remain at large until trial, the increasing tendency is to plead the figures for a claim for damages in more detail. However, you must of course hesitate to plead a figure until you are reasonably sure of it.

Regarding other drafts, an affidavit in a case may require figures to be pleaded in great detail, especially, for example, an affidavit supporting an application for financial relief on divorce. A draft order will of course need to have any relevant figures specifically included. If the figures are complex they should be presented in a schedule.

32.4.5   IN ADVOCACY

When presenting a case to a judge or jury it goes without saying that it is vital for the barrister to have total command of any figures in the case, be they sums of money, measurements or anything else.

Only if the barrister has personally gathered all the relevant figures and mastered them will he or she have any chance of explaining them clearly, let alone convincing anyone of the strength of the case. Even someone who is confident in dealing with figures in writing may have more difficulty in dealing with them orally.

There are various ways in which a barrister may have to deal with figures in the course of presenting a case in court. First and most simply, figures may need to be dealt with in opening and closing speeches. Secondly, figures will need to be dealt with in offering evidence, whether it be documents or witnesses. Clearly the barrister must be capable of examining or cross-examining a witness on figures. At every stage you need to be able to present any numerical information in a way which really communicates your meaning to the jury and the judge. Even if you understand the figures, helping someone else to understand them can be very difficult.

If you have complex figures to get across you need to find the best way of doing it. Long and complex documents are difficult to understand, and the good barrister should always try to look for summaries or clear ways of presentation that will help comprehension. Computers and video display units are already finding their way into court, and it is quite clear that they will increasingly do so in the future, and this is another area where facility may help with the presentation of the case.

32.4.6   IN NEGOTIATING A SETTLEMENT

Before attempting to negotiate a settlement you must have all the relevant figures to evaluate the case and identify the most and the least that the client might expect to win or pay. It is important to stress this. Sometimes the settlement is seen as a quick and easy way of avoiding a legal action, but of course no settlement should be contemplated until one has a clear idea of what the case might hope to achieve.

32.5   Collecting Evidence of Figures

Figures need to be ascertained just like other matters of fact, and admissible evidence will need to be found to prove them just as much as any other fact in the case. Having identified an area where figures are relevant, you need to sort out precisely what evidence you need and exactly where it may be obtained. Some the client will be able to provide. For others it is for the barrister to indicate to the solicitor what figures are required and for the solicitor to endeavour to find them.

The sources of figures, and of evidence of figures, are wide-ranging, from a full set of accounts to cash books, vouchers, receipts and even the backs of envelopes. In looking at figures it is important not to be blinded by big figures. The fact that a figure is large is not impressive — large figures can appear in the acounts of a company that is about to go into liquidation. You still need to be able to detect the truth behind the figures.

Not only do you need to identify a source for evidence on figures, you need to be aware of the problems that can arise in presenting such evidence. If you need to take an accountant through his or her evidence you will have to be familiar with all the appropriate terminology. You need to be able to present evidence in a form in which it can be understood. Most important of all, you will sooner or later need to be able to cross-examine on the figures presented by the other side, which requires a most thorough understanding.

It is important to be realistic about what figures may be available and what may not, and to bear in mind what figures may be available to your side and what figures will be available to the other side.

Having stressed the importance of figures, it is equally important for the barrister to be able to deal with the lack of figures — you will often come across a case where you need certain figures to advise in detail and they are simply not obtainable. You can only do your best. Try to think of all the sources from which figures might be obtained. If there are no sources, or if the figures are in any event theoretical, you will have to do your best to argue what the figure should be, from common sense, analogy or some other source. This can, for example, be a problem in arguing for loss of future profit.

This is a point that students often find difficult. If in a contract action there is a claim for future loss of profits, students tend to think that the claim is weak if it is difficult to assess what the potential profits might have been. This is of course a problem, but it is by no means fatal. The fact that a figure is difficult to assess simply means that you need to set about constructing a good argument for how it might be assessed. Look at profits over recent years, or profits of similar businesses.

A final point is the need to be aware of the procedural ways of getting figures that your client does not have. An obvious possibility is discovery, but there are many others that you should watch out for during the civil litigation course.

32.6 Typical Numeracy Issues in Practice

Dealing with figures is not just a matter of addition and subtraction. It may require an agile mind. A few practical points to watch out for are summarised here.

(a) *What numerical issues are there in a case?* Never be happy with just dealing with the obvious possibility of damages, or with simply dealing with the issues for which figures are given to you. Look out for all the possibilities. For example, there may be tax issues, interest issues, costs, etc.

(b) *What financial resources are there?* If your client is seeking maintenance you need to know not only what your client wants but also how to find out what might be available to claim from. If you are suing for damages, you need to look not only at what your client hopes to recover but also at what a potential defendant can afford to pay. If you are representing a defendant the question may well be what resources your client has to meet the claims against him.

(c) *Where has money come from?* This may arise as a legal issue in a trust case, but can equally be an important factor in other circumstances.

(d) *Where has money gone to?* A question you may well wish to ask if your client's money has disappeared in the hands of the other side! It may also be something you want to know of your own client's resources, or in a criminal case possibly not.

(e) *What is the relevance of an individual figure?* This may sound a strange question, but it may be important in analysing a case or tax question. What exactly does a particular figure given to you consist of? For example, is it capital or income, or can the figure be broken down in any way?

(f) *Is a particular figure reliable?* Don't accept any figure without question. Any figure may or may not be accurate, and may or may not be the right answer to the question you asked about figures. How good is the source of the figure?

(g) How accurate can a figure be? The difficulty of assessing figures in some circumstances has already been mentioned. Never give up just because a figure is difficult to assess. Real professional skills are being called on when a figure is not obvious.

(h) *What does a figure really mean?* Is a business really strong or weak? Don't be mesmerised by big figures or long lists of figures. Learn to know what each figure means and what figures are most important.

(i) *What can you do with the figures available to you?* Get the most you can out of a set of figures for the client. Figures are not often going to win or lose a case, but they may well make a vital difference to the client and to the professionalism of the job you do.

(j) *Be specific about figures.* Even if the figures given to you are vague, this is no excuse for you to be vague.

(k) *Be comprehensive with figures.* You do an inadequate job if you give a figure for damages without saying that interest will be recoverable too. It is no good giving a figure for damages without warning that it is likely to be liable for tax.

(l) *Be realistic about figures.* It is no use settling for a figure for maintenance for a client if you are not sure it will really cover client's needs. Is is no good offering a figure to settle a claim if you are not sure that your client can raise it.

(m) *Know what is suspicious in a set of figures.* There can be many factors in a set of accounts that could do with inquiry — a set of accounts is only a basic summary of the position of a business. Learn what may be suspicious and what to look for. Learn to find figures hidden in a set of accounts but which are not clearly labelled for what they are.

(n) *Always keep figures in context.* Although the emphasis here is on figures and money, always keep the relative importance of figures in context. A large possible figure for damages still needs to be seen in the perspective of how likely it is that the case will succeed. And remember that money is not always the most important thing for the client — sometimes they do have other objectives that need equal attention.

32.7 Statistics and Graphs

32.7.1 WHEN MAY THE USE OF STATISTICS BE HELPFUL TO YOU?

Statistical methods and statistical terms are used in reporting the mass data of social and economic trends, business conditions, opinion polls and the census. You should get used to reading statistics and utilise them whenever you seek to prove by inference that in your submission a state of affairs exists. Such information is particularly useful when seeking to establish racial or sexual discrimination, risk factors in such areas as sentencing, parole release from mental hospital, danger from chemicals and other environmental pollutants, risk factors in giving informed consent to medical treatment, future profit forecasts, blood test evidence, genetic fingerprinting evidence, etc.

32.8 The Language of Statistics

32.8.1 WHAT IS AN AVERAGE?

There are three different kinds of average: the mean, the median and the mode.

The mean is the arithmetic average arrived at by totalling the number of each of whatever it is you want to average and then dividing that by the total number in the sample. For example, you want to know the average (mean) number of cigarettes that Bar students who smoked, smoke on a particular Monday. If 400 of you smoke, and the total smoked by all 400 on the Monday in question was 8,120; the mean would be $8,120 \div 400 = 20.3$.

The median, using the same example, is the number of cigarettes which half the smokers smoke more than, and half smoke less than. In this example the figure could be less than the mean, and might be about 19.

The mode, again using the same example, is the number of cigarettes which the largest number of people in the sample smoke, so that if the greatest number of people in the group actually smoked 16 cigarettes on Monday then 16 is the modal number.

If presenting an average to the court always know what kind of average you are using, and if you are confronted with statistical information by your opponent, always ask what kind of average is being used.

32.9 What may Influence the Reliability of Statistical Information?

The major difficulty with all statistics is that they may be biased or based on too small a sample to give anything like a reasonable or believable result. Statistical data are generally developed from information collected in questionnaires. It is important to know: how many were sent out, how the respondents were selected, how many were returned, who did not return them and whether the respondents were likely to respond truthfully to the questions posed or whether there may have been a desire to give a pleasing answer. To be valid the sample must be representative and randomly selected.

32.10 Can the Significance of Statistical Conclusions be Tested?

Yes, it can: a test of significance lays down a set of rules for deciding when sample results are inconsistent with a hypothesis. You should check whether the statistics you want to use have been tested. These tests are tests of probability and in most cases nothing poorer than a 5 per cent level of significance is good enough, that is, 95 chances out of 100 that the result is real.

32.11 What Sources of Information Are There?

The government's statistics department provide monthly and annual figures which may be of use to you. Such publications as *Social Trends, Home Office Statistical Bulletin, Annual Abstract of Statistics, Regional Trends, Key Data, United Kingdom National Accounts, Economic Trends* and *Monthly Digest of Statistics* may all be of use to you. The *Guide to Official Statistics* will enable you to decide which of the published statistics may be particularly relevant to a case you are pursuing.

32.12 What is the Best Way to Display this Information

Explaining this kind of information to a court is something you should plan carefully. One way of doing so is to prepare a graph which can be displayed on an overhead projector, or on a large flip chart. Do not be timid in seeking to use presentational methods that will really assist understanding.

32.13 Numeracy Areas Dealt with on the Course

32.13.1 DAMAGES

Methods of assessing damages will be dealt with in the remedies course (see the **Remedies and Practical Background Manual**). The remedies course will give most emphasis to practial points on approaching the assessment of damages, and particularly complex issues in the assessment of damages. You are expected to know the principles for assessing damages in the core subject areas, and this may be an area where you need to do extra work. You will be expected to deal with general principles for assessing damages and with more detailed questions of whether particular heads of damage are recoverable in a particular case.

32.13.2 INTEREST

The recovery of interest will be dealt with where relevant in the remedies course, the civil litigation course and the drafting course.

32.13.3 COSTS

The recovery of costs will be dealt with where appropriate in the civil litigation and criminal litigation courses.

32.13.4 REVENUE LAW

There will be lectures and tutorials on revenue law for all students in the second term (see the **Remedies and Practical Background Manual**). This course will provide a basic grounding in the principles of tax law that are most relevant for the barrister. Students who have already studied revenue law are still advised to take this course bcause of the practical professional content.

32.13.5 ACCOUNTS

There will be lectures on accounts for all students in the second term (see the **Remedies and Practical Background Manual**). This course will familiarise you with the basic terminology of accounting, the elements of a set of accounts and the principles of and interpretation of a set of accounts. It is not intended that you will actually be able to draw up a set of accounts by the end of the course, simply that you will have enough knowledge to be able to deal with a set of accounts. A set of accounts can be a useful source of information once you know what it may contain. It can, for example, show how many of a man's possessions are actually owned by his company, and whether he is employing relatives in the business.

Inevitably the accounts course, like the revenue law course, has to deal with principles. A legal context will be used whenever possible, but no particular class should be underestimated simply because it has no obvious direct application to a particular type of legal case — the principles must be learned first.

32.13.6 MODULES

All the above areas will be developed as appropriate in the modules. For example, the **General Practice Manual** will look at particular tax implications in family cases, and the **Chancery Practice Manual** will look specifically at tax and accounts points relating to wills and trusts.

32.14 Helping Yourself to Deal with Figures

Always carry a calculator, be familiar with how to use it, and use it when figures arise. (A calculator may be taken into classes, assessments and examinations and will be expected to be used whenever appropriate.) Also, make sure you have a calendar available. When you are dealing with cases that happened some time ago a calendar covering more than the current year can be valuable.

Many other things can help with numeracy, the particular requirements depending on a barrister's practice. A ready reckoner can help with calculations. Tax tables are available, as are tables of current levels of social security benefits and so on.

In terms of doing personal accounts, the simple expedient of buying suitable business books for records pays dividends, and increasingly good software packages are available to help with the assessment of personal tax.

32.15 Dealing with Figures During the Course

You will be expected to deal with all numeracy issues whenever they arise on the course. Such issues will not always be obvious but must be spotted in dealing with an exercise, just as they would have to be in practice.

Once the teaching on revenue law and accounts has been completed, you will be expected to integrate such issues into any problem presented to you.

You will always be expected:

    (a)   to spot a numeracy issue,
    (b)   to deal with figures provided in a question,
    (c)   to deal intelligently with a situation in which figures are not provided,
    (d)   to do any necessary analysis of figures,
    (e)   to do any appropriate calculations.

32.16   Numeracy Problems

These problems are provided to illustrate the type of issue you may be required to deal with during the course. Some may be used in class, the rest can be used for private study.

Problem 1
Examine the following facts in detail, and identify as many areas as you can where information about numbers must be sought and dealt with.

In each case, identify where information about relevant figures might be sought by yourself or by instructing solicitors.

Mr Duff, aged 59, was injured in April 1993 when he was driving his car and it was hit by another vehicle. His father was a passenger in his car at the time and was killed in the accident. The accident was caused by the driver of the other car, Mr Young, who has since been convicted of dangerous driving with regard to the incident. Mr Duff is sueing Mr Young for negligence. As a result of the accident, which broke both his legs and caused serious internal injuries, Mr Duff could not work for six months. In order to be able to return to work as quickly as possible, Mr Duff used a substantial amount from his savings to pay for private medical treatment.

Mr Duff has had particular difficulties in that he is the manager of an interior design business. The business was incorporated in 1988 as Duff Decor Ltd, with Mr Duff as a 60% shareholder and his brother as a 40% shareholder. Business has suffered while Mr Duff has not been able to work. His brother is not good at business, so a manager had to be employed while Mr Duff was not there. In addition, a few months before the accident, £100,000 was borrowed to fund expansion of the business, and there have been problems keeping up with repayments on this loan.

Mr Duff's father left a will appointing Mr Duff and his brother as his executors. The main provisions of the father's will was to leave the residue of his estate in trust for his grandchildren.

Mr Duff left his wife and two children three years ago, and he has since lived in a flat. The wife and children are still in the former matrimonial home, and Mr Duff had been voluntarily paying maintenance to them. However, following his accident he has ben unable to make such payments, and his wife is currently in receipt of social security benefits. Mr Duff has heard rumours that his wife has formed a relationship with another man who has done substantial work on the home.

Problem 2
A has sued B for a debt of £7,187.50 due on 10 May 1992 and has claimed interest at 8% p.a. and £220.25 costs. B wishes to settle A's claim in full today. How much should B pay?

Problem 3
Albert died on 17 October 1990, leaving a widow, Barbara, and two children. Albert was a fitter earning £135.34 per week net at the date of his death with additional regular overtime. Albert consistently kept 25 per cent of his take-home pay and 65 per cent of his overtime for himself, the rest he gave to Barbara who spent it on running the household, keeping the family and paying rent and rates. Nothing was saved. Of the money Albert gave Barbara, 12 per cent was consistently spent by Barbara on Albert's upkeep, the rest on herself and the children and on expenditure for the family as a whole which has not diminished since Albert's death. Of the money Albert kept for himself, 5 per cent was consistently spent on gifts and entertainments for Barbara and the children.

Before Albert's death Barbara worked full-time earning £104.30 per week net, but since his death she has had to give up full-time work so as to look after the children. She quit her job on 1 November 1990 and took up part-time work from that date initially earning £55.98 per week net, rising to £58.32 per week net on 1 September 1991, and £63.85 on 1 September 1992. Her salary in full-time work would have risen to £110.06 per week net on 1 January 1991, £117.20 per week net on 1 January 1992 and £121.62 per week net on 1 January 1993. Had Albert not died his earnings would have risen to £147.61

per week net on 1 March 1991, £155.38 per week net on 1 March 1992 and £169.70 per week net on 1 March 1993. Overtime opportunities at Albert's place of work are spread evenly and fitters of Albert's seniority earned an average of £78.40 per month net in 1990, £79.15 per month net in 1991, £86.80 per month net in 1992 and so far in 1993 £69.20 per month net.

Albert used to do D.I.Y. work and repair work around the home. Barbara has so far spent £237.20 on workman's bills for work Albert would have done and has done no redecoration or home improvement some of which is now urgent and will cost £375. Barbara has spent more on baby-sitting since Albert's death: an extra £7.50 per week;

What is the total financial loss suffered by Barbara and the children in consequence of Albert's death as at 1 September 1993?

Problem 4
The defendant sold to the plaintiff 1.5 tonnes of Winterlite solid fuel at a price of £630, after falsely representing to the plaintiff that:

(a) Winterlite was suitable for use in her stoves.
(b) 1.5 tonnes of Winterlite would last throughout the winter.
(c) 1.5 tonnes of Winterlite would keep her home warm throughout the winter.

In fact:

(a) Winterlite was not suitable; the plaintiff should have used Glowworm fuel.
(b) The 1.5 tonnes lasted only five months of the winter. The plaintiff then bought 300 kg of Glowworm at a cost of £108 which lasted the remaining two months of the winter and kept her house warm.
(c) Winterlite did not keep her house warm and for the first five months of winter the plaintiff had to use additional electric heating at a cost of £695.

The plaintiff is suing the defendant for breach of contract and/or negligent misrepresentation. How much will she recover in damages?

Problem 5
A wife tells you that she needs maintenance from her husband. Both parties have made full disclosure of their financial situation and below you will find each party's schedule of income and expenditure. Is she right?

Wife	£
Gross income	15,708.00 p.a.
Net income, approximately	927.50 per month
National insurance	50.36 per month
Monthly expenditure:	
Gas	25.00
Electricity	15.00
Television licence	5.00
Contents insurance	13.00
Car tax and insurance	24.00
Car maintenance	34.00
Petrol	50.00
Dental treatment	10.00
House repairs, etc.	40.00
Investments: life assurance, etc.	154.25
Increase in national insurance contribution	68.00
Rates, water rates, buildings insurance, etc.	136.50
Food	200.00
Clothes	100.00

Husband	£
Gross income	34,000.00 p.a.
Net income, approximately	1,845.00 per month

Monthly expenditure:

Expenses of former matrimonial home, rates, etc.	136.30
Mortgage	719.00
Endowment policy	198.00
Gas	50.00
Electricity	20.00
Telephone	20.00
Contents insurance	10.00
Ground rent and maintenance charge	12.00
Television licence	5.00
Rates and water rates	58.00
Hire purchase: car, furniture	135.82
Savings	152.00
Food	200.00
Clothes	20.00
Holidays	150.00

Problem 6

The XYZ Building Society is unwilling to advance money for the purchase of terraced houses without front gardens in an area where members of ethnic minority groups live. Your instructing solicitors have presented you with a copy of a report compiled by the Commission of Racial Equality whch states that 86% of ethnic minority families living in that area live in terraced houses without front gardens, and that 46% of white families living there live in terraced houses without front gardens.

Your instructing solicitors believe that their client (a member of an ethnic minority group) can successfully claim that she has been indirectly discriminated against on racial grounds by the Building Society, which has refused to advance her a mortgage to purchase a terraced house without a front garden in the area. Explain how you can use the figures supplied to help to prove discrimination.

Problem 7

The defendant is charged with fraud. The prosecution wishes to prove that in May of a particular year her level of income and expenditure rose significantly, and has obtained copies of her bank statements. Do they bear this out?

BARTLETT'S BANK PLC 27 Old Steet London EC8Y 2HR		Account : J Park 14278693		
Date	Details	Withdrawals	Deposits	Balance
27 Mar	000621	50.00		3,018.88 2,968.88
28 Mar	CHEQUES		321.67	3,290.55
30 Mar	000620	98.27		
	PAYROLL		948.25	
	AC	30.00		4,110.53
3 Apr	HOLT FINANCE SO	59.28		
	BROADWAY RENTALS SO	22.90		4,028.35
5 Apr	000622	31.84		3,996.51

Date	Details		Withdrawals	Deposits	Balance
6 Apr		AC	75.00		3,921.51
7 Apr	W LONDON CTY CT	SO	100.00		3,821.51
10 Apr		000623	1,260.55		2,560.96
11 Apr		CC		13.60	
		000624	80.00		2,494.56
14 Apr		AC	50.00		
		000627	142.88		2,301.68
17 Apr	WESTLAND B/SOC	SO	392.27		
		000628	50.00		1,859.41
18 Apr		000625	27.00		1,832.41
19 Apr		AC	75.00		
	L. B. LAMBETH	SO	76.82		
		CC		500.00	2,180.59
20 Apr		000626	60.48		2,120.11
21 Apr		000629	100.00		2,020.11
25 Apr	S.ELEC	SO	43.00		1,977.11
26 Apr		000630	5,000.00		3,022.89 OD
27 Apr		CC		142.80	2880.09 OD
28 Apr	PAYROLL			948.25	
		AC	75.00		2,006,84 OD
2 May	HOLT FINANCE	SO	59.28		
		000632	50.00		2,116.12 OD
3 May	BROADWAY RENTALS	SO	22.90		
	CHEQUES			347.80	1,791.22 OD
5 May		000633	50.00		1,841.22 OD
8 May		AC	25.00		
	W LONDON CTY CT	SO	100.00		1,966.22 OD
9 May		CC		87.30	1,878.92 OD
10 May		000636	32.99		1,911.91 OD
11 May		000635	50.00		1,961.91 OD
12 May	BANK CHARGES		36.80		
		AC	75.00		
		CC		7.21	2,066.50 OD

Date	Details		Withdrawals	Deposits	Balance
16 May	WESTLAND B/SOC P. LANGTON	SO	392.27	2,500.00	41.23
17 May	INTEREST	000634	36.67 186.21		181.65 OD
18 May	STAR CLUB	DD AC CC	32.00 75.00	500.00	211.35
19 May	L. B. LAMBETH	SO	76.82		134.53
22 May		000637	75.00		59.53
25 May	S/ELEC	AC SO	75.00 43.00		58.47 OD
26 May		000638 CC	21.95	142.80	62.38
30 May	PAYROLL	000639 000640 000641	50.00 17.90 100.00	948.25	
	CHEQUES			338.92	1,181,65
1 Jun		AC	50.00		1,131.65
2 Jun	INTEREST		2.86		1,128.79
5 Jun	HOLT FINANCE BROADWAY RENTALS	SO SO 000642	59.28 22.90 50.00		996.61
7 Jun	P. LANGTON W LONDON CTY CT	000644 SO	250.00 100.00	2,500.00	3,146.61
8 Jun		000643	44.99		3,101.62
9 Jun		AC	75.00		3,026.62
12 Jun		AC	50.00		2,976.62
13 Jun		CC		28.50	3,005.12
16 Jun	WESTLAND B/SOC	SO 000645	392.27 50.00		2,562.85
19 Jun	L. B. LAMBETH	SO CC	76.82	500.00	2,986.03
20 Jun		000646	60.00		2,926.03

Date	Details		Withdrawals	Deposits	Balance
23 Jun		000647	23.90		2,902.13
23 Jun		AC	75.00		2,827.13

Key: SO STANDING ORDER   AC AUTOMATED CASH   OD OVERDRAWN
CC CASH AND/OR CHEQUES   DD DIRECT DEBIT

Glossary

This glossary contains the meaning of certain technical terms commonly found in medical reports.

Abduction: movement away from the mid-line
Adduction: movement towards the mid-line
Amnesia: absence of memory
Analgesic: pain relieving medication
Ankylosis: obliteration of a joint by fusion, either bony or fibrous
Aphasia: loss of power of speech
Arthrodesis: fusion of a joint by operation
Arthroplasty: production of movement in a joint by operation
Arthroscopy: direct vision inside a joint using a fibreoptic scope
Aspiration: sucking out fluid (e.g. from a point or a cavity) through a hollow needle
Ataxia: unsteadiness of gait
Atrophy: wasting of a body part from lack of vascular or nerve supply
Avascular necrosis: death of tissue through deprivation of blood supply; refers particularly to bones
—e.g. head of femur following fracture of neck of femur
Avulsion: wrenching away of a part, e.g. avulsion fracture, the wrenching away of a fragment of bone
by force applied by an attached tendon
Axonotmesis: interruption of conductivity in a nerve by 'physiological' (i.e. not physical) division of
the axons, resulting in paralysis and anaesthesia in the distribution of the nerve; spontaneous
recovery can be expected but will take some months (cf. neurapraxia and neurotmesis)
Biopsy: miscroscopic examination of tissue taken from the living body
Bi-valve: removal of a plaster cast by cutting along each side of its length, permitting replacement if
required
Brachial: pertaining to the arm
Brachioradialis: muscle of the forearm
B.S.R. (or E.S.R.): Blood (or erythrocyte) rate — a laboratory test upon the blood to detect the
presence of an inflammatory process somewhere in the body
Bursa: a cyst-like sac between a bony prominence and the skin —e.g. prepatellar bursa, inflammation
in which constitutes 'housemaid's knee'
Calcaneal: pertaining to the calcaneus
Calcaneus: the heel bone, or os calcis
Callus: the cement-like new bone formation which produces union of the fragments of a fracture
Cardiac: pertaining to the heart
Cephalic: pertaining to the head
Cervical: pertaining to the neck
Chondral: pertaining to cartilage
Chronic: long-lasting, the reverse of acute
Claudication: lameness; applied particularly to pain in the calf muscles resulting from defective blood
supply owing to arterial disease
Comminuted: a type of fracture of a bone in which there are more than two fragments
Concussion of the brain: to establish the diagnosis the loss of consciousness must be immediate and
complete though it may be of very short duration

Condyle: a rounded articular eminence

Cortex: the outer layer of a structure — e.g. the 'shell' of a bone; the surface of the brain

Costal: pertaining to the ribs

Crepitus: a creaking or grating, found in osteo-arthritic joints; also in recent fractures and with inflammation of tendons and their sheaths (teno-synovitis)

C.S.F.: cerebro-spinal fluid, which lies on the surface of the brain and spinal cord and inside the ventricles of the brain

Cuboid: a small bone of the foot

Cyanosis: blueness from deficient oxygenation of the blood

Deltoid region: the outer region of the upper third of the arm

Diplopia: double vision

Disarticulation: amputation through a joint

Disc, intervertebral: fibro-cartilaginous 'cushion' between two vertebrae

Distal: farthest point from the centre (opposite to proximal)

Dorsal spine: that part of the spine from which the ribs spring; known also as the 'thoracic' spine

Dorsiflexion: movement of a joint in a backward direction (syn. extension)

Dorsum: back or top — e.g. back of hand, top of foot

Dupuytren's contracture: thickened fibrous tissue in the palm of the hand causing contracture of the fingers

Dys-: prefix meaning difficult, defective, painful — e.g. dyspnoea, meaning shortness of breath

-ectomy: suffix meaning surgical excision — e.g. patellectomy, removal of the patella

E.E.G.: electro-encephalogram (graph of electric impulses in the brain)

Effusion: extravasation of fluid in a joint (or any cavity) — e.g. 'water on the knee' (i.e. synovitis)

Embolism: blockage of blood vessel by a clot which has migrated

Emphysema, surgical: collection of air in the tissues through puncture of the lung by a fractured rib

E.N.T.: ear, nose and throat

Epiphyseal line: the cartilaginous plate near the end of a bone at which the bone grows in length

Epiphysis: the end of a bone during the period of growth

Erythema: superficial blush or redness of the skin — e.g. as from a very slight burn or scald

Erythrocyte: red blood corpuscle

Eschar: crust of dead skin

Extension: moving a joint into the straight position (opposite to flexion)

External: outer side, syn. lateral (opposite to medial)

Fascia: a fibrous membrane

Femoral: pertaining to the femur

Femur: the thigh bone

Flexion: moving a joint into the bent position (opposite to extension)

Flexor: a muscle that bends or flexes a part

Fossa: anatomical term for a depression or furrow

Gangrene: total death of a structure through deprivation of blood supply

Genu: the knee joint

Gluteal: pertaining to the buttock

Haemarthrosis: effusion of blood in a joint

Haematoma: localised collection of blood

Hallux: the great toe

Humerus: the bone of the upper arm

Hyper-: prefix meaning increase above the normal

Hypo-: prefix meaning decrease below the normal; anatomical term for below

Ileum: the lower half of the small intestine

Ilium: the main bone of the pelvis

Induration: hardening of a tissue

Infarct: a wedge-shaped haemorrhagic or necrotic area produced by obstruction of a terminal artery

Inguinal: pertaining to the groin

Intercostal: between the ribs

Interosseous: between bones

Intracranial: within the skull

Intubation: insertion of a breathing tube through the vocal cords

Ischaemia: reduction of local blood supply to a structure

-itis: suffix meaning inflammation — e.g. osteitis, inflammation of a bone

Keloid: a scar which is thickened and deep pink in colour

Kyphosis: posterior convexity of the spine

Laceration: physical tearing of a structure, e.g. lacerated skin

Lateral: outer side, or external (opposite to medial)

Leg: that part of the lower limb between the knee and ankle

Lesion: a structural change in a tissue caused by disease or injury

Leucocyte: white blood corpuscle

Ligamentous: pertaining to a ligament

Lipping: ridge of adventitious bone at joint edges in arthritis (syn. osteophytic formation)

Lordosis: anterior convexity of the spine

Lumbar: the 'small' of the back — i.e. situated between the dorsal (thoracic) and sacral levels

Lumen: the cavity of a tubular structure

Macro-: prefix meaning abnormally large size

Malar: pertaining to cheek

Mallet finger: inability actively to straighten the terminal joint of a finger

Mandible: the lower jaw

Maxilla: the upper jaw

Medial: inner side, or internal (opposite to lateral)

Medullary cavity: the soft interior of a bone

Meniscus: the semilunar cartilage of the knee

Metacarp-phalangeal: pertaining to the joint between the fingers and the bones of the palm of the hand

Micro-: prefix meaning abnormally small size

Motor: pertaining to movement (applied particularly to peripheral nerve function)

Myelo-: prefix meaning pertaining to the spinal cord

Myo-: prefix meaning pertaining to muscle

Necrosis: death of tissue

Neurapraxia: interruption of conductivity in a nerve owing to pressure thereon, resulting in temporary paralysis and anaesthesia in the distribution of the nerve; full recovery will take place spontaneously in a matter of days or very few weeks (cf. axonotmesis and neurotmesis)

Neurotmesis: interruption of conductivity in a nerve by anatomical division causing permanent paralysis and anaesthesia in the distribution of the nerve; recovery cannot take place unless the nerve is surgically repaired (cf. axonotmesis and neurapraxia)

Nystagmus: oscillatory movement of the eyes

Oedema: accumulation of fluid in the tissues

Oesophagus: the gullet, the muscular tube connecting the back of the mouth and the stomach

Olfactory: pertaining to the sense of smell

Oligo-: prefix meaning fewness or lack of

Optic fundi: optic disc, where the optic nerve enters the retina

Orthopaedic: pertaining to bony deformity

Os calcis: see calcaneus

Osteitis: inflammation of bone

Osteoarthritis: degeneration of a joint from wear and tear

Osteophyte: ridge of adventitious bone at joint edges in arthritis (syn. 'lipping')

Osteoporosis: loss of mineral salts from bones, the result of lack of use owing to injury or disease and causing softening of the bone

Palmarflexion: moving the wrist in the direction that the palm faces (syn. flexion)

Para-: prefix meaning by the side of, near, through, abnormality

Paramedian: pertaining to a vertical line parallel with the midline, i.e. a line drawn down through the xiphoid process and umbilicus

Paresis: incomplete paralysis

Patella: the knee bone

Periarthritis: inflammation round a joint, due to infection or injury, causing pain and restricted movement

Phalanx: a finger

Phlebo-: prefix meaning pertaining to a vein

Plantarflexion: flexing the foot — i.e. 'pointing the toes'

-plegia: suffix meaning paralysis

Plexus: a network of nerves or veins

Pneumothorax: air in the pleural cavity — e.g. from the puncture of the lung by a fractured rib — and causing collapse of the lung

Poly-: prefix meaning much or many

Prolapse: falling down, or extrusion or protrusion, of a structure

Pronation: twisting the forearm, the elbow being fixed, to bring the palm of the hand facing downwards (opposite to supination)

Proximal: nearest the centre (opposite to distal)

Pulmonary: pertaining to the lung

Quadriceps: the main muscle of the front of the thigh

Recurvatum deformity: bent backwards

Reduction: restoration to a normal position – e.g. of a fractured bone or a dislocated joint

Renal: pertaining to the kidney

Retro-: prefix meaning behind or backward

Rhomberg's Test: a test of balance — the patient stands erect with toes and heels touching and eyes closed; unsteadiness occurs if test positive

Sclerosis: increased density, e.g. of a bone, owing to disease or injury

Scoliosis: lateral (i.e. sideways) curvature of the spine

Sensory: pertaining to sensation (applied particularly to peripheral nerve function)

Sequestrum: a fragment of dead bone

Sinus: a track leading from an infected focus — e.g. in a bone — to an opening on the surface of the skin

Slough: tissue, usually skin, dead from infection

Spondylosis: degenerative changes in the spine

Sternum: the breastbone

Subscapular: beneath the shoulder blade

Subtalar: beneath the talar bone

Supination: twisting the forearm, the elbow being flexed, to bring the palm of hand facing upwards (opposite to pronation)

Supraclavicular: above the clavicle

Suture: stitch

Synovitis: inflammation of the lining membrane of a joint

Tachycardia: increased pulse rate

Talar: bone of the foot

Therapeutic: pertaining to treatment, the application of a remedy

Thorax, thoracic: the chest, pertaining to the chest

Thrombosis: clotting (thrombus) in a blood vessel or in the heart

Tissue: anatomically a complex of similar cells and fibres forming a structure

Tracheotomy: operative opening into the trachea (windpipe) to assist breathing in certain chest injuries

Traction: method by which fractures, particularly of the femur, are treated — the lower limb is suspended by weights and pulleys and a continously pulling force is applied by means of further weights and pulleys attached to a metal pin (Steinmann pin) passed through the upper end of the tibia

Trauma: an injury, e.g. physical, emotional

Umbilicus: the belly button

Ulcer: localised destruction, by injury or disease, of a surface tissue (i.e. skin, mucous membrane)

Valgus: outward deviation — e.g. genu valgum = knock knee (the tibia deviates outwards from the knee)

Varicosity: dilation and pouching of the veins

Varus: inward deviation — e.g. genu valugum = bow leg (the tibia deviates inwards from the knee)

Ventilation: the movement of oxygen in and carbon dioxide out of the lungs, mechanical ventilation is ventilation by means of a machine.

Vertebra: one of the backbones

Whiplash injury: strain of cervical structure from the head moving violently in one direction and then bounding back in the reverse direction

Xanth-: prefix meaning yellow

Xiphoid process: the lower most bony part of the sternum

Further Reading

Anderson, T. and Twining, W., *Analysis of Evidence* (Weidenfeld, 1991).

Binder, D.A., and Bergman, P., *Fact Investigation: from Hypothesis to Proof*, West Publishing Co., 1984.

Bono, E. De, *Lateral Thinking*, Penguin 1990.

Bono, E. De, *Po: Beyond Yes and No*, Penguin 1990.

Bono, E. De, *Practical Thinking*, Penguin, 1992.

Bono, E. De, *Six Thinking Hats*, Penguin, 1990.

Bono, E. De, *Teaching Thinking*, Penguin, 1991.

Buzan, Tony, *Use Your Head*, BBC Books, 1982.

Gold, N., Mackie K., Twining W., *Learning Lawyers' Skills*, Butterworths, 1989.

Purver, J. M., *et al.*, *The Trial Lawyer's Book: Preparing and Winning Cases*, Lawyer's Cooperative Publishing, New York, 1990.

Sonsteng, J., Haydock and Boyd, *The Trial Book. A Total System for the Preparation & Presentation of a Case*, West Publishing Co., 1984.

Twining, W., *Theories of Evidence: Bentham and Wigmore*, Weidenfeld & Nicholson, 1985.

Twining, W., and Miers, D., *How to Do Things with Rules*, Weidenfeld & Nicolson, 1982.

Wigmore, J.H., 'The problem of proof', (1913) 8 Ill L Rev 77.

Wigmore, J.H., *The Science of Judicial Proof*, 1937.

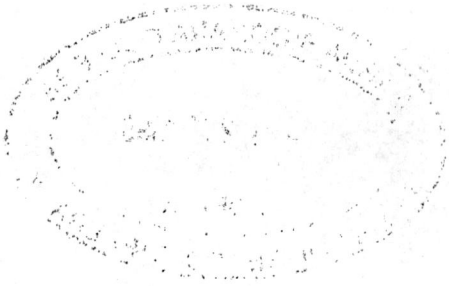